Documentary Report
of the
TANGLEWOOD
SYMPOSIUM

edited by

Robert A. Choate

MUSIC EDUCATORS NATIONAL CONFERENCE
A Department of the National Education Association
1201 Sixteenth Street N.W. Washington, D. C. 20036

INTRODUCTION

Tanglewood, summer home of the Boston Symphony Orchestra, from July 23 to August 2, 1967, was the setting for a unique Symposium which considered major issues related to the theme of "Music in American Society." The Symposium was convened by the Music Educators National Conference in cooperation with the Berkshire Music Center, the Theodore Presser Foundation, and the School of Fine and Applied Arts of Boston University.

Musicians, sociologists, scientists, labor leaders, educators, representatives of corporations, foundations, communications, and government, and others concerned with the many facets of music assembled for this purpose.

Why was such a conference organized with participants of such diverse background and viewpoints? It is obvious that the entire music profession as well as other arts are now facing urgent problems. These challenges arise from social, economic, and cultural developments of the last several decades and emanate from an emerging ideology and maturing of the nation as a whole. The following broad issues were identified in position papers that appeared in the March and April 1967 issues of the *Music Educators Journal,* which served as bases for discussion in MENC Division Conferences and for the participants in the Tanglewood Symposium. *What are the characteristics and desirable ideologies for an emerging post-industrial society? What are the values and unique functions of music and other arts for individuals and communities in such a society? How may these potentials be attained?*

The Symposium sought to reappraise and evaluate basic assumptions about music in the "educative" forces and institutions of our communities – the home, school, peer cultures, professional organizations, church, community groups, and communications media – to develop greater concern and awareness of the problems and potentials of music activities in our entire culture and to explore means of greater cooperation in becoming more effective as we seek new professional dimensions.

During the first week of the Symposium, in plenary sessions, panel presentations, and through subject area discussions, the Symposium members explored "value" systems: the role of the arts in society; characteristics of the "emerging age"; the music(s) of our time and trends in contemporary music; the impact and potentials in the behavioral sciences; the nature and nurture of creativity; and means of cooperation among institutions and organizations concerned with music.

For three days, in a "post-session" limited to music educators and consultants, implications of the Symposium for music education were formulated. Critical issues were identified, and recommendations for action suggested. A "Tanglewood Declaration" was drawn. Implications and recommendations for the music curriculum for educational processes, for evaluation, and for music in higher education and the community were made.

Gratitude is due to Louis G. Wersen, immediate past president of MENC, the Board of Directors, and the cooperating institutions that made the Symposium possible. Acknowledgment is made of the significant contributions of the Symposium participants, consultants, and members of Division discussion groups. Special acknowledgment is given to Diane Ruth, of the MENC staff, for her help in editing the *Documentary Report.*

The full meaning and effectiveness of the Symposium Project remains to be seen; the study is open-ended and ongoing. The responsibility for implementation lies with MENC officers and members at local, state, and national levels. Dimensions and potentials for developments in music education have been formulated. Appropriate action now becomes a professional imperative.

—*Robert A. Choate,* Director of the Tanglewood Symposium Project and Professor of Music, School of Fine and Applied Arts, Boston University.

PARTICIPATING SPONSORS

Berkshire Music Center,

Erich Leinsdorf, Director

Music Educators National Conference

Louis G. Wersen, President

School of Fine and Applied Arts, Boston University,

Edwin E. Stein, Dean

Theodore Presser Foundation,

John R. Ott, President

CONTENTS

I. The Role of the Arts in a Changing Society

Chairman
LOUIS G. WERSEN, President,
Music Educators National Conference

Speeches

Music in a Changing World
ERICH LEINSDORF, Music Director,
the Boston Symphony Orchestra

The Theoretic and Aesthetic Components in Western Civilization
F. S. C. NORTHROP, Sterling Professor of Philosophy and Law, Emeritus, Yale University

The Case for Aesthetic Education
HARRY S. BROUDY, Professor of the Philosophy of Education, University of Illinois

The Humanistic Curriculum
OLE SAND, Director of the Center for the Study of Instruction, National Education Association

The Role of the Arts in a Changing Society
WILLIAM C. HARTSHORN, Supervisor in Charge, Music Section, Los Angeles City School Districts

The Role of Music in Our Philosophy of Education
RALPH TYLER, Chairman, National Assessment Program

Discussion
MAX KAPLAN (Chairman) and Symposium participants

Music in a Changing World

Erich Leinsdorf

I was born and raised in Austria. The situation at that time was so completely different from that which exists for the young student today that I feel no reticence in drawing extensively on my own experiences to contrast them with the problems with which we are familiar.

Over the years I have retained a rather vivid memory of the time when music began to loom evermore as the primary source of my interest. (This was forty years ago, just after I had given up the serious intention of becoming a professional soccer player.) And I recall having ample opportunities to watch my own teachers and to witness how my friends studied. I do not think that I am putting a false golden halo around the past when I say that it seems to me life looked much simpler and much clearer to us then than it looks to today's youth. (And it goes without saying that what looks complicated to young people makes the life of the teacher ever so much more complex and difficult.)

Life in general did seem all very simple forty years ago although my entire youth was spent in constant economic turmoil — not merely personal but nationwide. When the First World War stopped I had just started school, and until I left Austria eighteen years later, I do not remember a week or a month when there was not an economic crisis in the country.

Austria at the time was a small fragment of the former Hapsburg Empire and had just about four million people, outside of the capital city of Vienna, whose population was an absurdly large two million.

In Vienna theatre and concerts were offered in great quantity, perhaps not as the older generation had remembered them from before 1914, but certainly more than I have seen in one city since, and that includes New York. Vienna had an opera house that functioned for three hundred days a year, playing fifty or sixty different works. It had a great dramatic repertory theatre, open three hundred days a year, where I saw more different Shakespeare plays than have been produced in the United States since I have lived here, which means nearly thirty years.

An environment like this is an aid to the teacher; it is part of a young student's education to be able to see how it is done by the "real" actors, by the "real" singers, by the "real" conductors, by the "real" orchestra players. We did not have one or two, but three or four or five cycles of orchestral concerts, with a diversified orchestral repertoire. Then there were innumerable recitals — song, piano, violin; chamber music concerts — quartets, trios, and so on. It was easy to attend concerts. Due to the economic depression there were plenty of free seats available. We went to the opera at a special student rate of fifteen cents or a quarter. We stood on our feet for many hours, but who cared? We could go three or four times a week for less than the present value of a dollar. We were poor, but our own economic problems did not prohibit our musical education outside the classroom, outside the studio, beyond the teacher, outside the regular process of learning.

The age of the airplane has altered the world tremendously, not only for the professional international artist, but for the student, the teacher, the entire world of music. It is important to ask "why this great difference?" I keep talking about this here at the Music Center to our own enrolled members. Through the jet age, through mechanical reproduction, all provincial standards either have already disappeared or will in no time be condemned. This is grim. It means that the teacher today has to turn out "finished products," ready to take their places on the international circuit. This is a burden. This is a strain.

Imagine this Music Center, Tanglewood, in the middle '40's. You know about the famous production of *Peter Grimes.* Look at the cast. Practically all the people, who later on became prominent, were already at that time promising young performers; but there was not much opportunity for them. There was the Metropolitan, there was the New York City Opera in its infancy, and there was the San Francisco Opera Company — all geared to the star system; and these young artists had nowhere to go. They could not go to Europe because of the war, so they came to Tanglewood and were discovered. They displayed their talents, and then began their careers. After 1947, with the travel barriers removed, young people like them went off to perform all over the world.

I remember one incident here three years ago, which will illustrate the situation as it is today. We were looking for a bass singer for one of our oratorio performances, and I heard a young man with a nice voice and nice personality, but a little green. The work I had in mind was a Schubert Mass. The solo bass part was short and not taxing. It was just the right kind of thing for this young man. I invited him to come to Tanglewood in July to sing it with us. He replied that he was sorry, but he could not be available because he had an engagement for thirteen weeks at one of the most prominent European festivals.

Today one goes from the classroom into the major leagues of the international circuit. I do not know how much this affects the educator; but I do know that it presents new challenges for pupil and teacher.

Let us, for example, look at how educational conditions have changed in the field with which I am most closely associated — the orchestral musician. One of the great players of the Boston Symphony of a former era was a friend of mine from Vienna, Victor Polatschek. As a youth he had studied at the Vienna State Academy with a teacher who was then the principal clarinet of the Vienna Opera and of the Vienna Philharmonic Orchestra. One day Mr. Polatschek was asked by his teacher to go to the Opera House and assist in a performance of *Rosenkavalier.* This kind of "substituting," with his teacher next to him (and later on without the safety belt of the teacher's presence) let him acquire know-how, experience, and security. He gradually got to know the repertoire; and by the time he was formally engaged as a regular player, he was no longer in doubt about what the job was all about, what the range of his involvement and the demands upon him would be. He had, as an apprentice, acquired professionalism in a very practical way. This kind of condition prevailed all through the 1920's and perhaps through the 1930's.

What is our situation today, and where do we get our musicians? For the second year in a row we have hired as new members of the Boston Symphony enormously gifted, able and fine instrumentalists, but so totally inexperienced that I suggested spending eight weeks here at the Music Center to gain some insight into the workings of an orchestra by having contact with section principals, by having some actual lessons — informal and formal instruction — and by gaining more ensemble experience, both chamber music and orchestral, in order not to be so inexperienced when the first rehearsal of the Boston Symphony commenced late in September at Symphony Hall.

I feel very warm sympathy and admiration for these young musicians, because technically they play their instruments so much more ably than did their colleagues of earlier generations; but in general they know so much less. This is an educational problem. I do not know how it can be solved. I do know that it cannot be solved in a private studio. One cannot give people experience by having them listen to a record of how other people play a particular piece.

The situation with the musician is similar to that of the high school boy who, at eighteen, joins one of the baseball teams in the major leagues instead of going down to the farm club where he first learns to bat and to field. We have not time for this. We are too shorthanded. We do not have enough candidates.

Only the other day Roger Stevens described to me how the admirable project sponsored by the National Arts Council — the Chamber Music Academy — had faltered under the protests of various orchestras who felt that their best talent would be taken away in an unfair competition.

We have to remedy this situation. We are caught in a double squeeze: the public wants more music, and the musicians want longer contracts. We have orchestras that look to longer seasons, but they do not have enough musicians. We are not only taking teen-agers into our major orchestras, but as fast as we take them we lose them to other orchestras which offer them positions as principals. This is all very nice story-telling material. This is all wonderful for some fine publicity writer. But it is not sound. Remember too that today our reportoire is many times larger than that which my friend Polatschek had to absorb. He did not have to know as many works as a young person today who enters the Boston Symphony, who in his first year will play a *minimum* of one hundred fifty to two hundred different pieces. Nobody can come equipped with that amount of knowledge; and even the best sightreader may, after a few weeks of this constant exposure to new material, become fatigued, cross-eyed, and develop migrain headaches.

The student, as well as the teacher, has to face reality. The demands in the professional world have not only increased by degrees; they have radically changed. There is today a premium on speed. There is today a premium on adaptability, for which perhaps our educational philosophy is not yet quite ready. I know mine is not.

I could ramble on, because in my years as a conductor, in both opera and symphony, I have seen the same problems over and over again. How often a gifted young professional, attractive both as a person and as an artist, falls by the wayside because the pace is too much; and within a decade of the start of his career capitulates and enters some other field, being unwilling and perhaps unable to face the exceedingly harsh realities and demands of the contemporary profession.

These are just some of our problems; and I ask you to provide some of the answers.

If I may make just one small suggestion it is this: as students finish their studies and enter the professional life they should be willing, prepared, and open-minded enough to accept what they are asked to do, even if they feel that their dream, their ideal niche (which they have designed for themselves), lies elsewhere. One does not know at eighteen, twenty, or twenty-two where one is most needed and where one's best abilities lie. As educators, do try, please, to suggest to the young (if such suggestion is possible and acceptable to them) to take what comes their way. They will in the end be more useful, happier, and will land where they belong more easily if they let the needs of the profession guide their steps and if they will consider the good of the community as important as their own personal pleasure.

The personal pleasure of any musician must be kept alive, lest music become a tired routine, but next to it should be the common good.

The Theoretic and Aesthetic Components

in Western Civilization

F. S. C. Northrop

In one of his works, Whitehead states that any profound analysis of Western civilization tends to become a commentary upon Plato. No matter what our reservations — and I have mine — about certain parts of Plato's philosophy, there is a fundamental and a deep sense in which one can believe this to be true. Einstein tells us that nobody who has not been thrilled by Euclid understands present twentieth-century mathematical physics. The great Newton, who founded the theroretical side of the modern world, tells us that he stood on the shoulders of the ancients, ancients who were the Greek mathematical physicists and philosophers. It is well to remember that Plato's Academy had over its door the words, "No one who does not understand geometry need enter here." Certainly Plato is one of the Western world's greatest humanists. This suggests that to put the aesthetic world over against the scientific world, branding the latter as unaesthetic, inhumane, and ethically neutral, if not positively evil, is a questionable practice. This practice arises from a fundamental error upon which the modern world was reared.

Plato, in his *Dialogues,* talks a great deal about the idea of the Good, but he never quite tells us what it is. Nevertheless, Socrates, in his account of the divided line in *The Republic* tells us how to get there, specifying the subjects one has to study. If one examines them with care, something that humanists who refer to Plato seem rarely to have done, one will find that every subject that one has to study to get to the idea of the Good is a mathematical science. The first is arithmetic; the second, acoustics or what the Greeks called music; the third is stereometry, without which the art of the Renaissance cannot be understood; and the fourth, mathematical astronomy. In short, for Plato and the Socrates of Plato's *Republic* music and mathematical physics were inseparable. The same was true also for the idea of the Good in ethics and politics, or in education.

Moreover, both Aristotle and Diogenes Laertus tell us that near the end of Plato's life a notice appeared on the bulletin board of his Academy announcing that Plato was going to give a lecture on the idea of the Good. They add that an audience gathered, buzzing with conversation, expecting to hear esoteric references to this topic, and many went away rather disappointed and somewhat irritated apparently because Plato referred to mathematical scientific subjects, and concluded by affirming that all things, that is, all subjects, are composed of and are to be understood in terms of two basic factors or ground principles. One of these he called "the indetermined dyad," or "the dyad of the great and the small," and the other he called *To En,* the One, which is illustrated by the imageless relation, ratio, or *logos,* which gives two imageful circles, one of which is greater and the other smaller, thus imageless formal or relational identity, the relation of diameter to the circumference of two imagefully different circles being *To En,* an imageless relational identity.

There are reaons for believing that the novel reconstructions, in our conception of the theoretic component of mathematical physics, discovered and mathematically specified by Einstein, Planck, Schrödinger, and Heisenberg in this century, continue this ancient Greek Democratean, Platonic, and Stoic conception, merely introducing richer and more adequate imageless, relational content, from which the old acoustical, stereometrical, and even modern Newtonian content derive as special cases. This is true, even though the new relational theory was so shocking that Heisenberg walked the streets for several nights before he dared publish his contribution to it, so revolutionary was it, with respect to his previous mathematical scientific thinking. The reason was that the Heisenberg principle modifies the role of one-hundred percent deterministic causality in mathematical physics. But nevertheless, Einstein's aforementioned observation remains true that this twentieth-century physics is a continuation of a way of knowing and thinking that goes back to Euclid and the ancient Greeks. Out of the arithmetical and the acoustical parts of Western mathematics, physics, and the contemporary acoustics taught in every physics lab, is a discovery of the so-called materialistic Democrateans as formalized in terms of ratios, variables of which are natural numbers by Theaetitus, after whom Plato named his dialogue on the theory of knowledge, which for him was the nature of the scientific method. We only obtain objectivity in human knowledge, be it humanistic or scientific, when we go to relations. Earl Bertrand Russell has expressed the essence of this point for our time, and he can hardly be regarded as a sentimentalist about the humanities or about science. What we know is that at the bottom of our world of mathematical physical science is a relatedness with certain formal properties. It is the old *Logos* of the ancient Greeks that has been generalized to possess and to discover. This new *logos* now possesses the much more complex formal properties of a field equation minus the old stereometrical conception of logos of Plato's Academy and the Democratean science of arithmetical acoustics which now forms the basis for our classical and contemporary music.

Yesterday afternoon we listened to three musical pieces by the incredible Boston Symphony. All three are classically Greek. Music is rooted in the science of acoustics, and its theoretic component is expressible and formulated in terms of ratios, the formal properties of which are such that only natural numbers make up the variables. In this sense, music is a less rich relational subject than, say, Renaissance painting, because the theoretical component in the paintings of Botticelli, Michelangelo, or Leonardo cannot be understood or expressed in terms of ratios between whole numbers. The discovery of the relation between natural numbers shook Greek mathematical physics to its foundations and made possible the discovery that there is a *logos* in all things that cannot be expressed in terms of ratios between natural numbers. Because acoustics can be expressed in terms of such ratios, classical and modern music of the West are rooted in the knowledge of this theoretic component.

After hearing Stravinsky, one thinks how radically, in some sense, is its aesthetic (defining "aesthetic" in the very strictest sense as a particular kind of art). Stravinsky has used the arithmetically-relational type of music to convey the non-relational, and in this sense he's radical. What is so remarkable about his music is both the degree to which it breaks from the classical and at the same time the degree to which it remains classical. Today there is music that is breaking from these old ratios. If music is really to generalize after the manner in which painting is generalized, I believe such a break must occur. Only then will the classical, and even Stravinsky, emerge out of the new as special cases, just as Newton's mechanics, in fact, comes from quantum theory as a special case, and not the whole universal rule. This is the heart of the pedagogical difficulties that artists face. More and more, it is becoming evident that Western scientific and humanistic thought was corrupt at the beginning of the modern world when the modern world made new and trustworthy discoveries, but misinterpreted them.

Some forty-five years ago, as a post-doctoral student at the Imperial College of Science and Technology in London, I was studying physics under Whitehead. One of the first statements he made was that *we cannot be too suspicious of ordinary language in science and philosophy.* I didn't understand then what that meant, but I believe that I do understand now. The truth of that statement lies at the beginning of our pedagogical difficulties when we talk about subjects and try to teach them, and devise the methods to get them into the schools.

The difficulty of taking children into art galleries or letting them hear musical pieces is well known. People come away from such experiences baffled. "I don't know what I'm to get out of it." Five- and six-year-old children do not ask this kind of question. A friend of Georgia O'Keeffe's who was connected with the Museum of Fine Arts in Minneapolis took some young children into the gallery. They looked at the classical paintings and came away unmoved. She then got the idea of taking one of O'Keeffe's pure, abstract works in which you cannot see a red barn with white snow on the roof, or flowers, or a skull on the desert plains of New Mexico, and she let the children see it. This work is pure in the sense that the aesthetic component suggests nothing beyond the surface given to the viewer. While adults are provoked to demand, "What does it mean?" the children were intrigued.

Dean Wenternetz of the Yale Medical School once remarked: "The condemnation of advanced education is that it kills the native born wonder with which children are born." This is tied to Whitehead's statement. But Whitehead said two things: First, you must spend your days and nights with Hume; and, second, you can't be too suspicious of ordinary language in science and philosophy. Now, the reason is clear. Ordinary language has what we logicians call a two-term syntax. To follow Whitehead, you must observe first graders, or even kindergarten children, as they tend to draw and paint in an impressionistic, O'Keeffean manner.

Why? Their brains have not been filled with Euclid for one thing. They don't read. They don't come equipped with Kantian, *a priori* forms of sensibility of space which they then read into the pure facts, the impressionistic immediacy.

Why did Whitehead say to me, "You ought to spend your days and nights with Hume?" What does Hume do for everybody? He did it for Kant and Einstein. Einstein understood this analysis, and Kant said it was reading Hume that "woke him from his dogmatic slumbers." Let me explain; dogmatic slumbering consists in confusing our theoretically and speculatively inferred, and usually outmoded common sense of scientific objects with directly observed facts. What David Hume does for you is to offer this suggestion: Whenever you have doubts about anything in science, philosophy, and other subjects, you have to regress. Let's push aside our theories as far as we can, and try to be hardboiled. We should say to ourselves: "I am only going to believe in what I directly observe. I am not going to believe in any speculatively-inferred objects. I'm going to leave this to philosophers."

Most people make the error of supposing that science and common sense get their objectivity by foregoing theory and speculation and just restricting themselves to observation. There isn't any greater error. Observation never gives us objects which are the same for all observers. Therefore, if anything is given in observation, it isn't objective; it isn't *directly* observed. This is a truth.

Now we must go to Hume and to what Kant meant when he said Hume had awakened him from his dogmatic slumbers. Kant meant that Hume had made him aware that what he thought to be *observed* objects were in reality only speculatively-inferred, only hypothetically and indirectly, at best, confirmed objects.

One of the best examples of dogmatic slumbering is that of the two West Virginia mountaineers who went to a Baptist church. They had just seen a very lucid and gloried baptism, where the converts had been soaked in a great big tub and thoroughly baptized. One mountaineer turned to the other and said, "John do you believe in baptism?" and John said, "Believe in baptism? Man, I've seen it!"

The person who believes that science gets its observation, its objectivity, by restricting itself to observation alone is just like John. He's seen baptism. He's seen material objects. He's seen electrons. You can no more see an electron than you can fly. Quantum mechanics has proved that if you can get an image of a scientific object, you're sure then that it isn't an object. In quantum mechanics, if you're going to insist that an object be imageable, then you will get a self-contradictory object. The object will have both wave and atomistic particle properties; that is, it will be both a continuing phenomenon and a localized particle at one and the same time.

What does this have to do with art? It has a great deal to do with it. The first thing that happened — and this was the great revolutionary advance the modern world made with Galileo and Newton — was that with the Greeks, the objective was purely spatial and geometrical. Therefore, time changed; and time had to be thrown over into the world of appearances. Whitehead once said to me, "The premoderns had flexi-forms, and it was the genius of Galileo and Newton to bring the flux into the formula." This occurred when Galileo drew a fourth line dimension perpendicular to the three stereometrical, spatial dimensions of the art of the

Renaissance. That was why the stereometrical, static Roman arch worked beautifully for Roman architecture. You'll find it in the Botticelli *Madonna and Child* reproduced in the *Meeting of East and West.* It is a purely rigid stereometrical art. There is no time dimension in it.

What this means is — and it is one of the things that is happening in the artistic world today, and best portrayed by music and moving pictures — is that the canvas tends to give you only a geometrical form at a frozen moment. It's difficult to get the time dimension into painting. Painters do it with a flame, and the flame was a symbol of the flux philosophy of the Greeks. (That is one way of doing it in a two-dimensional static effect on a canvas.) But music operates through time, and the theoretical component of the music of the future will use not only the space-time formula of Einstein, but also the quantum mechanic formula to make its aesthetic immediate flux of materials. The sculptor is doing this today by having incomplete figures, torsos that are partially unfinished, a man that isn't fully a man. This is about the only way you can get a flow in.

What did ordinary language do? The syntax of ordinary language is a subject-predicate, two-term syntax in which everything is described in terms of a noun possessing some predicate, which is attached to it by some form of the verb "to be." When working in this ordinary language, you get marked off in your essays in grade school if every indicative sentence does not have a noun and a predicate related to the noun by this two-termed relation.

Likewise, in the objective world of mathematical physics, there isn't a fact which isn't related to other facts by many terms and relations. We already have four key variables in our dimensional, mathematical physics; there are three in geometry. Thus, in a relation which has terms, there must be many terms or entities — not just one. The same is true of radical empirical, pure-fact, aesthetic immediacy. Every sense quality is related to other sense qualities by many-termed relations.

May I be autobiographical for a moment? I regard it as a terrific advantage as a philosopher that I am color-blind. Color-blindness doesn't mean that we don't see colors. It means, and makes unequivocally clear, that colors are not the predicates of the objects that the color out there seems to be the predicate of. For me, the "go" sign on the traffic light is a light — I don't know what the word "green" means. I haven't the foggiest idea. But I do know what the word green means scientifically; that is, the mathematical, physio-electrodynamic wave length meaning of the word. That's an observance. If you say the wave length for green is green, that's nonsense. That's just like saying electrons are pink. It's nonsense. Why is it nonsense? Because here one is in the world of imageless, relational constructs, or what in the *Meeting of East and West* I call concepts by postulation, derived from intellection. In this world of mathematical physics, all scientific objects get their properties analytically; or in contemporary tautological terms, nothing in Newton's equations implicates formal properties of relations.

Now we go to the error that Whitehead made when he said that you can't be too suspicious of ordinary language. He meant ordinary Aryan prose language. This isn't true of Burmese; the Burmese language doesn't throw you into this two-termed thing, this Aryan cultural way of describing facts and experience. Mass in Newton's physics is a variable in a relation that has the formal property specified in Newton's equations of motion. You thus treat mass as an entity, as a substance with property. In this way, ordinary language corrupts the concept of mass in mathematical physics, when in fact, even with Newton, it was a relational concept and there isn't any meaning to an isolated mass by itself having the property of extension.

Now we get into the notion of material substance, and you think of the world as filled with a lot of little mid-nineteenth century, gold, laissez-faire, unemotive, unaesthetic, unconscious, tiny billiard balls careening around, each one of them self-sufficient, having its extension and having its properties fastened to it as predicates, just as you think the predicate green is fastened as a predicate to the glass on the "go" sign of the traffic light.

For me, that blue out there is the same color as you and I would describe as the sky being blue — if it were. This expresses the fact that you are no different from me in this respect. A good occulist could take your eyes and operate on the rods and cones, and then you would correctly see blue on the "go" sign, too.

Why do I emphasize this, and what does it have to do with art? Every art deals with immediately-sensed predicates. Music has its sounds, painting its colors and shapes — all imageful predicates. If you use this Aryan prose thing-property-predicate, you have to find a noun to fasten the prediate to, and so you just unconsciously think that the green you see out there is fastened to the traffic light. It's the function of many-termed variables. I'll give another example. I have a view in New Hampshire that is a fabulous, panoramic view. I sit and look out at a lake. It's a beautiful, sunshiny morning, and if I don't watch this Aryan language, I will make the statement, "The water in Squam Lake is blue." And it is blue out there. I see it. Then I walk down through the woods, and before I plunge in, I cup up a handful of water and look at it; and it's colorless. Then, if I don't watch out, I'll say: "Oh, it only appeared to be blue; it's really colorless!" So it's made up of a lot of molecules that are colorless, and I've got my billiard ball atoms back again, and I understand physics, and the objective rule is nothing but a lot of colorless things. But still I've got that damned predicate, blue, and where am I going to put it? Well, my Aryan prose forces me to find a noun to fasten it to, so we make that a stowaway.

This leads us to the modern, spiritual man, a mental substance, or a spiritual substance. Thus, I'm a little, colorless, unemotive, or as Locke put it, "blank tabletish," a spiritual substance, only gotten inside. Theoretically I can look in, but I don't know why humanists feel they achieve creativity when they look at their insides. I find the dullest interior in there. It bores me to tears. Outside I find a very interesting world. I even think ordinary people are color-blind. How dull it must be for them to be in New England: every darn thing is green they tell me, everything! Now for me, the color of the pine tree has no more in common with the color of the maple than yellow and black have in common. They tell me the shades on the white houses are green. The grass is green. Well, the grass to me has no more the same color than a pine tree has, or the shades on white houses. Well, supposing people get bored with all these greens, and they get into their cars to get away from them. They only go for a block or two and they hit a traffic light, and they tell me *that's* green. No matter where you normal people go, all you get is green!

Whitehead expressed the truth of the matter. He said, *Every sense predicate ingresses into nature in many-termed relations.* The water is colorless if I can get it in a certain relation. A little later in the afternoon I'm sitting in my study looking at that lake, and terrific thunderclouds come up. The lake is a terrifying jet black. This is what Whitehead meant when he said that sense qualities ingress into nature in many-termed relations.

Now, take a painter. The painter gets his color fastened to something that suggests a vase, and the adults to to an art gallery, and they understand it. They see the point of such art. Why they want to go there I don't know. I live in the world of common-sense objects. We are inferring them all day long. Now, to me, classical art just puts me back in that world again. I don't want to go home and look at a lot of common-sense objects. I've been dodging the darned things all day to keep alive.

What has happened in modern physics has now happened in modern art. We've had to slough off those substances underneath the formula and have had to learn that in order to know what a scientific object really is, you will have to examine not only its formula, but also its relatedness, and from its relatedness therefore get its properties. What is true of inferred scientific objects is that they are four-dimensional, spatial, temporal, and not in a stereo-metrical state as they appeared in Renaissance art. The same is true of the data of the sense words; and thus both of them are many-termed relations.

Music, say Stravinsky's music, has difficulty in living, because if you try to find in our ordinary-language-syntactical world the predicated train whistles and nouns to go underneath every sound of a Stravinsky symphony, that will take a bit of doing. And you will soon give up and realize that this isn't the point. The point is that the sounds, and their sequence, in their own right, are to be enjoyed for their own sake, yet still under the disciplined control of an arithmetical ratio type of score and musical instruments. In the Orient, music is quite different. The reason, I believe, is that the oriental cultures have their inferred objects, just as ours does, but these objects tend to be defined in terms of immediately-sensed properties, devoid of Aryan prose thing-property-syntax. In the Orient, they don't corrupt their predicates by sticking material or mental substance nouns underneath them. This tends to throw their whole aesthetic world into a world of phantasm and helps them avoid the phenomenalistic scum which is now dulling our material substances and giving an even duller reality to our realm of mental ones. Thus, their phantasm leads them to mystical interactions with one another and with everything else coming out as appearance. In the arts the same thing has been going on, and it shows more clearly in painting. I'm sure the musicians can duplicate it, but I don't know the musical examples as well as I know those in painting. In Cezanne's painting, the apple's impression has beauty instead of having the beautiful located in a three-dimensional, perfectly proportioned apple. Cezanne paints the impression of the apple, and if the image doesn't have the shape of the apple, he paints the image. You can always recognize the old classical apple in a Cezanne apple, but if the impression is such that the shadow ends three-quarters short of what you conceive as the diameter of the so-called real apple, he still has painted that limited one.

Gradually you drop the apples, you drop the objects entirely. You can recognize a mountain in a Cezanne painting, but he's giving you that ineffable group of shades, colors, and forms in the impression that the mountain made on him, letting that object go. When you come back to this pure radical empirical immediacy, you see what Hume showed and what is meant by spending your days and nights with Hume.

Hume said, "What do you observe with?" And the answer is: "your different senses." Then, he takes every item of every sense and he shows that it doesn't give you public option. You get images that are relative to the perceiver. They are one thing if you are sitting there, another if you are standing here; and the same is true with any sound. He takes all the senses and he shows that we don't sense any relation or necessary connection, we just sense the sequence of perishing, particular images; and we don't sense either introspectively or the so-called outer senses or substance. This blows up the material of mental substance, and then you are intellectually prepared (but still talking inside an Aryan prose) to think about radical empirical immediacy: the pure facts of experience. Hume's empiricism is what we call radical empiricism: that you would truly know if you only knew with your senses and did not add any speculative inferences beyond. When we know in this radical empirical way, this is what I mean by "aesthetic component." I mean that form of art in which you are dealing with immediately experienced materials alone. It is this world the physicist begins with, and then his inferences from it to his many-termed relational order give him his scientific objects. As Russell has pointed out, what we know in physics is that intellectually known relations cannot be shown with images, cannot be defined away in terms of imageful. We know that, and it's complicated.

The first person to correct the erroneous ordinary-language-prose concept of mass in Newton's physics was Ernst Mark, at the beginning of this century. Next, Einstein told us that his physics moves out from Mark, that mass is a relational concept, a many-termed relational concept; and in the end the relation turns out to be such that mass can no longer even be conserved. In another sense, even Materialism, a relational theory about matter, can no longer claim matter as an absolute. Some Soviet Union philosophers of science have already said this; mathematical physics is said to be undermining Marxism in the Soviet Union as the old scientific and military leaders are replaced by others who know their mathematical physics in this new context. This same thing in Western art moved the old stereometrically static, geometrical world aside when *time* was brought into our theory of objectivity, and even Newton's physics became space-time oriented. Where once physics was only valid in what were called Galilean frames of reference, Einstein generalized it such that the laws of physics now contain *no* matter — regardless of where the observer stands when he observes, whether he be in one entity in the relational system or another.

Modern art has gone through this same process of dropping the substance underneath the aesthetic images. When we come back after spending our days and nights with Hume to pure, so-called "facts", what do we apprehend? We apprehend that all-embracing continuum with differentiating images, and they succeed one another in time, the differentiating images perishing. This gives us a continuum, a many-termed relational art in its first function; and when you come to this conclusion, oriental art and Western art find themselves in a common mold. This is shown historically in the impact of the Chinese painters on the French and English and American impressionists, and also in Zen Buddhism, which is in vogue at the present time in psychiatry.

Thus, we come down to two things that are ultimate in all things. First, the aesthetic immediate, a continuum of immediacy with its ineffable properties, which are not fastened to underlying substances in a two-termed manner, but are related in many terms. Second, that relatedness is different from the relatedness of inferred scientific objects. This is where Whitehead went wrong, I believe, and Einstein is right. In this same manner, this is the issue that was faced in ancient Greek and medieval mathematics and philosophy between the Aristotelian atomists and the Demo-cratean, Platonic, and Stoical mathematical physicists, moralists, and lawyers. The latter expressed it this way: in the many-termed relatedness of the objective world lies the world of mathematical relatedness and mathematical physics. These two are suggested by the many-termed relatedness of the immediately observed and sensed world, but they do not contain it. Thus, you cannot get the relatedness of mathematical physics out of the relatedness of the radical empirical, observed immediacy by abstraction, as Whitehead tried to do.

The sense world suggests the objective world, but does not contain it; and as Einstein has said (and I believe his epistemology of the situation is correct): "In mathematical physics, as in ordinary common sense beliefs, both rest on the belief in an external objective world, the same for all knowers; but we only know such a world by speculative means." What this amounts to is that you cannot define your scientific objects in terms of your sensed properties, or from your radical empirical immediacy. It is the essence of all the arts, whether they be of this radical empirical kind or of the speculatively-inferred, mathematical physical kind, that art is always dealing with immediate experience and material.

The physicist starts and presupposes the same world that the pure artist is dealing with, but he is using the data of the world not to observe objects for their own sake but to discover the relatedness of the objective world and its scientific objects that the sense world suggests.

In this sense, we come back to Plato's observation, in his famous lecture on the Good, that all things are made of two kinds of stuff. One is of immediate experience, ineffable and incurably aesthetic, the world of immediately experienced colors, flavors, sounds, odors, fragrances. The other is a world of ratios, objective, many-termed relatedness, and hence the civilization of the future. The first task of present art is to bring us back, so to speak, to pure fact. This is what the scientist is doing. He is breaking us loose from the old thought-inferred objects; and this function of the scientist is as important for the scientific profession to do as it is for those of the arts to do. Then we could start over again, deriving new inferred entities and a richer, theoretical, rational *logos*. Then music will serve in what I call its second function; that is, music will become the pure aesthetically immediate materials which convey the new *logos*.

We will have an art of the new Renaissance in which the aesthetically-immediate and the richer conception of the many-termed relational mathematics will be synthesized in a great aesthetic work. There will be new Michelangelos and Leonardos.

Practically, I think what this means is that we will have to learn to bypass the corruption of both the aesthetic and the scientific realms that now comes from the old thing-property ordinary language way of thinking. We must keep our youth in their pristine, fresh relationship with concrete immediacy and thus create a pedagogy of the arts and a pedagogy of mathematical physics, which must go forward together.

The Case for Aesthetic Education

Harry S. Broudy

In urging more and better aesthetic education before this conference, not only am I preaching to the converted, but to the missionaries themselves. This too is worth doing, I suppose, in order to restore zeal that even among the faithful occasionally flags. However, a more important reason for seeking justification for aesthetic education is that if our cause is just, it is not obviously so (and certainly it is not obvious to those who provide the time and money for public schooling).

Consider, for example, the following question: Is it desirable and necessary to teach English to all our citizens or prospective citizens? Everyone who has had to read college compositions and who has cringed at the linguistic stumbling of some of our elected officials would say "yes" vehemently. Yet, for all practical purposes, syntactical sloppiness does not hamper communication or even expression—if one accepts evidence from modern novels. For ordinary discourse, sloppy English usage must be judged as adequate. In their occupational life, people who use sloppy English in ordinary discourse speak a special jargon with as much technical precision as the situation demands. So why urge more and better English instruction?

The hidden premise is that something called "educated English" is better than the English most people, young and old, do in fact use. This premise need only be challenged in theory[1] — as it is ignored in practice—and the cry for more and better English instruction becomes a hollow echo of snobbery.

There is an embarrassing parallel in music education and in aesthetic education in general. That human beings have aesthetic experience and that they do not live, and probably cannot live, without art needs no elaborate proof. However, the art they choose to live with is plentiful and easily available in our culture, and it does for them just about what they want it to do. Popular music celebrates love, conflict, yearning, and victory. Young people thrill to it; older ones dream by it. True, some people—a large number, as a matter of fact—go to symphony concerts, the opera, and they enjoy string quartets. Indeed, if Alvin Toffler is our authority, the number is increasing into a veritable culture explosion.[2]

If everything is fine and everyone is happy with his aesthetic state, why the push for more and better music education, or for more and better art education in general? Do we have here also a hidden premise? Do we secretly believe that "good" music or "serious" music or "classic" music is better than popular music and that everyone should enjoy it, or at least help to support it?

I say "secretly" advisedly, because openly the philosophers vie with one another in challenging us to distinguish between the good and bad in both serious and popular music. And what theoreticians do by technical argument, teenagers accomplish with scornful hoots in the argot of the day.

Or is our reason for trying to justify a more widespread effort in the field of aesthetic education the reason that we lack facilities to train professional musicians? I am not competent to answer this question, but such a lack, if it existed, would not necessarily be remedied by an expanded program of general education in the arts. As a matter of fact, such music education as the public schools do provide, especially at the secondary level, is most often manifested in performing groups, and if this does not encourage young people to adopt music as a career, a more general sort of art education is not likely to do better. The searching out of talented youngsters and sequestering them in highly specialized secondary schools, as is done I believe in Russia and in some large city high schools in New York, might be a more direct solution to the problem of recruiting artists than a wide massive effort toward introducing more aesthetic education for everyone.

The economic plight of the serious artist may be genuine, as Baumol and Bowen show in their book, *The Performing Arts: The Economic Dilemma.*[3] If their analysis is correct, multiplying the number of performances is no remedy, because the creative arts cannot be mass-produced; that is, their production cannot be made more efficient; they can be *mass-reproduced,* but not *mass-produced.* And even if mass-reproduced, as on television, their creators cannot reap any reward until they are mass-consumed. Presumably they will not be mass-consumed unless an appreciative mass public is created. This might be done by more and better aesthetic education in the public schools. Relatively few non-college trained people support the performing arts. This is not a bad reason for aesthetic education—to create a mass public for the performing arts—and a persuasive one if it is in the public interest to preserve the serious arts, and if this is the only way of doing it. However, as Baumol and Bowen note, artists do not abandon their art because of poor economic rewards; clearly, they would not have embarked on such a career had this been the crucial factor. The arts will survive, thanks to the improvidence of artists.

Moreover, Harold Schonberg, of the *New York Times,* and others hold that a mass public for the serious arts is a misguided dream, perhaps a nightmare, to those who believe that serious art is produced by the few for the few. Somewhere between a mass public and the minuscule public of rich patrons is what might be called substantial publics. These substantial publics, there is reason to believe, are being created and sustained by our colleges and universities. Each has or aspires to have its own Greenwich Village, its own Bohemia. I dare say that more people are stirred to the liking and trying of literary and other artistic products in college than anywhere else. With ever larger proportions of people attending college, and being exposed to more and more artists in residence, the problem of a substantial public for the serious arts is in sight, whether we expand aesthetic education in the lower schools or not.

Another alternative is informal education in the arts. By this I mean the utilization of the powerful effect of milieu. One could envelop the population with art products—in stores, hotels, and, of course, schools. From this super saturation might crystallize a strong partiality for arts and artists. Of course, overexposure might produce the indifference of habit, but this risk, I assume, we might be happy to incur.

This alternative has merit, so much, in fact, that many sociologists and advertising experts consider it to be the only really effective way of inducing a mass effect of any sort. The mechanisms that seem to operate here are those of acceptance by familiarity; people become accustomed to strange musical and artistic forms, as they do to miniskirts or TV dinners or snails. Cage concerts and aleatory music concerts may be suffering from underexposure, and presumably in a genuine democracy of art all musical compositions would have a right to equal time.

I have dwelled perhaps overlong on the alternatives to the mass expansion of the formal study of art, or more broadly, aesthetic education, because insofar as they are plausible they reduce the strength of the argument for making aesthetic education an integral part of the required curriculum in the public schools. These alternatives are especially plausible if there is no discernible difference between serious and popular art, between the formally cultivated and uncultivated taste, that is, so long as we subscribe to the belief that in aesthetic matters taste is final. For to reiterate, there is no dearth of musical or artistic activity in the land if one does not differentiate among the activities.

With these observations in mind, I would argue that systematic reflection can extend the aesthetic experience, intensify our interest in it, and enhance the enjoyment of it. Educated language usage, educated judgment, and action in any domain is justified by the fact that it enlarges the range of whatever value is to be realized within that domain and the chances that we shall realize them. Furthermore, because mass engagement of the schools in the cultivation of taste entails a belief that such cultivation is possible as well as worthwhile, one has to show that an effective school program in aesthetic education can be devised.

Goals of Aesthetic Education

Cultivation has the connotation of deliberate and directed intervention. In cultivating a garden, one intervenes to destroy weeds and to increase the nitrogen content of the soil. Pruning, watering, hoeing—all are interventions; they utilize natural processes, but they produce what otherwise might not have been. Cultivation is the opposite of leaving matters alone to develop according to some given set of inner determinants or chance. Formal schooling is a prime example of intervention, of cultivation.

What then is to be cultivated in aesthetic education? It cannot be a preference for a fixed set of art products, for example, Shakespeare's *Hamlet* or Beethoven's *Ninth*. Even if one could secure consensus for such a set, it would mean the death of art, because all other art products would be doomed to rejection. Clearly what is meant is that works of art having certain properties are to become objects of preference. This would permit us to add new works to our preferred set, provided they met the criteria. Appreciation of good art would then be the goal of aesthetic education.

The difficulty with this way of defining the goal of aesthetic cultivation lies in the criteria themselves. Aside from the formal objections that it is misguided to seek a unique set of common defining properties of art, there is the fact that the criteria which have been suggested don't work.[4] Either they are formulas

organized into rules and canons which admit technically perfect aesthetic corpses (or perhaps more accurately, imitations of corpses, since they never were alive), or they exclude works that are admired despite lapses from the rules. This is the strongest weapon in the skeptic's armamentarium.

However, these difficulties do not destroy the educative possibilities of this way of looking at the goals of aesthetic education. For if there are properties by virtue of which we do judge a work of art to be good art—whether this constitutes a common defining set or by virtue of which works of art bear family resemblances to each other—then some art works could possess them in an eminently discernible way. This lies at the root of the claim of the classics to educative potency; it is a claim that cannot lightly be ignored.

Another goal for cultivation is the development of "adequate aesthetic experience." This defines the goal by qualities of experience rather than by objects or properties of selected objects; indeed, the objects need not be works of art; the rhythm of a rippling brook is as appropriate a target for aesthetic contemplation as the efforts of a symphony orchestra. This is analogous to stating the goal of education in terms of process rather than product. This has been expressed as teaching people to see as a painter sees, or to listen as a musician listens.

Unfortunately, it is no easier to get agreement on what constitutes a proper aesthetic experience than on the defining properties of good art. For one thing, some writers—John Dewey, for example—deny the existence of a distinctive type of experience to be called aesthetic. Further, can we agree on the artists who are to serve as models—as people who have the right kind of experience—and what portion of their experience is to count as relevant? For example, it won't do to regard their sex mores or political persuasion as part of the defining characteristics. As for applying these criteria, the difficulties are no less formidable than they were on the first approach.

A third approach argues that there are teachable skills of aesthetic discrimination and classification. Certain formal, stylistic, and technical properties can be discerned, and the discernment can be verified by interpersonal judgment. Statements actually used by critics can be regarded as hypotheses to be confirmed or disconfirmed by examining the work of art itself.

This approach has three real advantages: (1) It is teachable and the results are observable. (2) It avoids the need of committing the curriculum to any fixed set of objects as proper objects of veneration; any set may be used. (3) It is consonant with "aesthetic autonomy," that is, it does not drag in nonaesthetic values as an objective of aesthetic education.

However, this approach like the others cannot ultimately evade the value judgment. After all, analysis presupposes ideas as to what is important and what is good art. And is agreement on these matters among aestheticians and critics so marked that we can teach their judgments to school children? Without norms, it is impossible to justify aesthetic education; yet without some way of achieving agreement on norms one cannot justify aesthetic education either.

Whatever the theoretical difficulties, the practical solution is not all impossible. The solution is furnished by the method of justification used in every other department of instruction: we rely upon the expert or the consensus of the learned and, hopefully, the wise. Good chemistry for school purposes is what members of the American Chemical Society say is good chemistry. A roster of the learned societies furnishes the culture with definitions of norms within each of the intellectual disciplines. This principle is rarely invoked in the arts because:

1. The meaning of a work of art, it is argued, is contributed by the consumer. Each consumer feels what his experience (unique) more or less forces him to feel. There is, therefore, no fixed object to be judged. No man, therefore, can be more expert than another, and no one is qualified to tell another what he ought to feel. To this argument it can be replied that if one cannot tell another what to feel, one can teach him to see and hear what is to be seen and heard. Indeed, it is far easier to verify the presence of a fugue form in a piece of music than the presence of the air vibrations that make it audible.

2. Experts in the arts disagree in a scandalous fashion. One age repudiates the norms of a previous age. Many great artists were not appreciated in their own day. Stravinsky's work progressed from rejection to adulation in one lifetime.

Connoisseurs and critics may disagree with each other and with their predecessors, so there may be no one best symphony or folk song on every expert's list.[5] This fact leads many of us to jump to the conclusion that there are no experts and that there is no point in disputing about tastes. However, this misses the point entirely, for what qualifies a man to be an expert in any field is not a private crystal ball that enables him and his fellow experts to pick masterpieces in unerring unison, but rather arriving at a judgment by what experts agree is a valid method. This means that in matters of artistic judgment only experts can argue. There is no point in disputing about taste; one can only approve or deplore it. Dispute is properly confined to justifications for taste.

Whether one is referring to art objects or the kind of experience one is supposed to have in the contemplation of them, the expert is the only practical source of standards we have. Furthermore, although knowing about art is not the same as appreciating it or creating it, there is no special virtue in ignorance about the arts. Only the romantic illusion that art is made by divinely inspired frenzy and appreciated only by pristine innocence preserves this strange attitude toward knowledge about art. Such knowledge as we do have about art is as teachable as any other and like all knowledge is validated by the expertise of the expert.

What then are the characteristics of the expert that might serve as a guide for the cultivation of the pupil? Or to put it into instructional terms: What are the components of enlightened cherishing and how might instruction produce them?

Aesthetic Sensitivity

First of all, by developing aesthetic sensitivity. There are four dimensions:

1. sensitivity to sensory differences in the work of art,
2. sensitivity to formal properties in the work of art,
3. sensitivity to technical features in the work of art, and
4. sensitivity to expressiveness in the work of art.

Each art medium has its own store of sensory qualities that it uses to create objects which are "interesting to perception": sound pattens, visual shapes, color patterns, textures, gestures, images of all kinds. The artist becomes prematurely gray seeking the precise colors, shapes, and values for the effect he is trying to create. And while I am not saying that the perceiver can or should recreate every movement of the artist or suffer the pangs of creation, it does seem odd that he should not notice the differences that are so important to the artist. The connoisseur can be defined as the person to whom little differences make a big difference. The first step on the road to aesthetic education is, therefore, the sharpening of sensitivity to differences in the sensory manifold exhibited by a work of art. Training in this phase of aesthetic experience is certainly possible and almost prosaically straightforward.

By sensitivity to the formal properties of a work of art, I mean the ability to discern and react to patterns of composition, themes and variations, balances, similarities, and the other numerous characteristics comprehended under design. Here again, matters that are of first importance to the artist are often passed over unnoticed by the naive perceiver. Yet practice under guidance can improve sensitivity to the formal properties.

Little needs to be said about sensitivity to the technical aspects because when performance is the goal of instruction, technique usually receives its due. However, when appreciation is the goal, there is a tendency to denigrate technique, as if it detracted from enjoyment. This is arguable, to say the least.

The forth dimension of sensitivity, namely expressiveness, is more troublesome. By expressiveness I mean that elusive quality by virtue of which some works of art display import, albeit never literally or discursively. When we see a tree painted with inanimate materials as "lonely," then the painting is expressive. That is to say, it expresses something other than the visual outlines of a tree. By some peculiarity of human nature, and perhaps of physical nature as well, it is possible to paint "loneliness," it is possible to sing loneliness, it is possible to sculpt loneliness, and to dance it. It is possible to write a poem which expresses loneliness in words and in symbols which are themselves not lonely. The same applies to such qualities as: strength, energy, movement, sublimity, serenity, and grace.

Pedagogically, the problem is whether or not sensitivity to expressiveness can be cultivated. That it exists in most human beings is attested to by the universal tendency of children to perceive things as something else. The whole strategy of the fairy tale would backfire if this were not the case. So strong is this tendency that much of the training during the earlier years is directed toward sharpening the difference between reality and fancy in the child's experience. Having "disillusioned" him, we then have to reverse the process and restore his ability to see images as embodiments of feeling: a more mature and fruitful type of illusion. The artistic imagination is to be distinguished and should be distinguishable from the fancies of the child, the scatterbrain, the drug addict, and the lunatic.

One of the stumbling blocks to aesthetic education is the relentless pressure on the child to be literal, factual, and scientifically terse. These are indubitable virtues in modern man, and probably he could not survive without them. But if they do not wholly destroy the aesthetic capacities, they do inhibit the receptivity to the figurative, the imaginative, in short, the aesthetic mode of experience; it becomes increasingly awkward to shift into the aesthetic mood. What was simple and natural for the five-year-old is embarrassing to the twelve-year-old.

Aesthetic Skills

For a long time now the elementary school has been expected to give work in music and in art not only for enjoyment but also for the development of skills in the use of these media. One might reasonably expect that pupils by the end of the sixth grade will be able to read music, use voice, play some musical instrument, have had some experience with paint and crayons, and with the writing of prose and poetry that aspires to literary form. Dramatic skills and skills of the dance are less commonly practiced, although our expectations could extend to these also.We could be much firmer in asking the school to live up to these expectations.

Just how much of elementary school art is for skill, how much for play, and how much for therapy is hard to determine. Each approach has its advocates, but it is safe to say that technical skill is no longer the primary goal of aesthetic education in the elementary grades. There are many reasons for this, but the shift to free experimentation with diverse artistic media has certainly reduced the terror of the nonspecialized elementary school teacher when faced with the art lesson. On the whole, the gain for the program at this level probably outweighs the putative losses in technical skill.

However, whether aesthetic skills are achieved in the elementary school or elsewhere, achieved they must be, if for no other reason than that they force us to perceive an image in detail. How much performance is needed for appreciation I do not know, but I find it hard to believe that one can "see" as the painter sees or "hear" as the musician hears without some effort to translate what is "seen" into painted surfaces or what is "heard" into music.

Creative Performance

In addition to opportunities for developing artistic skills in the elementary grades, a complete program of aesthetic education should provide opportunities, curricular or extracurricular, in the secondary school for creative artistic activity at a higher level than that in the elementary grades. The word opportunity is used deliberately, because it is difficult to see how studio instruction in any of the arts can be required as part of general education. Differences in talent and inclination will diversify the artistic activities of the pupils at this stage of the schooling. Thus, although aesthetic education can be part of general education at the secondary school level, development of skill beyond a basic minimum level cannot be. A boy wishing to perfect himself in the piano should be able to take lessons at the high school if the school can afford to provide them; but this is a form of special training.

Aesthetic Judgment

In addition to sensitivity and skill, connoisseurship or enlightened cherishing requires aesthetic judgment, for it is in aesthetic judgment that we not only know what we like, but can also make some attempt at giving reasons for liking it. We approach aesthetic maturity when we can say, "I like this music, but it is not good art," or "This music is good art, but I don't like it." Only God and the aesthetically innocent are spared this discrepancy.

One can think of the aesthetic judgment as taking the form of criticism. I shall not go into the anatomy of criticism.[6] It will be sufficient to indicate some of the ingredients: classification of an art object of style, period, and the like; formal analysis of the aesthetic features in the work of art; application of some sort of standard to arrive at some reasoned evaluation about each dimension of the work and the total effect of all the dimensions.

One might say about the teaching of appreciation what T.S. Eliot said about the critic:

> So the critic to whom I am most grateful is the one who can make me look at something I have never looked at before, or looked at only with eyes clouded with prejudice, set me face to face with it and then leave me alone with it. From that point, I must rely upon my own sensibility, intelligence, and capacity for wisdom.[7]

This is fine for T.S. Eliot, who already had well-developed sensibility, intelligence, and capacity for wisdom, precisely what the pupil does not yet have. T.S. Eliot, one must suppose, had already introjected models that guided his aesthetic judgments. To what extent T.S. Eliot developed his own models I do not know, but one can safely wager that however much they were his own, they were modifications of standards that were developed from models espoused by critics from Aristotle on.

Although the introjection of models brings us back to the question of norms and the propriety of forcing them on the young, the problem is not fundamentally different in the arts than in other areas of instruction, *viz.*, to find the most economical way of inducting the young into a cultural domain.

Paradigm and Revolution

In every domain there are key concepts, modes of inquiry, standards of evidence, and problems to be solved. This is what I take Thomas Kuhn to mean by paradigm science. This is what provides the cognitive map for workers in the domains of science, and learners have to become familiar with this standard set of problems and solutions. In every developing domain there is a frontier that goes beyond the map, and every so often a creative explorer makes it imperative to produce a new map. This is what Kuhn would call a scientific revolution.[8]

I do not think we shall strain the analogy unduly if we speak of paradigm art and revolutionary art. The induction of the young to the artistic culture of the past must be through the paradigm art, that is, through those works that in each epoch supplied the models *from which the rules and principles were derived*. These might be classed as (1) summating works, (2) bridging works, and (3) anticipatory works.

By a summating work of art, I mean one that is considered by experts as somehow bringing together trends that had been developing for a period of time. In philosophy the great *Summae* of St. Thomas Aquinas are regarded as summating works. There is a sense also in which some of the dramas of Shakespeare are regarded as summating works with respect to the Elizabethan era.

By a bridging work, I mean one that contains elements of the past, but also introduces elements quite different from them. I take it that this is the sense in which Herman Melville's novels or T.S. Eliot's poetry or Gustav Mahler's music might be called bridging works. Bridging poems, pictures, and dramas are loved by historians of art, because they provide grist for the mill that grinds out doctoral theses which are intended to (and very often do) show that what claims to be new really isn't.

Finally, the anticipating works are those that broke sharply with the tradition of their time; that is, with the then current paradigms which seemed strange and weird to contemporary taste, but which time has tamed.

We cannot use the paradigmatic approach in teaching contemporary art. Revolutionary music, for example, may be a bid to scrap the paradigms and force a new one upon composers. Musical experiments at any age are challenges to the paradigm, but there is no way of knowing ahead of time which of the challenges will win the field and which will not last out the decade. About all one can do with contemporary art in aesthetic education is to cultivate a tolerance for experimentation and a sensitivity to whatever aesthetic qualities it may create. Aesthetic analysis is as far as the school can go with contemporary art; it can hardly be critical about it, for there are no paradigmatic norms that apply to it. It is the duty of an educated public to harbor the new until it has made or failed to make the grade; the fact that some educated people do not like or enjoy the experiments has nothing to do with their aesthetic duty.

My assignment is not to justify art but education in the arts, and I have suggested that we ought to make our claim for it on the basis that a cultivated taste is better than a raw one. In claiming this one cannot evade the need for cultivation in every domain of human accomplishment, so that school board members are well within the bounds of propriety to ask about the contribution of aesthetic education to general education. For the school is a social institution that purports to give general cultivation, and, in the nature of the case, no part of the curriculum can become completely dissociated from any other part. Art for art's sake is a reasonable and defensible dictum within the field of art, but art for "goodness" sake is the principle that art has to be recognized, if it claims to be integral to the culture rather than peripheral to it.

The good life, not science, not the humanities, not the arts, is the purpose of general education. We justify art education because aesthetic experience does contribute to well-being in a unique way, by giving aesthetic satisfaction and by intensifying and perhaps illuminating every other mode of experience. It is not the business of a composer to preach over the dead, but his requiem mass may help make death vivid and significant as no verbal account can. Nor do we have to agree with Tolstoy's insistence on the moral import of art in order to appreciate the fact that art can exemplify and even communicate aesthetically the shape of feeling appropriate to moral situations. That the aesthetic, cognitive, moral, and religious experience were originally one is highly probable; the aesthetic as a distinctive domain is a late development of sophisticated abstraction. So there is something to be said for the common man's instinctive demand that the primordial unity be restored. This sentiment will have more weight with educators than with artists.

Enlightened cherishing, of paradigm art at least, blends easily with the other ingredients of general education, and yet contributes something other ingredients cannot. This is the direct apprehension of the images by which the most cultivated people of the past perceived their world. This is not the place to argue about the veridicity of these images, but even creative geniuses cannot escape the images of their time. In reading the *Iliad* we do not read the mind of Homer; we do not communicate with Homer, or he with us. But more important, perhaps in reading Homer aesthetically, we share his images. This way of appropriating the ethos of an epoch is permitted only by the arts, and only serious art allows us to share images with the most cultivated spirits of that epoch.

If this does not make an important contribution to general education, then much of what we have called civilization has been a mistake.

---

[1] As did the builders of the most recent *Webster's Dictionary*.

[2] Alvin Toffler, *The Culture Consumers: Art and Affluence in America* (New York: St. Martin's Press, 1964).

[3] William J. Baumol and William G. Bowen, *The Performing Arts: The Economic Dilemma* (New York: Twentieth Century Fund, Inc., 1966).

[4] See Morris Weitz, "The Role of Theory in Aesthetics," *The Journal of Aesthetics and Art Criticism,* Vol. 15, Sept. 1956.

[5] A good discussion about the causes of this disagreement is to be found in D. W. Gotshalk, *Art and the Social Order* (New York: Dover, 1962), pp. 177-180.

[6] For a convenient collection of discussions of this topic, see *Aesthetics and Criticism in Art Education,* edited by Ralph A. Smith (Chicago: Rand McNally, 1966), pp 299-406.

[7] T.S. Eliot, *On Poetry and Poets* (New York: Farrar, Straus and Cudahy, 1957), p. 131.

[8] Thomas Kuhn, *The Structure of Scientific Revolutions* (Chicago: Chicago University Press, 1962).

The Humanistic Curriculum

Ole Sand

Educators interested in a humanistic curriculum should develop a strong devotion to Saint Alexis. He was the small, bright-eyed lad who lived unnoticed in his father's house for over twenty-five years, and ultimately pined away on an out-of-the-way island in the Seine. Like Cinderella, with whom most of us have at some time identified, he and most humanists have been relegated to the chimney corner while their elder sisters have been clamoring for the sunshine in the post-Sputnik streamlining. I think the time has come to put the glass slipper on the right foot.

The papers of Broudy and Northrop quickened my heart; they not only shed much light on the importance of an aesthetic education and a humanistic curriculum, but also indicated that the warmth such an education engenders is not the warmth of a chimney corner. Their papers highlight two of the twelve questions raised by the National Committee for the NEA Project on Instruction, which are primary concerns of mine in the NEA Center for the Study of Instruction, and which many of you are applying in your programs. I should like to restrict my remarks to these two questions:

1. How can the school provide a program appropriately balanced for the individual and maintain it amidst various pressures for specialization?

2. How can schools make wise selections of content from the ever-growing body of available knowledge?

CSI exists to help bring together the world of scholarship and the world of decision, for we are all painfully aware that the present quality of communication can stand much improvement. Would it not be breathtaking if we could make ourselves and our wares as dramatic as Beethoven's *Fifth* or "Georgy Girl" or even the Monkees? Or is there a more quiet way of doing our job?

If I were to attempt to present the work of CSI in capsule, I would say that we adhere to and support a rather fundamental belief that improvement of an educational program can and must be accomplished through rational planning of curriculum and instruction, which, incidentally, is the title of a new CSI publication you will all want to liven up your next faculty meeting.[1] Too many of these sessions are best described as quivering in unison. I am reminded of one of my colleagues who had suffered a coronary. We urged him to take care of himself and not come to faculty meetings. He said, "Oh, no. I shall come to all faculty meetings this year because, if I should have the final attack, I would like it to be at a faculty meeting. The transition from life to death would be scarcely perceptible."

While rational planning is a point of view likely to raise few eyebrows in this audience, it is a goal that demands repeating since it seems to have gone just as unnoticed as Saint Alexis. The objective is to keep all of the forces that are brought to bear upon the humanistic, educational process squarely on target.

To this end, I shall attempt to spell out some directions in which education is going. The curriculum reform movement has dealt primarily with *what* to teach. I shall deal with two of several issues in that area—balance and content selection.

Balancing the Program. In today's world of breathtaking technological advancement, the all-important position once attributed to the humanities has been usurped by the sciences, and we are bequeathed a disturbing imbalance that threatens to leave today's student starved in the humanities. Willy-nilly, we are the sudden beneficiaries of the TV-Sputnik-sitdown-IBM-mushroom cloud era, and, as Broudy points out, "many of us cannot escape the feeling that if we do wholly surrender our fates to the new gods, we may be saved *from* our humanity rather than *for* it." [2]Northrop, in a provocative and penetrating study, echoes this sentiment:

> Ours is a paradoxical world. The achievements which are its glory threaten to destroy it. The nations with the highest standard of living, the greatest capacity to take care of their people economically, the broadest education, and the most enlightened morality and religion exhibit the least capacity to avoid mutual destruction in war. It would seem that the more civilized we become the more incapable of maintaining civilization we are.[3]

Ask one of your students about the sun. What will he tell you? It is 93,000,000 miles from the earth, approximately 866,500 miles in diameter, with a surface rotation of about 25 days at the equator. If he is to live in the shadow of bigger and better bombs, perhaps he must be taught all these facts. Yet, it will always be the larger purpose of education to lead him to appreciate the radiance of a sunset. And here, G. K. Chesterton has something to say to our point:

> There is a notion adrift everywhere that imagination, especially mystical imagination, is dangerous to man's mental balance. Poets are commonly spoken of as psychologically unreliable; and generally there is a vague association between wreathing laurels in your hair and sticking straws in it. Facts and history utterly contradict this view. Most of the very great poets have been not only sane, but extremely business-like; and if Shakespeare ever really held horses, it was because he was much the safest man to hold them. Imagination does not breed insanity. Exactly what does breed insanity is reason. Poets do not go mad; but chess-players do. Mathematicians go mad, and cashiers; but creative artists very seldom. . . . Critics are much madder than poets. Homer is complete and calm enough; it is his critics who tear him into extravagant tatters. Shakespeare is quite himself; it is only some of his critics who have discovered that he was somebody else. And though St. John the Evangelist saw many strange monsters in his vision, he saw no creature so wild as one of his own commentators. The general fact is simple. Poetry is sane because it floats easily in an infinite sea; reason seeks to cross the infinite sea, and so make it finite. The result is mental exhaustion, like the physical exhaustion of Mr. Holbein. To accept everything is an exercise, to understand everything a strain. The poet only desires exaltation and expansion, a world to stretch himself in. The poet only asks to get his head into the heavens. It is the logician who seeks to get the heavens into his head. And it is his head that splits.[4]

Science is not the panacea of life's problems. We must keep our debt to it in clear perspective. Its Nembutal® helps us sleep; its wrinkle-resistant wash-and-wear clothes us; its steel beams support the great Music Shed here at Tanglewood. But the test tube has yet to come up with a formula for increasing man's ability to think, to feel, to appreciate, to understand, to love. It is the task of the humanities to help us understand ourselves so we can understand our fellow men, and to help us live in this valley of the dolls that science has fashioned for us.

The many projects initiated by MENC should prove essential in constructing a curriculum appropriately balanced for each individual. Your deep concern about creativity resulting from music education is a giant step toward helping students learn life-long aesthetic attitudes through experiences in music and the other arts and humanities.

The humanities, of course, must serve the schools in equipping today's students to make the best possible use of the greatest blessing to emerge from technology—the gift of leisure. The school shares this responsibility with other educational agencies. Incidentally, Dewey's disciples sometimes confuse his sound advice about schooling the whole child with nonsense about the school taking responsibility for the child's whole education.[5] The school is still only one educational institution. We are not looking for perfect balance, of course. A little disequilibrium often produces people who are as exciting as Petula Clark, as productive as Thomas Aquinas or Martin Luther, as imaginative and creative as Serge Koussevitzky.

The teacher who teaches with zest, who speaks and listens well, who helps his students interact with more than boredom or rebellion is a humanist, an artist working with humanity, and his art is the one thing in this pep-pill world of ours most likely to beget in his students a thirst, a passion for the fullness of life. Is there anything in our philosophy of education that requires that the teacher be a poor listener or speaker, alien to the sheer *delight* of being, fearful of his bright young students, and complete with spastic mannerisms? Is Plato less for writing well? Would we be richer if Socrates had spoken badly, if he had not charmed his young listeners to a view of the world and a delight in their own unique being, no matter what he was discussing at the moment? Is it a *blessing* that too many articles in educational journals are completely devoid of style? When a concept has reached such definition that it can be adequately expressed in jargon, then it can be taught much more efficiently by a machine.

The only reason that a teacher should be a person, alive to the things that are, is that he must encourage speculation and lead it. To help a student learn about an unknown and vastly different country requires a medium, a metaphor in which the known and the unknown can meet, each taking meaning from the other, and such a medium is the essence of music, of poetry, of art. Students taught by a real humanist will become real humanists, readers, listeners, men of intellectual and emotional delight, ready for a kind of intimacy with the world which will breed not contempt, but freedom of mind, a way out of the slavery of mere conformism to society. President Kennedy put it well:

I look forward to an America which will not be afraid of grace and beauty. . . which will reward achievement in the arts as we reward achievement in business or statecraft. . . which will steadily raise the standards of artistic accom-plishment. . . which will steadily enlarge cultural opportunities for all of our citizens.[6]

Selecting Content. The second issue I should like to explore briefly concerns the selection of content. Never before have the forces of change spun with such incredible speed. In the nearly 2,000 years since the birth of Christ, there has been first a very slow and then a rapidly accelerating growth in the accumulation of knowledge. The first time man's accumulated knowledge of his world doubled was in 1750. It redoubled 150 years later; then again 50 years later; then again 10 years later.

So much has been learned that, as the Red Queen in *Alice in Wonderland* complains, "It takes all the running you can do, just to keep in the same place." Because of this explosion of knowledge, the problems of what to learn require a vastly different approach today. We must move from an overemphasis on memorization of facts toward discovery of facts. The Pepsi-generation, nourished by Sputnik and Romper Room and *Playboy,* will not settle for the old pre-packaged pap. Art must spark the realization of quantity and relationship and convergence, the way Walt Disney did it. Literature must be the "open-sesame" to the dignities and depravities of man's striving, the way *21st Century* does it. Music must open the boy and release the man locked inside.

Important national curriculum studies are becoming as commonplace as cocktails before dinner. They spring from the urgent need for bringing the school curriculum up to date, incorporating the useful, discarding the obsolete. Here are some of the recommendations of the National Committee for the Project on Instruction on what schools should do in the selection of content:

1. The objectives of the school, with a clear statement of priorities, should give direction to all curriculum planning. This applies to adding content, eliminating content, or changing the emphases on various topics and fields of study.

2. The curriculum must undergo close and continuing reevaluation, in the light of new knowledge. Everyone can contribute to this Herculean task—the teacher, the school administrator, the scholar, the informed citizen, the student.

3. The results and recommendations of curriculum projects sponsored by nationally-oriented groups must be studied by school staffs who will glean and use promising findings.

There is a real need for a systematic procedure for studying the results of these curriculum projects—a procedure that honors the importance of balance and continuity in the total school experience of students. No system will be complete unless it allows for change when change is needed.

In conclusion, let me urge you all to be a little reckless. Intercourse with the arts, humanities, and music should make a man promiscuous. We need disequilibrium in ourselves as well as in our curriculum. Show your students that you are real humanists—people eager to "go and catch a falling star," (Donne) "to touch, taste, savor, and be stung," (Buckley)—educators who hunger for loveliness. Many people see things and say, "Why?" I sincerely hope that you will dream things that never were and say, "Why not?"[7]

And if others urge you to be more reasonable, more cautious, tell them about Mr. Blue—a man who was different, so gloriously different that dull-witted people thought him fantastic and just a

16

bit grotesque. He was no Saint Alexis. No corner, I am sure, however dark, could have contained him. He was a real humanist who, like Cinderella, got the glass slipper in the end. He wrote the following letter to a friend:

> And even you preach caution to me! How I detest that word! How it has written its evil over our lives. Why, a man can't be spontaneously affectionate today without being suspected of weakness! We are advised to watch ourselves. We are counseled to keep our thoughts to ourselves. Silence, caution, reserve are urged as prime virtues. Our fear of exuberancy, of ecstasy, of any genuine passion, is being stamped on our faces and our lives. We become a thin-lipped, close-eyed people. A thousand fine inheritances are being compressed into a single character—and what a thin weak putty that character is! Once, I am told, men put on their shields and banners such brave words as Love, Audacity, Faith. Today we have written across a million pages and placards and billboards our slogans: Self-considerateness, Thrift, Safety first. We have about as much hunger for loveliness as a turtle. And about as much capacity for intense and varied living as a cabbage.[8]

You have tried to change all this. Be forever restless, forever trying.

(Appreciation is expressed to Rev. Joseph Devlin, S.J., CSI Research Associate, for his assistance in preparing this manuscript.)

[1]*Rational Planning in Curriculum and Instruction: Eight Essays* (Washington: Center for the Study of Instruction, National Education Association, 1967).

[2]Harry S. Broudy, "Aesthetic Education in a Technological Society: The Other Excuses for Art," *The Journal of Aesthetic Education,* Spring 1966, p. 13.

[3]F.S.C. Northrop, *The Meeting of East and West* (New York: Collier Books, 1966), p. 1.

[4]G.K. Chesterton, *Orthodoxy* (New York: Dodd, Mead and Co., 1954 [c 1939]), pp. 16-18.

[5] Lawrence A. Cremin, *The Genius of American Education* (Pittsburgh: University of Pittsburgh Press, 1965), p. 8.

[6]Drawn from remarks made at Amherst during a memorial service for Robert Frost.

[7]G.B. Shaw, *Man and Superman.*

[8]Myles Connolly, *Mr. Blue* (New York: Macmillan, 1954 [c 1928]), pp. 73-74.

The Role of

the Arts in a Changing Society

William C. Hartshorn

The assignment given me is to react as a music educator to the presentations given by Professors Northrop and Broudy. Each speaker has provided an experience rarely given to a music educator. Too seldom are those of us on the firing line of music education given the privilege of intellectual challenges of such depth, nor do most of us have time to initiate them and pursue them for ourselves.

In response to what I believe is Northrop's point of view, I will focus upon his theory of the dual components in aesthetic experience and the interrelationships that must exist between them. No doubt this is an oversimplification, but I find this dual component in aesthetic experience a factor that is almost always present, either explicitly or implicitly, in Northrop's writing.

Each of these components has very definite implications for the teaching of music in the classroom.

As I understand Northrop, the first factor in the aesthetic experience is an immediately apprehended factor, which can be directly inspected and is not subject to change. For purposes of brevity I may sometimes refer to this component as Number 1. It is made up of colors, sounds, odors, flavors, pains and pleasures, and sensed spatial and *temporal* reactions. These are the materials used by painters, musicians, and poets. Under certain conditions these immediately experienced items are conveyed as they are, purely and empirically, and this is art for art's sake. Northrop refers to this as "the aesthetic" in the nature of things.

The other side of this duality involves references to inferred meanings emerging from the aesthetic experience. This second component – which for the sake of brevity may sometimes be referred to as Number 2 – is designated by Northrop to be a theoretical component as distinguished from the component itself. The inference would seem to be that the first component in the aesthetic experience deals with the experience of perceiving the flower, the sunset, the work of art, the musical composition, and of responding to its immediately sensed qualities. The second component, which conveys inferred meanings, analogies, and symbolisms, together with theoretical elements, is primarily scientific and intellectual in contrast to the predominantly emotional nature of the first component. As Northrop points out, these two must be inextricably bound together.

This music educator is inclined to equate the first component with so-called pure music and to associate it with goals of music education which deal with purely musical and aesthetic values and which make no claim for music in the curriculum on the basis of nonmusical values. In like manner, the second component would seem to be associated with inferred meanings, such as those relevant to program music – within limits there is a perfectly legitimate place for this – and also with those avowed purposes of

music in the curriculum which deal with purely theoretical aspects of the art, with technical skills, and with individual and societal values which are nonmusical in character.

Northrop finds a major weakness in Western Civilization in its tendency to make the scientific, theoretical, and deductively affirmed aspects of the aesthetic experience predominant, thus relegating the immediately apprehended, directly perceived components of aesthetic experience in our classrooms. To what extent are we providing young people with genuine, directly perceivable aesthetic experiences that are consistent with Northrop's first component? What degree of importance and attention are we giving to the theoretical, the formal-structural, the technical, and the deductively established intellectual component? To what extent is music education promoting a lively interaction between the two components in the musical experiences of children and young people? Granted that both components are essential to a complete aesthetic experience, to what extent are we shifting the emphasis from one component to the other in terms of the varying natures and needs of individual students or groups of students?

In setting forth the relationship between the first and second components in the aesthetic experience, Northrop brings to bear principles of epistemology through which he develops epistemic correlations that relate a thing known empirically in its aesthetic component to what is known in the theoretical component.

The illustration he uses has a special meaning for music educators. He suggests that the blind Helen Keller was incapable of developing a concept of blue by either perception or intuition, but that she could have come to a certain understanding of the nature of blueness by an intellectually understood theory of wave lengths. For the music educator there are implications of major importance in his statement that any complete thing is made up of both 1 and 2 – 1 being the emotional, aesthetic, and ineffable and 2 being the unseen theoretic component (designated by thought) which is deductively checked and appraised. He further states that blue sky, the color of the rose, or of the sunset (and there are musical counterparts of these) are ineffable because no theory can ever designate them and that therefore this is what is meant by the spiritual.

On this philosophical basis the music educator can affirm the spiritual values of music and seek to promote them. Certainly the implication here is that the role of the music teacher is to get himself out of the way of the music and to perform only those functions which are necessary to clear the path between the student and his aesthetic experience and to avoid the perennial fault of talking too much.

Northrop states very clearly that the aesthetic component, or any part of it, must be immediately experienced to be known and that unlike the theoretical component, it cannot be conveyed syntactically and deductively by a postulational technique. No amount of verbal description can convey the sensed color blue to one born blind or the sound of music to one who has never heard.

These are days when general educators are placing high value upon the development of self-realization, of a self image in which one can find satisfaction and a wholesome sense of pride. This is a special need of minority races, which education should seek to fulfill in a way proven psychologically sound. Northrop has stated that the most important ground of freedom is in the aesthetic component of man's nature: to be one's true self is to give expression to the ineffable emotional spontaneity of the aesthetic component of one's essential nature and to bring the more theoretically known constitution of one's self to the act of aesthetic expression. It would appear that one of the major goals of the music educator should be to provide for more young people well motivated, carefully directed, and specifically focused experiences with the sound of music itself through which they can become truly self-identified with the work of art they are experiencing, so that it possesses them more completely than they could ever conceivably possess it.

In response to Dr. Broudy's speech, certain questions come to mind:

To what extent do we really believe in general education in the arts? Why?

To what extent do we really value music as a part of general education? Why?

Is the fact that only a small minority of young people have any organized instruction in music in the secondary schools due to some philosophical belief, to a deeply entrenched common practice, to a lack of creativity in scheduling, or to a combination of any or all of these factors? Is this of any concern to us, and if so, how should we go about attempting to correct the problem?

Are the protagonists for an extended program of music in general education motivated only by a desire to provide a wider audience through support of professional musicians, or is there also a deep-seated conviction that the quality of living in our society can be enhanced by the intrinsic values that may be realized through music education for all young people?

If the answer to the last part of the previous question is affirmative, how can the program of instruction be varied to meet the widely divergent societal, cultural, and intellectual backgrounds of the young people who attended our secondary schools, to say nothing of the more impressionable youngsters who are in our elementary schools?

Do we agree with those who believe that serious art is by the few and for the few? Is aesthetic education to be limited to a cultural and intellectual elite? Dr. Broudy argues on behalf of systematically organized experiences which will extend the aesthetic education of young people, but he also tells us that we must show that an effective program can be devised.

Dr. Broudy warns us against an approach in which we select a specified body of music literature consisting of particular titles of compositions which, if studied by our pupils, would give them a repertoire for appreciation and therefore take them one step on the road to being educated in music. In contrast to this approach, he recommends that the music literature studied be selected on the basis of its embodiment of certain principles, and perhaps it may be assumed that he would want our students to investigate these principles to understand the way they operate in a piece of music.

Broudy's first goal of aesthetic education is the development of a cultivated sense of discrimination and therefore an appreciation of aesthetic objects, including music, which meet certain criteria.

Broudy suggests that another goal for aesthetic education is the development of adequate aesthetic experience, where he places special value upon the quality of *experience* rather than upon the properties of selected objects. He places a value upon critical thinking and apparently supports the goal of teaching young people to listen as a musician listens.

Perhaps the best education in music we can give young people is to help them discover for themselves, through processes of inquiry, how to approach a piece of music on its own terms. Those terms are purely musical. They deal with the constituent elements and the relationships that exist among them.

The third approach to aesthetic education suggested by Broudy has to do with the teaching of skills and aesthetic discrimination. This would deal with formal, stylistic, and technical properties of pieces of music. Here again these should not be taught as facts but as processes within the work of art.

Broudy's statement that the thing which qualifies a man to be an expert in any field is the validity of his method of arriving at a judgment would seem to argue on behalf of aesthetic education as a process of inquiry, for if that process is consistent with the nature of the subject under investigation the result should be valid.

Restrictions of time permit the mention of only one other topic in Broudy's paper, and that had to do with aesthetic sensitivity. First he mentions sensory differences in the work of art, and this points up the absolute and basic necessity of perception as the first step in aesthetic conceptualization—the direct experience, in our case, with music itself. Second, he mentions aesthetic sensivity to formal properties in the work of art. Third, Broudy mentions sensitivity to technical features in a work of art. For the performer this can be related to the development of technical skills and of theoretical aspects. It would seem that these are interrelated, at least to some extent, with formal properties. Finally, Broudy advocates development of sensitivity to expressiveness in a work of art. He concedes that this is troublesome. Herein lie dangerous pitfalls for the music teacher who probably has had little opportunity, if any, to develop any kind of aesthetic theory.

Finally, Broudy says, "The good life, not science, not the humanities, not the arts, is the purpose of general education. We justify art education [and I might interpolate here music education] because aesthetic experience does contribute to well-being in a unique way by giving aesthetic satisfaction and by intensifying and perhaps illuminating every other mode of experience." And Northrop assures us that aesthetic experience is a need of human nature as essential as is food.

The Role of Music

in Our Philosophy of Education

Ralph W. Tyler

My role here at Tanglewood is related to my own special work in studies of learning and especially studies of what school and college students learn — what kinds of difficulties they have in learning, and ways in which their learning can be improved. If I use that background as a basis for responding to the excellent presentations of the morning, it may lend a different perspective.

The brilliant and clear exposition of the theoretic bases of aesthetics, which Professor Northrop gave us this morning, is very important for those who are concerned with college and school learning, because it presents a more general theory of art experience and aesthetics than the ones characteristic of the nineteenth and early part of the twentieth century. For example, classical music is only a special case in this broad theory, which uses a more adequate conceptualization to guide students' action to appreciation of a wide range of music, including contemporary music and music not yet produced. It is also helpful to me because it gets around one of the difficult questions we find that help us to distinguish students who are relatively successful in school and college work from those who have greater difficulty, and that is their own conception of scholarship.

There are many students, and unfortunately they are in the majority in school and college, for whom answers to questions are already in existence. They are in books, in encyclopedias, in teachers; and the student's role is to find those answers and to give them back, or to remember them with the hope that they may be useful not only on quiz programs but in other ways. The more modern notion of scholarship, which guides many of the new curricula that are being developed (for example, the Physical Science Study Commission—the earliest one to be given financial support by the federal government), is the nature of scholarship as inquiry. Man is the one who makes knowledge, and his ability to make knowledge increases as he gains more perspective, as he develops better tools to work with, as he has more experience with phenomena. This knowledge is always a continually growing one, and we do not expect to have someone give us the answers, and then assume our world is complete when we finish school. Knowledge is something that keeps growing, and we will never know exactly what the world is like in that sense. We are always seeking knowledge, and this seems to me to provide us with the basis for viewing music and the other arts.

I did not hear in Professor Northrop's statement a detailed consideration of some of the other features of music that are also part of the expectations of many school people and, even more, of the lay public. These other features are the role of music in acculturation — that is, helping a person become a communicating, meaningful, contributing part of the particular society in which he lives. There is a sense in which music plays a very important role in helping us feel a part of America, or part of Western civilization, or just part of humanity. We cannot overlook the extent to which young people gain a pride and sense of contribution to their society through music.

Another objective, which is not specifically aesthetic, is the way in which music provides the means for reliving meaningful emotional experiences that we have had. The human life is always lived, as Dr. Northrop pointed out, "in time perspective." We are not living only in the present. Much of the difference between the educated person and an uneducated one is the extent to which he is already thinking about the future and planning his life. In thinking about the future, we are reacting to the specific sense stimuli of the present, and we are also carrying the memories of the past. Music can provide clues for the re-enactment of things that have been very meaningful, especially with the emotional concomitant. This is not the *aesthetic role of music,* but it is the *role of human music.* Think how many times YOU have memories reinstated by the music you hear.

And a third role of music which has not been discussed thus far is in the communication of special forms of expression. One time at our Center at Stanford, Freda Fromm Reichman, the famous psychoanalyst, came to give a lecture. She began to raise questions about how one communicated with human beings, especially about their emotional problems and their emotional life, and how little of that could be ascertained if you simply transcribed their words on paper. This began to interest a number of other people—anthropologists and linguists among others—that is, the role of various forms of communication by which we really communicate. A film was made of a psychiatrist interviewing a patient while the patient's daughter was present, and she was one of the problems. Their interview was first analyzed in terms of what could be put on paper, then by the psychiatrist's analysis, next by a linguist in terms of the aural sound track, and then by looking at the tenseness of the body and the various forms of kinetic expression.

Certainly, we have a much wider range of communication than that which would be expressed by writing our thoughts down to be read. And music seems to me to be one of these forms of communication, especially for emotional states, that has an important role in the lives of all of us; and it seems to me that we should be looking at that, too. It may not be a major role, but as a person psychologically looking at the learners, it seems to me that this potential should be reviewed.

Turning to Professor Broudy's discussion of what he called the justification, this seemed to me much more a statement of what our aims and objectives for music education, or aesthetic education, should be. We are inclined to work in the field of learning of school children and college students and to apply certain considerations to the judgment. They are such considerations as the sense to which this learning can be relevant to the individual so that he can engage in it significantly and do something with it, and the extent to which he can contribute as a member of society, and I think that both of those were dealt with effectively by Professor Broudy. He implied that they are cohesive with the contemporary philosophy of American education.

An important objective in terms of the contemporary philosophy of American education is the learning which "opens" people rather than "closing" them. Now one of the difficulties of building a curriculum based on an analysis of manpower needs of the United States, which tends to be one of the things often considered in engineering, science, and vocational education, is the preoccupation upon specializing the person, on having him that way as a democratic concern. Everything that a student learns ought to be something that makes it possible for him to *have more alternative choices* rather than fewer; it opens doors rather than specializing him to a point where he has no alternative except this one thing for which he has been trained. The kind of emphasis that we have here upon development of aesthetic sensitivity, including a sensitivity to formal aspects, to technical and to expressive aspects, affords all kinds of developments that help to open up new doors. I do not see them as being limited to a particular form of music. New music develops. One can benefit from having acquired or cultivated these kinds of sensitivities.

Another objective in our philosophy of education is that a provision and opportunity for continued learning in music be afforded. What we are trying to do is to get people started on a lifelong road of learning and provide the possibility to keep learning. Not having things answered now and we are through, but having gathered clues to continue the developing, increasing confidence that one can learn, increasing ways of getting new understanding and so on — these, it seems to me, are the criteria met by the kinds of objectives that Professor Broudy pointed out.

There is a third objective in the contemporary philosophy of education. Learning provides opportunities to integrate thought, feeling, and action rather than separating them so that we pride ourselves on knowing something but will not act without thinking and feeling. The effort to provide that opportunity and the importance of providing this kind of integration is certainly implied by the way in which Professor Broudy pointed out the role of critical reflection and analysis as well as a synthesis in hearing and being sensitive. Now he did make a point about taste — which seems to represent important aspects of any educational objective in this field. We hope that if music education becomes an effective thing, there will be an increasing interest on the part of the student in continuing his musical experience, and there will be the development of taste. But I do not think that Professor Broudy meant that having a paradigm of norms necessarily means *closed* norms. We need to find norms that are sensible, that make a difference to us, norms from which we get more meaning and more satisfaction. Students should realize that we do not have a closed system of norms, but a normative system that is quite capable of growth, development, and modification.

The importance of the performing skills in building sensitivity to really hear what is going on and to appreciate various technical aspects should never be overlooked. Efforts to teach music appreciation without any opportunity for production on the part of the student have not been very effective compared with the opportunity for some development of performing skills.

The relevance of objectives like these can be perceived by students. By first listening to things that they already want to listen to, and moving step by step away from that, they can discover that this kind of learning offers a means of enhancing their aesthetic experience, of getting more meaning from a wide variety of sounds. These kinds of objectives are not only desirable from a philosophical point of view, but they can be very meaningful to students and can become a basis for an effective learning program. I think that this concept in the role of music education is a challenge for all of us because it offers a means of moving ahead that can be important, but we have a long way to go to implement it and to obtain adequate support for it.

Discussion

Max Kaplan, Chairman

Max Kaplan: After listening to the speeches today, it seems to me that the dialogue we had hoped for has already begun. I am pleased to turn to anyone in the room for questions.

David McAllester: I would like to set the stage by referring to an incident that happened in Japan where a decision was made as to what was music and what was not music by a court decision. There came a case where somebody was accused of plagiarism of a kind of soap opera that is heard on Japanese radio. When the plagiarism case came to court, they decided to throw it out on the grounds that this "pop" opera was not music. And ever since that time, nobody has studied this music in Japan. Yet, to a Westerner, it is certainly music; but in Japan it is not. It has been ruled out by legalism. Now, I think that Mr. Broudy did the same thing with "calendar art." Perhaps Mr. Broudy's barber would be a better judge of calendar art than Mr. Broudy. I do have a serious point here. Thinking of the arts of the future, any decision to rule out a particular form of expression may leave us lagging far behind, in the future, if we go by established canons as to what is and what is not art.

Kaplan: I take it that you are asking Dr. Broudy to respond: (1) on legal determinism in aesthetics and (2) with specific reference to his comment on who is the expert.

Harry Broudy: I'll try to make this brief. First, we had a similar famous incident — the "Brancusi Birds." It became a question as to whether or not these sculptures were to be admitted into this country as an art object or something else; and it made a difference in the duties. So there again, a legal decision had to be made: were these "Brancusi Birds" art or not?

I think that I tried to indicate the problem of a closed definition of art. I also thought I indicated that our definitions of art were always after the fact. That is why our best, our safest, our most reliable definitions are those made by experts in the art of the past, when nothing can really change them, because this is the art from which principles and norms are derived. The second point is that I did not ask a court to make the definitions. I said that the experts of a given time were practically the only people who can make them for reasons I tried to detail.

The third point—the barber. You recall, I did not rule this [calendar art] out as art. I merely put in a small, snide remark that his taste in pictorial art, I thought, was deplorable. Now, I was making a judgment about his taste. I did not say calendar art was not art. I then tried to contrast his taste in fishing rods. Actually, the calendar art objects were more beautiful than the fishing rods. Aesthetically, they had much to commend them, even to gentlemen of a fairly advanced age. The point that I was trying to bring out is that the barber knew why he liked one fishing rod rather than another, but he had no idea in the world (and did not think it

necessary to have any idea) as to why he liked one calendar better than another.

As to the last point, the implication of the question was that this rigidity is going to freeze art, that academy art kills art, that authorities kill art. Brevity compels me to be dogmatic in these matters, and this is why I try to use the difference between paradigmatic art and contemporary art. I would quite agree with the speaker that as far as contemporary, avant-garde, experimental work is concerned, there are no authorities because there are no paradigms. This is what is meant by being authoritative — having a paradigm that is accepted by the experts of an age — and where there are not any, there is no point in talking about it. I would not, however, conclude that it is either useless or mischievous to study the past in terms of the paradigms, because strange as avant garde is, it would be a violation of a very important, philosophical principle to suppose that there is a real and absolute discontinuity between the art of the past, the present, and of the future. I would merely appeal to the other agencies to induct them into the heritage of the past as well as getting them ready with all the openness we have for the future.

Kaplan: I take it both by his physical appearance and his reply that the same barber will be employed as in the past. Any further questions?

Wilson Coker: I would like to ask Professor Northrop to discuss further, if he would, the importance of relations, structural matters, and the basic aesthetic response one might have to them. I am concerned as to whether or not he regards relations (such as before and after, louder and softer) as fundamentally the aesthetic relations one responds to with feeling as much as with inferential thought.

Northrop: With respect to the matter, I am always left cold by the prevalent Kantian and neo-Kantian theories of art, which analyze in terms of matter and form, because the word "form," the relation of how this radical empirical — immediately experienced materials — is different from the "form" of the stereometric in Roman architectural art of Botticelli, for example, in his *Madonna and Child.* The forms are two quite different things, and the canons for judging aesthetic values are different in two ways. I believe that Professor Broudy's value judgment problem can be handled objectively. Differences in matters of taste do not turn around any conflict in different tastes, but rather turn art around where the artist is a major concern, and with radical empirical, aesthetic immediacy for its own sake. This is the aim of an O'Keeffe. It was the air of the French Impressionists as they moved away from the more geometrical, perfectly proportioned form of Renaissance objects to radical empirical immediacy in painting the image of the object, and letting the object go. Now, form in those two cases is different; and if you mean by the difference between early and late, or by louder and softer, in the radical empirical sense, then I would say that it is quite a different type of *form* from what you get in mathematical physics, or the form that goes into the laws of acoustics in a musical piece where the notes come in earlier or later. The former *form* is: "you just have to experience that" (which will not be the same for any two perceivers).

I do not know whether that answers your question or not; but roughly speaking, theoretical component form is self-imageless, and it is defined in terms of its formal properties, more like symmetry reflects in its transitivity, the same kind of stuff that mathematical is built out of.

Father O'Connor: Dr. Northrop: What would you say to some of the current episodes in art in which form and content have become one and the same? Also, of some of the imageless fashions that we have gone through? Now we are stepping back 'out into image relationships, insofar as artistic endeavor goes. For instance, the whole pop music, even in terms of some of the Eastern musics that we are now encountering like Ravi Shanker, have become syntactical in the sense of noun, subject-predicate, and the rest of the traditional Western apparatus.

Northrop: I have not immersed myself too much in contemporary art. I have a one-track mind, and I have been off in the legal and political, theoretical world. I immerse myself in the Impressionistic period of painting. To answer your question: the primary thing to note about the difference between oriental and Western music is that Western music operates with a *linear time sequence.* Take all three pieces of music played yesterday — there is a theme and it moves toward a climax. It is linear. *Oriental music is cyclical.* Now I believe that that goes back to a difference in scientific content — scientific, empirical knowledge of the two cultures. I believe that the oriental scientist has his affectual, more of a natural-history-type of science; and for him, time is immediately sensed time and is cyclical. You have the continuum of immediacy, and the first cycle is a sequence of lightness and darkness. Now never in his thinking is this connected with astronomical bodies. It is just the immediately-experienced radical empirical sequence of darkness and light that we call day and night. And then within the dark period of the sequence, he notes the sequence of two-dimensional, yellowish patches, which we call the new moon, the quarter moon, the half moon, the three-quarter moon, and then the full; and that goes in a cycle. Then, relative to that, you get the cycle of the year. Then in the year, he notes the sequence of different, perishing colors; the fresh-for-you greens of spring, and the summer colors, and the fall colors, and the whites and blacks of winter; and this goes in a cycle. And human beings to in the same cycle of youth, maturity of life, the fall, grey-haired stage, and the blackness of night. And this goes over and over in every generation. Now, oriental music picks up that theme, of a cyclical theory of time.

The linear theory of time comes from mathematical physics. Another source of it is our calendar and the Christian religious tradition, which tends to line us up culturally in a linear time.

The reason why I believe that contemporary artists in the West and in the Orient find themselves reinforcing one another is because of the breakdown of the traditional conception of the theoretic component in Western scientific and philosophic knowledge, which has happened with the modern world. When a great traditional synthesis breaks down, you move right back to radical empirical immediacy. So, in mathematical physics, when the Newtonian theory was shown to be limited by Einstein, the philosophy of science went to radical empirical positivism. And scientists in the Vienna circle then thought that they could define away electrons and the metric of space/time in terms of immediately sensed data. You move down into what Sorokin calls a sensate, positivistic culture. The Orient, I believe, lives all the time in the immediate, radical empirical world; and this is why the two reinforce one another.

In the West there is this factor in our music coming in from a theoretical side — permuting your scale enables you to permute your radical empirically sensed sounds in ways in which they were never sensed. This was the thing that so impressed me about the Stravinsky yesterday. That is one of the things that art does. Just listen to the sequence of sounds, and you will get a permutation of sound you never imagined before. This is what is happening. We are in an experimental, existential world in which the humanists have lost the theoretical component of our culture. This theoretical component goes back to Kant, Locke, and Descartes' separation, signing the humanities to the mental substances, the sciences to the material substances, so that you can never get your humanistic world and your scientific world together.

We are in a theoretically-disillusioned, humanist world. Now the scientists have recovered. First they found that you cannot define electrons away in terms of radical empirical images of sense data. Then the scientists went to common-sense, naive objects in which you have physicalism — what you mean by electrons, and backhanded statements about naively sensed scales. You cannot account for the electron theory of metals with that theory, because in the electron theory of metals, it is the scientific object that is defining the scales — the common sense metal object. Carnape, who initiated the Viennese movement, now frankly says: "You have to take the relational constructs of your question as primitive." You cannot define them away in terms of the radical empirical or the common-sensical naive realist. When your theory is broken down in your humanistic world, then your youth are running around, experimenting with everything. There is no formula to guide them, there are no legal or moral controls, and you have all kinds of flirting with all kinds of feelings and emotions. I was with some young people last week, and they thought that they had the answer. And I said, "We really would like to know how your philosophy works, and until we see you at the age of thirty-five" — I did not say seventy-four, I said thirty-five — "aren't you going to be so bored with your sensations that you will be drooling idiots?"

Well, I think this is a little bit of the world which we are in. Traditional theoretic components for the humanist are broken down.

O'Connor: Don't you present an enormous problem then for music education in a sense that we cannot define a possibility of an aesthetic in our present instance? How are we to manipulate this undefinable into the mechanics of good instruction in teaching in small classrooms?

Northrop: It is right here, I think, that your paradigms come in and your tradition. You have to preserve, you have to re-educate people to the importance of theory in things. That is the only place where you can get your standards. This re-education has to come in, and they are going to be bored in wallowing in their own private, introspective emotions and the sensations they get from a drug.

Gerard Knieter: This question can be answered either by Dr. Broudy or Dr. Northrop, but I think that the origin of the remarks would probably be traced to Dr. Northrop. Both are philosophers, and I would welcome an answer from either.

In the initial commentary, you pointed out the historicity, the relationship of contemporary acoustics and philosophy with Plato. If memory serves me, one writer pointed out that Plato believed "music was the mathematical preparation for the study of philosophy." The stress on acoustics as the basis, or a propositional syntax, for music is highly questionable on a contemporary scene. Do we consider the aesthetic base of music from an acoustical, from a mathematical point of view, or do we consider the syntax of music from a *musical* point of view, where its ultimate meaning rests not in an analog to another subject, but in itself?

Northrop: I agree with everything you say by understanding, but what you mean by music is the *character* of music to determine your theory of music. This is the radical empirical meaning of music, and that is quite independent and cannot be any theory of acoustics. The theory of acoustics is the creation not of the Platonic, Greek mathematicians, but the Democrateans. The theoretic component that accompanied classical music is rooted in the ratios of the mathematical physics of acoustics. You only have to connect the score, the marks on paper of the composer's score, not unlike the mathematical equations and relations, and you have operational definitions which, in terms of the intervals and the strings of your musical instrument, are based on the acoustical relations connected with the scores. This is an example of an epistemic correlation between the intervals and the ratios built right into your musical instruments and into the piano that relate it to the score, but not to what you hear. You do not need to know, you do not sense the molecules of the air vibrating in your eardrums. You hear a sequence of immediately experienced sounds put together in a very unusual set of permutations. Your acoustics enables you to hear those sounds as permutations and sequences that do not come in nature.

The Orient has music that does not depend on the laws of acoustics at all. They are implicit in the oriental drum; the theory of the music is quite different. You can have a different theoretical component. People are now experimenting with musical magnitudes that acoustically are not ratios of whole numbers, and this is possible. I have no doubt that the music of the future may well take this direction, but then you are opening up new formulae. You have a new theoretic component; but I do agree with you that it does not have anything to do with the theoretically inferred factor.

You are quite right in saying that you do not have to have acoustical theory. I think that in much contemporary music the reason why a lot of it seems chaotic and meaningless to us is that it has dropped the old theoretical criteria for what you call good music. Contemporary music is just presenting unusual, immediately experienced, emotional sounds for their own sake.

Broudy: I think there is one other aspect in this relation with theory and the phenomenological fact of the music, or the music having its own autonomous system of organization, with relation to Plato. I am sure that Professor Northrop will agree that this business of the ratios was also part of the scheme for perfection for Plato, that he had more than a small suspicion that the Good, the true, and the beautiful were isomorphic with respect to ratios, that number was somehow the difference between chaos, the formless, and that which was informed, intelligible, and beautiful.

Now, in addition to music trying to become free from the mathematical order (that is, taking an order from mathematics) it also has tried to become free from the moral order which Plato had hitched to the ratios. After all, for him the basic modes of music had definite, extra-aesthetic values. One ratio was better than another for a certain purpose. They were tied to character, the lofty, and the soul. I think that modern music has tried to get its autonomy from both kinds of external order: the mathematical order and the moral order. It has tried to formulate its own criteria in terms of formal properties. There are certain pleasing sounds, directly pleasing, which seem to exhibit some formal properties. These properties might be in terms of ratios, but they might not be. If I understand you correctly, the autonomy of music is the right to determine its formal properties from what seems musically adequate and not from any other source.

Knieter: It is possible that we have a forced correlation. In other words, there is simultaneously a scientific operation of the acoustical laws concurrent with the evolution of compositional practice. Although we have assumed it, I am not sure that because these operate simultaneously, we have in fact a cause and effect relationship. If we study the compositional practice through the ages, we find that composers compose, and when they are finished composing theoreticians analyze, formulate, and theorize. Instead of going back to the music, our practice, historically, has been to go back to the theoretical treatise.

My concern with the forced correlation might be illustrated by this small anecdote of a graduating class in 1927. It is reported that in the divinity schools around the country, enrollment increased by seventeen percent. During that same year the consumption of alcohol also increased by seventeen percent. Now, many conclusions can be formed by these figures. I might assume that there were happy graduation parties, or we might not form any connections. My concern here is that the professional philosopher with the mind of the scientific logician has been able to bring about equations of events through history, as Dr. Broudy pointed out, putting moral order alongside of music and putting value judgments on scales. The very scale that Plato condemned as being the most immoral is our major scale. The question that I probe challenges the entire philosophical position of Western aesthetics. I am really marking now, with a big question mark, the fact that these things have existed through the centuries, and that they are parallel. I am not sure that there is a cause and effect relationship. It is true that instrument construction, that true discovery of historical sharps and flats move with acoustical principles. I am not sure that composers were aware of this; it may have been an intuitive discovery.

Northrop: I think you are quite right. A Mexican has written a paper and made a great study of the Spaniards preceding the French Impressionist movement. They had read the radical empirical theory. As a result of reading a paper by a French mathematical physicist, one artist developed colors purer than what other painters were using. He did not use the paper at all to build up an electromagnetic theory in painting; he used it for just the opposite — to present pure color in a manner in which you would see a color for its own sake and not as an embodiment of a theory.

Kaplan: Thank you, gentlemen. It is unfortunately an additional burden of the chairman not only to help give birth to our ideas, but sometimes to seek polite ways of integrating the inner substance of these ideas to external, theoretical circumstances.

It strikes me that the general drift of the afternoon has been again to emphasize the two ways of approaching the world and knowledge and art. The questions which arose were basically concerned with: "How do you teach this immediate experience?" and "To what degree do you rely upon forms and techniques and traditions of the past?" To satisfy the conscience of this sociologist, I would elaborate by asking: "What are the changing social circumstances in an emerging American society and in the future as we can project it?" Of course, the question then follows: "How do you relate both the theoretic, however taught, and the external social changes, however they develop and emerge?"

This session has provided a highly nourishing set of ideas, questions, and issues, which I presume will dominate discussions for the rest of the week.

II. Potentials for the Arts in the Community

Chairman
> ALVIN C. EURICH, President,
> Aspen Institute for Humanistic Studies

Speeches
> **The St. James Program**
> DOROTHY MAYNOR, Founder and Executive Director,
> Harlem School of the Arts, Inc.
>
> **These Essences**
> WILLIAM H. CORNOG, Superintendent, New Trier
> Township High School District, Winnetka, Illinois
>
> **A Program for Leisure and Recreation**
> OLGA MADAR, Executive Board Member,
> United Auto Workers
>
> **Arts Councils and the Expanding Arts Scene**
> GEORGE M. IRWIN, Chairman,
> Associated Councils of the Arts

The St. James Program

Dorothy Maynor

My credentials for addressing a gathering of this kind are questionable. I may not be thought of as an educator, though I completed graduate work in public school music. Nearly thirty years ago, this very place, Tanglewood, served as a sort of launching pad to get me into orbit as a concert soprano; and that was my profession for a quarter of a century. If there are those here in this gathering who subscribe to the view that singers, on the whole, are a weak-minded lot, and the even more popular notion that sopranos resemble birds — not only in their throats but in their heads as well — if, as I say, that happens to be the view of anybody seated before me, I can well understand your outrage at my having the brass to open my mouth in this company of experts. You are due an apology, which I at the outset must humbly offer.

With this reservation. The experts themselves are not doing too well nowadays. Certainly not in urban affairs, where we who live in cities are daily under threat of strangulation. Certainly not in international affairs, where the mood is increasingly suicidal. Certainly not in education, where chaos mounts in direct ratio to budgets and trappings. Maybe we would be better off if the experts gave up. Maybe common sense, if you please, practical horse sense, should have a hearing. That is about all I have to offer here.

That and one other thing. I live in America's most slandered community — Harlem. The excesses, the woes of Harlem are taken to typify the woes of the Negro all over this nation. Every day, I hear and see and smell the signs of something rotten — not in Denmark, mind you — but right here in America. For a quarter of a century, I have lived in this ghetto and I have watched from day to day the downward spiral of the life around me. Never mind the high-sounding talk about the Great Society. Take, if you will, the word of an eye-witness: the frustration, the bitterness, the impatient rage are among the facts of the life I live day in and day out. Where this will ultimately lead, what effect it will have on the life of this nation defies prediction. While I claim no special wisdom in this area of our national life, I do present myself as one just in from the front line of battle. From my personal watch tower in Harlem, and as I am made aware of events in Los Angeles and Cleveland and Chicago and Boston, and now more recently, in Newark, East Harlem, and Detroit, I am forced to think solemn thoughts about the future of America. It would be tragic indeed if, while we are striving to weave a cloak of democracy for Vietnam and the rest of the world, the fabric of democracy were torn beyond repair within our own borders. This is no time for for name-calling or hand-wringing or tongue-clucking. We have a lot of unfinished business here at home. It demands a high place on the agenda of every one of us. It is not the responsibility of any one segment of the nation. Each of us has a job to do; we must address ourselves to that job with the urgency and the determination that has been the distinctive mark of this nation all through its history. We pride ourselves on our inventiveness and our know-how. These traits have served us well in our mines and factories and laboratories. They have made us the richest, the most powerful people, the most pampered people this planet has ever known. But unless we can apply this resourcefulness to the problem of living together, all these other accomplishments will count for nothing.

Under any circumstances, our task would be a difficult and challenging one. Unfortunately, we are required to deal with this crisis at a time when most of the tools available to our fathers and mothers are being discarded. The stabilizing influence of religion cannot now be counted on. Law and order are openly ridiculed. In many quarters, family life is a thing of scorn. Personal integrity is no longer taken for granted. In other words, the roof has fallen in; what is cynically called the "Establishment," like London Bridge, has fallen down. And amid the rubble we find survivors who are tough-minded and hardboiled. This is true, not just in ghetto areas such as mine; it is strikingly true in the great, sprawling suburbs of this country.

But the toll those changes are taking in Harlem, and Watts, and in Newark's Central Ward, in East Harlem, and Detroit is especially devastating. By the tens of thousands, the black people of America are disclaiming any allegiance whatever to the value system by which white Americans have professed to live. They see it as a complex of sham, of make-believe that the white man has used for his own advantage. Whatever good there may be in the middle-class American way of life has been denied the black man. The vain effort to attain these values, as we are hearing more and more now from the black masses, only adds to our bafflement. The only thing left for us is to give up, to drop out. Your system according to this line of reasoning, is false, a form of addiction. So we will turn to other forms of addiction — pot, or LSD, or whatever.

As I have said, this mentality is not peculiar to the black ghetto. But it is increasingly prevalent there. And it is all the more difficult to cope with and insidious because those who argue thus have a lot of truth on their side. The testimony of three hundred years of criminal injustice toward the Negro in America is a pretty hard thing to refute. No honest man would try to refute it.

And yet I am confident that there are black Americans — I certainly am one — by the hundreds of thousands who have not given up on the "Establishment." There is a noisy minority whose avowed purpose it is, so it seems, to wreck and dismantle the whole shebang. They will stop at nothing — murder, arson, agitation, you name it. It is a sad thing that their methods do get attention, while the pleas and the plans of the men and women of reason and moderation go unheeded. It is not to justify looting and burning to point out that again and again, in city after city, the looters and the burners got the attention of the mayor or the governor or even the President that the more moderate leader would never have been given. The real culprit is often the indifferent or the prejudiced public official or private citizen who could not care less — until the reputation of his neighborhood or his city is soiled by news of an upheaval that disrupts business or makes it unsafe for his family to walk the streets. These are the inciters to riot and destruction.

Still, the great masses of the black people of this land know fully well that such gains are only short term, hand-to-mouth advantages. This is not the way to build a democracy. The ingredients that make up the good life are much the same from age to age; they apply to all people, white or black. There is no substitute for patient, daily, disciplined effort. Self-mastery is the tuition that all of us must pay in the school of life. That some find themselves in circumstances where the tution is higher because of race or color or an unfriendly environment is simply one of the grim facts of life. Tantrums will not help; only a child thinks they will. They may attract attention, or win small concessions, or patronizing behavior on the part of parents or bystanders. But these are childish ways, unworthy of mature, resourceful, imaginative men and women.

I know, and the great masses of my people know, that we have no option but to identify ourselves with the great mainstream of American life. The scandal is that so many white Americans are engaged in a systematic, considered crusade to see to it that this does not happen.

Because I feel that this is no time for standing idly by, giving mere lip-service to these things, some three years ago, at the suggestion of my husband, who is the pastor of the St. James Presbyterian Church in Harlem, I formed what we called a School of the Arts, in the hope that at least a few boys and girls in our area might be given some clue to their own possibilities and selfhood. We certainly did not expect to turn them all into creative artists whose efforts will, in the next few years, adorn the museums and concert halls of New York City. Most of them will not show rare talent as musicians or dancers or painters or actors, although we provide instruction in all these areas and we have assembled an excellent staff of inspiring teachers. Maybe the lightning will strike once or twice, and out of our school there may come some boy or girl whose talents in one thing or another will command acclaim. But we are not counting on that. What we are counting on, and in some small ways our hopes are bearing fruit already, is that a lad who seems to have little or no purpose, who has never been taken very seriously by his parents or by the other kids on the block or even by his teachers in the public schools, that such a boy or girl might, just by learning to concentrate on mastering an instrument, or in the blending of colors, or in the careful use of the English language that our drama teacher insists on — in some way this child may be taught to dream and to realize that dreams are quite real. And if this is kept up for a while, that child will one day look in the mirror and see something that he never saw before — the making of a real human being. I suppose we are not trying to teach the arts so much as we are trying to create horizons. One of the prices we city-dwellers pay for living as we do is that the vision is blocked in every direction. There is something quite unnatural about living on this earth year after year and never seeing a sunrise. Doubtlessly, there are thousands of native New Yorkers who literally never have seen the sun come up out of the sea or from behind the hills. It certainly is the case with our boys and girls in Harlem. Life affords them no vista, no ample view of themselves.

That is what I want them to have. And I firmly believe that the arts are a splendid means of providing this.

There are many reasons, both in the past and the present, why the ideal of family life was not attainable within the Negro community. This was certainly and obviously so back on the plantation; it is so in urban ghettos today. But here, too, we must keep trying. There is no substitute if you are trying to create a real person, for the love and the security and the guidance and the dicipline that is every child's birthright. Withhold that, and you have left the salt off the table. One of the things that we insist on at our school is that there be responsible participation on the part of the parents in this effort to bring out the best in the child. We aim to get both parents; unfortunately, the father is often missing. But at the very least, we must have the mother; we will not settle for less than that. We want her to know — she will have heard this many times before, but she may not have felt it in her bones — that the odds against her child's amounting to anything at all are insurmountable unless she takes her role as a mother with the utmost seriousness. I don't mind telling you that some of my greatest problems and a few of my proudest victories have been with mothers who, out of indifference or ignorance or frustration or necessity, have not been on the job as mothers. It is a grateful thing to see a mother coming to a full awareness of what her place is in the life of her boy or girl. Until we can multiply instances of this kind, creating the setting for this and supplying whatever may be needed to bring this about in cases beyond number, our ghetto problem will be with us. I am by family life as one of our statesmen said when asked about democracy as a form of government: "It is a terrible form of Government; but it is the best we have." Although a good many radical voices denounce everything that has come out of the white world, anybody who denounces the family, if his aim is to produce character and responsible citizenship, has taken leave of his senses. If the black man wants to denounce it simply because he got it from the white man, I still say he is wrong. Now and then God sends a gift by the Devil.

Our school has had some successes that can be proudly mentioned. Governor Rockefeller recently gave us an award for what he considered our contribution to the cultural life of the State of New York. The New York State Council on the Arts and the National Foundation on the Arts have provided us with some money. Private sources, both foundations and individuals, have been generous. The children are required to make nominal contributions. We need money; a good deal of my time is devoted to trying to find support for the school.

Our project is as dust in the balance, when measured against the great and urgent need now confronting us. It requires perseverance and a faith that must be renewed each day. I wish there were some way to make a great leap forward that would lift us over the drudgery and the disappointments that are the lot of those who take the course that I am trying to follow. I don't know of any other way. Until I find another, I am committed to this one. I have no choice.

These Essences

William H. Cornog

The great Dutch historian Johan Huizinga published in the year 1938 an extraordinary book, *Homo Ludens, A Study of the Play Element in Culture.* In it he developed beautifully the thesis that an understanding of man's nature and culture is incomplete unless one sees man not only as *homo sapiens,* and *homo faber,* but also as *homo ludens:* Man the Thinker, and Man the Maker, but also Man the Player. Huizinga writes:

> From the point of view of a world wholly determined by the operation of blind forces, play would be altogether superfluous. Play only becomes possible, thinkable and understandable when an influx of *mind* breaks down the absolute determination of the cosmos. The very existence of play continually confirms the supralogical nature of the human situation. Animals play, so they must be more than merely mechanical things. We play and know that we play, so we must be more than merely rational beings, for play is irrational.[1]

By irrational insights, by release from determinism and reason and fact, man finds meanings, purposes, delights, and even satisfactory, if illusory, answers to what reality harshly insists is inscrutable and unanswerable. Myth solves mysteries, and poets sing the heart to faith and resolution. For as Huizinga says:

> Play lies outside the antithesis of wisdom and folly, and equally outside those of truth and falsehood, good and evil. Although it is a non-material activity it has no moral function. The valuations of vice and virtue do not apply here.[2]

But, on the other hand, it is true (Huizinga confesses) that the Chinese conceived that the purpose of music and dance is to keep the world in its right course and to force nature into benevolence toward man.

Nothing is more clearly an act of Man the Player, in his verbal expression, than the making of poetry; and nothing more clearly an example of the play of the human mind than making music.

The essence of poetry is that it is an essence, and so is every form of art. Art — whether it be poetry, music, painting, sculpture, drama — is an extraction from random or reasoned nature, a distillation of meanings, often an illusory idle breeze carrying the seeds of truth deep into the mind and heart.

Because I know poetry far better than I know any of the other arts of *homo ludens,* I shall let a poet say it for me. Keats expresses it well in the Proem to Book I of *Endymion:*

A thing of beauty is a joy for ever:
Its loveliness increases; it will never
Pass into nothingness; but still will keep
A bower quiet for us, and a sleep
Full of sweet dreams, and health, and quiet breathing.
Therefore, on every morrow, are we wreathing
A flowery band to bind us to the earth.
Spite of despondence, of the inhuman dearth
Of noble natures, of the gloomy days,
Of all the unhealthy and o'er-darkened ways

Made for our searching: yes, in spite of all,
Some shape of beauty moves away the pall
From our dark spirits.
. . . .
Nor do we merely feel these essences
For one short hour; no, even as the trees
That whisper round a temple become soon
Dear as the temple's self, so does the moon,
The passion poesy, glories infinite,
Haunt us till they become a cheering light
Unto our souls, and bound to us so fast,
That whether there be shine, or gloom o'ercast,
They always must be with us, or we die.

Now, you can teach a computer a language and a computer can teach you a language, in so far as a language can be defined as a conventional set or arrangement of signals or symbols. But you can't get a computer to play with words and talk about these essences which "always must be with us, or we die." Computers can also be programed to compose music; indeed, I have been privileged to hear a performance. As a piece of scientific virtuosity, it enthralled me, but musically it was an ersatz essence. Still, it showed man at play, and at play anything goes; and that is how new art, new styles, new fashions, new instruments, and all changes come into the culture.

The play of one man's mind in the arts defies convention, or reason, or order, or fact, or utility, or truth. But although it does this, it is not without a serious intent. Man's play is not always, nor even dominantly, child's play. Aristotle described man as a political animal. He also called him *animal ridens,* a laughing animal; and a later and post-Darwinian translation of this has been God's little laughing ape. Much of man's play is for laughs, and all the best of it is for leisure. This is what art is all about, and this is what the teaching of the arts in schools is all about.

The Greeks knew this better than any people ever have, and Aristotle knew this, or said this, better than any other Greek. The word "school" comes from the Greek word *scola* meaning leisure. Did you know that the Greek word for education and for child's play is the same word: *paideia?* Thus a pedagogue, loosely translated, is a go-go playboy.

Aristotle says so well what most of us say stumblingly on education and music, particulary in Book VIII of the *Politics.* For Aristotle, the first principle of all action was leisure, and it was as important for a man to use leisure well as it was for him to work well. Music, although originally included in education, was cultivated mainly for the sake of pleasure. One of its greatest attributes was that it provided intellectual enjoyment of leisure.

Man the Player is playing like mad outside the schools, outside the whole respectable scholastic world — in literature, in art, in music — and this has always been so. The schools have not always known where the action is. Part of the revolt against formal schooling has been given form and expression in extracurricular freedoms. Let's face it. School can be dull to *homo ludens*, if not to *homo sapiens*.

Clearly that part of education which is especially the province of playful man, as opposed to thinking man, cannot suspend judgments and postpone relevance. With patience a rational scholar plods after truth. But the dancer, the musician is immediately engaged, body and soul. What the player plays must be played now, and heard now, and felt now. Poetry, said Wordsworth, is emotion remembered in tranquility. Not music. Not dance. Not play-acting. The relevance must be present, the note of the meaning clear. The name of the game is: I dig you.

Are you getting the messages from those most visible, center stage, in our culture? They have something to communicate to the Establishment, or any part of it that will listen. Some of the musicians in that center stage, whom our young people applaud (to our Aristotelian annoyance), may look like the inmates of the asylum of Charenton, but if you have seen Peter Weiss' great play, *Marat-Sade,* you know that we denizens of the rational world may be enjoying only an illusion of sanity.

Indeed, the world we live in, as it is sometimes reflected in the culture it produces, resembles more and more an asylum managed by a decaying coalition of madmen and scoundrels.

It is difficult in such a world for a completely rational man (if there is one) to find his identity. Literature is currently full of descriptions of the identity crises of heroes and anti-heroes. The search for identity is very hard to carry on at a time when the race of man itself has lost its bearings. Man can no longer believe, as he could in the enclosed and clockwork cosmos of old, that he, man, is slightly lower than the angels. Science has packed the angels off to the dustbin of folklore and introduced man to his true brethren, the algae.

In a world of faith withdrawn and in the thousand-suns dawn of nuclear science, what hope is there for art which, for man the player, has always been supremely an act of faith? Shall art lose its centrality in man's life? Shall it decay to a bauble to ornament the practical, gray, and virtuous life of man the thinker and man the maker?

But, people will argue, there will always be some music, some art, some poetry; won't there? That's the nature of man: everybody enjoys art, and art is for everybody.

Up to a certain point. It has its place today: somewhere between water-skiing and cook-outs.

There are at least three classical or categorical positions one can take on the place of these essences, the arts, in the life of a man, or in the life of a school: 1) There is no longer any convenient place for them. *Sapiens* is preempting more and more time. Get lost, *ludens.* 2) The arts deserve some place in one's life and in a curriculum, if only for *auld lang syne,* or *ars gratia loquendi.* 3) The arts are an indispensable part of man's life and education and a place must be found.

If you take the first position, the dialogue is over. If you take the second, you are making a timorous compromise that will betray you. There is no place to go from this position except down to defeat.

. If art is indispensable and its support must be assured, what allies do we have beyond man's laughing, playful, inexhaustibly artistic nature, which is a powerful and, I think, an unbeatable ally,

but an in-and-outer? Sometimes the artist will take a messianic or self-salvatory position, but not often. And he usually doesn't care who is for him or who is against him and leaves all the fighting to the professors, the patrons, and the proud possessors.

Art as a commodity has an assured future. Foundations, business, government, and private collectors and speculators, by subsidy, commissions, and trading, will cherish art in sickness and health, for richer, for poorer, in a stable but unexciting marriage of merit and the marketplace. An opera company may go under, or a symphony cancel a season, but not without causing a twinge to civic conscience and a bruise to civic pride.

Now, the schools can't buy paintings or support symphonies. Art as a commodity is not their affair, and need not be. At least I hope we're not in the business of training consumers of art. However, the schools have (or should have) a great deal to do about three major aspects of art, whether it be music, or painting, or drama, or poetry, or sculpture, or whatever. We have a special obligation to reveal art as heritage, art as experience, and art as prophecy.

These essences, the arts, speak of man's past, of man's encounters with mystery and love, evil and madness, hungers beyond the body's hunger, and horrors more fearsome within the mind than ever lurked in cave or covert. And they sing of triumph and despair and the bitter joys of conflict. To learn what it means to be a man, a man must read somewhat in the record; and the best reading, that closest the the heart of the creature, is that which the creature wrote in play.

But, reading the record is not enough. Art is experience. Music is playing. Poetry is writing. Drama is acting. Despite Aristotle's reservations about the need to perform (which seemed a menial job to him) the school, to whatever extent it can, should regard the arts as performing arts and offer as many as possible a chance to exercise that *ludens* part of their humanity.

Beyond these purposes of revealing the arts as heritage and as experience, the schools, it seems to me, cannot escape the duty to allow students to discover that art truly is prophecy, that its comments upon man's nature are so insightful at times as to be prophetic. The Latin word for poet is *vates:* a seer, a man possessed, a visionary. If you would know what man can be, read the poets. If you would know the illimitable range of man's playful mind, observe not merely the past but present art, music, and drama.

If you want to know what youth are thinking and feeling today, you cannot find anyone who speaks for them or to them more clearly than the Beatles. And you should also listen closely to the Rolling Stones, the Mamas and the Papas, the Jefferson Airplane, Simon and Garfunkel, and the Grateful Dead.

Among the prophetic poets, I have most liked Coleridge. His "Kubla Khan" seems especially "with it" today, or even farther out than that. He was the first of the psychedelic poets, and I don't think anyone around now can match him.

> In Xanadu did Kubla Khan
> A stately pleasure-dome decree:
> Where Alph, the sacred river, ran
> Through caverns measureless to man
> Down to a sunless sea.

So twice five miles of fertile ground
With walls and towers were girdled round:
And here were gardens bright with sinuous rills,
Where blossomed many an incense-bearing tree;
And here were forests ancient as the hills,
Enfolding sunny spots of greenery.

. . . .

Five miles meandering with a mazy motion
Through wood and dale the sacred river ran,
Then reached the caverns measureless to man
And sank in tumult to a lifeless ocean:
And 'mid this tumult Kubla heard from far
Ancestral voices prophesying war!

The shadow of the dome of pleasure
Floated midway on the waves;
Where was heard the mingled measure
From the fountain and the caves.
It was a miracle of rare device,
A sunny pleasure-dome with caves of ice!

A damsel with a dulcimer
In a vision once I saw:
It was an Abyssinian maid,
And on her dulcimer she played,
Singing of Mount Abora.
Could I revive within me
Her symphony and song,
To such a deep delight 'twould win me,
That with music loud and long,
I would build that dome in air,
That sunny dome! those caves of ice!
And all who heard should see them there,
And all should cry, Beware! Beware!
His flashing eyes, his floating hair!
Weave a circle round him thrice,
And close your eyes with holy dread,
For he on honey-dew hath fed,
And drunk the milk of Paradise.

Keats was right: "Nor do we merely feel these essences/For one short hour. . . . They always must be with us, or we die."

---

[1]Huizinga, Johan. *Homo Ludens, A Study of the Play Element in Culture* (London: Routledge & Kegan Paul, Ltd., 1938), pp. 3-4.

[2]*Ibid.*,p.6.

A Program for

Leisure and Recreation

Olga Madar

I don't know a thing about music, so I'm not going to talk about music at all. I'm going to trust the judgment of this Symposium in terms of what we ought to do about this. However, I think we have a kind of mutual problem.

Our union (UAW) has been interested in technology, not only in how it affects people on the job, but also in its impact on the amount of non-work time available to people. We are concerned about channeling the benefits of this improved technology to help secure a better life for all people. What you are committed to do here at this Symposium, to make recommendations and give directions for action by music educators, should be important in achieving a happier and better life for our people. So our interests are the same.

We too believe in securing cooperation from the community at large, and we look upon ourselves as citizens of the community first and as union members second. We hope to achieve the good things of life in cooperation with the rest of society.

Recently, our International Executive Board asked me to prepare a new program — one that we could, in conjunction with our local unions, put into action so that the influence of our union could be felt on a community level. I would like to comment briefly about this program; perhaps it will be helpful to you in reaching people and getting their support and in getting more members of our society helping to shape and influence the kinds of policies and programs we have in our communities. Truly, it seems that what you are talking about here will be in a vacuum until we can reach out to the masses of people.

The United Auto Workers has had a department of recreation practically since its inception in the late 1930's. At our first convention (1938), the union members expressed their concern for helping to interest the membership in music, particularly in folk songs that would relate the kinds of struggles taking place in the shop and the problems they were having in the picket lines. Also enunciated at that first convention was an interest in bands and a concern about children in crowded city streets. As a result of that early discussion, we established in our local unions a standing committee on recreation. At that time we set aside six cents per year per member out of the union dues to finance a recreation program. Later, it was increased to twelve cents. All well and good.

What happened to our local recreation committees is the same kind of thing that has occurred in our communities generally. Recreation meant doing the kinds of things and developing the kinds of programs that they knew best. The leadership people who volunteered their time to the local union recreation committees were people who had been involved in sports programs. As a result, they developed sports programs for the few, the skilled few. And you know what happened. We spent most of our time with those who were skilled rather than those who weren't. So, we have been working for the past twenty years to broaden the horizons and to have "recreation" mean something more than just sports for a few.

We've had a difficult time with semantics. For so many years our program has been called the Department of Recreation. After a suggestion from our union president and action of the International Executive Board, we are now a Department of Recreation and Leisure Time Activities. And I've got news for you: it *works*. In the brief time since that happened, the program has more meaning for the union members. Immediately they go beyond the concept of the sports program in talking about other kinds of activities.

Another thing occurred. We have learned that there is a tendency to isolate non-work time activities into categories. For example, as we talked about the development of programs for senior citizens, for older people, we talked about isolated kinds of events rather than trying to program and work with individuals in terms of total needs.

We learned that we could be more successful if we looked at the program not just in terms of non-work activity, but from the standpoint of health needs, financial needs, and other kinds of needs in terms of satisfaction to the individual. We realized that we really weren't programing to enable people to use their time away from the job in a satisfactory fashion. We also learned that many of our members felt, "just give us the money, give us the time, don't worry about us, and we'll take care of the situation." Now, there's no question that they would. The problem is whether or not they are really going to secure the full potential from that time.

You see, our whole emphasis has been in relation to work and the values of work. All of us involved in activities in non-work time, in leisure-time activities, have suffered from the attitudes built in our society, which we help to perpetuate as individuals. It isn't a new problem created by the advancing technology. We've had this problem for a long time. We've talked about the "new leisure." We talked about it in the 1930's. We talked about what the federal government was going to do about it. Then we turned to the old Department of Social Security for help, and they washed their hands of it. We turned every place for help in trying to do *education for leisure.* The one continuing problem has been the need for a different attitude toward uses of time away from the job so that people can use that time, not only in a way satisfying to themselves, but for the community generally.

Therefore, we've put this question of the uses of non-work time on the front burner; and we've also stressed the whole question of our environment, because these two, of course, are related. As a result, in addition to the Department of Recreation and Leisure Time Activities, we also have a Department of

Conservation and Resource Development. We are going to try to reach out through our 1200 local unions in which we have standing committees.

One of the first things that we are asking the local unions' Conservation and Recreation Committees to do is to use all of the communications media techniques and procedures at their disposal to interpret and inform the membership of the philosophies, policies, programs, and procedures as adopted by the International Executive Board, as they relate to conservation and recreation.

Apparently everybody is having difficulty carrying on a dialogue about non-work time, leisure time activities, recreation, and all the rest. The scholars are having trouble; everybody is having trouble. Most of all, we are not reaching out to the masses of people. This is the thing that's jarring us all, including the music educators. The masses want what the elite have, just as we want the guaranteed income. The executives and the bosses have it, and there's nothing too good for us. If the bosses have it, then we ought to have it too. And it's the same way in terms of all the advantages.

The committees will be asked to contact the appropriate community governmental and voluntary agencies that determine the community recreation, park, conservation, and natural resources deficiencies and needs, as well as assets, and the information that is to be studied, and evaluate it for possible local union action; and that means social action.

To do this job on an international level, we will be increasing our staff from six to twelve. They will be located geographically, working with our local unions in the geographic areas. The reason I mention this to you is so that now you know you've got a UAW local union, you know how to reach the people. If you want to get their involvement, to down and talk to the leadership about this.

For many years, in cities like Detroit, all over the country where we've had social unrest, there have been a number of people, too few, who have been working to provide the kinds of services that the middle-class, white neighborhoods enjoy. There are areas of the city where the governmental agencies and the voluntary agencies have *not* placed their resources, and certainly in the cultural arts they have done very little. Indeed, they have done very little in terms of recreation programs (including sports programs) in some areas of our cities— despite the fact that we have been trying for years to put special emphasis and leadership into the central cities to make up for all those years of deprivation. It hasn't happened, although in some instances belated attempts have been made.

I feel badly staying here while this [riots] is going on in Detroit. I want to see for myself what's happening. And maybe in seeing and watching with the rest of the citizens of Detroit, at long last we may wake up. My only hope is that it isn't too late.

What you are going to be doing here is going to be very important in the future. I wish you well in your deliberation, because the kind of world we have in the future will depend upon what you do and say here along with other groups of a similar kind. Beyond that, and even more important, is not only what you do and say here, but how all of us can work together so that the kinds of things that are happening in Detroit and all over the world may sometime in the future not happen. I have hope.

Arts Councils and

the Expanding Arts Scene

George M. Irwin

The expanding arts scene cannot be discussed without, at the same time, considering the importance of the position of those in the arts whose responsibility it is to manage and direct the affairs of our arts institutions.

As one who has been on both sides of the fence, as artistic director as well as administrative director of arts institutions, I am continually impressed with the need for a strong partnership between the artist and the manager in the development of any arts activity. At the same time, I am concerned that board members of arts groups too often will accept less than adequate administrative or management know-how, while at the same time seeking the highest possible standards in the artistic areas.

With the rapid growth of symphony orchestras, art museums, theater and dance groups, we have the problem of developing the professional manager as well as the professional artist. You are acquainted with the responsibilities of symphony managers, art museum directors, and theatre and dance managers, and I think you know that theirs is an increasingly complex job. Today there are simply not enough trained administrators to go around. This same problem exists in the field of arts councils, both at the community and state levels. In the work of arts councils, several ways are suggested in which the problems of administration can be dealt with in view of these new responsibilities.

The growth of arts councils in our country occupies a unique place in our amazing post-war cultural development. The formation of community arts councils seems to have been truly a grass-roots effort as responsible citizens became more concerned with the role of the arts and the programs of art institutions in their cities. In 1950, there were less than a dozen such councils; by 1955 the number had more than doubled; in 1960, at least fifty were known to exist; and in 1967 the national office of Associated Councils of the Arts listed over 250 such councils in varying stages of development. Since 1960, state arts councils have increased so that now all fifty states have some such body, either created by legislation or by executive order of the governor.

Associated Councils of the Arts, established in 1960, is a national private organization seeking to develop and promote cooperative solutions to the problems of organization, administration, growth, and support of the arts at the local, state, and national level. It cooperates with the National Council on the Arts on projects, and seeks an increased dialogue among national arts groups on behalf of all the arts.

A community arts council is usually a membership organization made up of individual cultural institutions and individuals, banded together to share services and solve common problems. Often the stimulus for the creation of a community arts council has been the need to minimize confusion and overlapping in the schedule of performances and exhibits. One of the most effective contributions to audience building is a year-round community calendar of cultural programs. (This should also involve those of colleges and public and private schools.) The publication of a community calendar and the development of central information centers to handle publicity is the next step.

The same coordinated approach can be applied to the operation of facilities for the arts. The sharing of such facilities focuses attention on the programs of all groups using the buildings. The total community cooperation concept can also be effectively applied to public campaigns for the construction of arts centers as well. Such appeals are substantially enhanced when a potential donor can be told that the entire cultural resources of the community, rather than one art form only, will benefit from his generosity. If public funds are involved, the same approach can be used with equal effectiveness.

In at least a dozen cities across the country, annual united fine arts drives are proving a successful way to develop support for the arts. In most every instance, these united drives have repeatedly raised more money more effectively, eliminating multiple campaigns and utilizing volunteers to better advantage than was possible in preceding separate drives. A united drive also frees the managerial and artistic personnel from fund-raising and permits more time to develop their individual programs. Leaders in various arts groups can achieve substantial benefits by working together on arts festivals, community surveys, and perhaps the long-range planning of a city's total fine arts programs. Also, by acting as a united public voice for their members groups, arts councils can deal more effectively with the rapid changes taking place in our cities. These problems of growth and changing economic conditions directly affect the arts and are not confined to the metropolitan centers alone. The problems of parking, suburban growth, deteriorating areas where arts buildings are located, downtown redevelopment programs, and the impact of television are intimately involved with the community's support of music, art, and drama. Construction of public facilities suitable for arts presentations, the creation of architecturally attractive buildings utilizing sculpture, open spaces and fountains, are concerns of an alert arts council board.

New ways must be developed for taking arts programs to the audience. Arts councils, by cooperation with the schools, can help develop broad arts educational programs. By cooperating with teachers of the arts, and coordinating the mechanics and communications necessary to transport children to arts institutions, and artists into the classrooms, for example, the administrative burden on our overloaded school systems could be considerably eased. Even more important, however, the efforts of an arts council in bringing together school authorities and professional arts directors can result in coordinated educational programs using the best resources in all institutions involved. The use of professional artists in school programs not only opens new vistas for both teacher and student, but provides expanded employment opportunities for the artists. New programs are stimulated. This is similar to the reinvestment of business capital or the development of industrial research programs. Increased cooperation, which involves the artist more directly with the student, is a responsibility and a concern of colleges, as well as elementary and secondary schools.

In observing some current trends (the artists-in-residence programs of colleges and universities for example), it seems to me that there is an increasing awareness, though not nearly enough, on the part of college administrators that the arts cannot be taught in the same ways as mathematics or English. There must be a further separation of curriculum between the liberal arts students and those students with special talents which call for careers as performing or creative artists. State arts councils can make significant contributions in this direction.

One word of caution must be made in all this concern for new methods, new arts, and new money: innovation in itself does not build quality programs. We must be concerned with value and content and not be carried away by the fashion of the moment. The really encouraging part is that more and more educators and arts administrators are willing to consider the new ideas. Thus, a cultural environment can be created that encourages the work of our composers, artists, and playwrights. The concern for the development of high standards, both in program and facility, is an important aspect of an arts council.

State arts councils or commissions are official government agencies, charged with the responsibility of improving the general cultural welfare on a statewide basis. These organizations consist of an appointed citizens board and may include an executive staff to carry out policy. State arts councils generally are not membership organizations. Most state councils are less than two years old, but official interest in the arts on the part of top state officials has been significant. The pioneering and continuing efforts in support of the arts by New York Governor Rockefeller since 1960 and the personal interest taken by Illinois Governor Kerner in the last four years have been instrumental in the establishment of these programs.

State arts councils can significantly assist major cultural institutions to expand their programs through touring. They have the flexibility of developing special technical assistance programs to aid the individual arts groups, utilizing the professional talent available; and they can direct attention to the arts through publications, and the sponsorship of conferences involving all aspects of the state's cultural institutions. Touring assistance, both in the performing arts and visual arts, often means the difference between a fine concert, play, dance program, or outstanding art exhibit being presented in the community or passing through.

We are all aware of these rising costs of doing business in the arts: this extends to all phases of arts production. As we look for new monies to support expanding programs, we are continually faced with the responsibility of putting our cultural house in order besides getting the most of ticket money and contributions.

One of the more exciting, as well as controversial, new areas of support for the arts is found in programs at the federal level.

These are contained in Title III of the Elementary and Secondary Education Act of 1965, administered by the U. S. Office of Education, and the initial programs of the National Council of the Arts, created under the National Endowment on the Arts and Humanities Act of 1965.

Although opportunity for the arts exists under Title I of the Elementary and Secondary Act, as well as sections of the Higher Education Act, it is interesting to note the scope and diversity of projects approved under Title III. Of the 653 projects in all fields under Title III, 170 of them call for arts resources amounting to approximately $12,100,000 of the total $44,600,000 funded for all projects and subjects.

The programs funded in the last two years by the National Council of the Arts have been especially significant, not only for the broad scope which they touch, but an unusually high degree of success. Grants have been made to well over a hundred novelists, poets, painters, sculptors, composers, promising graduate students in the arts, choreographers, biographers, and playwrights. Efforts to expand audiences have resulted in support for the Martha Graham Dance Company, American Ballet Theater, New York Shakespeare Festival, Chicago Hull House, Laboratory Theater Companies in New Orleans and Providence, the Academy of American Poets, the Metropolitan Opera National Company, the National Repertory Theatre, international conferences, arts programing on educational television, technical assistance programs expanded by American National Theatre and Academy, American Symphony Orchestra League and the American Educational Teacher Association. Arts in educational programs at Fordham University, Writer's Workshop in Los Angeles, as well as grants to all state and territorial arts councils, underscore the scope of the National Council's programs. In initiating new programs the Council has been concerned with pilot projects in architecture and allied fields, launching studies to explore the feasibility of establishing an American Film Institute, an institute concerned with environmental design, an association of American dance companies and an American Lyric Theater workshop, low rent studio living quarters for artists, and with expanding metropolitan museum resources to smaller communities. All of these grants and programs amounted to $8½ million.

Other government programs are often overlooked. While the cultural exchange program of the State Department is fairly well known, I doubt that many arts managers know that the National Park Service offers courses for museum administrators, or that the Department of Defense makes available its arts collection to communities. The U. S. Information Agency is helping financially with the APA-Phoenix Repertory Theater Company to travel to Expo '67 in Montreal; and federal urban renewal programs can help with housing for the arts. Even the Office of Economic Opportunity has funded several programs involving the arts. There are currently 120 federal programs providing funds and services for artists and arts programing. A report listing these will be available late this summer from the Superintendent of Documents in Washington.

In considering the national scene, the amounts of federal money available to the arts are quite small, and this has been intentional. I am firmly convinced that federal support of the arts should not become a major factor in arts programs, and the best way to use federal funds in this area is to stimulate and encourage without in any way dominating an arts program.

Corporate support of the arts, which is new money for the most part, will increase as the corporate managers are impressed with the management abilities of arts organizations as well as their artistic offerings. We are faced squarely with the problem of communicating to large numbers of people the innermost values of the arts. The language of planning, research, market studies, cost analysis, and customer service applies here, and certainly is understood by the prospective corporate donor. He may have some difficulty in defining the arts and their role in our lives today, even though he may be increasingly aware of their importance, but he can certainly understand and recognize a well administered arts organization. Only when the local arts organization has done the best job possible in managing itself, in setting artistic goals and standards, and in showing that it recognizes its total community role can that group expect corporate officials to contribute corporate money, or the time and talents of company personnel.

However, in the recent *Rockefeller Panel Report* on the Performing Arts, it is pointed out that although there is growing interest in and support of the arts by corporations, their contributions to all fields have taken only one percent of their taxable income. Also, the report states that only slightly over half of all corporations in the United States give anything to the arts. Of the total contributions made by all corporations, only a tiny fraction, at most three to four percent, goes to the arts.

I believe that more and more business leaders are recognizing that today's corporation has a social responsibility as well as an economic one, that there are new ideals and responsibilities which go beyond the profit motive. This greater responsibility is, in effect, a recognition of the corporation's role as a citizen of the community and the entire area which it serves.

In this time of expanding arts, the *educator* occupies a unique role and has a major responsibility to contribute to improved communications between the arts and the corporations. From my observations of twenty years, it is my impression that music educators have done a less than adequate job in community participation and establishing professional acceptance. While not overlooking outstanding examples, I am struck by the fact that too many music educators refuse to accept community responsibility, are overburdened with apathy and withered professional idealism, and all too often are inadequately trained for the important position of teaching. Even considering overcrowded classrooms, disinterested students, lack of cooperation among colleagues, supervisors, and administrators, meager teaching materials, misassignment, rigid seniority rules, heavy extra class duties, mountains of paperwork, and uneven compensation schedules, it still seems that music educators are failing to take advantage of the opportunities.

Some responsibility for this problem must be accepted by the schools that produce the teachers. A recent study by the National Education Association states that a beginning teacher finds the real world of the classroom a far cry from what was expected. Why can't the training of teachers, as it applies to practice teachers, be more effectively managed so that the hours of the practice teacher during his few weeks of field experience are professionally supervised and encouraged for maximum benefits? In most states a thorough reform is needed of the curriculum used to train teachers of the arts.

Courses in educational methodology still override professional attainments in a given art form. The cooperative role of a state arts council with the state office of education is immediately apparent. Why does the music educator stand aside in his role as community citizen and let the doctor, the lawyer, the businessman, and the housewife serve on the boards of the local symphony, theater, or arts groups, or be active in the Community Chest?

The failure of teachers to accept community responsibility is all the more amazing when one considers the potential enhancement of not only professional reputation, but also of effective action to minimize school problems. Arts councils, as citizens' groups, may often have greater influence in local school affairs than the efforts of teachers within the profession. I cannot emphasize too much that one major critical issue for long-range development of the arts in our country is the quality of teaching the arts in our schools.

It is important, too, that public schools and colleges make their facilities available to adult arts groups. Few communities can afford duplicate structures for such activities. The local school could make a significant start by having its own cooperative arts committee with genuine cooperation among the music, art, drama, and dance departments. An alert public school system should also look around and consider sharing professional performances with neighboring schools systems. Such results could be far more stimulating and effective than the total of individual noncooperative programs.

As teachers of the new artists and new artists and new leaders, educators, as well as artists and patrons, should heed the words of August Heckscher, former director of the Twentieth Century Fund:

> The ultimate dedication to our way of life will be won not on the basis of economic satisfaction alone, but on the basis of an inward quality and an ideal. The younger generation especially is looking for something at once more demanding and more genuinely satisfying than what passes for happiness by current standards. To minimize or frustrate this quest is to risk weakening the fabric of our whole society.

III. Toward the Year 2000

Chairman
WILEY L. HOUSEWRIGHT, Dean, School of Music,
Florida State University

Speeches
The Emerging American Society
MAX LERNER, Professor of American Civilization,
Brandeis University
Discussion

**Reflections on the Impact of Science on Cultural
Interactions Among Nations**
THOMAS F. MALONE, Chairman,
the U. S. National Commission for UNESCO

The Quest for Quality
ALVIN C. EURICH, President,
Aspen Institute for Humanistic Studies
Discussion

The Arts in Higher Education: Valid or Valueless?
SAMUEL B. GOULD, Chancellor,
State University of New York, Albany

The Emerging American Society

Max Lerner

The province that has been suggested for my presentation is essentially that of a contemporary Cassandra. It is not a very favoring province. If you turn out to be right by the year 2000, they will have forgotten about it. If you turn out to be wrong, they hoot you down the corridors of time.

I do not pretend to have made many extensive researches in this area of prediction. I do want to suggest for you a study which is now in progress: The Commission on the Year 2000.

The Commission on the Year 2000 was established with foundation funds under the American Academy of Arts and Sciences. This Commission has been working for some years under a committee headed by Daniel Bell, Columbia sociologist, and a set of working papers will be published shortly. *The Year 2000* (a framework for speculation on the next thirty-three years) is co-authored by Herman Kahn and Anthony Wiener, of the Hudson Institute. You may recall Mr. Kahn as the author of some very provocative studies on nuclear strategy. He has since broadened his writing to include the larger frame of global politics and of social forces inside American civilization. I have spent some days now with the study but do not pretend to have mastered the material which is in it. I say this in order to state again unequivocally that I am not in any sense an expert in what is now an emerging field of specialization — analysis of present trends and their projection into the future. This of course was a propitious occasion for the study because this year we are entering the last third of the twentieth century, and the question which this group has put to itself is the question of what we can expect in this final third, what the world and America will be like in the year 2000. I was, therefore, extremely happy to have your invitation to come here to talk about this topic as it converged very much with my own incipient interest. I will not be rhetorical in any sense. We have relatively little time and I want to present as many of these issues as possible.

I listened yesterday to Professor Northrop's exciting talk. It was interesting to me that he spoke of the difficulty of getting the time dimension into the spatial relations of physics, and into painting and sculpture. In the social studies and the social disciplines, the time dimension has been studied for some time — at least in the Western disciplines. Wyndham Lewis in *Time and Western Man* indicates the extent to which Western man has been time-oriented. The whole of Marx's theory incorporates the time dimension. The dialectic which Marx took over from the Greek philosophers moves through time so that you get historical materialism. The two crucial elements of Marx's theory are first, a theory of historical and social change which assumes a self-contained entity (that is, that change takes place out of whatever is within the society) out of its inner contradictions, its inner tensions, its inner struggles. Very few elements come from without. The change is linear. The change is presumably away from what is less desirable toward the more desirable.

The second element in Marx's theory is that it is apocalyptic. There is much struggle, bloodshed, violence, and overthrow; and

out of the elements of struggle that are contained in the historical dialectic, you get the more desirable societies. While we have not followed Marxism in American social theory, we have embodied the time dimension very strongly so that much of our thinking is "time thinking."

I have just mentioned the element of the apocalyptic, of the struggle, in Marxism. In my own perception of "emergence" in American civiliation, I have seen relatively little of that. The struggle is undoubtedly there. As I see it, American civilization emerged out of the breakup of the pent-up energies of European civilizations. We were the inheritors of a whole complex of forces within European civilizations — dynastic and religious wars, hierarchical church control, land scarcity, land hunger, the hunger for scientific freedom, the eagerness to get away from stratified European societies. All of that represents the ground, so to speak, in a figure-ground relationship, if the settlement of America is the figure. As Walter Frank put it, "the settlement of America took place out of the unsettlement of Europe."

It is important to understand that there were very crucial revolutionary elements within European society which could not be contained within the frame of Europe and for which America represented a new area of expressiveness. This is one of the factors that gave American experience its revolutionary character, using "revolutionary" now in a sense of drastic and accelerated pace of change.

Now, there are two meanings of the concept of revolution that we need to distinguish. One is a classical meaning of which I have spoken as the apocalyptic in Marx's thought — that is, revolution as overturn, overthrow, a transfer of power by direct action, violent action from one class to another, from one ruling group to another. Even in that sense, America is revolutionary in its origins. We represented the first revolution against colonialism in modern history. But there is a second sense of the term revolution, which for me is deeper and more sophisticated, and that is revolution as an accelerated pace of change, so accelerated as to achieve a series of breakthroughs — changes so drastic as well as so rapid that in a sense you have to remake your intellectual map, your social map. You have to redraw it because the change has been so drastic and rapid.

In traveling around the world in recent years, I have had the experience of talking with young journalists, professors, and diplomats; and they have said to me, "Mr. Lerner, this reactionary America of yours!" And I say to them, "Watch out. You have, of course, the right to disagree with the decisions of our decision makers. Many of us do as well, but don't say 'reactionary' because actually America is the most 'revolutionary' society in the world today."

This rocks them back on their heels. America the most revolutionary society today? And I say, yes — if you mean it in the second sense of the accelerated pace of change that leads to a succession of breakthroughs in various segments of the society, and in society as a whole. In that sense, we are more revolutionary than the Soviet Union. We are more revolutionary than Communist China. We are more revolutionary than Castro's Cuba.

I have had some experience on this score. I worked on the first draft of my book, *America as a Civilization,* for ten or twelve years. I found out when I was through that a number of things which were written in the beginning were no longer true or valid. During the very period of writing, what I was describing — the *emerging* American civilization — had changed so rapidly that it was necessary for me to rewrite. It has now been ten years and I am quite sure if I were to take the task of doing a new edition, I would find that the pace of accelerated change has been even greater, even more rapid.

Now this kind of change is not very comfortable. When my friend Ellsworth Bunker, whom I knew in India and who is now Ambassador in Saigon, assumed his duties, he called his staff together and suggested a book for them to read: Eric Hoffer's *The Ordeal of Change.* Obviously this ordeal of change is one that the developing countries, like Southeastern Asian nations, are passing through; but we also as a developed country are passing through an ordeal of change. It is a very difficult ordeal because it involves a transvaluation of values. It involves coming to grips with these revolutionary changes. It involves coming to terms with the fact that many of our codes have become archaic. A good many of our intellectual structures are obsolescent.

But it is an ordeal in another sense and that is that revolutions in the first sense are likely at some point to become involved with revolutions in the second sense. We have always thought of the terms revolution and evolution as somehow opposite, but now we are beginning to understand that one of the things Hoffer says in *The Ordeal of Change* is that revolutions in the violent sense do not take place in societies which are stagnant. They take place in societies of relatively rapid change. We are witnessing it right now in our cities. We witnessed it in Newark. We witnessed it in Detroit. Given the history of our Negro-White problems, the pace of change has accelerated in the last generation and certainly within the last five or ten years. I got my first inkling of this before I had read Hoffer. I got it from reading Tocqueville. In the study of the French Revolution, he points out that the violence of the French Revolution did not come at the point when the condition of the peasant and of the city masses was at its worst, but at the point when conditions were considerably improved. Revolution in the first sense comes very often at the point when rapid changes are taking place. Now, why? This is what I call the "Tocqueville effect," because it is an approach which can be used in many areas. What happens when you get rapid social change and improvement of conditions is that there is a corresponding effect: a much more rapid acceleration of expectation.

Now this is particularly true when the changes that take place take some time to filter down and relatively little is left residually. This has been true in the case of our Negro populations in America. When the anti-poverty movements, the educational movements — while well intentioned with much money behind them — have filtered down, there is relatively little residue, although some. But the expectations continually increase, and it is the gap between what these Americans feel they have and what they have come to claim that is increasing. And as the gap increases, of course, you get situations of revolutionary violence in

the first sense as well.

Now, having started out on this very grim note, may I say very quickly that I do not regard the general problem that is posed in social predictions as being a very relevant question. Generally when my students say to me, "Are you an optimist or a pessimist as you look toward the future?," I say, "What do you think this is — Wall Street! You think this is a question of whether I am bullish or bearish on stocks and stockmarkets. It is not in our stars but in ourselves that we shape our future. I am neither an optimist, nor am I a pessimist. I am a *possibilist."* And let me explain what I mean by that. When I read history, or write history, or teach history, I teach it as a choice of alternatives. I read it in terms of the kind of choices that have been open for decisions.

You remember Robert Frost's poem, "The Road Not Taken," about the poet coming to two roads diverging in a wood. In a sense there are always diverging roads in the wood of history; and the question of what happened in the past is not only that of what actually occurred, but also of what might have happened if different choices had been made of these divergent roads. But, of course, the same thing applies to the future. This is why, when I think of these changes in American civilization, these silent revolutions that are taking place, I think of them in terms of the extent to which we can organize our will and intelligence and channel these changes into productive, creative, human uses.

Revolutions in neither of these two senses carry any ethos with them. They are neither good nor bad. The ethos comes from us. The ethos is imposed on them, and it is incumbent always on us to ride the whirlwind and command the storm so as to master the revolutionary changes and to guide them into channels of human constructiveness. If you are talking of social prediction, as this group is, then you are talking of probabilities of what will probably happen, whether it is desirable or undesirable.

When I say I am a "possibilist" I mean that we need to make moral choices, as between alternatives, and in making those moral choices we need to organize our will and intelligence; and I would say that *there is a range of possibility in the future.* Obviously it is not limitless but within limits, especially given the immense extent of American resources: human resources, technology and science, and a power structure probably unparalleled in history. Given all of that, our range of possibility in the future is probably greater than that for any other civilization.

And this is why your group should try to look toward the year 2000, that is, try to see what trends will be emerging in this last third of the century. Discussion is important on two scores: we will be needing to make decisions, and our decisions will probably be more decisive. It will become almost a matter of folk wisdom that the American President can push a button which could be terribly destructive. (The kind of decision Kennedy made in the missile confrontation involved the entire world.) The same is true of economic decisions that some of our economic leadership in government, industry, and trade unions are making. That is one reason why we need to project present forces and trends to see what the *alternative* futures are. There are a whole complex of alternative Americas ahead, in alternative worlds. There is not a single America.

When I was teaching in India for a year I had a chance to talk to Indian students and teacher audiences, and at the end I used to say: "Tell me, what is your picture of my country and my culture?" Always they gave me a picture of a reactionary America — fearful, frustrated, making alliances always with the reactionary forces in the world, and afraid to carry out the basic assumptions of equalitarianism and freedom. This was not long after the McCarthy era. And I said to them: "Obviously the picture you have given is valid, but it is not the only one. There are other Americas. There is the revolutionary America that stretches all the way from the American Revolution, the Jeffersonian revolution, the Jacksonian revolution, the Civil War — when for the first time in modern history brother fought brother so that other men could be free — the Bryan movement, the Populace movement, Theodore Roosevelt's New Nationalism, Woodrow Wilson's New Freedom, Franklin Roosevelt's New Deal, Harry Truman's Square Deal, John Kennedy's New Frontier. I would add Lyndon Johnson's Great Society if I were there now, not out of any partisan spirit (certainly I do not identify with our external war adventure), but in terms of continuity, the continuity of American history; there is this America too as an alternative America.

And I would say to my Indian students: "In a sense, every American carries both Americas within him like two burning cities in the human brain and in the human heart, and what happens to the emerging America will be decided by the struggle between these conceptions."

Now I can extend that two to a large number. It is not just two very clearly, it is a whole set of alternative Americas; and our decisions will be very decisive for the rest of the world, too.

This kind of study is important for another reason. Given our wide range of possibility, possibilism in the future, our crucial problems are likely to be not power problems or affluence problems, but problems of moral choices and aesthetic problems —problems of the kind of society we want, the kinds of values in it, and the kind of life style that we somehow can shape.

As a kind of a footnote, it may be of some relevance to say: It is not good to be entirely future-oriented unless you have a very firm understanding of possibility in the past.

When I was finishing up one of my books, *The Age of Overkill*, which is a study of nuclear weapon systems, war technology, and the impact on our world of nation-states, one of the problems I had to grapple with was the question of whether American civilization would survive. It is not anything we can take for granted. It would be very smug and complacent indeed for us to take it for granted. There have been great civilizations in the past, not like ours — not as great, not as powerful or affluent, but in some ways greater. What happened to them? They are dead. Why? I came to some tentative conclusions: 1) Some of them died of over-reaching: trying to reach too far on too narrow a base of power. 2) Some of them died out of rigidity, as prehistoric animals died when the environment changed and they did not change with it. 3) Some of them died because of failure to respond to challenges, whether challenges without or challenges within. And finally, 4) some of them died out of failure of belief. The young people no longer believed in the institutions, in the ethos of that civilization. Harold Laski, one of the former leaders of the British Labor Party, once said: "When the leaders of the people ask their followers to die for a dream, those followers have a right to know on whose behalf that dream is being dreamt."

In a sense, at the core of every civilization there is a dream. I use dream now in a sense of myth; and I use myth not in the somewhat vulgar sense of something that is not true. I use myth in a way which Sorokin used it. Myth is something, whether true or not, whether valid or not, that moves men to action and passions. In that sense, at the core of every society there has to be a myth, a dream. And if you ask young people to die for a dream or to live for a dream, they have a right to know on whose behalf that dream is being dreamt. What kind of future will be merging for them, what kind of claims can they make on that future, and what are the chances that these claims will be fulfilled?

This is why the most difficult, and elusive, and yet important projections into the future are not the technological projections, the economic ones, living standards or population projections, the military projections, the political projections, but the projections I am now talking about. It is a kind of civic religion, a world view, life goals, and values. If I had to find a single word that suggests the whole complex, I would use the word *ethos* — a whole stance toward life and what is desirable in life. I find relatively little, if I may say so, in this study of the projection of ethos into the year 2000. It is terribly difficult to do. It is a kind of thing that cannot be done by computer methods or by ordinary research methods. It can only be done by speculative leaps, with some knowledge of present trends.

In this ethos there are a number of problems. The central problem appears to be that of commitment. I put it in terms of two dangers: 1) The danger of becoming "a true believer," or the danger of fanaticism. The worst killers are those who kill with a sense of commitment, who believe, who are sure, that they have a pipeline to God and who rationalize killing because of this pipeline. I use Eric Hoffer's term, "the true believer." 2) At the other extreme there is anomie — valuelessness, the absence of value. There are aspects of anomie, secularism for example, total intellectualism, total rationalism, total mechanism. A number of philosophers of history (Sorokin, Toynbee and Spengler among others) have tried to indicate that civilizations move through cycles. Sorokin thinks at the present time that we are in a late, sensate stage in the development of civilizations; and that means total breakdown of religion, of ethos, of commitment, and presumably there is a recoil against which there will come some form of very strong fanaticism.

I do not accept these cyclical theories. I think they are suggestive, but I am enough of a possibilist to believe that we can break the cycle, if indeed the cycle is there, or considerably extend various phases of it. If we are asking where we are at the present time, in terms of these two extremes, my answer is that we embody elements of both, that we have the anomie, which we call alienation, among considerable groups of our population and particularly among our younger people, but that we also have "the true believers." And when both of these are present in a civilization, you have a situation of great danger. My own feeling is that toward the year 2000 each of these extremes will be intensified and the situation, in that sense of the struggle between the two, will probably get worse rather than better.

Science and technology have been eroding ideologies. They have been eroding "true believer" fanaticisms. It has become a truism to speak of the end of ideology in our present world, a truism to point out that the Communist ideology has been eroded, particularly in the Soviet Union and in Eastern Europe, and that the Western ideology, the democratic ideology, is being eroded.

Projecting again toward the future, my own feeling is that there will be an extension of this trend and that the erosion of ideology will move from the Soviet Union and Eastern Europe on to the present area of fanaticism, Communist China; but I do not think it at all impossible that new fanaticisms will arise. We have seen instances of "true believer" fanaticisms in the Middle East. Very recently we have seen them in Africa. They may arise again somewhere in the Communist world. It may take the form not of a democratic ethos but of an antidemocratic ethos. The reason why rightist movements in America today are of more than temporary interest is that they indicate the possibilities and the potentials of that kind of development of "true believer" fanaticism.

Today, among American youth, there is a split essentially between the hippies and the New Left. The hippies are non-activist; essentially they are quietist. They want to let the forces of the world go on while they build their own little private preserves. The new leftist is hyperactivist. Both forces are at work among young people. The same is true among Negroes. You will find among a number of Negroes a disenchantment with the whole value structure of America and, as a result of that, a very considerable anomie, which you find also in small activist groups where you get a "true believer" fanaticism.

What kind of a future can the younger generational groups lay claim to as they look toward this future? I want to put this question rather quickly now in a succession of areas.

1) *On the area of war and peace.* This study gives us some very concrete predictions about what is going to happen to technology, but it is by no means concrete on the question of war and peace. The author of this study, Herman Kahn, probably knows as much about nuclear tensions as any man in the world today, and yet the best he can do is to present a set of what he calls "scenarios." In a number of them a nuclear war has broken out by 2000 — a war, let us say, that starts in Central Europe between the two Germanies. A war between China and America. A war between the Soviet Union and America. War between China and the Soviet Union. War between one of the larger Asian countries and one of the Western countries, which may start as a conventional war and end as a small nuclear war. All of these Mr. Kahn sees as scenarios of possibility. He ends up with a tentative hypothesis that the possibility of a nuclear war is less likely than any other of the possibilities. This does not mean less than fifty percent chance; but given a whole range of alternatives the chances of a war are not very high.

The scenarios contain a considerable amount of realism, and they are hair-raising reading in that sense. Mr. Kahn suggests (and I myself would agree with this) that by the year 2000 there will be two super powers, the United States and the Soviet Union, and eight relatively great powers in terms of the Gross National Product. In terms of power, these eight nations are likely to run in the following sequence:

3.	Japan	7.	United Kingdom
4.	West Germany	8.	India
5.	France	9.	Italy
6.	China	10.	Canada

This is in terms of Gross National Product, of military and political power. But, the real question that bothers us is nuclear proliferation and political disarray. Here the best resources of the predictors are relatively futile. I believe the chances are that we will *not* have a nuclear war. In the next ten or fifteen years, let us say by 1985, if we have not organized by that time a way of preventing nuclear warfare, the chances of it not happening by 2000 are, I believe, relatively small. For me the breathing spell, the time we have at our disposal, is not great; and it is not the next thirty-two or thirty-three years. I think it is more likely to be ten or fifteen years. Now, time for what? Not for a condominium between the United States and the Soviet Union which we once thought of. Efforts of the two powers at the present time to ban proliferation of weapons for the non-nuclear powers is meeting great resistance from Germany and Japan; they do not want a world dominated by two powers.

But what is more likely, in my mind, is what I call a "concert of powers" — what Professor Brejinski calls a "community of the developed nations." (He is in the State Department so he has to use somewhat more polite language: a "community of the developed nations.") By "concert of powers," I mean that those nations that have power, perhaps these ten, get together and decide that they are not going to allow the use of nuclear weapons by any of their own members or by any other nation. This involves a meeting of minds to start with, between the Soviet Union and America, and it involves an extension of that meeting of the minds to Communist China and to the other countries. Whether we can wrench ourselves free of past hostilities of ideological conflicts, and particularly of our thinking about the nation-state, one-hundred-percent sovereignty, whether we can wrench ourselves free from those patterns of thought in time to develop this kind of "concert of powers" is a very open question. Here again, I am only a possibilist. I think it will be possible to prevent a thermonuclear war by the year 2000. It is not guaranteed.

2) The point at which predictions are most concrete are in technology. I recommend to you a list that the authors Kahn and Weiner give of a hundred likely technical innovations by the year 2000. This is fascinating and almost science fiction reading, and they vouch for the very high probability that these hundred innovations will have come to fruition. They then give a series of twenty-five less likely innovations, and finally ten far-out innovations. Taken together I get men in the year 2000 who are omniscient, omnicompetent, omnipotent, and omnipresent. These are the dreams, the technological dreams of innovation. It is really a picture that H. G. Wells talked of: of men like gods. Of course, there is a danger that all of us are aware of, and that is another part of the landscape. Along with these men like gods will be robots that act like men and, in turn, assign to men the role of being like robots. This is one of the problems we have thought about a good deal and are still concerned with — the problem of the computer era ahead. There is no question that the remaining part of the century will be technologically oriented — computer geared, information directed. There will be a plethora of information. The problem of our libraries will be the retrieval of information, and a good part of the problem of computers will be the selection of information. There is no question at all that the possibilities of the computers in terms of the achievements that men can direct them to do are almost limitless.

3) The problems that are raised in our minds, now, is what this does to human beings. My own feeling (a personal speculation)

is that *the most crucial philosophical problem ahead of us is the problem of a choice between two conceptions of the relation of man to his machines: One, the mechanization of the human being, and two, the humanization of the machine.* In this struggle there can be no compromise, no qualification. There must be total commitment toward the humanization of the machine. I try to say to my students as we look toward the future: "You are going to have to live on a landscape with these machines and with huge units, but you do not have to live by them."

W. H. Auden once spoke of the differences between two groups of people as "those who live and those who are lived." You do not have to live by them. And it is those who are lived that are very likely to take over the ethos of gigantism. The ethos of the computer, assuming there is an ethos in the functioning of a computer, involves some stretching of terms. My own approach to the machine is that I am not a Luddite. I do not believe in machine smashing. I believe in using machines; but fundamentally I think that machines are not gadgets or artifacts outside of the human being. The machines we are developing in the educational process, that we are using in automation, in cybernetics, even the war machines — every one of those machines embodies the human imagination as well as the human intellect. It would not be what it is if it did not have the human imagination and intellect in it. And just as we have built our intellect and imagination into the machine in making it, so there must be the same building of intellect and imagination into the machine in using it. Norbert Wiener said to one of my classes, "Of the two books I have written, the one I am most proud of is not the book on cybernetics, which began the whole cybernetic revolution, but a second book called, *The Human Use of Human Beings.*" Wiener understood the possible consequences of technology; he understood that there could not be any real control over technology unless you built the human imagination, the human intellect, the human moral choice into the machine.

I end with a whole array of problems:

1) The problem of the inner city — the kind of things that are happening in the inner city today, partly because we have abandoned it, partly because it is now populated by groups who have had a bitter experience.

2) The problem of postindustrial America, moving beyond the industrial revolution to the point where we are going to have tertiary and quarternary industries rather than primary or secondary; that is, communication industries, educational industry and service industry rather than production industries.

3) The whole question of time: the leisure revolution, which all of us are very concerned with. The basic problem, or the essence, of the leisure revolution is the release of time for more and more people. What we get created is not another leisure class society, as in Periclean Athens, or in Imperial Rome, or in Renaissance Italy, or in Elizabethan England, but one in which more and more time is available for more and more poeple and not just for the elite groups. There is an elegant paradox here. As we look toward this cybernetic future with more and more time available and more and more people, there will be less and less time available for the few. In past leisure class society, a relatively small elite group had their leisure made possible by sitting on top of a pyramid of the exploited many, the work-driven many. But in the society that is emerging there will be more time made possible for the many because of the work being done by the efforts of a few. Because of the nature of leadership, the nature of the elite will be such that it will not be possible for them to have the kind of leisure that is possible for the others. And this, of course, leads in turn to two other themes which I hope we will have a chance to discuss: the generational struggle and the value revolution.

4) The generational struggle, which is going on in America, is one of the most crucial struggles because it represents the presentation of claims by the younger generation on the future. It represents their revolt against the things that, as they put it, "we have been hung up on"—the value structure of our society which we have tried to transmit to them—ethical, political, economical, and aesthetic. For example, I believe the hippies represent a more enduring phenomenon than the New Left, because the New Left simply takes more radical attitudes of more or less conventional patterns. The hippies, however, represent a revolt against all the "hang-ups," against the whole value structure, against the pursuit of the "fast buck," against the nationalized mass killing that we call war, against the "bitch goddess success," against gigantism, against the power structure, and against affluence.

5) The value revolution is the most crucial revolution we are going through, because if we are going to do anything with the time which is released to us, we have to make these moral and aesthetic choices about values. The urgency of making these choices is being pushed on us now by the generational struggle. In that sense, it is a very creative thing. There has been a breakdown of communication between the generations. There needs to be a restoration of communication, of confidence, of dialogue; and if there is that kind of restoration in the dialogue between generations, it may be possible by the year 2000 to have worked out a more meaningful value structure in America than we now have.

DISCUSSION

Question: One of the implications of what you say in terms of being a "possibilist" deals with the ways in which the masses are released from work, are more and more affluent, respond to and are educated for so-called creative aesthetic enterprise. Eric Hoffer makes much of this. You wrote about this in your *American Civilization.* Have you had any further thinking about these problems?

Lerner: This is a very searching question. I did not get a chance to talk of the elite revolutions that have been taking place in the last few decades. Eric Hoffer wrote an interesting magazine article recently in which he said, in effect, that every member of the masses is pushing his way into the elite. While that is a rather exaggerated way of putting it, there is very little doubt that one of the things that is happening as a result of our educational and cultural breakthrough is increased education. If we look toward the year 2000, there will be undoubtedly a population with something like 100 percent secondary school education and somewhere between 80 and 90 percent with a university education, even though the quality of the education may not be quite what we have been accustomed to.

It is difficult to speak of a mass culture. Fundamentally, I think the term mass culture becomes obsolescent, and the whole dichotomy between elite and mass culture begins to fade away. There is much flux there. I myself do not make very much of this dichotomy. I would say what is happening in the United States today is a "storming of the gates" of educational opportunity. The remarkable thing about college students really has to do with their parents. So large a proportion come from families that never had a high school or a college education. As we go on toward the end of the century, this will be less true because more and more of the parents will have had a college education. However, it is very difficult to talk of mass culture in that sense or of an elite culture. I think these terms will become obsolescent. In every society there are always two basic elites. One is the commanding or power elite and the other is the creative, intellectual elite.

Problems that I pose are rather different: 1) There are questions about the relation of the elites to each other. 2) There are questions about the dialogue between the power elite particularly and the rest of the population, who cannot be thought of as mass, but nevertheless are not in the power elite. Now, on the relation of the elites to each other, there is the danger of hostility between these two elites. George Orwell once wrote an essay called "England, Your England." He wrote it while there was a hail of Nazi bombs on London. This essay was addressed to his former radical friends — he had been a communist before the Spanish Civil War. What he said to them was: "Look, this is England — your England; you have created it by your passivism, by your contempt for the military, by your being willing to appease the Nazis and all the rest of this. You created it. This rain of bombs is the result of the hostility between the commanding elite and the creative elite."

And this is terribly important because in America today, the hostility between these elites is more bitter than ever. The point at which there was greatest acceptance was under John F. Kennedy. Kennedy's greatness lay not so much in the decisions that he made (except for that decision on the missile confrontation in Cuba, which was a very crucial one), but in the incandescence of his appeal to young people, because he stood in both elites. You may remember what Robert Frost said to Kennedy on inauguration day. He said, "I hope, Mr. President, that this will be an Augustan age of poetry and power; but I hope, Mr. President, that you will be more Irish than Harvard."

The interesting thing about Kennedy was that he did have this quality of incandescence, as a symbol for the young, showing them that it was possible to have a relationship of confidence between the elites. We do not have that now.

As we move toward the year 2000 there will likely be three elites — bureaucratic, meritocratic, and democratic. *Bureaucratic* in that they will become larger parts of larger organizations: corporate, governmental, and the like; *meritocratic* because of their intellectual merit; and *democratic* because they are not self-perpetuated, but will be drawn from the people of various social strata. I recall a phrase from Jefferson in one of his letters to John Adams. (There was a wonderful correspondence between the two men toward the end of their lives.) He said, "In any democracy like America, you cannot expect the democracy to survive unless you develop an aristocracy of virtue and talent." What Jefferson was talking of was a democratic elite — democratic because this aristocracy would be drawn not from the aristocracy of privilege, but from the people themselves. (His whole scheme for education

in Virginia, of course, was part of this.) And this is likely to be true in the future. A democratic, as well as meritocratic, and a bureaucratic elite is likely to emerge in both of these areas—virtue and talent. For that reason, it is all the more important that these young people should never lose touch with what they came from.

These are my caveats about the relations between the elites. On the other score, there is the whole problem of the dialogue between the various strata of society and between the power groups and the non-power groups; and a good deal depends on the maintenance of that dialogue. This seems to me to be the relevant question for the future.

Question: Is it possible that you might consider communications more important than "a tertiary industry of the future" as you defined it? I ask this especially in view of your comments on ethos, your comments of a few moments ago on the elimination of mass culture by the assumption of a complete educational activity. Would it not seem then that the communications industry might become the primary industry?

Lerner: We are using the terms primary, secondary, and tertiary in different senses. All I meant by tertiary or quaternary is the way in which the terms are usually used by sociologists and economists, which means further removed from actual production. That's all. Primary industries are production industries; and communication and service industries and education are tertiary in that sense.

Question: The other sense might be *the* primary industry.

Lerner: There is no question about it. In sheer industrial terms, in terms of investment involved, education is already becoming the number one industry. Education and communication will undoubtedly, by the year 2000, outstrip all the other industries in that sense; and in the sense of how crucial they are in the whole body politic and in the creativeness of the society, I could not agree with you more. The big media are, of course, part of our educational and cultural breakthrough.

I think it is worth defining the term communication a little more sharply than we tend to do. I have recently been traveling in this country and I have often been asked whether there is intelligent life beyond the earth. It is a fascinating question, but I have another question in a higher degree of priority: Not "Is there intelligent life up there in space?" but "Is there intelligent life down here on earth?" And not "Will we ever be able to communicate with life in space?" but "Will we ever be able to communicate here on earth: communicate between the ideologies, between the nations, between ethnic groups, between the generations?" Now, if you talk of communication industries, (meaning the transmitting of what has happened) this is very rapid and, in fact, instantaneous.

One of my theories about the present rash of riots is that it is partly the result of instantaneous communication and the infection effect. For example, what has been happening in Newark, and what is happening at the black power conference in Newark has an impact on Cairo, Illinois, on Detroit, Michigan, and so on. That is communication in one sense, and I sometimes wonder whether we have not sold ourselves to the devil in getting instant communication.

Now, there is a second meaning of communication, and that is: How much of an actual dialogue is there? To what extent do we really understand each other? In that sense, of course, with the development of the media, there has been at the same time a breakdown of communication which is very serious—particularly inside the structure of the family and within the community. This is one of the reasons we get the riots. Another reason is that we have never allowed the Negro to be really a part of a community; and if you do not allow a whole group to be part of the community, how can you expect genuine dialogue, genuine communication? You cannot expect it. Out of the breakdown of communication comes hostility and all the rest.

There is a third sense of communication, such as what McLuhan is talking about: the impact of the nature of the communication media on the autonomic nervous system. This is what McLuhan means, presumably, by "the medium is the message." What is really important is the impact with the medium itself on the nervous system, rather than the literary and intellectual message that is conveyed.

There are these three senses of communication, and we need to be precise about which one we are using.

Question: It has been observed that man represents an intermediate step between the anthropoid ape and the human being. If man is also emergent, is he becoming more human? This may be an alternate question; I do not know, but would you care to discuss this?

Lerner: I have spent a little time recently on this kind of problem. One of the great revolutions taking place has been the uncovering of man's past to an extent that we had not known before and an extension of the total lifespan of man on earth — much, much longer than we ever thought, running into millions of years now.

May I reflect somewhat on the future? The history of man on earth has turned out to be so long that the chances are that he has pretty much established his basic constitution. What is likely to change in his basic constitution in the course of the next 32 or 33 years is relatively small; even what is likely to happen in the course of the next few thousand years is small. But, what man can do is to change the environment, not only in terms of nature, but in two other senses: 1) the social environment, which is really at our command to change, and 2) the intellectual environment, the internal furniture of the human mind and, indeed, the moral choices. It is in the changes of environment in these three senses that our best possibilities lie, rather than in any hope for changes in the basic constitution of man.

May I say that as you formulated your little epigram at the start, I was a good deal amused. My own feeling is that man is not evil, nor is he good. For me, man is a bundle of potentials in terms of his basic constitution. He has developed the rational in only the recent timespan. He has developed that on the bases of both the rational and nonrational elements. For example, love is not rational, it is nonrational, a feeling of paternal affection. Below the nonrational elements are the irrational and the destructive elements that you seem to be talking about, at the lowest level of the irrational. The level of the irrational which contains most of our instinctual life also contains some very creative elements. When we talk, for example, of creativity, whether in music education or in literature education or in social science education, we are really talking of leaps that are made by people who are capable of tapping their unconscious and putting the irrational to the service of their intellect in the human social uses. In that sense, again, even the rational is not wholly destructive. It is a bundle of potentials, and for some reason I find it difficult to take this particularly

pessimistic point of view of human potentials. What we can do now is to create new environments.

Question: We are, of course concerned with change. Would you address some remarks to the idea of social function and use of the arts as an interaction of change and stability in a continuum which is evolving? My hypothesis is that within the frame of continuous change we have the creativity that man develops through the arts, and this has a stabilizing effect interpersonally, socially, and individually. What I am really asking for is a check-out on this hypothesis, if history gives you any indication one way or another.

Lerner: I have a colleague who is going to be on this platform, Professor Maslow, of Brandeis, whom I find to be very provocative in his thinking. It is part of his hypothesis that education has not yet really addressed itself adequately to the whole question of the peak experiences that are potential in man's development. Many of these peak experiences are obviously in the area of the arts. There is no question about it.

I would say that what we have had in our culture has been far more pragmatic, utilitarian, goal-oriented, production-oriented, and so on. This is why I say that what is happening with the hippies is so meaningful, because they are rejecting that whole orientation, and talking in terms of something that runs much more in terms of play. Their whole conception of man is *homo ludens,* not *homo faber.* To me it is wonderful to see a generation coming up which is interested in human expressiveness, not in order to produce something, but in terms of a kind of total harmony of body, mind, and spirit, just for the sheer hell of it, for its own sake. My definition of play is this total body, mind, and spirit for its own sake, for human expressiveness. And the area of the arts is, to a very considerable extent, part of play and part of the fulfillment of the mythos and the dream — human aspiration expressed in other than productive terms. These are peak achievements for those who create them, and I would add that they are peak achievements for those who are exposed to them. We are today, as part of our cultural revolution, witnessing a real cultural breakthrough in terms of art museums, symphony orchestras, and chamber music across the country. We are witnessing also, on the television medium, what I call a "horizontal humanism"; that is, making available to millions of people for the first time the best that has been created in music, in theater, and in the other arts. I call this horizontal humanism because it means opening to the total population these peak experiences. The importance of this is not to be minimized. It is not creative in the sense of "vertical humanism." A kind of experience that the creative artist himself has is a very different kind, but there is a relationship between the two. A society which becomes more and more accustomed to this kind of exposure is a society in which these experiences become more valuable, and ultimately, a society in which the vertical creativeness takes place.

I did not get to hear my friend, Mr. Leinsdorf, but I read his talk; and I was very interested in his talking of Vienna as a place where you go to concerts as an ordinary experience, so that out of it evolved a kind of vertical creativity from that particular area. We are, I think, on the verge of this kind of experience; but there is no guarantee. It is quite conceivable that the totality of horizontal humanism, which may saturate the society, may nevertheless result in a corresponding increase in vertical creativity such as existed in a little state like the Greek city state. We just do not know.

Reflections on the Impact of Science
on Cultural Interactions Among Nations

Thomas F. Malone

The sombre and distressing news of the past few weeks and months brings a clear message that the ills that have beset the world for centuries are still with us. There is a change in the state of man that is quite possibly the most profound in either written or unrecorded history. It is of this change that I will speak with you this morning. I venture to do so because I believe that this change does present new dimensions of opportunity, that they are the consequences of human thought, and they have their origin in science and their consequences in your area of interest.

I am convinced that the state of man has changed over the past two decades — profoundly, dramatically, and irrevocably. In probing this statement, however, we must carefully distinguish between basic change and symptoms of change. The transformation in transportation and communications that give new meaning to the term, "one world"; the specter of a nuclear holocaust, the promise of nuclear power; the agricultural revolution and the associated urban explosion; the hope and the danger of new science and technology; the challenge to the human mind and spirit of space exploration; the ominous shadow of environmental pollution; the widening and frightening gap in economic development between the advanced and the advancing countries; the domestic problem of poverty; the frightening phenomenon of alienation that threatens to estrange modern man from his fellow man and from the world which he has inherited; the growth in population that conflicts with achievement of human aspirations in the short term and adequate space for all on this planet in the long term; the 700 million illiterates; the 1½ billion undernourished in a world which has the potential for plenty for all; the future of international organizations—these and all the other characteristics of a modern society are measures of the condition of man, his problems and his prospects. In some, however, they are the consequences of progress or lack of progress in six areas that are the province of the human mind, and therefore are of concern today. I am speaking of: 1) the physical sciences, 2) social sciences, 3) the life sciences, 4) informational sciences, 5) culture, and 6) that realm sometimes called philosophy of ethics, or morality. Our symptoms arise because of an unequal balance in progress in these six domains of the human mind.

So, I would like to do three things: first, a few words about perspective; second, a few words about implications; and third, a few gratuitous thoughts that occurred to me from contact in science that possibly may be of interest to you.

To think intelligently about the year 2000, or any time ahead, we have to look back and see where we have been. Very briefly, the world is about 5 billion years old. Life of some kind appeared about 3 billion years ago; man, about 2½ million years (and the time interval is increasing); modern man, that is, with about the intellectual and physical *potential* that he has today, about 50 thousand years ago. We must be aware of this time scale. Looking ahead, there is ample energy in the sun, and even allowing for explosions we can say another 2½ million years. It may be twice that or four times that, it really does not matter; but 2½ million years is a nice, symmetrical number; and that is the only reason why I select it, because it is the right order of magnitude.

So much for time; now for change. Knowledge doubled approximately between the time of Christ and 1750. It doubled again by 1900, again by 1950, again by 1960, and no one has calculated more recently. This has many implications. I would pick four or five out of the whole span of man's existence: 1) the development of logical reasoning; 2) the inter-human capability of speech; 3) the invention of writing; 4) the mastery of energy and matter, which is important to me as a scientist and engineer because it multiplied the muscle power to produce the goods and services that are the starting point for the things in which you people are interested; 5) the invention of the computer. (No more dramatic illustration of its significance can be cited than the machine on the moon a few weeks ago, a quarter of a million miles away, digging a little trench upon instructions from earth.) I rank these as the five major developments in the long history of man.

This brings me to the principal point I wish to make: That progress in the physical sciences, the life sciences, and in information processing over the past few decades, slight as it may be compared with the progress that may be expected in the future, has brought us to a sort of turning point in the affairs of man that opens up new dimensions of opportunity. In the first place, even limited mastery of matter, energy, life processes, and information has now made it possible, in principle, to produce all the goods and services required to meet the basic human needs of all mankind. We have not realized it, but we have it in our grasp. This productive power now frees us to devote some portion of our time and energy to expanding and extending our understanding in the other three domains of knowledge — the social sciences, culture, and the realms of morality, philosophy, and ethics — the "why" of man's existence.

It seems clear that a deeper understanding of the events that take place inside the heads of human beings, that regulate the behavior of one individual relative to others, and of institutions relative to other institutions, and a profound reexamination leading first to an understanding, and then to renovation and renewal of the institutions and organizations by which society conducts its affairs, have taken on new urgency, simply because knowledge is expanding so rapidly in these other areas.

With each increment of knowledge in these other domains, the problem of directing its application toward beneficial ends becomes more difficult, the consequences of failure more disastrous, and the time for decisions more brief. Yet, it is to the social sciences and to the very foundations of human knowledge and behavior, to the basic roots of morality, that we must turn to make these decisions and to make them wisely. Hence, the need for renewal, which John Gardner pointed out when he spoke of our need to be concerned not only with form and structure, but with a careful reexamination of values, principles, ideals, attitudes, motivations, aims, and beliefs.

The list of institutions demanding understanding and renewal is virtually endless — political, educational, familial, religious, industrial, our urban complexes, our transportation systems, the mechanisms by which we preserve the quality of our environment (an environment in which our growing population is expanding), and particularly the international institutions that have now enlarged responsibilities in a world shrunken by advances in communication and transportation. Just as our understanding of the physical universe and of life processes, and information will expand explosively in the years ahead, I am convinced that the increasingly difficult knowledge problems in the social sciences, in morality, ethics, religious belief, and philosophy will yield to man's intellectual assault. For the first time in the history of the 87 billion people who have lived on this earth, this intellectual assault can be mounted because we can meet our basic, primitive needs. We are going to regard the last 2,000 years as the primitive era of Christianity, and the last 200 years as the aboriginal period in the social sciences.

A few gratuitous thoughts: First, the importance of associating means and ends. To me, science is an exciting adventure of the human mind and spirit, and I love doing it; but it has things it can accomplish. For six long, frustrating, disappointing years, I have been traveling about the world on a mission started by President Kennedy to lay the foundations for cooperation in a rational assault on the problem of controlling the behavior of the atmosphere. If we do not lay the base of cooperation now we are going to be in trouble — twenty, thirty, fifty, a hundred, or a thousand years from now. After six years we are two-thirds of the way there. We have not got Red China in yet. This little effort is but one brick in the kind of edifice, such as in what this Symposium is doing, the keystone to this arch that is being constructed, brick by brick, where both the intrinsic interest in an area of intellectual activity and the things it can accomplish are both recognized.

Finally, I would urge proper attention to the element of creativity. I am aware that social scientists look at physical scientists with envy, that the life scientists are looked at with envy, because they get all the money and do all the exciting things. I suggest that emphasis on creativity is a reason these other areas have moved ahead. Do not misunderstand. You have creativity. I emphasize that this is your most powerful tool in moving ahead and in getting the support from the private sector, the public sector, and involving the interests of young people.

The Quest for Quality

Alvin C. Eurich

We've heard some very significant things at this Symposium about the job we have to do in the years ahead. We've been greatly stimulated. Now I think, we see, new possibilities.

Max Lerner said this morning that he is not an optimist nor a pessimist; he is a possibilist. He wants to make plans for the future, for he thinks they can be carried out. Professor Gabor, of the University of London, wrote on the same theme in his book, *Inventing the Future*. He distinguished between predicting the future and inventing it. Dr. Malone also pointed out that is now possible to make plans for utilizing our enormous resources and then to carry them out. This approach represents a striking change between our predictions today and those made by previous generations.

My wife, Nell, has spent a number of years making an analysis of Utopian literature. Her book, *Science in Utopia: A Mighty Design*, has just been published by the Harvard University Press. In her analysis of Utopias, she analyzed the predictions made in science. These were dreams. Many of them have come to pass. There was a dream, for example, of a scientific laboratory for schools and colleges more than a century before our first scientific laboratory was established. The predictions of Utopias were not always thought possible. They were considered wild dreams; but now we make predictions of things we believe possible of attainment.

Another important observation made by Max Lerner was that our projections must include a whole area of life, the ethos not touched by the computer; an area of life from which music springs; an area of life concerned with values and with the destiny and purposes of man. These observations are particularly pertinent to the work of this conference, because they imply that the future of music in society and the future of music instruction in the schools depend on the plans we make and the degree to which we apply our energies and ingenuity to carry them out.

Today something strange, new, and remarkable is overtaking the status and prospects of the arts in America. I am deliberately using neutral, non-judgmental adjectives to characterize this change, for among those most concerned with this phenomenon — critics, philosophers, anthropologists, sociologists, psychologists, teachers, artists, and the performers themselves — the precise nature of this change is a subject of endless argument.

The terms "cultural explosion" and "culture boom" are by now, in this age of instant communication, tiresome cliches. All of us have been flooded by a stream of magazine articles and books testifying to the magnitude of this development: the proliferation of art galleries and museums, the multiplication of orchestras and other musical groups in the country, the staggering increase in concert and museum attendance, in the sale and use of musical instruments, and in the publication of musical compositions of all kinds, old and new.

The statistics defy argument. They clearly show the extent of change. No one is inclined to deny the sheer magnitude of America's consumption of culture, or what we can loosely put under that catch-all phrase. It has been indubitably strange, new, and remarkable. But there the consensus ends. The argument starts the moment we begin to evaluate the new development, to try to assess its real import for the quality of American life and to project its impact on America's future. John D. Gardner's much quoted question: "Can we be equal and excellent, too?" is highly relevant to our consideration of the present arts scene.

Little in our country's history prepared us for what we now see around us on all sides. Those extraordinary men who invented America two centuries ago demonstrated their commitment to the arts in their own lives as well as in their own words. It was not just the philosopher-statesmen, like Jefferson, but men of action too, like George Washington, who said that "the arts and sciences are essential to the prosperity of the state and to the ornament and happiness of human life." But their views and example could hardly prevail as their countrymen transformed the wilderness into towns and farms, fended off their enemies, forged a nation.

For generations, by and large, the audience for the arts — painting, poetry, music — were for the rich and cultivated, a graceful adjunct to their lives. Then, as now, the creators of art came from all classes. The act of creation, the creative impulse: these are classless. You might almost say that the archetype of the creator has been the poor, struggling painter or composer in his garret or crumbling cottage. This gives us pause when we think about the quality of production, because quality in art, in the creative enterprise, has perhaps seldom come from the people who have the wealth.

In formal education the arts have suffered from successive waves of fashion and emphasis, now up, now down, in academic or artistic status. Though music was one of the seven liberal arts of antiquity, it has long been treated as an extra or professional specialty in our colleges and universities. In the lower schools, to be sure, the arts have displayed more staying power, but only by comparison with higher education. Once children proceed beyond the primary grades, painting and music become more and more a filler for the "tag end of Friday," as one of our veteran settlement house workers has put it. Like many other good elements of John Dewey's educational program, the arts have been increasingly de-emphasized in the near hysteria that gripped the schools in the post-Sputnik period. I do not want to be misunderstood. I am not impugning the progress wrought by recent reforms in science and mathematics instruction, nor am I underestimating the need for increased academic rigor and intellectual improvement in the schools. But all the accelerated stress on intelligence and scholastic aptitude tests, on college entrance requirements, on the national need for trained manpower — all these have strictly emphasized the academic and scholastic parts of the curriculum and slighted the arts, particularly music.

It would be foolish, obviously, to suggest that the health of the arts has ever been conditioned exclusively or principally by formal education or by the patronage of the rich and powerful. For from the beginning of time, the "people" have been creating and enjoying their own brand of culture — what we somewhat condescendingly refer to as "fold" culture, or nowadays as popular culture. Not until fairly recent times have we come to appreciate fully, and then only with the help of the archaeologist and the anthropologist, the excellence and the artistic merit of the ballads and street plays and primitive carvings that the elite of previous generations disdained or ignored. William Cornog suggested the other day that perhaps our children are the ones who can help us understand better those more primitive types of art which have more lasting value.

It is not my intention here to deal, except in passing, with the intricate aesthetic and sociological questions raised by the contrast of "high" art and "folk" art. My point, rather, is that today — and this is the new and remarkable development of our time — the division between the two is becoming blurred. They are blending into each other. In the process, no doubt, something precious has been lost, but I believe there are some compensating gains.

Today we are witnessing the rise of something that is quite without precedent in history, something which I think holds infinite promise and hope for the human race. It could be that the popularization of the kinds of music and painting and other arts that once were the prerogative of the elite may vastly improve the quality and hope and potential of everyday life for everybody. To the nay-sayers, like Dwight MacDonald, this is self-evident nonsense and Philistine heresy. But I disagree.

The cultural boom now really presents the opportunity to emphasize quality. We need not accept the attitude that the arts in a democracy must inevitably tend toward mediocrity if they are to attempt to reach more than the already enlightened few. Our passion for democracy is not inimical to a passion for excellence. Presenting the arts to the many does not necessarily mean that we must lower our artistic standards. As we often see in our political setup, the democratic way is slower and more laborious; but it is not impossible and, in fact, the end product usually is far more durable and satisfying than what would be produced more quickly within a more authoritative system.

Just because a democracy has never produced a great culture does not mean that it cannot. But there is an all important proviso — it is a very big "if." The democratization of the arts will work. By that I mean it will give rise to excellent works and sensitive audiences, but (and here is where we must overcome the IF) only *if* we actively and purposefully strive for quality in everything we do. Quality is something all of us concerned with progress of the arts, all of us taking part in this symposium as well as well as thousands of others, must plan for carefully and work for constantly. Activity, a lot of activity on the part of everybody, does not do the job; it is only half the job. The other half is lifting the activity, lifting the sensitivity, to a much higher level of quality.

Bob Choate and Max Kaplan, in their comprehensive introduction to the issues that concern this symposium, raised the question very briefly for formal education: "Is it possible to maintain qualities of artistic excellence in a program of education which by mandate must be for all children? Or, as so many critics insist, is a 'mass culture' of necessity of low caliber, if not utterly impossible?"

In order to work for quality — whether it be in steel production, public health, government, or in the arts — we have to avoid sweeping, windy generalizations, high-sounding platitudes. We have to know what we are talking about, and that means we have to set our objectives very clearly — objectives not only for what we are trying to do in the program, but also for quality.

Music in our society, and music education in particular, entails two quite distinct and interrelated problems. We want to prepare professionals of high quality, to be sure: performers, conductors, composers, scholars, teachers, critics. Yet, at the same time, we want to nurture and encourage amateurs in music who will constitute the sensitive and appreciative audiences of the future and who are bound to have greater and greater spans of leisure time. The music programs of our schools and colleges plus other community resources, such as our museums, community centers, musical organizations, have important responsibilities in meeting both these goals.

It seems reasonable to assume that every child is born into this world, barring severe physical or mental defects, with a potential for creativeness and probably for "musicality" (an awkward word, but there seems to be no better one). It should be the endeavor of parents, teachers, and other adults concerned with a given child to encourage and nurture this capacity, whatever form it takes. Certainly we have the responsibility to identify that minority gifted with special talents and give them the most appropriate and the best possible opportunity to develop those talents to the fullest.

But we bear a responsibility for *all* children (a fact which has been pointed out several times during this conference) and for the aesthetic component of every child's development. Music should not be a specialty for a gifted few nor an optional "enrichment" for the great majority.

Not long ago Music Educators National Conference asked several distinguished educators to summarize the ideal picture of a musically literate high school graduate. These are their words:
He'd be able to listen to music with intelligence and sensitivity. He'd know how to sing and to follow music notation. He could play at least one instrument — if only a recorder. He'd understand the importance of design in music, music's relationship to other areas of human endeavor, and the place of music in contemporary society He'd have respect for the value of music as a means of self-expression, he'd want to continue his musical experience, and he'd have a degree of musical discrimination.

We all know how far we are from this ideal, but it is an ideal worth working for and surely not beyond our capabilities. The main question is, "How, then, should we go about trying to attain higher quality in music education?" (This question holds not only for music but for other areas, too. Some of the steps we might take are obvious ones. All I am doing is reminding us of the more important.)

I've already referred to the *first* step: to improve quality, we must have clearly defined goals. Unless we know what we want to achieve not only in the range of activities in which we engage but also their quality, there is little possibility of achieving it. With skills in music this is relatively easy; but with interests, motivation, or a sense of values in music, it is much harder. Musical discrimination, as stated by the experts, is an essential ingredient of higher quality.

A *second* major step, which is particularly crucial when we are concerned with the great majority of the people, is to realize the importance of diversification of programs. Since people have a wide range of abilities, no single, set program will reach all of them. As Professor Broudy said yesterday, "People differ greatly in their tastes; they start at different points." What kinds of programs do we need in order to reach not just groups within the mass but individuals? Here I think the motto of the State of University of New York, which we inscribed on the seal during my presidency, is a very important guide to keep in mind in any instruction or area of living: "Let each become all he is capable of being." If we have that as our goal, we must develop diversified programs adapted to each individual.

A *third* element in the program to improve quality is people. This implies the selection of people who can exercise different functions in differentiated programs. It implies the training of people and, of course, the best utilization of them. We all have been concerned with people, but we have not utilized to the fullest extent the resource that we have in our communities, particularly in the arts and in music. Commissioner Harold Howe recently talked about the importance of drawing performing artists into the schools. These artists can fulfill a special function in the arts in the schools, because they have talents which most teachers lack. In other words, there are resources available in the community that can be used in the schools, and they should be heavily drawn upon in our quest for the highest possible quality. (Incidentally, Howe pointed out that it is important to draw upon these resources without requiring the artists to obtain the "necessary" teaching certificate.)

A *fourth* area is the imaginative use of materials and technological aids. Are the schools and colleges devising well thought out and carefully constructed programs, stressing really good music from the earliest grades, whether it's the classics or jazz or folk songs or (yes!) the Beatles? Are they tapping available community or regional resources? Are they making full use of technology in this age of technology?

Here are just a few of the possibilities of technology. Phonograph recordings are, I am sure, being used extensively. The quality, variety, scope, and availability of records is multiplying. But are the schools financially able to take advantage of these advances? Perhaps the major recording and manufacturing companies could be persuaded to do more than they're doing about supplying equipment at minimal prices for educational use. Tape recorders, I'm sure, would be invaluable to the struggling student. Ways should be found to make them more widely available, too.

Even with the expanded use of recordings, the student should not lose contact with the excitement of live performances. The sight and sound of a musical performance are especially rewarding to a student learning to play. In an attempt to extend this experience, schools can use films and television to great advantage, even though the fidelity of the sound production is lower. *The Young Person's Guide to the Orchestra* by Benjamin Britten is a prime example. Films also can be used most effectively in teaching music history. Documentaries can help the student relate the music of a period or place to other facets of a particular culture. People must be encouraged to produce and make available such films.

Max Lerner referred to the use of television in our instructional procedures. Through television we can bring to large numbers the best talent in any field. A few years ago, for example, one of our networks put on a performance of *Hamlet*. It was estimated that more people saw Hamlet that evening over television than all who had seen the play from the time it was written up until that night. This demonstrates the potentiality of our technological age — with its wealth of television, radio, films, records, tapes — in making available the best talent to encourage the ideal of high quality for millions.

A *fifth* and essential step in achieving higher quality is to make some provision for continuous evaluation and appraisal. We need to look critically at what we are doing in order to see the deficiencies of our programs, to see at which points we are not achieving the highest possible quality. This can be done by specifically assigning responsibility to someone for carrying out that evaluation and giving him full support. This also involves more adequate training and preparation of critics, particularly in the field of music.

The *sixth* and final step, which goes along with evaluation and appraisal, is the need to provide for continuous research and development: experimentation, trying out of new ideas, focusing clearly on improvement and the development of long-range plans. I separate evaluation and appraisal from the development of long-range plans, because by keeping them distinct we tend to employ the special talents of people. It does not generally hold that the best critic is the best person to develop a long-range plan. By assigning these as separate responsibilities, more concentrated attention is given both to the criticism and the development of plans.

You can readily add other steps, I am sure, which should be taken. I suggest these six in the hope that they will stimulate further discussion of all ways by which we might improve the quality of our programs. And in our concern with quality we have to keep in mind that those who are directly involved in a particular field such as music are not always in the best position to determine how to improve its quality. This can be seen clearly by looking at some other developments in American education. Our medical education, for example in the early part of this century was greatly improved. How? It started with a study made by Abraham Flexner, a high school teacher of Latin and Greek, who never studied medicine. During the course of his study he visited every medical school in the United States (155 at that time). He was an outstanding critic, pointing out specifically the inadequacies of these schools. Over the next 25 years we closed more than half of the medical schools in the United States, dropping from 155 to 72. Only through a deep concern with quality did we greatly improve medical education and develop the strongest system that now exists anywhere in the world.

Or take the field of automobile safety. Here we have a critic from the outside, Ralph Nader, who made the public aware of our lack of concern with the safety of our automobiles. When considering all the research being carried on by the automobile industry, all the money being spent, one would think that more attention might have been given to the development of safety devices. Why was this not done? Essentially because the research and development were concerned with finding new procedures or new types of equipment that would help sell automobiles. That was its orientation, and that is one of the dangers of tying together both evaluation and appraisal with development. By separating evaluation and appraisal from development, we have two independent observations which are exceedingly important in any field in raising the quality of the work being done. Considering the enormous numbers of people we are working with in the field of music, our central issue always ought to be: How good are we doing?

These, then, are some of the means by which we can put ourselves on the right course to build a rich artistic — specifically a rich musical — life for Americans. The quest for quality is never-ending. The tired, worn-out, listless, apathetic people have had their day. They cannot contribute to the quest for quality. They merely get in the way and impede progress. The quest requires the imagination, creativity, and vigor of all of us. Any long-range program must keep these qualities central to its development and execution.

DISCUSSION

Father O'Connor: Dr. Eurich, will you make a few comments on the philosophies, the underlying terms you use? The whole notion of "quality" — what good are we doing, and all this sort of thing — is really not connecting with the scene today; and we are not concerned with those problems any more. Our attitude toward the arts in the realm of mass art are artificial abstractions which do not relate to where we are. What we are trying to do is to communicate an art; and if it communicates successfully, then it will be good art. Quality is no longer this kind of absolute which exists outside of what we are doing, because we talk to the younger generation and this is certainly not their concern. They are in another world; and contemporary artists are too, generally. I feel that these abstractions have no reality for us.

Alvin Eurich: In my concern with *quality* I am not restricting the word, quality, to the object.

O'Connor: Take the fine arts, the "in" arts which are a tradition, for example, Beethoven and Bach: these are problems when we get into the world where we live today.

Eurich: I was not thinking of excluding them at all. It is a problem of semantics, using customary words that seem to leave out the whole area that is important in the arts today, and I certainly do not want to leave out that area. I would regard communication as one of the major objectives and purposes of the arts; and if that becomes a major objective and purpose, then you have to raise the question: How well are we communicating?

O'Connor: I thought that you mentioned in connection with folk art and fine art that something precious had been lost.

Eurich: I was talking about the merger.

O'Connor: Well, I'm not sure what preciousness was lost. These are statements which I find difficult to take because I'm not sure whether they are true, and I suspect that the ideology which exists behind this thinking is that we have a really strong divergence.

Eurich: The only thing I am thinking of there is that we want the quality and the product of the art; and I am just raising the question, *"Are we losing anything in the quality of the product by broadening the scope of the arts?"* I indicated that I am wholly in favor of broadening the scope of the arts, but I do not want to lose anything we have had that has been good in the process.

O'Connor: It won't be lost if there is a program that is carried out, but the idea of quality will be the communication, not that it has internal forms of beauty or associations — which historically have been the defense of the fine arts.

Eurich: But, I'm saying that we should have both rather than one form or the other.

David McAllester: Dr. Eurich, I would like to pick up the same question, but in another way. In a search for quality, it seems to me that we sometimes miss quality which is right under our noses because of certain cultural instincts, and then speak of the popular arts in a sense of high finesse technique, and so on. These things are present in the popular arts as well as in the folk arts, and we are just barely beginning to become aware of that. There are skills and sophistications: for instance, *The Singer of Tales,* Albert Lord's book on Yugoslav ethics. In this analysis of the poetry of these ethics we discover qualities of sophistication of poetry which were never written down and which almost stagger the imagination. Here is an area where we have missed high quality for some hundreds of years, right under our noses.

Freda Goldman: Mr. McAllester, raising the question on what quality is, you are using the standard definition of quality?

McAllester: I am.

Goldman: And this is the definition Mr. Eurich uses. If I heard you correctly, you are throwing that out. I'm not. And if you throw it out, the burden rests upon you to tell us what will replace something that has been for so many centuries. I imagine we can still use it in relation to the happenings around us. Do we have to throw out the *quality* as we have understood it?

McAllester: I suspect that we do . . . yes!

Goldman: This is a fascinating question, and I would love to listen to you talk about it, but this is Mr. Eurich's subject.

O'Connor: Yes, but he uses the expression, the "quest for quality," which creates big problems. If we addressed an artistic community today, where artists work in a very isolated way, they would be highly critical, because this is not what they are trying to do.

Eurich: I related that, however, in my first statement: what do we want to achieve through the arts? Now, I did not attempt to set up these codes. If we are going to have quality, then we need to be very clear in what we are trying to achieve, and then evaluate our activity to achieve the highest level possible. If it's communication we want, then we want to be sure we are communicating.

Allen Britton: Mr. Eurich, I think there can be no question that Father O'Connor and Professor McAllester have raised what is probably our most significant problem. At the same time, I would like to say that there is no question that everything you said is good and proper, true. The problem is: we use terms that in themselves embody the very problem. For example, you did use the terms "folk art" and "high art"; and this implies that the art produced for rather a degenerate European aristocracy was far superior to the art practised by the general mass of people.

I would like to say one more thing. I have the misfortune, I guess, of being a historian of music, particularly of American music. I want to remind you that it is simply not true that music was for the rich in the United States. From our very beginning, American people, including both white and Negro people as well as the Indians, produced and maintained probably the most vivid, living musical culture that exists anywhere in the world.

Eurich: This is one of the finer points I hope to make: mainly, the points which I referred to in the creative areas in music. When I was talking about the rich and the affluent, I was talking about the patrons of the arts in this country. I did point out the difference between that and the creative activity that came from the poor. I could not agree with you more on the matter of words.

Another point, which I left out and want to mention here, is the kind of things I was talking about in terms of the creative element in terms of getting high quality, which is something really for the young and for the older people with young spirits. Here is where we need to look for our really creative efforts in the future.

The Arts in Higher Education:

Valid or Valueless?

Samuel B. Gould

There are educators who earnestly and sincerely question the validity of the arts in higher education. Why this is so is not too difficult to determine. The major reason, of course, is the time-honored one that so much of what one wishes to deal with in the arts touches upon technique as opposed to philosophy. The conservative view in higher education is that all such matters are better left to the responsibility of others. The traditional disciplines approached through traditional courses attended by traditionally selected students represent what is rightfully the concern of colleges and universities. Nothing else is necessary; indeed, anything else may be dangerous since it may confuse the mission of higher education. There are other times and places and methods for exploration of the arts, and there are other kinds of students who should be accommodated elsewhere.

A number of factors are beginning to mitigate against this point of view, so much so, in fact, that I think the educational conservatives are, in the long run, fighting a losing battle. Some of these factors relate to the arts and others do not, but all are pertinent. Most obvious of the related ones, of course, is the tremendous surge of interest in the arts in America, one that has been identified over and over. It is impossible to have such interest and not have the question arise as to whether higher education has a role in coping with it directly or indirectly. It has now become increasingly difficult for institutions of higher learning to avoid reexamining their responsibilities as this wave of activities continues to build in height and power. For some this marks the first time they have faced the issue of whether more than the traditionally accepted patterns are necessary or desirable. And the conclusions being reached are unquestionably in the direction of new responsibilities, even though these are as yet incompletely defined.

One fact to be remembered, for example, is that higher education of the future is bound to be more urban in character. Colleges and universities will be part of urban communities more and more as time goes on, and will be more closely allied to other cultural and intellectual entities of these communities. The tie between universities and art museums or music and dance groups or libraries or theatrical enterprises will be a strong one. This will inevitably cause changes in the universities themselves as well as in the nature of the associated groups. Faculties and students will be involved as never before in the encouragement of such groups and in coordinated efforts with them. This is bound to have an effect upon traditional attitudes.

The increasing diversity of missions is another fact of modern university life. Higher education is being called upon to serve in ways never dreamed of a few short decades ago. It is logical to suppose that part of this diversity will include the arts, not only in

the milieu of aesthetic appreciation, but in training as well. There is nowhere else to turn if the current and future demand is to be satisfied even in part. Some people argue (and with some cogency) that if higher education is called upon to produce professionals and technicians in so many of the more practical walks of life, why should it not be similarly involved in developing people capable of coping with the public need in artistic matters, especially in a time of increasing leisure? And even the realization that the problems of artistic development are different and far more difficult does not deter these people from pressing their case.

Still another factor to bear in mind is that universities are tending toward becoming university systems, and even colleges are tending toward cooperative arrangements as a way of gaining strength. This new phenomenon in education also has its implications for the arts, for it makes possible and practicable endeavors which a single institution would not have ventured upon by itself. Not only does the exchange of campus talent and the sharing of resources provide a new dimension, but great professional organizations and individual performers become available to appear on many campuses under such arrangements.

Finally, we can look for a trend toward more flexibility and even a new formlessness in the organization and curricula of higher education in the next few decades. Many of the old sacred cows now being attacked so vehemently by students will be relegated to oblivion. Content and methods of instruction will undergo great transformations. Individualized education will take on a new pre-eminence. It will be realized more and more that the most important function of our colleges and universities will be to live in a world of rapid, even breathtaking change, and emphasis will be centered on ways of adapting oneself intellectually, culturally, and socially to such a swiftly moving society. And as part of such a trend the door opens more easily to the inclusion of the arts as one of the changing patterns to be studied and to be dealt with.

All this is by way of a rather sketchy premise. There is much more that could be said about the university of the future which would further strengthen my belief that there will be much more receptivity to the arts than ever before. But I must hurry on to the real specifics of our discussion.

Is there validity in the inclusion of the arts in the regular patterns of higher education, or is their value overestimated? This is the question before you during this entire Symposium, inherent in all that is being examined. With your permission I should like to offer four propositions suggesting such validity and, in doing so, point out a number of assumptions that, if allowed to go unexamined, are dangerous and could lead us to false and unrealistic hopes. These are not *my* propositions, they are everybody's. I am merely gathering them together here, summarizing them, and commenting upon them. It is only in such comments that I may be saying anything you have not already heard many times.

The first of these propositions offers the conviction that *the arts are an essential in higher education to provide a balance to the present emphasis on science and technology*.

I need not ring all the changes on this theme since you are all thoroughly familiar with it. There is no question that the scientific and technological progress of our time has so captivated the imagination of youth that the humanities have been relegated to a secondary position. The imbalance of material rewards in favor of the scientist and technologist, whether in personal income or research support, has been evident for a long time and has embittered the humanist. In addition, from a nonmaterialistic viewpoint, the scientist has become the hero of our era.

There is no way to stop the onrush of scientific and technological achievement, nor would we encourage any lessening of such efforts even if we could. They are essential to us and represent a vast and vital territory where the search for truth continues. But many thoughtful people feel that a corresponding attention to the arts and humanities would serve to put our new discoveries into proper perspective, to remind us that the value of these discoveries is in direct relation to the attitudes and understandings of the people who use them, to introduce value judgments by which all these discoveries may be appraised. Most of all, many are disturbed lest the preoccupation with science will create generations of insensitive specialists, absorbed in the specifics of their work and forming a species of esoteric priesthood, supremely confident in its mission and unintelligible to the uninitiated. The arts as an essential of education are, therefore, necessary to shape the whole man of this century and the centuries to come.

Notwithstanding the cogency of this proposition, there is a word of caution to be uttered about the presupposition that the man of science knows little and cares less about the arts. My own experience with scientists in the academic world challenges this, and perhaps it is paralleled by yours. I find again and again that the man of science is very often much involved with arts passively or actively and that his appreciation of their work adds an important component to his life. Some of the most passionate devotees of the arts whom I have known are men and women whose major lifework is scientific or technological. On the other hand, I find few humanists who willingly make the effort to acquaint themselves in more than cursory fashion with scientific progress. They find it mysterious, complicated, and sometimes boring. And by their aloofness they make the obviously necessary rapprochement between science and the humanities all the more difficult.

A second proposition often stated is that *involvement with the arts makes man a more sensitive, discriminating, appreciative, creatively aware creature and is therefore not only desirable but essential in higher education*.

The habit of listening to good music, attending the theatre or concerts or ballets, developing interests in sculpture and painting, or participating actively in any of these art forms is one that can be instilled in early youth. Great efforts to inculcate such habits from childhood on have been made in our country, and these are steadily increasing. We could all cite dozens of examples. During higher education these efforts are being continued, hence the

steady stream of professional artists now moving from campus to campus, and the building of fine theatres and concert halls in universities. Granted that the goal of quality is not always reached in these endeavors, the fact remains that they are worthwhile and promising.

One could easily challenge the comment I have just made. There are those who feel that the broadening of popular interest in the arts (or its democratization, to put it another way) has been a deterrent to the appreciation of quality and to the lifting of artistic levels. They fear that the present proliferation of arts councils, cultural and performing arts centers, symphony orchestras, and the like, has the effect of dragging the arts toward mediocrity rather than excellence.

I would agree that the danger certainly exists. But I do not subscribe to the theory that a democratic nation, concerned for all its citizens, cannot work in the interests of excellence. We need not accept the dictum that the arts in a democracy must inevitably tend toward mediocrity if they attempt to reach more than the already enlightened few. We are a young nation with our cultural traditions still incompletely identified and shaped. Our passion for democracy is not inimical to a corresponding passion for excellence. We should not accept passively the theory that presenting the arts to the many inevitably causes the former to be debased. Our task is rather the slower, more tortuous one of encompassing a population in our efforts to instill a desire for the best. Just as we have done before what the world considered impossible or rashly conceived, so once more and in still another way can we show our peculiar bent for strengthening the sinews of democracy.

Higher education must share in this demonstration. But if it is to do this, it must recognize that its efforts cannot be other than educational. It must be a front-runner in experiment and research just as it presumably is in other more traditional disciplines. If it is to be a major worker toward the goal of quality, it must avoid the temptations of commercialism, attractive as these may be, and give due attention instead to artistic productions in many forms which should be heard and seen but which would never see the light of day otherwise. This is not an easy course to follow, since it will inevitably be marked by a certain percentage of failures and thus a considerable amount of criticism. But if higher education follows any other course, it will simply be contributing toward the strengthening of artistic mediocrity.

One more comment needs to be made about this proposition relating to the effect of the arts upon man. All of us are prone to think euphorically about the aesthetic effect of the arts and to accept as an unquestioned fact that by adding new cultural dimensions they make for a more humane citizenry. This *can* be true, but there is nothing sure about it, any more than one can be certain that more education generally always means more humanity. Great ideas and great works can sometimes be used for ignoble purposes. One can be sensitive to art and insensitive to everything else. I cannot forget Hitler sitting in his lofty eyrie at Berchtesgaden and listening to Wagnerian music by the hour while he conjured up new ways to humiliate the dignity and spirit of man. And there are other historic parallels to recall. So much depends upon how the arts are presented and taught as a part of education.

I say this not to be critical but to be realistic. All that is good and true and inspiring in the arts can come to nothing of consequence when they are presented pedantically and out of context with all that surrounds man's life. This is equally true of all disciplines, of course; but if we are to be more than modest in what we claim to be the influence of the arts, then we must be extraordinarily watchful about how they are dealt with in education.

A third proposition for the validity of the arts in higher education is based upon the belief that *colleges and universities can perform valuable services as repositories and disseminating points for library materials, art objects, and performances in the varied art forms.*

There is a certain logic in the assumption that colleges and universities lend themselves admirably to the function of coordinating community or regional interests and needs in the arts. Their approach normally is more catholic than that of other agencies and their motivations are more impartial. In at least one aspect, that of developing and making available library resources for the study of the arts, they are the ones to whom all others should be able to turn. This is an extremely valuable service, contributing much to the growth and quality improvement of the arts.

Similarly, there is a strong feeling these days that colleges and universities should assume positions of initiative and leadership in becoming the coordinators and disseminators of art exhibits and performances of many kinds. It is felt that no other agency can do this as effectively, and in so doing, not only influence and elevate public taste, but also make certain that the new, more experimental, more esoteric, and sometimes even the more bizarre examples of the arts are seen and heard.

I do not quarrel with this point of view; indeed, I second it heartily. But if our story is to be complete, certain caveats should be entered. The first of these is a reminder of the danger that when the college or university takes on such a role, it tends to destroy community initiative and vitality. A general air of passive acceptance can soon permeate the community where the higher educational institution dominates. Some communities willingly resign themselves to the idea that the university, like the Lord, will provide and that their own role is one of being a recipient. This is true not only in the arts but in many other areas as well. If there were time, I could offer many illustrations of this, all of them disquieting if one is sensitive to the necessity for community responsibility and action. The final result all too often is that there is a gradual disintegration of friendliness and understanding, and the university in spite of all its good intentions ultimately finds itself branded as an interloper rather than as a catalyst.

The delicacy with which cooperative and coordinated arrangements should be established, therefore, and the care with which they should be developed cannot be overemphasized. Specific situations will always differ, of course, but unless the principle of sharing is clear to all — whether in planning or providing resources — animosities can be born and nurtured that will widen the gap between university and community, rather than close it.

Equally crucial is a realization that such responsibility undertaken by higher education has great implications in regard to the resources to be mustered. All the goodwill in the world must not blind us to the fact the university resources are always limited, and priorities always have to be set. The total demands upon modern higher education are staggering. Many of them relate to the most fundamental needs, such as those of accommodating the increasing thousands of students who seek an education. The American taxpayer is not yet at the point of sophistication where he will eagerly or even willingly support programs in the arts as high-priority items. Furthermore, he is somewhat dismayed to discover how expensive such programs are when related to their increasingly elaborate facilities requirements. This is true of the curricular and performing aspects; it is even more disturbing when one thinks of objects of art to be gathered for display. It becomes more and more obvious that closer ties between universities and museums must be established so that resources may more easily be shared, since few colleges or universities can undertake more than the most modest galleries or works of art of their own.

A final proposition about the place of the arts in higher education is that which assigns to universities *a responsibility for encouraging and sharing in the training of potentially professional artists.*

This has become a truly controversial issue, argued by those who see no such role for the university at all and those who feel that the university must do far more than it has ever done. There are many underlying considerations in this, not the least of which is the still knotty question of what kind of financial security the professional artist can expect in modern society once he has been trained. Still another is that professional schools of a non-university character are not proliferating and are indeed having difficulty over mere survival. It seems evident that if the well-nigh explosive interest of our people in the arts is to be served and satisfied by high quality of artistry, more professionals are needed. But where they are to be trained and how they are to be remunerated are still unsolved problems. Today's picture of the artist as drawn by the Rockefeller Panel, and even more specifically by the Twentieth Century Fund Report, is not a promising one. Its effect is to cause the young man or woman with unusual talent and artistic ambitions to pause and think carefully before embarking upon a professional career. By what means can he be persuaded?

The university itself has its own reasons to pause. To enter upon a training process that will produce the highest quality in results requires a revision of many time-honored conceptions of admission policies, curricular planning, and all the rest. How many universities are ready to admit students who are artistically brilliant but academically mediocre? How many are ready to make special provisions for such students? How many are ready to develop the kinds of organizational changes that give students of arts adequate time for practice or rehearsal or studio work in view of the other more traditional demands upon their time? How many are ready to devise special curricula to meet these needs? And even more crucial, how many can hope to get such curricula accepted by the general faculty? How many are prepared to allocate sufficient budgetary support to such highly specialized and costly activities? These are hard, practical, almost brutal questions, but they must be answered or we are all deluding ourselves when we escape into the realm of philosophical conjecture.

There is still another facet to the total problem. Anyone close to the artistic life knows that to make even a start toward the guarantee of quality one must identify talent early and see to it that such talent is trained properly from the very beginning. This is essential in all the arts. It is unrealistic to begin professional training at the university level unless it has been preceded by years of carefully supervised work. An essential, therefore, to any involvement of higher education is the closest kind of relationship to all the rest of education. Talent not only *can* be identified early; it *must* be. And once identified, such talent must be placed in an appropriate setting for growth. It may even be necessary, for example, that the university establish a campus school of a specialized type to provide for such a need, especially since there is no more than a handful of such specialized opportunities for elementary and secondary school children in this country. And in making such provision, the general education of these children also cannot be neglected. Otherwise we shall be turning out the very kind of narrow specialist we decry so much in other disciplines.

The fact that these difficulties exist should not deter higher education from efforts to fulfill the kind of responsibility suggested by the proposition I have just identified. They must be reckoned with, but they are not insurmountable. My own university is attacking them and so are others. We do this because it is essential to the well-being of America and to its development as a cultured, humane nation. And we do it with the full realization that the path to the achievement of such a goal will be filled with obstacles and even with heartbreak.

IV. Prospects for the Future: Television, Symphony, Opera

Chairman
  LOUIS G. WERSEN, President,
  Music Educators National Conference

Speeches
  **National Educational Television:
  Fulfilling the Artistic Potential**
  CURTIS W. DAVIS, Director of
  Cultural Affairs Programing, NET

  **The Problems, Concerns, and Projections of the
  Symphony Orchestra in the United States**
  MILTON KATIMS, Conductor,
  the Seattle Symphony Orchestra

  The Future of Opera in the United States
  SARAH CALDWELL, Artistic Director of the
  National Opera Company and of the
  Opera Company of Boston
  Discussion

National Educational Television:

Fulfilling the Artistic Potential

Curtis W. Davis

Some of you may have read the striking closing lines of Suzanne Langer's article, "The Cultural Importance of the Arts." They seem to me highly pertinent to the theme of this conference:

> Art education is the education of feeling, and a society that neglects it gives itself up to formless emotion. Bad art is corruption of feeling. This is a large factor in the irrationalism which dictators and demagogues exploit.[1]

Since television, like any performing art (and you may be somewhat surprised by that parallel) carries a heavy freightload of feeling, whatever its intellectual content may be, the potential good or bad effect of TV on anyone's aesthetic sensibility and growth is indisputable. Because it also reaches out so widely and apparently unselectively, TV is potentially the single most influential shaper of attitudes in the world today. In this respect its pervasive capacity outstrips that of the family, the school, the newspaper and other publishing media, the radio, the church, and even the movies, which are now becoming a division of television. No wonder we hear talk of the dictatorship, or tyranny, of television.

The sway of a great performing arts medium over the populace has not always been an evil, and indeed I for one feel that it is not one today. There has been some reference these past 24 hours to Plato; in point of fact, 2400 years ago in Athens the great mass medium was the theater. Many a Greek citizen's understanding of history, religion, his society, and himself was shaped substantially by the views of Euripides and Aristophanes. The suppression of some of the works of these writers in present-day Greece is testimony to their continuing profound effect. In our time, television has taken over this influential role. Unfortunately, TV has all too often regarded itself and has been treated by others as a by-product, a carrier, a publisher—some of you might substitute a "sewer pipe." It can be something else: a stage within its own precepts and conditions, an art drawing as any other upon all human experience and knowledge to provide its greater and lesser masterworks. Television need not be a parasite.

I remember talking once to John Grierson, the great Scotsman and documentary filmmaker, who had his own highly successful series on Scottish television dealing with films and filmmakers. I was hoping to bring some of his programs into the United States. Mr. Grierson advised me to forget it, and start my own series. "After all," he went on to suggest with his noted bluntness, "I make my living now off of the beautiful things produced by others. Now you don't *really* want to be a parasite's parasite!" This seems to me to be a good working definition of a prominent dilemma for TV in its current stage of development as an expressive art or medium.

The treatment of music on TV in this country is evidence of its dilemma. Too often we have had to settle for a poor copy of something done far better elsewhere. Television is not a concert hall or a classroom. It is not a recording, a movie, a radio broadcast with pictures, or a journal. It may, quite often, be a legitimate observer of any of these other modes of communication. More rarely it seeks its own form, style, and vocabulary. When Leonard Bernstein first walked out onto a TV studio floor in 1954 for *Omnibus,* and stood on an immense blowup of the first page of the score of Beethoven's *Fifth Symphony,* and then summoned live musicians to stand on each of the staves to which they belonged, he was doing something belonging to no other medium. The language of music on TV has not progressed very much further since then, at least here at home.

Bernstein is, of course, one of the three B's of our 21-inch world; the other two are Bell Telephone and the Beatles. All three of them display a comparable sophistication in achieving popular appeal. In the first two cases, it may be because we've come a long way from that point thirty years ago when Clifford Odets' "Golden Boy" had to choose between the concert platform and boxing, between the ring and the string you might say. For most of us, Odets' view of a man facing the undesirability of a musical career—a popular American attitude until recently—seems ingenuous now. It is a view tinged with romantic idealism, comparable to that of the elderly newsstand lady in the quip about the young finalist in a string competition who lost his way in New York's subway system. Looking at his watch, which told him he was already four minutes late, the young man went up to the newsstand keeper and asked, "Please, can you tell me the fastest way to get to Carnegie Hall?" Looking at his fiddle case, the old lady replied, not unsympathetically, "You've got to woik, woik hard, prectise, prectise!" She must have seen the John Garfield movie of Odets' play.

If I am to believe some of what I've heard these few days, that music has begun moving now, if not yet toward the core, at least well away from the periphery of American life, the trend has not yet appreciably shown up on television here. Other countries are way ahead of us, particularly Great Britain, Germany, and Japan. One need only read the quarterly bulletins of the International Music Center in Vienna, with its reports of a multitude of major music telecasts in fifteen to twenty countries, to sense this sharply. The annual output of music telecasts by BBC on Channels 1 and 2 runs to more than 150 hours of prime evening time. By way of further contrast, the Japanese government network, NHK, which is rather like the BBC, boasts over one hundred staff producers of music programs, many working interchangeably in television and radio. In the United States, commercial TV, with such rare exceptions as Bell and Bernstein, pays attention to music only as a phenomenal activity to be classed with the human fly, who used to climb the outsides of buildings as if they were Mount Everest. Another way of putting this view is to formulate Sullivan's Law–which I will name for the fifth great stone face after Mount Rushmore: Ed Sullivan–a law which runs E = MC^3. This translates to: Excitement equals the Musician times the altitude, velocity, and volume of his pursuit of high C.

Now let's be fair: music on TV is not *all* Jan Peerce singing your favorites by John Lennon. One organization which has been trying to do something else for music on the home screen is National Educational Television. Over the past dozen years we have televised over one hundred orchestral and chamber recital concerts, including many with our host here this week, the Boston Symphony. We are the first network to have given national television exposure to the orchestras in Cleveland, Pittsburgh, Los Angeles, Detroit, Salt Lake City, and Minneapolis, among others; and here I must express our deep gratitude to Herman Kenin and the American Federation of Musicians, national and local, for their superb cooperation. We inaugurated the *Master Class* on television in 1960 with Pablo Casals, and went on to produce series with Heifetz, Lotte Lehmann, and Segovia. The idea has been copied elsewhere, and the BBC series with Yehudi Menuhin is now running on NET. Next year we will have more from that source with Carl Ebert. NET has, of course, done any number of informational series, two of the most popular being *The Fine Arts Quartet in Rehearsal* and *Aaron Copland on Music in the 20's.* There have been popular music series, such as *Jass Casual* from San Francisco and *The Ragtime Era* from Denver with Max Morath. There have also been many specials in the fields of opera, dance, concert, jazz, and folk music. I'll take time to name our production of *Lizzie Borden,* the opera by Jack Beeson based on the New York City Opera performance, and *Intolleranza* by Luigi Nono, which we co-produced with Sarah Caldwell and the Boston Opera Company; *Othello* with Del Monaco and Carteri, from RAI-TV in Rome; *An Hour with Joan Sutherland,* for which NET received an Emmy nomination; *Night Journey* and *A Dancer's World* with Martha Graham, whom only NET has thus far broadcast here; composer portraits, such as *Sibelius;* a contemporary documentary, *Duke Ellington: Love You Madly,* and *Charles Ives: The Fourth Symphony,* and *Carmina Burana,* choreographed by John Butler and danced inside and outside of a fourteenth-century Dutch castle by the Netherlands Dance Theater.

One thing should be clear about NET music programs and inferred about all of our work: we are not in the business of classroom TV. Our programs are designed for the evening prime time part of the affiliated station schedule. At the moment we are serving 120 affiliates in all the major U.S. cities. By 1970 this number should be over 160. As of November (1967) we will inaugurate a regular interconnected "live" network service, initially on Sunday evenings, to handle the new current events show put out by NET's Broadcast Lab. Some fifteen percent of our total programing is now in color, and by 1970 at least fifty percent of it will be in color.

I'm already dipping into the future, and that's just as well, for despite some individually good things, by NET and the commercial networks, the potential achievements to be expected for music on TV are just beginning to show up clearly. I've already said that we have fallen well behind producers in other countries,

and NET can take its share of the blame. Too many of our past programs have come uncomfortably close to the music appreciation class I remember all too well, in which the teacher said: "Children, today we will listen to Schubert's 'Trout' Quintet. Now you all know what a trout is. . . ." I don't know if any of you saw the BBC documentary *The Golden Ring* when it was aired by NET this spring. It was made from film and tape coverage of the recording sessions in the winter of 1964 of Wagner's *Götterdämmerung,* at the Sophiensaal in Vienna. There was enough technology and data on recording logistics in this 90-minute show to satisfy any hi-fi bug; but it was also the best lesson in Wagner I've ever seen. Senior high or junior college level classes in music appreciation should have made it required viewing. Nothing like it has yet been accomplished by an American TV producer. And it had Nilsson, Windgassen, Fischer-Dieskau, and Solti, along with the Vienna Philharmonic, as its stars.

It is toward preparing broadcasts of the caliber of *The Golden Ring* that a major effort on our part must be trained and directed, for it is here that television finally can make its most distinctive and lasting musical contribution. I must note the steps taken in this direction over the past season by Bell Telephone, which are splendid. NET will move strongly in this direction in 1968 with a major music series, NET Festival, designed as a companion to our already popular NET Playhouse. Portraits of William Steinberg, Erich Leinsdorf, Georg Solti, Carlos Chavez, Igor Stravinsky; Festival programs from Glyndebourne, Monterrey, Spoleto, and Marlboro; concerts by Dietrich Fischer-Dieskau, the Amsterdam Concertgebouw, the New Orleans Philharmonic, I Solisti Veneti, the Boston Pops, Lili Kraus, and Glenn Gould are only a few among the programs in various stages of production and preparation. We will also launch a far-reaching study of the needs for televised music in the coming decade, with special attention to the younger audience. One major consultant whom NET has persuaded to assist us here is Peter Herman Adler, co-founder and music director until 1959 of the NBC Opera, and now Music Director of the Baltimore Symphony. NET will continue its program of doing commissions with the Lincoln Center, offering opportunities to artists in several fields to make creative use of television. This spring we completed the second in this series which will bring you John Butler's *Five Ballets of the Five Senses.* The program is notable for its five original score segments, subcommissioned from Benjamin Lees, Eric Siday, Gunther Schuller, Leon Bibb, and Robert Starer. Future commissioned productions in the NET-Lincoln Center series include works by Leon Kirchner, Agnes de Mille, and Roy Harris.

Yet all of this is but the first step, for in this coming decade our medium will change radically, and with it so will our thinking. There is no doubt that better sound quality is one of *the* next steps which television set manufacturers will have to undertake. The taste for good audio has been fully developed now by hi-fi technology. What may be less well known is that home screens will leave the box, and be hung on the wall; they may be as large as six-by-nine feet. Home video tape will be refined, and with it the pre-recorded tape cartridge, both of which may virtually replace film as a working material, in the school as well as the home. Satellites will bring ten, fifteen, even thirty channels within reach of all.

Glenn Gould said on television in Canada recently that in a

generation the concert hall will vanish, except as a museum, with perhaps just one in each of several major cities, just to remind us. Performers will restrict themselves largely to concertizing in the mass medium of TV, and to recordings. Gould also foresees the day when he can put out a tape album of twelve different interpretations of Beethoven's "Moonlight" Sonata, all by Gould, and let you edit your own version, choosing the tempi, phrasing, and dynamics which most closely coincide with your own view.

Some sense of the growth of the TV medium can be deduced from the BBC audience survey report that its telecast last winter of Beethoven's *Missa Solemnis* was seen by three million people in Great Britain alone. That is remarkable enough; yet if only one percent of the viewership was moved to buy the recording, it could mean some 30,000 sets leaving dealers' shelves. That is a sale which no record company would take casually. Of equal value is the fact that so many were allowed to share in a great musical performance. It is not the numbers but the principle which counts here, for if I may carry beyond Mr. Eurich's comment this morning, it is the fact that numbers are the only thing which matter to the profit-minded broadcaster which troubles most of us; whereas, even with many millions there today to see *Hamlet* or the *Missa Solemnis,* only a fraction of that viewing public is likely to take either as a peak experience.

Once the technology of TV catches up with the artistic quality of the performing arts event (which should become the rule by 1975), we will be confronted with a greatly altered set of conditions—and we had all better be ready for this. Anticipation of swift growth is one reason why it seems to me essential that the communities of music and television must come together, must develop a receptivity and understanding of one another, if we are to accomplish anything of value whatever.

Right now we are already behind schedule, and there are times when I fear that music and TV have signed a mutual nonassistance pact. One crying need is the training of production staff people with the competence and insight needed to produce fruitful results; and for this they must have experience both in TV and in music. Television has at times misused music; however, I can show you miles and miles of footage, most of it mercifully buried now, to drive home the fact that music educators and other professionals have almost consistently misused TV. We are going to have to become buddies, and this puts me in mind of Mr. Cornog's comment on "Peanuts" last night. Just as one's *potential* can be a burden, so can one's label as an educator. Yet this burden is one which we share, after all, and with pride. There was another "Peanuts" strip, one where a fiercely glowering Snoopy is seen in panel 1 peering out of the topmost branches of a tree. In panel 2, Charlie Brown comes by and hails him with "Hi, buddy." In panel 3, Snoopy still glowers, alone and silent. By panel 4 he concludes, "Vultures just hate to be called buddy."

Well, let's not us buddies call one another vultures either.

------

[1]Suzanne Langer, "The Cultural Importance of the Arts," *Aesthetic Form and Education,* ed. by Michael F. Andrews (Syracuse: Syracuse University Press, 1958).

Problems, Concerns, and Projections

for the Symphony Orchestra

in the United States

Milton Katims

My concerns are related to the problems and programs of the symphony orchestras in our country. This is a rather large order. It might be most helpful to take you behind the scenes of an orchestra in an average-sized city in the United States and give you some glimpses into the mind and heart of the conductor.

The other day, when I mentioned the subject of symphony orchestras to a colleague of mine, his sole comment was: "How often and in how many languages can you say MONEY?" My immediate reaction was to think how right he was, and I began to recall ways to speak that magic word. But, just as quickly, second thoughts began to take shape. Of course, money—the funding of an orchestra—is of paramount importance; but by no means is it the single concern. To a certain extent an orchestra is comparable to a good baseball team where the club with the largest purse buys the best players and wins the pennant; but this analogy is too easy. Finances are but one important part of the whole symphonic scene.

The finest orchestral ensemble gathered together, with unlimited funds, placed in an environment (a community) which is not ready for it, not ready to be an active and integral part of this symphonic picture, not ready to provide fertile soil, would be performing in an aesthetic vacuum. It would wither away for lack of proper care and sustenance.

Many of you can probably recall that when the NBC Symphony was disbanded, it refused to die and reformed itself into the Symphony of the Air. At that time it was offered intact to a rather large city with no professional orchestra of its own. Despite the obvious advantages to both the city and the Symphony of the Air, it was not to be—that community just was not ready for such a large and sumptuous repast.

There must be constant action and interaction between any cultural institution and the community in which it is to thrive. The desire, the need for the emotional, spiritual, and intellectual fruits of the arts must spring from the people themselves, with just the right amount of inspiration and perhaps some subliminal guidance from its cultural leaders. The people themselves must indicate by their interested and active attendance, by their financial support, that they appreciate and want what the arts have to offer. They themselves must realize that the arts are at the very core of their social structure—not some peripheral cloak to be donned when all other needs have been satisfied, not some luxury that exists on a take-it-or-leave-it basis.

To my way of thinking, the healthy situation is one where a parallel growth of the symphony and the active participation of the community go so closely hand-in-hand that it's impossible to ascertain which is leading which. In achieving this situation, the challenges are many: some confront the conductor, some the managerial staff, or the board of trustees, the orchestra players, and the Musicians Union. Challenges confront the music critics; and some of the most important are yours, as music educators, to face.

Consider first some of the many challenges that constantly confront the conductor. We must try to increase and to keep as large an interested audience as possible. In Seattle we are doing fairly well in this area; we have the fourth largest subscription audience in the country. Box-office revenue provides a little over seventy percent of our budget needs. Ever present is the primary need of building an audience which not only buys the tickets, but which really fills the concert hall, hopefully welcomes exposure to all repertoire, and which stimulates the orchestra and conductor to ever greater heights. Every performing artist is instantly aware of the quality of his audience and responds to it in equal measure.

What are some of the ingredients of such an audience? Naturally it will include musicians, both professional and amateur, and teachers. It will include those who have had some prior knowledge and experience with music as well as those who come into the concert hall only with a fresh eagerness and curiosity for a new experience.

In Seattle, we have formed about seventeen or eighteen symphony league study groups in various parts of the city. Each group meets in someone's home shortly before a subscription concert to hear a discussion (with live or recorded illustrations) of the music to be performed. Also, being quite aware that people often arrive at their seats too late to read the program notes, we provide our audiences with advance notes, covering the following program. These can be read leisurely at home before the next concert. Both of these procedures are conducive to creating an audience which is somewhat more knowledgeable and is hopefully increasing its enjoyment of music.

The symphony conductor is constantly challenged to intrigue the community with new and fresh ideas, with imaginative approaches at all levels. The alchemy of a successful conductor is somewhat mysterious, not unlike that of a good teacher. They both combine the describable and the indescribable. But no matter what the ingredients of his success are, it is most important for a conductor to know his community and the psychology of its people in order to guide its musical taste. Being concerned with the obvious musical responsibilities is only part of the challenge a conductor must accept. Any orchestra (within certain limits) is only as successful and as good as its conductor; and a conductor must be in the right city at the right time of its development. (I don't think Seattle was really ready for Sir Thomas Beecham when he was there in the early 40's.) I venture to say that in most cases where an orchestra is faltering, probably the wrong man is on the podium. Communication is a key word in the success of any conductor—communication on and off the podium. You can't intrigue an audience by living in some ivory tower with your opera cloak pulled tightly around you. It helps to be somewhat gregarious, to actually get to know something of the hopes and dreams of your audience if you expect them to come panting into the concert hall for Bach, Berg, and Boulez. Of course, a good balance must be sought. With the tremendous responsibilities of the conductors (he's usually held accountable for almost every note his orchestra plays) he must avoid spreading himself too thin. If, in his studies, preparations, and performances, he isn't always growing and maturing, his players know it—and soon enough, his public.

Building an ever finer orchestra, maintaining high quality, and devising provocative programs that will interest the greatest number of people sum up the large part of a conductor's responsibilities. In my own programing, I pay no attention to the screams of anguish from the small fringes of listeners at either end of the taste spectrum (those that want nothing but music of the past and those who want nothing but music of the here-and-now and tomorrow). New dimensions and greater audience interest can be achieved in symphonic programs by the periodic introduction of unusual elements: paintings, dancers, and dramas—semi-staged works like Honnegger's *Jeanne d'Arc* or Schoenberg's *Erwartung*.

The challenge of building a finer and finer orchestra puts the conductor squarely between his board of trustees (getting enough money for his players) and the Musicians Union (getting the necessary understanding and cooperation when replacements become necessary—either because of resignations or the need to add to the orchestra). As in any team effort, as qualitative levels rise, individual capability must keep pace. When musicians of such quality are not to be found locally, the conductor must look elsewhere. This is a vital area, also a responsibility and challenge to the Musicians Union, which under the sensitive leadership of Herman Kenin has made fine strides and enjoys the respect of the community. However, in a number of areas it needs to do some soul searching, needs to realize it must share some of the challenges which face the symphony orchestras in our country. The problem of "importation" is a serious one; the rules vary enormously in different locals. In its efforts to protect the local players, the union fails to realize the vital need for qualitative levels, fails to take the long-term point of view, anticipates the benefits for the many in favor of the few. There is also a great need for more uniform regulations in the Musicians Union so that personal rules are not so inconsistent.

In his efforts to engage the finest available talent for his orchestra, the conductor is, of course, competing with every other orchestra in approximately the same budget bracket. But that's not all. He is also competing with the music departments of state-supported universities. It used to be advantageous for both the orchestra and the university to work closely together—sharing key musicians who combined the performance schedule of the orches-tra with teaching at the university. But now, with most of the orchestra reaching out to the goal of an all-year-round contract (with the companion need for widening the geographical areas of symphony service) the possibility of combining the two has become increasingly difficult, and in certain instances impossible. This need not be the case.

The solution may lie in a vastly enlarged orchestra—larger than its need for any one concert. Its personnel, on a revolving basis, might then be capable of serving both orchestra and university. Also, the growing recognition that the symphony serves an important educational function in the community might also help to meet rising orchestra costs: the symphony orchestra could share with the university some of the state subsidy.

The movements toward increasing the length of the season and seeking new audiences in ever-widening geographical areas will create further challenges. We will eventually have in our country fewer (but larger) major orchestras, each one regional in its scope. A better-educated public, with higher earnings and with more leisure time, has demonstrated an increased desire for performances of good music. Through improved recording techniques people are becoming accustomed to finer sound and performance, becoming more selective and reluctant to settle for less than the most "professional" performances. Orchestras of quality will have to cover more territory to serve a larger number of audiences. In so doing, the regional orchestra, mobile enough to serve educational needs in the largest geographical area, will have the greatest justification for government subsidy.

What about some of the other responsibilities of the conductor, for instance: the contemporary composer, the young, aspiring soloist, the potential orchestra players? These are uniquely the conductor's bailiwick. The composers writing now (particularly the American composers, who depend almost entirely upon the conductors of American orchestras for performances) must look to us for support. In this area we are assisted by various foundations. This past spring, we premiered the works of four young American composers under a grant from the Rockefeller Foundation, and since then I've conducted three more world premieres by American composers—one with the help of Title III, one in Tokyo, and the most recent one, two weeks ago on the La Jolla series. It is only through such performances that an audience—if it will assume this responsibility—can hear a work, react, respond, and really be the ultimate judge of a work either by wanting to hear it again, possibly starting it on its way to immortality, or letting it fall into discard.

First performances, particularly by young composers, *should automatically* be recorded on tape for purposes of study and for use in bringing the work to the attention of other conductors; but this is unfortunately not the case. Although the Musicians Union almost always does give its consent, it defers to a vote by the members of the orchestra for the final decision. If but one member of the orchestra votes negatively, the composer is deprived of this very essential aid in the development of his career. This is another challenge and a responsibility that should become automatic. The likelihood of such tapes being used commerically or exploited in any way is most unlikely, especially when you consider the technical quality of such tapes. Where would we recreative musicians be if it weren't for composers?

In my programing for youth concerts I endeavor to engage

gifted young soloists, as do many of my colleagues. It's a double-edged sword. It gives the young soloist that first big chance, and hopefully inspires members of his audience, because they relate more readily to a soloist their own age. Right now, in Seattle, plans are being finalized to carry this idea one step further. Next season, seven of our regular Monday and Tuesday evening subscription concerts will be preceded by a series of "Prepeats" on the previous Sunday afternoon. The series will be called "Stars of the Future." At these concerts, in place of the nationally and internationally known soloists to be heard at the evening performances, gifted young artists will appear as soloists—in most instances playing the same solo vehicle. Here, too, this series will not only serve as the launching pad for a new career, but will also add another week to the orchestra schedule, thus seeking a new audience. These Sunday afternoon concerts should bring into the concert hall many people hitherto unable to come on weekday evenings.

And what about the young potential orchestra player—the young musician with somewhat less lofty goals? Where is this instrumentalist to gain his experience, or at least acquire a taste for playing with a professional orchestra? Unless there happens to be a training group in his city, there is no way except to play in the school, college, and community orchestra—all too often inadequate as the sole training ground for a professional career. In Seattle, we do have a very good junior symphony, which not only arouses their interest but also does a good job of training them. In addition to this, I introduced a new project which might be of further inspiration to these young members. Each season, along with all the other series of concerts (subscription, youth, out-of-town, and Little Orchestra), we play a series of about eighteen Family Concerts in different parts of urban and suburban Seattle. With the assistance of the music educators in the school systems who actually make the selection, I invite the two best high school instrumentalists to sit in with us for the performance of the final work on the program. Having one of the major Seattle banks sponsor this idea to the extent of medals for the chosen players and funds to underwrite the added rehearsal time also serves to bring an important business group into a closer understanding with and support for the Seattle Symphony.

Thus far I have touched on many challenges of the Symphony, and only by incidental inference have I made any reference to the great need for funds—direct financial support from the community. I'm sure I don't have to spell out the need for a maintenance fund in the operation of a symphony orchestra. Until very recently, before the advent of Title III (unlike European and Japanese orchestras under direct government subsidy), American orchestras depended almost entirely upon an annual passing of the hat to make up its deficit. To the greatest extent it still must depend upon voluntary contributions from individuals, businesses, corporations, and unions, with token amounts from cities, counties, and in some instances from state governments. With concert ticket prices at top levels (higher prices in most cities would reduce the number of poeple able to afford them), with ever-mounting costs, maintenance fund goals have been pushed higher and higher. Obviously, new areas of income for the orchestra must be developed. Some of these avenues are already being explored. Government-subsidized use of the orchestra for education is as valid and logical as the use of taxpayers' money for schools and libraries themselves. A real understanding and enjoyment of fine music can be inculcated in our young people only through live performance, right in the schools where proper facilities are available—performances aimed not only at the music-oriented youngster, but at the entire student body.

Title III, the federal program in which the Seattle Symphony Orchestra was one of the first to thoroughly develop a format, is an important step in this direction. Hearing exciting live performances and sharing this experience with others are essential parts of education. Those of you who have witnessed any such concerts in your own schools know just how important, how thrilling, this whole program can be. Our concerts this past spring, under the joint auspices of Title III, the Rockefeller Foundation, local sponsorship, and our own operating funds made it possible for us to travel not only throughout the State of Washington but also to play concerts in Oregon, Idaho, and Montana, with plans for Alaska now in the making. With the federal government now joining state, county, and municipal authorities in support for the arts, we must decide whether or not we want to adopt the ideas of a "British Arts Council," or governmental subsidy (as in European countries), or develop a system that will better reflect the American way of doing things. My own firm belief is to retain, but definitely, the American community active participation in every cultural effort. Some formula of matching funds should be worked out so that the subsidies from the four levels of government are geared to the amount of effort and support from the local community itself, which must continue to be directly involved and not allow itself to sit back and let Uncle Sam do it completely.

Other sources of income to be developed are the direct sponsorship of concert series by industry for their employees and families and by unions for the benefit of their membership. A larger income for the symphony player could be realized through recordings, but only if the cost of recording can be adjusted to compete somewhat with that of European and Japanese orchestras—another challenge for the unions to meet in cooperation with the symphony.

One of the weak lines in symphony operation is the dearth of experienced management. The dynamic and creative imagination of a manager, working closely with the conductor, adds to the success of any orchestra. The rapid expansion of orchestras has resulted in fewer managers with experience. With the exception of the Ford Foundation and the American Symphony League training program, there is no way to learn the business except by coming up through the ranks. I'm sure I don't have to point out how enormous the responsibilities are of handling a "business" with budgets that range upward of $500,000. Not the least of the manager's responsibilities is his working with and guidance of a board of trustees, who are not professionals in the field of music.

Other sources of funds for specific activities of the symphony orchestras are the foundations. The Rockefeller Foundation, to a limited extent, has involved itself in an effort to assist young American composers and, at the same time, extend orchestra seasons by one or two weeks. This basic idea could be developed. Take an American composer out of the specialized, all-American category. Help put his music where it should be, if it has any merit, on regular subscription programs. Added rehearsal costs, taping, and the like, should be underwritten by the foundation. Right now, all of the major orchestras are engaged in the large Ford Foundation program, with a conditional grant of $84,000,000 to those orchestras which are successful in matching grants. The fascinating projection here is that this whole program may in itself eliminate those orchestras with unsuccessful drives, those who cannot keep pace.

Music reviewers are one group of men and women who must shoulder part of the responsibility for the growth, or lack of growth, of symphony orchestras. They must face the challenge of combining the truth as they see it, reporting what they have heard, pointing out in a healthy and constructive manner areas for improvement, while leading the way for the constant growth of the orchestra's image in its city. It is they who must also be catalysts directing the public, with sincere fervor, toward emotional fulfillment *via* the arts. It helps to have a mature person in the position of arts reviewer — one who realizes the need to help shape the cultural destiny of his city. We all know, too well, the glaring exceptions of "angry critics" who have torn their cities into destructive and querulous factions, which often reflect and echo their own frustrations.

If I do a great deal of soul searching, ask myself honestly what all of these challenges of the American orchestras really add up to, I must answer that there are none that cannot be met successfully. If all of the people involved operate at their highest levels, we can storm the firmaments, providing we have the one element that matters the most: a good audience, an audience coming up constantly from the roots, the roots that you music educators must nourish. We must have an American school system where the study of the arts is an integral part of education. The schoolboy interested in music and the arts rarely finds himself in Juvenile Court. It isn't easy to superimpose "culture" on a fifty-year-old man. The time to make the arts an enjoyable and meaningful part of a person's life is at the same time he is learning his math and science. We are a nation rocked with crime, with young people in trouble, trying to find themselves. Yet, we provide them with practically no emotional outlets except the violent crime and amorality they view daily on their TV screens. What in the world do we expect if we do not, in their formative years, open up horizons of emotional fulfillment and inspiration, if we do not ignite the child's imagination, fire his artistic potential from the first moment he sets foot in the classroom, if we do not impress upon his parents the need for creating an artistic environment in the home!

Only when we have achieved some of these goals will we be developing a civilization which can look inward with joy and satisfaction. Only then will we be forming the whole man. I leave much of this project, the dreams, the promise of it, in your very capable hands. No words express more eloquently and sum up my aspirations more succinctly than these spoken by John F. Kennedy: "I look forward to an America which will not be afraid of grace and beauty. . .which will reward achievement in the arts as we reward achievement in business or statecraft. . .which will steadily raise the standards of artistics accomplishment. . .which will steadily enlarge cultural opportunities for all of our citizens."

The Future of Opera

in the United States

Sarah Caldwell

It is very pleasant to be here in the Berkshires; I think that the greatest musical inspiration of my life came from being a student at Tanglewood–working in the incredibly stimulating atmosphere which Dr. Koussevitzky created in the early days of Tanglewood. I think that those of us who were fortunate enough to be a part of that owe a great debt to Dr. Koussevitzky to carry on his remarkable form of inspiration–the awareness that the responsibility for the artistic life is our own.

The American National Opera Company is a new company, which has grown out, in a sense, of the work of the Metropolitan National Opera Company. It, like many things today, did not really grow. It happened. When last fall, the Boston Opera produced *Moses and Aaron* by Schoenberg we were most fortunate in receiving a grant from the National Foundation of the Arts. This grant came to us with great dispatch as a result of an agonized visit which I made to Washington to see Mr. Roger Stevens. Without Mr. Stevens' quick action, we would never have had *Moses and Aaron.* But we did have it. Mr. Stevens had the bad judgment to come and see the final performance, and he seemed to like it very much. We told him at that time that we now had a really expensive idea for him, and perhaps it was too expensive to discuss that night, but could we have breakfast the next morning? And as a result of this breakfast, the American National Opera Company happened.

The biggest problem in producing opera today is money, or the lack of it. The lack of money has driven many of the most gifted people in this profession into other lives. Some of our finest singers, as we all know, have gone to Germany, have taken root there, have become part of the traditions of the company in which they perform and of the cities in which they live.

While all of this is certainly proper and understandable, we in this country have been robbed of the opportunity that should have been ours: to work with these people, to build operatic traditions and a style, a form of our own.

One of the most interesting things that has happened is that we develop certain facilities that are not developed in other countries. The singers who stay in America (those who are not currently employed at Sears, Roebuck) do make a living, a few of them in music; but they make a living by becoming enormously versatile. They are adept at doing things rapidly, because all our performing organizations have financial problems–and none of us has remotely the amount of rehearsal time that it takes to develop a really remarkable artistic achievement. The end result is that we all develop facilities. And so the American artist, who has gone through the last ten years performing with dozens of opera companies in this country, or performing in major symphony orchestras, or touring in community concerts, or singing on radio-television, is a product of the world in which he has lived. He has developed the facility but he has not developed the artistic depth that his colleagues had ten years before. At that time a singer had the opportunity to grow, to become part of an opera house, to watch performers better than he was, to perform and study and mature. It is this kind of animal–this remarkable singing actor that we want to have the opportunity to develop in this country.

Like all American companies, in order to exist we must travel; and while our lives in the next few months will parallel those of most American performers anyway, we still have this very special luxury of a rehearsal period of three months in which we are working together to prepare three new opera productions.

This company has been brought together very rapidly, American style. There were bookings available, the atmosphere in the country was right and we were fortunate to have the good services of Mr. Hurok in booking the company. It had to be done now or not done at all. So, in a very few months, we have assembled a company with the help of some very wonderful people. I have been to Germany several times, auditioning in Italy, or auditioning American singers, and the most striking thing to me is the tremendous eagerness these people have to come home, and the sacrifices they are willing to make to try to help build such a company.

We have spent a great deal of time auditioning an orchestra, and we are very proud and happy with the results of these auditions. We have some very distinguished musicians from many of the symphony orchestras; some have recently retired, but for the most part, this orchestra is made up of very brilliant young people. Musicians are going to work together for a rehearsal period of three weeks to prepare Alban Berg's *Lulu,* and *Falstaff,* and *Tosca.* This is not a bad three weeks' work.

When we leave the Berkshires, we are going to the Midwest so that we can get the full atmosphere of this country. We have been invited by the city of Indianapolis to spend our last five weeks rehearsing there, and we will produce our operas there.

We have the very exciting experience of taking opera many places where opera has been before, but also performing opera in many communities and for many people who will never have heard opera.

When we chose the repertoire, we did it from the conviction that the entire country is composed of people interested in music and theatre and that those people interested in let's say such relatively obscure works as *Lulu* are not really confined to New York City. We felt that the general country was far more sophisticated than it is sometimes given credit for being. I am terribly pleased that so many, many cities have booked *Lulu,* and we hope that they will find it exciting and provocative, disturbing and shocking, and wonderful as it indeed is.

I think that the limits of opera producing are outlined by financial problems. All opera producers now are essentially fund raisers. None of us devotes to his artistic work nearly the percentage of time and attention that he should. We are all involved in the financial problems of trying to get the time and the money to pay the artists. And something is happening. The artists and the performers are getting impatient. They have all kinds of ridiculous ideas; they want to be paid like other people are paid. They want to make a decent living; they want to own automobiles. They want to have insurance policies. While certain performers are willing to make sacrifices for a short while, they cannot build a stable, artistic life with the kind of financial rewards and the ridiculous kind of monies that are available to the people who perform. And this is why it is so difficult to get a group of people willing to make the sacrifice to try to build a fine company.

I think that opera is a very exciting thing, and the reason why I love the work I do so much is because it leads me into many worlds. And I believe that one can give operatic performances of the nature that will hopefully share with the audience the kind of excitement we feel in producing it.

About two weeks ago at three o'clock in the morning, I was on top of the church of St. Angelo in Rome. It was a very frightening experience and I only went there because four men went ahead of me and they were not a bit afraid. You walk across a drawbridge in the dark, and then go up some stairs, and it seemed as if I were climbing forever. But the purpose of this trip was to make tapes of the bells of Rome as Puccini heard them. Puccini had made a special trip to Rome to listen to the bells. *Tosca* is full of bell sounds, and as we are unable to take the bells of Rome to the States, at least we could tape them and somewhere assimilate these sounds. We also had a photographer who made a number of photographs in the church of St. Andrea dello Valle where the first act of *Tosca* takes place. Puccini deliberately, for some reason, changed the church from Sardou's play. And one of the things that we wanted to find out is why this might have happened. And we also wanted to hear the very sounds of the church, so we asked the church organist to play for us. We then realized why Puccini had chosen this church because it was without question the loudest organ that I have ever heard, and when these sounds fill the chapel the whole place was shaking. It really was tremendously exciting and I think that this was the effect that Puccini wanted to create in the "Te Deum" at the end of the first act.

The future of opera in America lies in developing forms which fit into our world. In our production of *Lulu,* we are going to make some experiments in mixed media. We will use some closed-circuit television, some special movies using some psychedelic lighting, and try to find ways in bringing this piece to life so that it will have meaning to us today.

This kind of work we have done in the past has made it very clear that the most important thing we can do is to develop an audience. We are terribly interested in building audiences before it is too late. We have had some very interesting experiences with Title I, and I would like to tell you about them because I think that they are very significant for the development of music and may assist in securing government support.

We have a Pilot Project with Worcester, a city near Boston. We went to Worcester because they were interested in opera, interested in what opera might do for the children of the community. A group of 200 disadvantaged children came to our entire opera season and at the end of this time, with a great deal of preparation before each performance they saw the *Rake's Progress,* they heard a ballet by Bartok, *The Miraculous Mandarin,* and they heard Puccini's *Tosca.* Out of this they then produced an opera of their own, which is one of the most charming things I have seen. They made scenery, they made costumes, they did their own staging, their orchestra played (the world's smallest concert master). And the major effect that came from this was the 200 very small junior high school students suddenly had a number of worlds open to them. They learned much and became curious about a variety of things which I believe they would never have been curious about had it not been for this experience. We hope that we can stimulate this kind of activity throughout the country. Mr. Schaffer who is our Director of Student Programming, now looks at every teenager and says, "There goes a little opera lover;" and we are hoping that we can make this the case. We are trying to commission new pieces, and there are several theories as to how opera in this country will develop. One is that through a National Company, opera may grow, and grow stronger and that regional companies will grow as off-shoots of a National Company. I hope that this National Company can take roots in the cities in which it performs. But I hope that ultimately these cities can be stimulated to have companies of their own, and that the outgrowth of the National Company will be many small companies, which we hope can be nurtured and made to flourish.

DISCUSSION

Question: If the National Opera Company has such trouble being funded, wouldn't it be prohibitive for many local ones to even dream of getting a start unless there is quite a new concept of opera in terms of number of performers and things like that?

Sarah Caldwell: I think we need a new concept of money. If every small city in Europe can have its opera company, surely we can be entitled to such excitement.

Robert Choate: Earlier today, Dr. Gould was talking about the possibility of a program within the state university system, the community colleges. Do you feel that universities and colleges may be experimental bases for opera companies which might grow out of the communities? Is this feasible?

Caldwell: It is very feasible. It depends almost entirely on the attitudes of school and college administrators. Many interesting things can be developed.

Wayne Hertz: We are worried about money too. [Mr. Hertz is chairman of the music department of Central Washington State College.] We have the same problem; and in the process of developing the department, or a school, opera is often left until all other parts of the curriculum are satisfied. I can tell you in our own instance this is one of our next adventures. We have been in existence as a department for a long time. Talent is not our problem. It is the money that it takes to produce. We need sympathy.

Louis Wersen: I wonder if Mr. Katims would say something about the opera project in Seattle.

Milton Katims: No. Opera, as I indicated before, is separate from the Seattle Symphony, and that was my decision to make because I had been very instrumental in forming the opera company. Again, the question with regional opera is that in the average community it must depend upon well-known box office leading singers who are brought in. My quarrel is that you cannot possibly expect any kind of an ensemble to result from singers, who have obviously done these roles many times, with many different directors and opera companies, to suddenly be able to merge and fuse as an artistic whole with the local singers and local directors. That's the problem there. It is always a compromise.

John Roberts: How closely do you work with your public school system in the building of an audience for the symphony and the opera company in Seattle?

Katims: The board of education allocates a certain amount of money. It is about 12,000 to 15,000 dollars for our projects.

Roberts: What are your relations with the staff and curriculum of the Seattle schools?

Katims: We have a direct working cooperation. I know exactly what Jack Schaeffer would like to achieve in the schools. What I did when I first came to Seattle was to go into the schools and take part in a rehearsal of an orchestra. I conferred with music educators in the schools. We have talked about the type of thing they would like me to do in planning programs for the young people. I have tried to encourage, as I indicated before, young instrumentalists, too, by active participation with us. There is no official liaison other than these actions. I have taken the orchestra into the high schools, and we have youngsters come to the opera house for a particular number of concerts.

Roberts: We try to fill their requirements to the greatest extent possible, and I will guide them too if I think that there is another direction in which they should be going.

Karl Ernst: There is an interesting development on the West Coast with opera. It is known as the Western Opera Association, which takes anything from a reduced version with a piano to an aria. They did the *Barber of Seville* a few months ago in a high school gym with seventh-and eighth-grade students. The whole production was compressed to about one hour with narration. They use a portable stage that can be transported by bus. At the end of the opera, all the characters, including the director and the make-up artist, meet in front of the students seated around the gymnasium and carry on a conversation. They move around and after fifteen minutes or so the students have the chance to meet all the characters. When they go to a small town they might put on an afternoon performance or a morning one, and if the town is big enough and wants to support a full-length version with a small orchestra, they are prepared to do this. Prices are reasonable. This seems to be quite an interesting way of getting it operated, to the smaller communities particularly.

Ernestine Ferrell: On the arts and the humanities, is not there a move to establish regional opera companies? I would like Miss Caldwell to tell us whether she has any knowledge of this.

Caldwell: I believe that there has been a grant throughout the Southeast.

Freda Goldman: I think that one of the things that might help is to redefine audience education a little bit. This is what I am very much concerned with. I think it's wonderful to teach the children and to help them become good audiences, but they do not have much of an impact on the community. The money is only going to come if the *value system* is changed so that money for opera or music is considered a very legitimate outlay of funds and has a priority. This means that we teach them not only taste but the economics and politics of music. I think this is a very important thing, and few people are concerned about it. Educating an audience means educating children, and I think this is very good. But I think that the problem has to be started somewhere in the middle. Right now, if the atmosphere is not created through the adults, who are the decision makers, the future of the arts may not be as hopeful.

Katims: I think you are right in what you have to say, but you are overlooking one very important factor, and that is that these children create the audience of today. They go home if they are excited and tell their parents about what they have experienced; and in so many cases, those youngsters have literally dragged their parents to performances—first to family concerts and then to the subscription concerts. In essence, they can sway some of the votes that you talk about.

Goldman: I think that you also invest in the other. You must think of it from both angles.

Katims: Are you suggesting that economics, or opera economics, be taught along with appreciation of the arts? It would seem to me that if you appreciate and really value and enjoy pearls, you will go out and buy the pearls. You will find the money for them. If you can create an audience which really feels it has a *need* for the product, you create a consumer for that product.

Goldman: I think that is true.

Wersen: Remember the admonishment earlier today: "Invent the future"; so we must have some inventors in this crowd.

William Hartshorn: More about the California company: the reaction down there was just wonderful; but not all opera comes from California, comes from San Francisco. For 21 years we have had a company in Los Angeles that has done nothing but opera; and within the last 15 years, we have had annual attendance between 60,000 and 70,000. This year it was 69,400. Children pay a small sum.

In respect to the education of the audience, one of the things that disturbs me about this is that going to the opera has become for these children almost as much a status symbol as it is with the adult society. The only thing that mitigates against this and retains my belief in the intrinsic merit of the whole thing and the value for the individual child is that we do educate that audience. We have about 450 elementary schools. The first year we did *The Magic Flute.* The following year my budget permitted me to buy enough recordings so that every elementary school in Los Angeles now has a recording of the opera. For a period of about six weeks before the opera series begins, that is the course content in the elementary schools of Los Angeles. In this way the literature becomes part of the curriculum in the school system. These children learn the story and the music. They learn to sing.

We have to be realistic. This does not solve the operatic problem in the city of Los Angeles; but I can testify that when young children in the fourth and fifth grades have a chance to know operas that are appropriate to their age level—*Hansel and Gretel, Bartered Bride,* and the *Magic Flute*—they love it.

Wiley Housewright: Miss Caldwell, could you look into the future and tell us what you see in terms of opera between now and the year 2000? We would like to know what the music is going to be like, and what technical changes will be made, where the people will be coming from. We know where the musicians are coming from, but the technical directors and all these other people who are involved in an opera production—what will be the changes in this rather static situation that we have had for so long?

Caldwell: There will probably be a much closer involvement with television, as Mr. Davis has pointed out. I think that the potentials are great. We must take advantage of every opportunity in all aspects of our community institutions.

Housewright: Have you any idea as to what the repertory might be?

Caldwell: I withdraw.

Page Bailey: There has been a tendency for the economic situation to create a climate in which composers tend toward smaller forms.

Herman Kenin: I know so little about opera. I agree with Miss Caldwell and Milton Katims that our principal problem is money. There is an audience for opera in this country, and it is getting wider and wider. Money has been the problem for as long as I can remember it, and I was surprised to hear Milton Katims say that 71 percent of the money needed came from the box office. I think that is the highest in the country. Milton must have brought a very imaginative program to Seattle.

Wersen: I think we are inclined to feel a little bit down about those who do not help us, but I dare say that there would be no National Opera Company if it had not been for Miss Caldwell's belief in it; and the money factor did not stop her from doing it. She actually had a view. She thought big. She proceeded and some money did come in. So, Sarah, I do not think that your problem is as bad as it sounds. It does take someone to spark this; someone has to think with dreams, as Dorothy Maynor said the other night.

I am wondering, Miss Maynor, have you done anything with opera in your little school?

Dorothy Maynor: No, we have started with the piano, art, dance, and strings. We will eventually come to opera. I think that will be when we have our own building and theater.

V. Perspectives on Music and the Individual

Chairman
> KARL D. ERNST, Chairman, Division of Creative Arts, California State College at Hayward

Speeches
> **Music, Education, and Peak Experiences**
> ABRAHAM H. MASLOW, Professor of Psychology, Brandeis University
>
> **Expanding Dimensions in Music Education**
> E. THAYER GASTON, Professor of Music Education, Director of Music Therapy, University of Kansas
>
> **The Rationale for Nationwide Assessment of Music Instruction**
> RALPH W. TYLER, Chairman, National Assessment Program

Music, Education, and Peak Experiences

Abraham H. Maslow

Something big is happening. It's happening to everything that concerns human beings. Everything the human being generates is involved, and certainly education is involved. A new *Weltanschauung* is in the process of being developed, a new *Zeitgeist,* a new set of values and a new way of finding them—certainly a new image of man. There is a new kind of psychology, presently called the humanistic, existential, third-force psychology, which at this transitional moment is certainly different in many important ways from the Freudian and behavioristic psychologies—two great comprehensive, dominating psychologies.

To sketch this briefly and to indicate that I am talking about a life philosophy, the beginning of a new century, it is evident that there are new conceptions of interpersonal relationships. There is a new image of society. There is a new conception of the goals of society, of all the social institutions, and of all the social sciences, which are a part of society. There is a new economics, for instance, a new conception of politics. I have written in the past several years of revolutions and have tried to apply these revolutions to religion, to science, and to work. There is a newer conception of education popping along that I will mention briefly, because it will be the background for my iconoclastic ideas about music, music education, and creativeness.

First, I would mention psychologies of learning. If one took a course or picked up a book in the psychology of learning, most of it, in my opinion, would be beside the point—that is, beside the "humanistic" point. Most of it would present learning as the acquisition of associations, of skills and capacities that are *external* and not *intrinsic* to the human character, to the human personality, to the person himself. It is a matter of picking up coins or keys or possessions or something of the sort in order to pick up reinforcements and conditioned reflexes that are, in a certain, very profound sense, expendable. It does not really matter if one has a conditioned reflex; if I salivate to the sound of a buzzer and then this extinguishes, nothing has happened to me; I have lost nothing of any consequence whatever. We might almost say that these extensive books on the psychology of learning are of no consequence, at least to the human center, to the human soul.

Generated by this new humanistic philosophy is also a new conception of learning, of teaching, and of education. Stated simply, such a concept holds that the function of education, the goal of education—the human goal, the humanistic goal, the goal so far as human beings are concerned—is ultimately the "self-actualization" of a person, the becoming fully human, the development of the fullest height that the human species can stand up to or that the particular individual can come to. In a less technical way, it is helping the person to become the best that he is able to become.

Such a goal involves very serious shifts in what we would teach in a course in the psychology of learning. It is not going to be a matter of associative learning. Associative learning in general is certainly useful, extremely useful for learning things that are of no real consequence. And many of the things we must learn are like

that. If one needs to memorize the vocabulary of some other language, he would learn it by sheer rote memory. Here, the laws of association can be a help. Or if one wants to learn all sorts of automatic habits in driving, responding to a red signal light or something of the sort, then conditioning is of consequence. It is important and useful, especially in a technological society. But in terms of becoming a better person, in terms of self-development and self-fulfillment, or in terms of "becoming fully human," the great learning experiences are very different.

In my life, such experiences have been far more important than classes, listening to lectures, memorizing the branches of the twelve cranial nerves and dissecting a human brain, or memorizing the insertions of the muscles, or the kinds of things that one does in medical schools, in biology courses, or other such courses.

Far more important for me have been such experiences as having a child. Our first baby changed me as a psychologist. It made the behaviorism I had been brought up in look so foolish that I could not stomach it any more. It was impossible. Having a second baby, and learning how profoundly different people are even before birth, made it impossible for me to think in terms of the kind of learning psychology in which one can teach anybody anything. Or the John B. Watson theory of, "Give me two babies and I will make one into this and one into the other." It is as if he never had any children. We know only too well that a parent cannot make his children into anything. Children make themselves into something. The best we can do and frequently the most effect we can have is by serving as something to react against if the child presses too hard.

Another profound learning experience that I value far more highly than any particular course or any degree that I have ever had was my personal psychoanalysis: discovering my own identity, my own self. Another basic experience—far more important—was getting married. This was certainly far more important than my Ph.D. by way of instructiveness. If one thinks in terms of the developing of the kinds of wisdom, the kinds of understanding, the kinds of life skills that we would want, then he must think in terms of what I would like to call *intrinsic* education—*intrinsic* learning; that is, learning to be a human being in general, and second, learning to be this particular human being. I am now very busily occupied in trying to catch up with all the epiphenomena of this notion of intrinsic education. Certainly one thing I can tell you. Our conventional education looks mighty sick. Once you start thinking in this framework, that is, in terms of making a good human being, and if then you ask the question about the courses that you took in high school, "How did my trigonometry course help me to become a better human being?" and echo answers, "By gosh, it didn't!" In a certain sense, trigonometry was a waste of time. My early music education was also not very successful, because it taught a child who had a very profound feeling for music and a great love for the piano *not* to learn it. I had a piano teacher who taught me that music is something to stay away from. And I had to relearn music as an adult, all by myself.

Observe that I have been talking about ends. This is a revolution that is a repudiation of nineteenth-century science and of contemporary professional philosophy, which is essentially a technology and not a philosophy of ends. I have rejected thereby, as theories of human nature, positivism, behaviorism, and objectivism. I have rejected thereby the whole model of science and all its works that have been derived from the historical accident that science began with the study of nonpersonal, nonhuman things, which in fact had no ends. The development of physics, astronomy, mechanics, chemistry, and biology was in fact impossible until it had become value-free, value-neutral, so that pure descriptiveness was now possible. The great mistake that we are now learning about is that this model, which developed from the study of objects and of things, has been illegitimately used for the study of human beings. It is a terrible technique. It has not worked.

Most of the psychology on this positivistic model, on this objectivistic, associationistic, value-free, value-neutral model of science, as it piles up like a coral reef or like mountains and mountains of small facts about this and that, was certainly not false, but merely trivial. I would like to point out here that in order not to sell my own science short, I think we do know a great deal about things that *do* matter to the human being, but I would maintain that what has mattered to the human being that we have learned has been learned by non-physicalistic techniques, by the humanistic science techniques of which we have become more conscious.

In speaking of the world situation at the opening ceremonies of a recent Lincoln Center Festival, Archibald MacLeish said:

> . . . What is wrong is not the great discoveries of science—information is always better than ignorance, no matter what information or what ignorance. What is wrong is the belief that information will change the world. It won't. Information without human understanding is like an answer without its question—meaningless. And human understanding is only possible through the arts. It is the work of art that creates the human perspective in which information turns to truth. . . .

In a certain sense I disagree with MacLeish, although I can understand why he said this. What he is talking about is information *short of this new revolution,* short of the humanistic psychologies, short of the conceptions of the sciences that not only repudiate the notion of being value-free and value-neutral, but actually assume as an obligation, as a duty, the necessity for discovery of values—the empirical discovery, demonstration, and verification of the values that are inherent in human nature itself. This work is now busily going on.

What Mr. MacLeish said was appropriate for the era from 1920 to 1930. It is appropriate today if one doesn't know about the new psychologies. "And human understanding is only possible through the arts." That was true. Fortunately, it is no longer true. It now is possible to gather information that can contribute to human understanding, that carries imbedded within it value hints, vectorial and directional information, information that goes some place instead of just inertly lying there like flapjacks.

"It is the work of art that creates the human perspective in which information turns to truth." I deny that, and we had better argue about that. We must have some criteria for distinguishing good art from bad art. They do not exist in the realms of art so far as I know. They are beginning to exist, and I would like to leave one hint, an empirical hint. A possibility is beginning to emerge that we would have some criteria for discriminating good art from bad art.

If your situation is like mine, you know that we are in a complete and total confusion of values in the arts. In music, you try to prove something about the virtues of John Cage as against Beethoven—or Elvis Presley. In painting and architecture similar confusion is present. We have no shared values anymore. I don't bother to read music criticism. It is useless to me. So is art criticism, which I have also given up reading. Book reviews I find useless frequently. There is a complete chaos and anarchy of standards. For instance, the *Saturday Review* recently carried a favorable review of one of Jean Genet's crummy books. Written by a professor of theology, it was total confusion. It was the approach that Evil now has become Good because there is some kind of paradox while playing with words: if evil becomes totally evil, then it somehow becomes good, and there were rhapsodies to the beauties of sodomy and drug addiction which, for a poor psychologist who spends most of his time trying to rescue people from the anguish of these kinds of things, were incomprehensible. How can a grown man recommend this book as a chapter in ethics and a guide to the young?

If Archibald MacLeish says that works of art lead to the truth, Archibald MacLeish is thinking about particular works of art that Archibald MacLeish has picked out, but ones his son might not agree with. And *then,* MacLeish really has nothing much to say. There is no way of convincing anybody about this point. I think this could be some symbol of the way in which I feel that we are at a turning point. We are moving around the corner. Something new is happening. There are discernible differences—and these are not differences in taste or arbitrary values. These are empirical discoveries. They are new things that have been found out, and from these are generated all sorts of propositions about values and education.

One is the discovery that the human being *has higher needs,* that he has instincts—like needs, which are a part of his biological equipment—the need to be dignified, for instance, and to be respected, and the need to be free for self-development. The discovery of higher needs carries with it all sorts of revolutionary implications.

Secondly, the point I have already made about the social sciences: many people are beginning to discover that the physicalistic, mechanistic model was a mistake and that it has led us . . . where? To atom bombs. To a beautiful technology of killing, as in the concentration camps. To Eichmann. An Eichmann cannot be refuted with a positivistic philosophy or science. He just cannot; and he never got it until the moment he died. He didn't know what was wrong. As far as he was concerned, nothing was wrong; he had done a good job. He *did* do a good job, if you forget about the ends and the values. I point out that professional science and professional philosophy are dedicated to the proposition of forgetting about the values, excluding them. This, therefore must lead to Eichmanns, to atom bombs, and to who knows what!

The great discoveries Freud made, we can now add to. His one big mistake, which we are correcting now, is that he thought of the unconscious merely as undesirable evil. But unconsciousness carries in it also the roots of creativeness, of joy, of happiness, of goodness, of its own human ethics and values. We know that there is such a thing as a healthy unconscious as well as an unhealthy one. And the new psychologies are studying this at full tilt. The existential psychiatrists and psychotherapists are actually putting it into practice. New kinds of therapies are being practiced.

So we have a good conscious and a bad conscious—and a good unconscious and a bad unconscious. Furthermore, the good is real, in a non-Freudian sense. Freud was committed by his own positivism. Remember, Freud came out of a physicalistic, chemicalistic science. He was a neurologist. And a sworn oath that is in print called for a project to develop a psychology that could be entirely reduced to physical and chemical statements. This is what he dedicated himself to. He himself disproved his point. And about this higher nature that I claim we have discovered and that, of course, exists, the question is, how do we explain it? The Freudian explanation has been reductive. Explain it away. If I am a kind man, this is a reaction formation against my rage to kill. Somehow, the killing is more basic than the kindness. And the kindness is a way of trying to cover up, repress, and defend myself against realizing the fact that I am truly a murderer. If I am generous, this is a reaction formation against stinginess. I am really stingy inside. This is a very peculiar thing. Somehow there is the begging of the question that is so obvious now. Why did he not say, for instance, that maybe killing people was a reaction formation against loving them? It is just as legitimate a conclusion and, as a matter of fact, more true for many people.

But to return to the principal idea, this exciting new development in science, this new moment in history. I have a very strong sense of being in the middle of a historical wave. One hundred and fifty years from now, what will the historians say about this age? What was really important? What was going? What was finished? My belief is that much of what makes the headlines is finished, and the growing tip of mankind is what is now growing and will flourish in a hundred or two hundred years, if we manage to endure. Historians will be talking about this movement as the sweep of history, that here, as Whitehead pointed out, when you get a new model, a new paradigm, a new way of perceiving, new definitions of the old words, words which now mean something else, suddenly, you have an illumination, an insight. You can see things in a different way. That, for instance, as one of the consequences generated by what I have been talking about, is flat denial. Empirical, mind you. I am not being pious, or arbitrary, or *a priori,* or wishful. This is an empirical denial of the Freudian contention of a necessary, intrinsic, built-in opposition between the needs of the individual and the needs of society and civilization. It just is not so. We now know something about how to set up the conditions in which the needs of the individual becomes synergic with, not opposed to, the needs of society, and in which they both work to the same ends. This is an empirical statement, I claim.

Another empirical statement is about the peak experiences. This is the most dramatic and probably the most relevant for this particular audience. We have made studies of peak experiences by asking groups of people and individuals such questions as, What was the most ecstatic moment of your life? Or as one investigator asked, Have you experienced transcendent ecstasy? One might think that in a general population, such questions might get only blank stares, but there were many answers. Apparently, the transcendent ecstacies had all been kept private, because there is no way of speaking about them in public. They are sort of embarrassing, shameful, not scientific—which, for many people, is the ultimate sin.

In our investigations of peak experiences, we found many, many triggers, many kinds of experiences that would set them off. Apparently all people, or almost all people, have peak experiences, or ecstasies. The question might be asked in terms of the single, most joyous, happiest, most blissful moment of your whole life. You might ask questions of the kind I asked. How did you feel different about yourself at that time? How did the world look different? What did you feel like? What were your impulses? How did you change if you did? I want to report that the two easiest ways of getting peak experiences (in terms of simple statistics in empirical reports) are through music and through sex. I will push aside sex education, as such discussions are premature—although I am certain that one day we will not giggle over it, but will take it quite seriously and teach children that like music, like love, like insight, like a beautiful meadow, like a cute baby, or whatever, that there are many paths to heaven, and sex is one of them, and music is one of them. These happen to be the easiest ones, the most widespread, and the ones that are easiest to understand.

For our purposes in identifying and studying peak experiences, we can say it is justified to make a list of these kinds of triggers. The list gets so long that it becomes necessary to make generalizations. It looks as if any experience of real excellence, of real perfection, of any moving toward the perfect justice or toward perfect values tends to produce a peak experience. Not always. But this is the generalization I would make for the many kinds of things that we have concentrated on. Remember, I am talking here as a scientist. This doesn't sound like scientific talk, but this is a new kind of science. A dissertation will soon be published which will show that out of this humanistic science has come, I would say, one of the real childbearing improvements since Adam and Eve. It is a dissertation on peak experiences in natural childbirth. And this can be a potent source of peak experiences. We know just how to encourage peak experiences; we know the best way for women to have children in such a fashion that the childbearing mother is apt to have a great and mystical experience, a religious experience if you wish—an illumination, a revelation, an insight. That is what they call it, by the way, in the interviews—to simply become a different kind of person because, in a fair number of peak experiences, there ensues what I have called "the cognition of being."

We must make a new vocabulary for all these untilled, these unworked problems. This "cognition of being" means really the cognition that Plato and Socrates were talking about; almost, you could say, a technology of happiness, of pure excellence, pure truth, pure goodness, and so on. Well, why not a technology of joy, of happiness? I must add that this is the only known technique for inducing peak experiences in fathers. It had occurred to us, as my wife and I had first gotten to these surveys of college students, that many triggers were discovered. One of them was that while women talked about peak experiences from having children, men didn't. Now we have a way to teach men also to have peak experiences from childbirth. This means, in a certain condensed sense, being changed, seeing things differently, living in a different world, having different cognitions, in a certain sense some move toward living happily ever after. Now these are data, various paths to mystical experiences, but I'd better pass them by as they're so numerous.

For our purposes, let's proceed to music in this relation. So far, I have found that these peak experiences are reported from what we might call "classical music." I have not found a peak experience from John Cage or from an Andy Warhol movie, from abstract expressionistic kind of painting, or the like. I just haven't. The peak experience that has reported the great joy, the ecstacy, the visions of another world, or another level of living, have come from classical music—the great classics. Also I must report to you that this melts over, fuses over, into dancing or rhythm. So far as this realm of research is concerned, there really isn't much difference; they melt into each other. I may add even, that when I was talking about music as a path to peak experiences, I included dancing. For me they have already melted together. The rhythmic experience, even the very simple rhythmic experience—the good dancing of a rumba, or the kinds of things that the kids can do with drums: I don't know whether you want to call that music, dancing, rhythm, athletics, or something else. The love for the body, awareness of the body, and a reverence of the body—that kind of thing that gets mixed in there—these are clearly good paths to peak experiences. These in turn are good paths, (not guaranteed, but statistically likely to be good paths) to the "cognition of being," to the perceiving of the Platonic essences, the intrinsic values, the ultimate values of being, which in turn is a thera- peutic-like help toward both the curing-of-sicknesses kind of therapy and also the growth toward self-actualization, the growth toward full humanness. In other words, peak experiences often have consequences. They can have very, very important conse- quences. Music and art in a certain sense can do the same; there is a certain overlap. They can do the same there as psychotherapy, if one keeps his goals right, and if one knows just what he is about, and if one is conscious of what he is going toward. We can certainly talk, on the one hand, of the breaking up of symptoms, like the breaking up of clichés, of anxieties, or the like; or on the other hand, we can talk about the development of spontaneity, and of courage, and of Olympian or God-like humor and suchness, sensory awareness, body awareness, and the like.

Far from least, it happens that music and rhythm and dancing are excellent ways of moving toward the discovering of identity. We are built in such a fashion that this kind of trigger, this kind of stimulation, tends to do all kinds of things to our autonomic nervous systems, endocrine glands, to our feelings, and to our emotions. It just does. We just do not know enough about physiology to understand why it does. But it does, and these are unmistakable experiences. It is a little like pain, which is also an unmistakable experience. In experientially empty people, which includes a tragically large proportion of the population, people who do not know what is going on inside themselves and who live by clocks, schedules, rules, laws, and hints from the neigh- bors — other-directed people — this is a way of discovering what the self is like. There are signals from inside, there are voices that yell out, "By gosh this is good, don't ever doubt it!" This is a path, one of the ways that we try to teach self-actualization and the discovery of self. The discovery of identity comes via the impulse voices, via the ability to listen to your own guts, and to their reactions and to what is going on inside of you.

Mathematics can be just as beautiful, just as peak-producing as music; of course, there are mathematics teachers who have devoted themselves to preventing this. I had no glimpse of mathematics as a study in aesthetics until I was thirty years old, until I read some books on the subject. So can history, or anthropology (in the sense of learning another culture), social anthropology, or palaeontology, or the study of science. Here again I want to talk data. If one works with great creators, great scientists, the creative scientists, *that* is the way they talk. The picture of the scientist must change. The image of the scientist, which most high school kids have, as one who never smiles, who bleeds embalming fluid rather than blood, and whom the high school girls are horrified by and wouldn't want to marry. "Marry one of those monsters who will do experiments on my babies?" they might think. This conception of scientists is giving way to an understanding of the creative scientist, and the creative scientist lives by peak experiences. He lives for the moments of glory when a problem solves itself, when suddenly through a microscope he sees things in a very different way, the moments of revelation, of illumination, insight, understanding, ecstacy. These are vital for them. Scientists are very, very shy and embarrassed about this. They refuse to talk about this in public. It takes a very, very delicate kind of a midwife to get these things out, but I have gotten them out. They are there, and if one can manage to convince a creative scientist that he is not going to be laughed at for these things, then he will blushingly admit the fact of having a high emotional experience from, for example, the moment in which the crucial correlation turns out right. They just don't talk about it, and the usual textbook on how you do science is total nonsense.

My point here is that it is possible; that if we are conscious enough of what we are doing, that is if we are philosophical enough in the insightful sense too, we may be able to use those experiences that most easily produce ecstacies, that most easily produce revelations, experiences, illumination, bliss, and rapture experi- ences. We may be able to use them as a model by which to reevaluate history teaching or any other kind of teaching.

Finally, the impression that I want to try to work out—and I would certainly suggest that this is a problem for everyone involved in arts education—is that effective education in music, education in art, education in dancing and rhythm, is intrinsically far closer than the core curriculum to intrinsic education of the kind that I am talking about, of learning one's identity as an essential part of education. If education doesn't do that, it is useless. Education is learning to grow, learning what to grow toward, learning what is good and bad, learning what is desirable and undesirable, learning what to choose and what not to choose. In this realm of intrinsic learning, intrinsic teaching, and intrinsic education I think that the arts, and especially the ones that I have mentioned, are so close to our psychological and biological core, so close to this identity, this biological identity, that rather than think of these courses as a sort of whipped or luxury cream, they must become basic experiences in education. I mean that this kind of education can be a glimpse into the infinite, into ultimate values. This intrinsic education may very well have art education, music education, and dancing education at its core. (I think dancing is the one I would choose first for children. It is the easiest for the two-, three-, or four-year-old children—just plain rhythm.) Such experiences could very well serve as the model, the means by which perhaps we could rescue the rest of the school curriculum from the value-free, value-neutral, goal-less meaninglessness into which it has fallen.

Expanding Dimensions in Music Education

E. Thayer Gaston

We cannot consider music without man, nor man without music. It is a form of human behavior, unique and powerful in its influence. This basic theme at no time denies or disputes that music is an art. It is the most abstract of the arts, yet a thoroughly structured segment of reality. Music education is a process, both artistic and scientific, that induces a greater profundity of humanness, usually manifested by changes in behavior.

Behavioral Sciences and a Multidisciplinary Approach to Music Education. The disciplines of psychology, sociology, and anthropology are known as behavioral sciences—the scientific study of man's behavior. They are relatively new when compared with some of the so-called exact sciences. The behavioral sciences have provided a majority of the research data for music education. However, little is yet known of the processing of musical stimuli by the human organism. Therefore, because little is known of what happens inside man when he is engaged musically, the only recourse is to observe and study his overt behavior.

It is true that behavioral sciences have, at times, excluded other sources of knowledge and guidance. For example, constructs have been set up that bore little relation to physiological function, thus setting up guidelines external to man. To propound a psychological theory that has little or no relationship with organismic states is nearly certain to result in false theory. Some behavioral scientists have been so pessimistic of ever learning the inner functions of man that they have made few attempts to utilize available data. Such pessimism is a mistake, because no single science will ever explain man. In the conclusion of his address as president of the American Psychological Association, Neal Elgar Miller said, "A combination of behavioral and physiological sciences is increasing our knowledge of these [brain] processes and their significance to psychology."[1]

Bakan has protested the purely behavioral approach.[2] Murphy has gone into detail to show the potential contribution of genetics, biochemistry, neurology, and other disciplines.[3] There are other reasons why the understanding of human behavior, specifically music education, will profit most from a multidisciplinary approach. "All problems of life are ultimately biological. . . ."[4] Scott, Masserman, Allport, and others have declared the multidisciplinary approach to be essential.[5]

Music education, broadly conceived, should follow the paths of the behavioral sciences in solving many of its problems. To believe that problems in music education of a sociological, anthropological, or psychological nature can be solved by the art of music is hardly a wise belief. Music education should be buttressed at every strategic point and in every critical area with whatever will be helpful, not only from behavioral science, but also from other sciences and fields of knowledge.

There is a second reason for encouraging a broader approach by music educators, particularly in their training. All music educators must begin their music study many years before entering college. If one cannot communicate musically, he cannot teach music. For this reason, the music educator must be a good musician. But somewhere along the way, he picks up several unfortunate ideas. One is that science, mathematics, and liberal arts contribute no benefit to him as a musician. This is a false premise, however, not only for the musician but doubly so for the music educator. A cursory remembrance of Ancient Greece or the Renaissance period in Europe will show that knowledge enriches art, certainly teaching. There is no conflict between music and science: *all truth is compatible, not conflictual.*

Even aesthetics is no longer the child of philosophy. *Webster's Third New International Dictionary* describes well the modern situation: "Aesthetics, the science whose subject matter is the description and explanation of the arts, artistic phenomena, and aesthetic experience and includes psychology, sociology, ethnology. . .and essentially related aspects." Music education will be better and more practically informed if it looks first to the behavioral and other sciences, and then to philosophy.

The Development of Man. "Man is the most mysterious of all experiences. This is why art and science strive to make him comprehensible. . . . Man has both a nature and a history."[6] We cannot understand man well unless we know how he became what he is. I speak now of all mankind and of all his musics. To know other men is to know ourselves better—to know other musics is to know our own music better. There is only one species of man, and we all belong to it. All that lives is our kin. The basic mechanisms of reproduction, chromosomes and genes, are found in all plants and animals. We live in a universe, not a *diverse*. The earth, seas, animals, and man (an animal) all share the same building materials: atoms, molecules, and elements. We are creatures of cosmic law and so is our behavior. Music is not mystical; it is only mysterious.

The beginnings of man go back at least two million years. Crude tools and the work of Leakey provide the evidence.[7] How did the progenitor of man develop the characteristics of humanness that eventually set man apart from all other animals? To begin to answer this question, *it is not necessary to separate the biology and culture of man.* They go hand in hand. Biological and cultural evolutions are parts of the same process.[8] This means that the part of man's culture which we call music has a biological basis as well as a cultural basis. The evolvement of cultural capacity is no less than the evolution of mankind.[9]

One of the essential conditions for the organization of men into cooperative societies is the suppression of rage and hostility. This could not come about until the cortex of the cerebrum had developed sufficiently so that it could exert some control over the more primitive parts of the nervous system. Even today, for example, one has to stop and think in order to control anger and destructive rages. The development of the cortex as a control of the autonomic nervous system is essential for development of human society.[10]

Only in the primate family, that family of mammals to which

man belongs, is the female receptive to the male in significantly longer periods between one oestrous and the next. This is a vital necessity for the beginning of the family, for the female can not only attract the male but she can also hold the same male. This is the biological basis for the formation of family relationships of longer duration. No longer is the female periodically forced into blind, instinctive behavior, accepting a different male at each period of oestrous. The cortical, so to speak, becomes dominant over the endocrine factor. Sexual dimorphism (difference in size between male and female) becomes more apparent. Division of labor occurs. The relationship between male and female modifies aggressive behavior and results in increased communication. All of this leads to a uniqueness of humans among all animals, the mother-child relationship, without which there would be no culture as we know it.

The central nervous system in apes and monkeys is developed better at birth than is that of the human baby. In spite of its increased brain size, the human baby is far more helpless at birth than any other neonate. It is highly dependent on the mother for a long period of time. Because the father provides the necessary protection and food provision, the mother can devote her time to care of the baby. She has time and circumstance to teach her child, and the child has time to learn. From this comes the early stages of cultural development, because "...it is this helplessness and prolonged dependence on the ministrations of the parents and other persons that favor in man the socialization and learning process on which the transmission of culture wholly depends."[11]

The effect of the break-up of the mother-child relationship, even in monkeys, has been shown by Harlow.[12] The effects on the young monkeys are disastrous and last a lifetime. Another important genetic factor adds to the time the mother may spend with her individual young: primate mothers do not have litters.[13] There is usually one baby, although there may be twins in a few species. Each child, therefore, receives far more attention from the mother.

The two most distinguishing characteristics, then, of man's development are his society and the immense complexity of his brain. They are highly interactive, and each is dependent on the other. In the society of man, he is seen to have constantly drawn closer together, and he has become more interdependent. His brain makes possible speech, communication, abstract thinking, and significant nonverbal communication in the form of music.

Man and His Senses: Music. "Einstein said something that needed to be said and that has been said better by no one else: 'The most incomprehensible thing about the world is that it is comprehensible.' "[14] This means that the most difficult thing to understand about man is how he comes to know the world about him. Without this comprehensibility of the outside world, there would be no music, because from this outside world—the world that man senses—comes the raw data of all that man will ever do, think, or feel.[15] Basically and completely, it is man's sensory experience of hearing that makes possible his music. In spite of all the genetic equipment and all the potentiality of the newborn, it is doomed to an isolated nothingness without the senses. And yet, the sensory operations and perceptions of the baby are part of body perception. They are biological functions.[16]

The end organs of our senses, of hearing, seeing (in part), touching, smelling, and tasting, are all differentiated skin. They develop from the ectoderm of the embryo, and although each sense brings its own particular quality of reality to us, no one can say that auditory stimuli are less real than other sensory stimuli. Our senses provide us with the basic material of what is to be our intelligence and, just as certainly, what is to be our aesthetic sense. The full fruition of our potential for humanness can never be attained without a rich musical environment.

As one follows the development of man and sees the many organizations of his experience, the place of music, as a necessity in all cultures, becomes clear.

> *All mankind must organize,* must seek causes and endings. In a multitude of religions and philosophies, man explains how things came to be and how they will be. There are no races, tribes, or peoples who cannot do this. And each individual of every race, tribe, and people, began this process of abstraction by receiving sensory stimuli.[17]

Great emphasis has been placed upon this universal demand of organization, because it provides a necessary insight into the propensity and demand of human beings for music. There are "sense hungers" for sights, sounds, shapes, textures, and rhythms. These needs are particularly evident in children, and the satisfaction of these needs is essential to normal growth and development. The impulses to see, to hear, to touch, and to taste are as natural and demanding as the desire to understand.

Man, with his cerebrum of billions of cells, must not only organize the incoming stimuli that inform him of his environment, eventually he must also create new designs and new forms for his use. From this process comes his aesthetic sense. No culture, no tribe, has ever been satisfied with only the sounds of nature. Man has made new sounds and has placed them in orderly fashion in some system or organization that is *generally and predominantly rhythmical,* but only sometimes melodic and/or harmonic. Each child born into a culture learns the music of that culture if he learns any music. His music is one of his folkways. Murphy has said this about the elaboration of the sensory:

> There is, however, no group of human beings which has not cultivated devices for enriching contact with the sensory world.... The word ordinarily used to describe this class of satisfactions ... is aesthetic. ... The *potentials for becoming a human being,* as compared with a less complex kind of animal *lie largely in this enrichment and elaboration of the sensory and motor ranges of experience....*[18]

Man cannot escape the formation of aesthetic constructs. The great potential of his nervous system takes him beyond bare animal adaptation. Furthermore, *aesthetic experience may be one of the best devices to help him adjust and adapt to his environment.* The chief significance of aesthetic experience, however, is that a man would be less complete as a human being without it. *It is toward this humanness that our discourse moves,* because "what matters most for understanding him (man) is that 'humanness' which sets him apart from the rest of creation."[19] To understand "humanness" is to understand more profoundly what is necessary for the health and happiness of man. Music is of the essence of humanness, not only because man creates it, but also because he creates his relationship to it.

Although this discussion will say more about the ubiquity of music and the various ways in which the human potential is accomplished, the main purpose, thus far, has been to lay a foundation for understanding man and music. Such an understanding is basic to knowledge of man's humanness and the relation of music to it, to research and practice in music education. Music is an essential and necessary function of man. It influences his behavior and condition, and it has done so for tens of thousands of years.

The Functionality of Music. "Music is a uniquely human phenomenon which exists only in terms of social interaction. . . ."[20] Social interaction or social behavior of the right kind is a characteristic deficiency of the behaviorally disordered (mentally ill) and the handicapped. It is precisely with such people that music, because of its nature, has been beneficially influential along with the music therapist in persuading the ill and handicapped toward better patterns of behavior.

Thus we introduce a neglected dimension of music education, the functionality of music. Most music in the world is functional music, that is, music that is made for a primary purpose other than the music itself. In most cultures, all music is functional music. Even in our culture, most music is functional—church music, dance music, background music, and so forth. Because of television, the time is short until various ethnic musics will become a part of the material of music education. If its functionality is understood, it will be understood and adopted. Thus the child will learn of his fellowmen and will enrich himself.

From the vantage point of over twenty years of research, clinical practice, and the training of music educators and music therapists, the following principles of music therapy and music education may be stated. For the sick and the handicapped are more like the well than is commonly understood.

All mankind has need for aesthetic expression and experience. Masserman has said that ". . . *all organisms are actuated by their physiologic needs,* including those leading to aesthetic expression."[21] Most handicapped children are primarily in need of more and different sensory stimulation. For his own needs, he must make other sounds. As his aesthetic sensitivity develops, he must elaborate, make more intricate and complex his sensory and motor behavior. Of importance is the fact that as he matures, he will formalize his soundmaking into distinct and recognizable patterns. This is music. The expression and experience of music in all cultures and races is an essential of man's health, because his healthy life is one of interdependence. Those few, or many, individuals who would not be interdependent were dropped from the stream of life long ago.

The cultural matrix determines the mode of expression. Linton has indicated clearly that each cultural group develops its own mode of expression.[22] Just as each culture or ethnic group evolves its own language, so does each develop its own music, and each individual must learn that music of his culture. Man must learn to be human, and he does so in terms of his own tribe or culture. If people are to be influenced, then music that is understood, at least to some extent, by the patients, should be employed.

Music and religion are integrally related. One of the clearest and most evident uses of music is with religion. The coincidence of music and religion is strikingly widespread. This is true because the purposes of religious service, and the performance of music, are practically identical. The great valance possessed in full degree by both music and religion is to draw people together. Both music and religion are at their peak function when they are group activities.

Music is communication. Music is communication, but nearly always it is or functions as, *nonverbal communication.* In reality, it is the *wordless* meaning of music that provides its potency and value. There would probably be no music, and no need for it, if it were possible to communicate verbally that which is easily communicated musically.[23]

There is so much nonverbal communication in our everyday and special-day life that we are often unaware of it or of its importance. We are unaware that some of our most valued and functional communications are carried on because they cannot be verbalized. How do you verbally communicate a kiss, a smile, a frown, a gesture of farewell, or a condescending stare? How can you say in words the feelings elicited by the National Anthem, a marching band, a Strauss waltz, Brahms' *Fourth Symphony,* a Bach prelude? Even the best verbal substitute for nonverbal music is poverty stricken. Music is a most intimate type of nonverbal communication, deeply cherished and nurtured by mankind.

Music is structured reality. Even though music is nonverbal communication, only to the unknowing and the uninitiated does music seem to be unstructured. From the example of the Mayan Indian who was severly punished when he broke rhythm[24] to the example of the school band musician who must, and can, distinguish discrepancies in accuracy of time as small as a sixteenth of a second, we observe that there is little question of structure in music. Melodic pattern, pitch, tempo, rhythm, and dynamics all demand a preciseness that is astounding when carefully considered. All of the end organs of the senses—the ear, the outward part of the eye, inner parts of the nostrils, the taste buds, the pacinian corpuscles (for touch)—come from the same part of the embryo. All are differentiated skin; all bring to us aspects of reality. To hear a chord of music is no less real than to smell a rose, to see a sunset, to taste an apple, or to feel the impact of striking a wall. In addition to the enticing aspects of music, its reality and its structure make it a therapeutic medium of much value.

Music is derived from the tender emotions. Man's genetic and cultural development brought him into more and more interpersonal relationships until these relationships became second to no other influence in his life. So important are his fellows to man that he can never know himself until he knows his fellowman. He cannot understand his relationships except from the group. A person cannot become human without the group.[25] The vast majority of all music is concerned with the positive relationships that draw man closer to his fellowmen: love, loyalty, patriotism, and religion, to name a few. Consider popular music, folk songs, religious music, art songs, opera, and other types of music. Nearly all of them have to do with love in one form or another. Musical activity is a source of social cohesion, a coming together. The value of the adaptation of the individual to the group can hardly be overestimated in a society.[26] Group music brings a feeling of belongingness.

Music involves the individual so totally and in such unique fashion that "closeness" is felt, and painful "aloneness" may be alleviated. Music is nonpunitive and, in nearly all cases, nonthreatening. The desire for "closeness" furnishes much of the motivation for group singing, such as in church, service clubs, convocations, and similar situations in our own culture. It is not the beauty of the singing that matters in most of these cases, although the pleasure of singing may be a motivational factor also. In our culture, as well as in other cultures, *music is nearly always an expression of good will, a reaching out to others,* and is so interpreted. Music is thus a powerful expression of the interdependence of mankind, and, from the lullaby to the funeral dirge, an expression of the tender emotions.

Music is a source of gratification. The performance of music generally brings an intimate sense of gratification. Such gratification springs from feelings of accomplishment and mastery. It is a matter of achievement, and always, *in noncompetitive situations.* Music has order and predictability, and both are essential for competence. Thus it is that the individual may subtly but compellingly be moved toward proper behavior, which will make it possible for him to rejoin society on a more significant level. Music and the therapist or teacher are important parts of the process and environment that persuades the individual toward beneficial changes of behavior.

In all uses of music, no laws of nature are abrogated. Music and its influences may be studied scientifically, using methods of the behavioral sciences. To study music education by such means requires adequate, multidisciplinary knowledge, without which our vision is restricted to the one, old construct of greatest familiarity. "There is much yet to be discovered in us, in our behavior towards one another, and in our group activities."[27] The two best hopes for personal growth and happiness are the strengths of our positive interpersonal relationships, and our love for and increase of knowledge.

---

[1]Neal Elgar Miller, *American Psychologist,* Vol. 20 (1965), p. 183.

[2]D. Bakan, "The Mystery-Mastery Complex in Contemporary Psychology," *American Psychologist,* Vol. 20 (1965), pp. 186-191.

[3]G. Murphy, "The Psychology of 1976: An Extrapolation," *American Psychologist,* Vol. 18 (1963), pp. 689-695.

[4]E. W. Sinnott, *The Biology of the Spirit* (New York: Viking Press, 1955), pp. vii-viii.

[5]G. P. Scott, *Animal Behavior* (Garden City, New York: Doubleday, 1963). J. H. Masserman, *Principles of Dynamic Psychiatry* (Philadelphia: W. B. Saunders, 1961), p. 108. G. W. Allport, *Pattern and Growth in Personality* (New York: Holt, Rinehart and Winston, 1961), p. 193.

[6]T. Dobzhansky, *Mankind Evolving* (New Haven: Yale University Press, 1962), pp. xi and 18.

[7]L. S. B. Leakey, *The Progress and Evolution of Man in Africa* (New York: Alfred A. Knopf, 1962).

[8]Dobzhansky, p. 22.

[9]F. S. Hulse, *The Human Species* (New York: Random House, 1963), p. 221.

[10]W. Etkin, "Social Behavior and the Evolution of Man's Mental Faculties," in M. F. Ashley-Montagu (Ed.), *Culture and the Evolution of Man* (New York: Oxford University Press, 1962), pp. 131-147.

[11]Dobzhansky, p. 196.

[12]H. R. Harlow, "The Nature of Love," *American Psychologist,* Vol. 13 (1958), pp. 673-685.

[13]Hulse, p. 132.

[14]Dobzhansky, p. xi.

[15]W. von Buddenbrock, *The Senses* (Ann Arbor: University of Michigan Press, 1958).

[16]F. Dautsch, *Body, Mind, and the Sensory Gateways* (New York: Basic Books, 1962), p. 2.

[17]E. T. Gaston, "The Aesthetic Experience and Biological Man," *Journal of Music Therapy,* Vol. 1, No. 1 (1964), p. 4.

[18]G. Murphy, *Human Potentialities* (New York: Basic Books, 1958), p. 34.

[19]R. DuBos, *Man Adapting* (New Haven: Yale University Press, 1965), p. 3.

[20]A. P. Merriam, *The Anthropology of Music* (Evanston, Illinois: Northwestern University Press, 1964), p. 27.

[21]J. H. Masserman, *The Practice of Dynamic Psychiatry* (Philadelphia: W. B. Saunders, 1965), p. 431.

[22]R. Linton, *The Tree of Culture* (New York: Alfred A. Knopf, 1955), p. vii.

[23]E. T. Gaston, "Music in Therapy." In J. H. Masserman and J. L. Moreno (Eds.), *Progress in Psychotherapy* (New York: Grune and Stratton, 1958), pp. 142-148.

[24]V. W. von Hagen, *The Ancient Sun Kingdoms of the Americas* (New York: World Publishing Company, 1961), p. 281.

[25]M. F. Ashley-Montagu, *The Humanization of Man* (New York: World Publishing Company, 1962), p. 280.

[26]Dobzhansky, p. 217.

[27]P. Ostwald, *Soundmaking* (Springfield, Illinois: Charles C. Thomas, 1963), p. 158.

The Rationale for

Nationwide Assessment of Music Instruction

Ralph Tyler

The purpose of the project on assessing the progress of education is to provide the intelligent lay-public with census-like data on the educational levels of important sectors of our population. This purpose is to give information to the public about where we are in education, what progress we are making, and where our problems are. The National Assessment Program serves the same purpose as public health data serve when giving us a notion of what sectors of the population, for example, have higher incidents of heart disease or cancer. It is not to be mistaken for the task of developing means by which the doctor may carry on his diagnosis. We are not primarily providing information about the individual, but rather are concerned with what could be called census-like data.

Today, education is a necessity for everyone in order to participate in our complex civic, social, and industrial life. The public is asked to support programs for extending both the quantity and the quality of education. Without perspective regarding the progress we have made and the difficult task we face, our citizens have an inadequate basis for making judgments. As a result, decisions are frequently made on hearsay, or widely publicized assertions, rather than on a reasonably clear picture of the actual educational situation.

A Brief Background

It was in the summer of 1963 that a number of leading citizens, who had grown increasingly conscious of the need to expand our educational efforts, were asking questions about the educational status of both children and adults and the progress being made. They found no comprehensive and dependable data about the population as a whole. There were reports on numbers of schools, buildings, teachers, and pupils, and about the monies expended; but there wasn't any sound and adequate information on educational results. When dependable data are not available, personal interviews, distorted reports, and journalistic impressions become the sources of public opinion; thus, schools were frequently attacked as well as defended without the necessary evidence to support either claim. Therefore, some of these concerned men and women asked the Carnegie Corporation of New York, a private foundation, to call conferences of school people and experts in measuring educational results to see whether it was possible to meet this need for dependable information. Three such conferences were held during the winter of 1963-64, and the general opinion expressed by the conferees was that such data could be obtained—although it would require new appraisal instruments and new procedures.

Following up these conferences, Carnegie Corporation in the summer of 1964 appointed an exploratory committee on assessing the progress of education. I was asked to serve as chairman. The committee's assignment was to confer with teachers, administrators, school board members, and others concerned with education, on how such a project could be helpful to the schools. The committee was also charged with developing and testing of instruments and procedures for assessing the progress of education. The committee has been working on these assignments for nearly three years.

Last year the Fund for the Advancement of Education joined in supporting the project. Discussions soon stressed that the initial assessment include more than the three R's and that it ultimately cover the range of the modern school's important educational tasks. In harmony with this suggestion, instruments have been constructed by four leading test development agencies in the fields of reading and the language arts, science, mathematics, social studies, citizenship, the fine arts—which includes a section on music, on the visual and graphic arts, and on literature—and vocational education. In subsequent years other important areas will be included. (Nothing thus far has been included, for example, in health and physical education.) Because the purpose of the assessment is to provide helpful information about the progress of education that can be understood and accepted by public-spirited lay citizens, some new procedures are being developed.

In each field, scholars, teachers, and curriculum specialists have formulated statements of the objectives which, they believe, faithfully reflect the contribution of that field and which the schools are seriously seeking to attain. There are six objectives which were formulated by music specialists and music teachers in this effort to say: What is it that ought to be assessed?

1. Being able to perform a musical piece, theme, or figure in any medium.

2. Reading standard musical notation, scheme, and its accompanying figures—numbers and verbal symbols.

3. Listening to music with understanding and enjoyment.

4. Being knowledgeable about composers, performers, periods, styles, instruments, and works, and about the place of music in Western culture.

5. Actively seeking musical experience.

6. Developing preferences and making judgments about music and its performance.

For each of these major fields, prototype exercises were then constructed to give students an opportunity to demonstrate the behavior employed by the objective. These lists of objectives and prototype exercises, which help to define them, were then reviewed by a series of panels of public-spirited citizens from various parts of the country—cities, towns, and villages. Each panel spent two days reviewing the material and making a judgment about each objective in terms of these questions: Is this something important for people to learn today? Is it something that I would like my children to learn? It might surprise some people to know that regardless whether they were in rural small-town areas, in cities, or in surburban areas, or whether they were in the North, South, East, or West, all of them considered these objectives in music to be important things that they would like to have their children learn.

This process resulted in very few revisions of the original listing of objectives, but the procedure was designed to ensure that every objective being assessed is (a) considered important by scholars; (b) accepted as an educational task by the school; and (c) deemed desirable by leading citizens—thus eliminating criticism.

The National Assessment will not be very meaningful unless separate measures are obtained for populations within the total country, which vary among themselves and thus present different degrees in kinds of progress and different problems to be solved. The particular populations that need to be treated separately may change over the years ahead, but for some time, age, sex, socioeconomic status, geographical location, and rural, urban, and suburban differences will probably be significant. Hence, our plan is to assess a probability sample for each of 256 populations defined by the following subdivisions: boys and girls (we need to keep them separate because achievements are different in boys and girls); four geographic regions: the Northeast, Southeast, Middle West, and Far West; four age groups: nine-year-olds, thirteen-year-olds, seventeen-year-olds, and adults between the ages of 26 and 35 (this adult age was chosen to represent the time when almost everybody has finished formal schooling yet near enough to the time of schooling so that it reflects somewhat current educational efforts). There are four divisions by large city, small city, suburban, and rural classifications; and finally two socioeconomic levels: upper and lower (using the levels that the schools now are asked to identify in connection with Title I of the Elementary and Secondary Education Act).

The fact that populations are to be assessed, and not individuals, makes it possible to extend the sampling of exercises far beyond that of an individual test in which one person takes it all. This comprehensive assessment requires so many exercises that if it were to be taken by one person he would need more than ten hours to complete them. However, with a population sample, twenty persons each spending 30 minutes would together take all the exercises, and we would have information about the population without any one person having taken them all. In this case, a population, for example, of 10,000 persons would furnish a sample of 500 for each of the assessment exercises and no one would have given more than 30 minutes of his time. Assuming that an assessment would be made every three to five years in order to ascertain the kinds of progress taking place, it is very unlikely that many of those individuals who participated in the earlier assessments would be involved in the subsequent ones. Hence, from the point of view of the child or adult, no serious demand would be made on his time. Furthermore, it is unlikely that the children taking exercises in later years would be drawn from the same classrooms as the earlier ones, and the demands made upon a teacher, in releasing a child for half an hour, would be minimal.

The assessment will involve little or no inconvenience to individuals or to schools. Since the assessment does not require that all participants be in classes, the exercises to be used are not limited to the usual items. Interviews, questionnaires, performance tests, and observational procedures are to be employed to furnish information about interests, habits, skills, and practices that have been learned. Because school objectives commonly include these areas, it is necessary that an assessment is made to the levels of attainment.

The assessment exercises will differ from current achievement tests in another important respect. Our present achievement tests seek to measure individual differences among pupils where you are trying to say, "which shall get a scholarship," or "which shall be given some other special opportunity"; or they are used to establish reliable average scores for grades or school. Hence, the items of the test are concentrated on those which are typical of average performance. We, however, are interested in the progress being made by the whole distribution. How about the disadvantaged kids: what progress are they making? How about those who are most advantaged and seem most gifted: what progress are they making? So it has been necessary to develop new exercises, and we are discovering that our contractors (although they are the people that make the major tests in the country) have great difficulty in constructing exercises. They are required to develop exercises at each level in which the three parts represent achievement characteristics of the lower third, the middle third, and the top third respectively of that age level.

The four contractors have virtually completed their tasks of constructing the thousands of assessment exercises required. We have on hand 10,900 exercises for the various fields of study in the four age groups. (In the field of music, we have about 800 exercises.) As these exercises came into the office, they were sent out for review by teachers, supervisors, subject specialists, and test specialists. Also, we are using another lay review to identify any exercise that might be considered objectionable by parents and educated members of the public. We do not find those typically in the music field, but the public tends to be sensitive to three areas: sex, politics, and religion.

Since last December, the new exercises have been tried out in schools in 41 of the 50 states. The purpose of the tryouts is to see that the exercises are practical to administer and meet the specifications—particularly that they represent a wide enough range of difficulty to furnish information about progress being made by all children.

The contractors working on the adult level are testing out responses obtained by going to the individual home (to see whether a 35-year-old can sing and what sorts of things he can do). They find, interestingly enough, that adults are quite happy to show what they can do. Whereas we thought no child should spend more than half an hour, it is very difficult for the interviewer to get away from an adult in less than an hour and a half. Adults do like to demonstrate what they know, what they understand, what skills they have, and the like.

To summarize the educational attainments of these several populations, we do not plan to compute test scores; although these scores may be useful for some purposes, they are abstract numbers that are almost meaningless and are often misinterpreted by the public. Instead, the following sorts of things would be reported: From the sample of seventeen-year-old boys of upper socioeconomic status from rural and from small town areas of the Midwest region, it was found that 93 percent could read a typical newspaper paragraph; 76 percent could write an acceptable letter ordering several items from a store; 52 percent took a responsible part in working with other youth in playground and community activities; and 24 percent had one or more of the occupational skills required for initial employment—always showing what they can do rather than abstract numbers. It is anticipated that the assessment would be in charge of a commission of highly respected citizens. They and the commission staff would prepare reports of the findings of the assessment much as we now obtain reports of the findings every ten years of the decennial census. These reports would be available to all people interested in education, providing them with significant and helpful information on what has been learned by each of the 256 populations. In the following years, the subsequent progress made by each of these populations would also be reported.

Some Criticisms

The project is encountering some difficulties in getting itself understood. It is being confused with a nationwide individual testing program, and several common fears are expressed by those who make this error. They note that tests used in the schools influence the direction and amount of effort of pupils and teachers. If the whole class is going to be tested on something, and if it makes a difference, some will be admitted to college, or they will get prestige for having made a higher score than some other community. This, of course, affects the interests and efforts of teachers and pupils. In this way, if national tests do not reflect the local educational objectives, pupils and teachers are deflected from their work. This criticism does not apply to the assessment project because no individual student or teacher can make a showing. No student will take more than a small fraction of the exercises; no scores will be obtained on individual performance. The student will not be assessed at any later time, and he can gain no desired end, such as admission to college or a scholarship.

The second fear is that such an assessment enables the federal government to control the curriculum. This is also a misunderstanding. The objectives to be assessed are those which are accepted by teachers and curriculum specialists as goals toward which they already work. These were not obtained from the federal government, but from various groups. (In the case of music educators, objectives are obtained from music educators themselves and scholars in the field of music.) They have been reviewed by lay leaders throughout the country so as to include only aims deemed important by public-spirited citizens. Therefore, this project will report on the extent to which children, youth, and adults are learning things now considered important by both professional school people and the informed public.

A third fear sometimes raised is that this project would stultify the curriculum by not allowing changes over the years in instructional methods and educational goals. It should be made clear that the project will assess what children, youth, and adults have learned and not how they have learned it; hence, the assessment is not dependent upon any particular instructional methods. For example, we shall report the percentage of thirteen-year-olds who can comprehend the plain sense of a typical newspaper paragraph. We will not be reporting the methods of reading instruction that are used in various schools. In another illustration, we shall report on the percentage of adults who participate regularly in civic affairs, but not on the methods used in teaching high school civics. The matter of changing educational goals, however, is a relevant question because the objectives determine what will be assessed. Our plan calls for review one year in advance of each assessment.

Through various conferences with school people and interested laymen, the committee has been able to identify concerns and problems with which such an assessment must deal. As the plans are shaping up, it appears to be possible to conduct the project in a way that will not injure our schools, but will provide greatly needed information. How will this information be useful?

The data obtained from the assessment will furnish information on no geographic area smaller than a region. Let us suppose that you are an administrator in a city of middle size (that is, with a population between 50,000 and 200,000) located in the Midwest. You have just read the report of the recent national assessment, and you note such hypothetical data as the following on reading achievement for males in the Midwest region among cities of middle size:

1. Comprehension. The percent who can get the plain sense of a simple newspaper paragraph: nine-year-olds—upper socioeconomic levels 73 percent, lower 21 percent; thirteen-year-olds—upper 86 percent, lower 32 percent; seventeen-year-olds—upper 96 percent, lower 45 percent; adults—upper 90 percent, lower 31 percent.

2. Reading. The percent who can bring the necessary supplementary information to bear on expository materal: nine-year-olds—upper socioeconomic levels 41 percent, lower 13 percent; thirteen-year-olds—upper 58 percent, lower 24 percent; seventeen-year-olds—upper 68 percent, lower 36 percent; adults—upper 64 percent, lower 21 percent.

3. Interest in reading. The percent who devote two hours or more a week to voluntary reading: nine-year-olds—upper socioeconomic levels 64 percent, lower 41 percent; thirteen-year-olds—upper 89 percent, lower 46 percent; seventeen-year-olds—upper 83 percent, lower 42 percent; adults—upper 76 percent, lower 26 percent.

Knowing that the assessment report will have been widely publicized, you realize that most of your board members, parent-teacher associations, and other citizen groups would have read it. Hence, wherever you have a chance to speak or to write, you might make the following points: "No doubt you have seen the report of the recent National Assessment and notice that in this region most children from upper socioeconomic levels learn to read and maintain their interests in reading; but for children coming from lower socioeconomic levels, where they have less encouragement and less chance to develop reading interest and skills in the home, only about a third of them reach the level of competence and interest in reading characteristic of most persons from the upper levels. In our school, we maintain a continuing appraisal of the progress of children in reading." Because the National Assessment will provide background data, the public will have a broader perspective from which to view the local problems and there will be less tendency than there is now to attack the local schools groundlessly. Hopefully, the public will see that most difficult educational problems are not localized (and there is not "the devil of this superintendent" or "these teachers we have here" that cause the problems).

These hypothetical data, I think, give some notion of what could be done by the superintendents and other administrators, although the purpose of the assessment is especially to help the public to get a better perspective upon which to act intelligently. With the wealth of such information from an assessment report, the local school officials can be aided in getting public understanding.

Another value in the assessment will be its demonstration of a wider range of useful evaluation procedures and studies than those previously employed. It is demonstrating the feasibility of using samples of students so that the range in depth of evaluation can be greatly extended. In my opinion, this may be our most important contribution to the development of more adequate evaluation within our schools.

VI. Economic and Community Support: Perspectives

Chairman
OLIVER DANIEL, Assistant Vice-President,
Concert Music Administration, Broadcast Music, Inc.

Speeches

The AFL-CIO and the Arts

Herman D. Kenin

We are considering a number of questions regarding support for the arts, and while we will address ourselves to all of them in the course of this Symposium, I'd like to deviate slightly from these areas to give you not a prophecy, but a series of examples. I'm sure that all of you are aware of the present government support for the arts, on the federal, state and local levels. I am also sure that you are all familiar with the work being done by various foundations, and the welcome support that the arts have received from some large corporations and businesses.

However, there is one rather large element of the American public which has not been mentioned in these discussions so far, and I'd like to address myself to that. Organized Labor, with justification, has taken pride, and credit, for the increased leisure time available to all of us. Labor has been in the forefront of the social progress movement for some time now, and we will continue to work toward reducing working hours and improving the standards of living of not only our members, but of all Americans.

We have not abrogated our responsibility to help make this leisure time a rewarding experience. There was a time when Americans were content to sit and rock when a day's work was done. Today, however, the only ones content with "rocking" are the youngsters.

There is no doubt that this country is currently experiencing a cultural boom. Yet in the midst of this growing demand for cultural opportunity, the economic plight of the performing artist is almost as desperate as it has ever been. This is particularly true in the area of music. The economics of symphony orchestra management is such that many of our nation's largest organizations must depend, in great measure, upon donations, grants, and sponsors for their economic stability.

I'm sure that most of you have read press reports of symphony musicians who have "disrupted" performances and seasons. I'm also sure that all of you are familiar with the great economic handicaps under which these symphony orchestra members live. They do not earn, in our society, a wage comparable to their skill or to the hours that they work. A vast number of them are forced to teach, or to hold several jobs, in order to make ends meet. This is a fact of musical life, and I state it not by way of apology, but simply as a truth which must be considered.

A question in the brochure that was sent me prior to this conference asks: "Does the precarious economic future for the professional musician hold any implications for the college music department?" The fact is that the precarious economic future of the professional musician holds grave implications for everyone who loves music.

There is a great difference between a Beethoven, or Mahler, or Sibelius symphony performed by one of our nation's leading orchestras and the same composition as performed by a high school orchestra. The composition and the notes are the same, but what we hear, what we experience, is vastly different.

And unfortunately it is not inconceivable that, in the future,

despite the growing demand for cultural opportunities, the quality of musical performances, on the whole, may decline. I'm reminded of a story that my good friend, Congressman Frank Thompson, told some time ago. He was visiting a musician friend, an orchestra member, and Thompson asked whether the musician would encourage his son to follow in his footsteps. The musician replied, after giving the matter some thought, "If he really loves music, I wouldn't stop him. But I'd never let my daughter marry a musician."

Unless there is increased support for the arts, and for music—and unless it is forthcoming quickly, a great many promising talents may be discouraged from continuing their music studies. There exists now a shortage of qualified instrumentalists, a shortage which will continue unless more is done to encourage talented youngsters.

We of the American Federation of Musicians have been aware of this problem for some time. As professional musicians, we are concerned not only with the welfare of our members, but of the "industry," as it were, of our art. This shortage has been particularly acute in the area of string instrumentalists. With this in mind, the AFM began a project some nine years ago to give talented young performers an opportunity to improve their skills, and to expose them to the best of professional musicians, thus encouraging them to continue. The project is called the AFM Congress of Strings. I think that it is unique in the annals of Labor, and in many ways is a project which has few equals anywhere.

The member Locals choose a group of talented youngsters, at open auditions, and provide them with an eight-week summer program of instruction and performance. In past years, 100 students have been chosen annually, and the Federation and its Locals have provided transportation to and from the Congress site, instruction, room and board, as well as recreation facilities.

These students have studied under some of the finest string instrumentalists in America—drawn from the first chairs of the nation's symphonies; and they have performed, in concert, under the finest conductors—William Steinberg of Pittsburgh, Josef Krips of San Francisco, Eugene Ormandy of Philadelphia, Howard Mitchell of the National Symphony, and our host at this gathering, Maestro Leinsdorf.

This year, the program has been expanded. With the aid of a grant from the Rockefeller Foundation, the Congress of Strings has established branches at the University of Southern California and at the Saratoga Performing Arts Center. This arrangement enabled us to increase the number of students and, we believe, to upgrade the high quality of the program.

As for results: after only eight years the Congress of Strings has provided at least one regular performer for every major symphony in the United States and Canada, and dozens upon dozens of members for smaller organizations throughout the nation.

The AFM has sought other means of aiding music, and we have been successful in this as well. Back in 1945, when few people had given much thought to ways and means of supporting musical performances with funds other than those obtained at the box office and from wealthy patrons, the American Federation of Musicians, under my predecessor, the fiery and beloved James C. Petrillo, emerged from a negotiating session with a landmark contract. Included in its provisions was recognition, by the recording industry, of their responsibilities for the technological job losses by musicians as a result of the proliferation of recorded music. This recognition took the form of a penny-a-record royalty, paid to the Federation.

It was Union money—and could be spent in any way the Union saw fit. The subject of disposal of these funds was debated at our convention. We had a dream, and it was toward this dream that we worked. This money, we felt, should go to musicians—but more, it should go toward the future of live music. Toward that end, a trust fund, "The Recording and Transcription Fund" was established. It began sponsoring free public performances in 1947.

At that time, the Fund was operated entirely by the Federation of Musicians, and, in order to permit all of its funds to go toward live music, the Federation undertook to pay the operating and administrative expenses out of its own treasury. With the passage of the Taft-Hartley Act in 1947, the fund was outlawed, and the recording industry stopped its contributions to the music fund. Shortly afterward, the AFM renewed its drive to continue this program. It took a second long and bitter hiatus in the making of records by AFM members, but in 1949 another agreement was reached with the recording industry to continue the public services of the Recording and Transcription Fund. This new operation, under the name of the Music Performance Trust Funds, has operated since that time, under the direction of an independent trustee, Samuel Rosenbaum. To date, more than $76 million has been spent by these Funds for live music.

Let me also explain that there are no welfare benefits or other features provided by the Funds. The musician works for the pay he receives. Expenses for these programs, other than the pay of the musicians, are borne by the co-sponsors of the event. Locals of the AFM throughout the nation serve as a grass-roots source of aid in encouraging worthy performances, and of coordinating programing with the trustee and local organizations anxious to co-sponsor musical events. Thus, the encouragement and development of live, creative music in all its forms is carried on in virtually every city and town throughout the United States and Canada by the AFM and the Music Performance Trust Funds.

Now, let's consider for a moment what these activities accomplish. Certainly they provide some small cushion for the professional musician against the continuing inroads of automation and "canned music." Also, these activities provide audiences throughout the country with the opportunity to attend free, live performances. As music lovers, you all know that there is a perhaps indefinable, but no less real, difference between a live and a recorded performance. Sam Rosenbaum has often compared the difference in experiences to that of kissing your girl over the telephone and the real thing. There is a magic, a communication, between orchestra, conductor, and audience that cannot be achieved on the record.

Finally, in addition to the public service aspects of these performances—in hospitals, children's homes, and the like—there is a more important achievement, in terms of the future of music. These performances help to build audiences, and that is of major importance to us all.

Whenever the question of increased federal support for the arts arises, we tend to think in terms of how many performers, or performances, or workshops, these monies will support. Yet there is another justification for these funds—one which, I believe, is of the utmost importance. Each time live music is heard, each time live music is performed, a new audience is "indoctrinated." And if these funds, whether they come from government, or foundations, or corporations, stimulate an interest in music not only for future professionals, but for the audiences of today and of tomorrow, then they have been successfully utilized.

For some time now, those of us involved in support for the arts have been complaining about the "tyranny of the box office." Unless the "old chestnuts" are performed, audiences won't pay; and orchestras must turn elsewhere for their support. This, I think, is something we should examine very carefully. These old chestnuts are accepted, and desired by audiences in general because they are familiar. Their acceptance is not necessarily an indication of merit. Few composers have been truly popular in their own times, the work of few men has lasted and entered the area of the classics. By and large the greatest composers and the greatest compositions were ahead of their times. They were building upon what had been accomplished, they were seeking new musical approaches; and because they were able to go beyond the standard, they achieved a measure of greatness.

It takes time for an audience, for a listener, to evaluate a piece of music. A new composition, particularly when it is avant-garde, is strange, and it must be heard several times before it can be judged, let alone appreciated or loved. This is not so with a play—although in the theatre innovation may sometimes be a disturbing influence for audiences. Perhaps it is only in the area of art, and only within the last few years, that we have an audience, a "box office," that is willing and ready to accept the newest innovations readily. And even there, the general public has been slow to accept the value of modern art. (Incidentally, I include myself in that "general public" which finds it difficult to understand the beauty of a six-foot high soap box.)

I don't know that it would be fair of us to expect the general listening public to accept, unquestioningly, modern music—or even musical compositions that don't fall into the chestnut category although they are fairly well known. Rather, we must concern ourselves first with the problem of educating the public to a fuller and more comprehensive appreciation of music. And, I believe, programs such as the Music Performance Trust Funds free concerts, the New York Philharmonic series of concerts in the park, sponsored by the Schlitz Brewing Company, the various programs being carried out under foundation grants, as well as the projects utilizing funds under the various titles of the Elementary and Secondary Education Act, provide us with the best opportunities for educating the public.

It is to this goal that we must dedicate ourselves. Perhaps there will always be need for "outside" economic support for music, and for the other performing arts; but this need may be lessened by the establishment of wider audiences. When it comes to justifying federal support for the arts, a large audience eager to listen to music is the best justification in the world for a recalcitrant congressman—particularly if that audience is in his home district.

The U.S. Steel Corporation and Music

W. Homer Turner

Over the past half century, this nation has witnessed a major cultural renaissance attributable to many interrelated, inchoate, and subtle factors. Among the more tangible, objective factors are the substantial growth in leisure time, an ever-lengthening life expectancy, increasing individual economic well-being, advancement in communication media, growing individual mobility, and a new sense of pride by the citizenry in the national culture. This renaissance seems to be related to efforts designed to catch up culturally with the far swifter material march of the society. Meanwhile, there is an ongoing search for a quality of surprise and ecstacy in human experience, a blending of a sense of dignity, power, and mysticism, and a quest for functional machine-made beauty in design and in other common experiences of daily life.

Never before has mankind had such easy access to the entire world of art; but even with increased opportunity, enthusiasm, and participation, most of the organizations and activities related to cultural affairs perennially require subsidy. Until recently, most of the subsidy required for all cultural needs was provided by individuals, voluntary groups, or local governments. Today, only one-half to two-thirds of the resources required can be derived from prior endowment accumulations or as income from admission fees. Consequently, the balance of the required resources must be supplied by institutions and individuals in the private sectors, or, alternatively, by some level of government. The corporation and the corporate-financed foundation, as major institutions in the society, must determine their proper share of the subsidy.

Motivation for any such assumption of responsibility for aid is a balanced compound of the general and long-term self interests. David Rockefeller, at the Fiftieth Anniversary Conference of the National Industrial Conference Board, phrased it as follows:

> Almost imperceptibly over the past several years, the modern corporation has evolved into a social as well as an economic institution. Without losing sight of the need to make a profit, it has developed ideals and responsibilities going far beyond the profit motive. It has become, in effect, a full-fledged citizen, not only of the community in which it is headquartered, but of the country and indeed the world.

The distinguished scholar Richard Eells, adjunct professor at Columbia and himself a talented musician and composer, in his book, *The Corporation and the Arts*[1], adumbrates the whole spectrum of motivation and action in today's corporate—derived support of the arts. Eells observes that as a social institution, the corporation is tied to the ecological urban problem; and thereby it is concerned also with the aesthetic aspects of it. Corporate-financed foundations, precisely as with other general welfare foundations, are motivated in making grants exclusively by public interest considerations. As a matter of both law and chosen policy, they become involved with donor self-interest only as a nondesigned byproduct. But for those not yet perceiving the societal position of the modern corporation, it can be shown that there exist direct business interests as well in cultural matters. First, there is the direct interest in increasing the profitability of capital invested. A music center established in a

semi-rural area, for example, is estimated to have increased the income of the community by several million dollars yearly.

Second, there is the interest in the raising of the local cultural level. Thus, often a new thruway interchange, or the clearance of slums, is balanced by the building of an art museum. On occasion, a cultural enterprise will have an impact which amounts to a complete reshaping of a community, thereby favorably altering local business production and marketing environment.

Third, there is the concern of enterprise with its reflection. One corporation asserts that its institutional reputation for appreciation of the fine arts, acquired through reproduction of modern paintings in national advertising, aids worldwide acceptance of its goods and services. Another company's broadcasts of performances of great operas is a further case in point. Still another organization combines, for special color television presentations, great masterpieces of world art with distinctive musical compositions of a renowned artist.

Fourth, encouragement of the arts, through music especially, can improve the morale of employees, help attract qualified personnel, and encourage their channeling of leisure time into rewarding and enriching activities; and, because of the more satisfying quality of life resulting, become more productive in multiple ways.

With no desire to engage in controversy, I invite my co-panelist representing a union, Herman Kenin, to comment upon the challenges for union statesmanship help recently cited by Nancy Hanks of the Rockefeller Brothers Fund—distinguished analyst and articulate catalyst for all the arts. Before a contributions research group affiliated with the National Industrial Conference Board she observed:

> Operating at a continuous deficit, the market mechanisms restraints found in private industry do not regulate the allocation of resources. The amount of funds available to pay salaries depends in considerable measure on the ability of the fund raisers. This "unknown," plus the fact that very few arts organizations yet have the ability to do any meaningful long-range planning, throw a great question mark into bargaining.
>
> There are several new distinct trends that will vitally affect labor relations in the arts. The first is the increase in government support, with accompanying labor regulations as well as funds.
>
> Another trend is that toward year-round employment. At present the unions are devoted largely to protecting the interests of individual members because of the very high unemployment rate. As this changes, the unions may evolve more toward being professional associations, which could cause considerable wrenching in the union struction.
>
> As the unions and their members become increasingly professional, it is quite evident that there will have to be better means of communication developed between management and the artists. We have example after example of the artists wishing to have more say-so as to where they will perform. Earlier they would do most anything to expand the length of the season.

Union leaders do have a truly unusual opportunity, through

wise actions and thoughtful long-range policy developments, to advance or to retard the sound management and prudent directional efforts of all the arts, especially music.

The "Why" of Aid to Music

Here it may be useful to attempt a statement about the motivations for support of music. In the whole panorama of aesthetic expression, music alone—without visual or verbal interference—has capacity to fire the mind in a manner distinctively penetrating. The power of music, in this repect, transcends national, racial, linguistic, and other barriers.

To enlarge music's useful role, it is needful only to increase the number of persons coming under its influence. There are many modes of experiencing music, and a chief one is symphonic music performed by a professional orchestra. The magnificent advances in technology, and the availability of recordings, radio, television, and other means of reproduction and dissemination should not cause anyone to forget the immense value of direct participation in *live* performances. Unfortunately, the opportunity to experience live performances remains an undeniably limited one; of our 800 major cities, only about one in five has heard a professional orchestra within the past four years.

Attending live performances helps introduce hearers to the deeper meaningfulness of music. One might liken direct listening to music to the intimate vision of beauty enjoyed by the skin diver exploring beneath the sea, as contrasted with the more remote observation of the voyager on the ocean surface.

The performance of great music is differentiated in still another respect. Most art works stand completed. Music, however, like the theatre or the ballet, depends upon a third element, in this case an orchestra, between the composer and his audience. Unlike some unfortunate human relationships, familiarity with music does not breed contempt but unites the hearer with qualities touching the infinite and the mysterious. Fritz Kreisler once declared that the world is a great child, and tires easily, only to be restored to freshness by great music. Haydn, pursuing the same thought, awakened the drowsy ones at a certain point with special arrangements in his *Surprise Symphony.*

Symphonic music may be likened to a pyramid. The base and greater part of the pyramid of musical performance is the receptive public, enjoying the natural heritage open to almost every human being. The pyramid apex is the creative source: the composer. The section in-between comprises the interpretive conductor and the performing artists, who relive in execution the composer's work. To all these society owes a large debt, for without them availability of superlative music would be vastly restricted.

The symphonic orchestra is a culmination of the best in cooperative effort. This cooperation is not unlike that which is attained when all the wanted elements of superior architecture are brought together. Both symphonic music and Gothic cathedrals—the one of physical grandeur, the other invoking lofty and intricate emotional response—are immensely significant to the race. Being so significant, their financing must be assured.

Within the last year more than 300 new organizations devoted to the encouragement of the arts have been established throughout the nation, of which there were 12 new opera groups, 45 new music organizations, and 16 concerned with art and music education. Altogether today there are about 1,400 orchestras in the profes-sional, semiprofessional, or amateur category (more than half of those in the world) and between 650 and 750 opera companies.

In 1920 the United States had fewer than 100 such orchestras, and in 1900 only ten of them. An increasing number of symphonic groups may be now characterized as first-rate, with scores of others on the way to developing superior quality. Americans spend more at symphony concert box offices than at baseball ticket gates. They spend as much for recordings of concert music and high-fidelity equipment as they do for *all* spectator sports.

In the past fifteen years, about 1,000 works of some 300 American composers of "serious music" have appeared on long-play-ing records. There are more than 75 national musical organizations in the United States with nearly one million members active in the cause of concert music, and about 200 other organizations dedicated to the general advancement and appreciation of music. One estimate is that there are 35 million persons in the U.S.A. interested in concerts. During a recent season, the American Concert League reported more sold-out houses and higher ticket sales than at any other prior point in history.

Ten large cities—New York, Los Angeles, Chicago, Philadelphia, San Francisco, Pittsburgh, Washington, Cleveland, Houston, and Dallas—already provide live symphonic music to millions; and other distinguished city orchestras, including Boston, Detroit, Minneapolis, St. Louis, Rochester, Buffalo, and Baltimore, extend the coverage. Still other cities will enhance the future, spurred on by the Ford Foundation grants.

One acute observer finds that there are three basic pressures working to increase financial aid. The *first* factor is the increment in the number of amateur and other performers involved; the *second* is the enhanced trend to integrate arts into the educational system; and the *third* is the growing concern of citizens for the quality of their environment.

The "How" of Aid

There are at least two basic means of supporting and advancing the creative arts, including music. The artists may be provided aid directly, or the special apparatus related to them may be enhanced. The true artists have been defined as those with an overwhelming urge to create material objects or sound which will illuminate or represent some interior vision, fused of spirit and sensation. Their work awakens knowledge of a kind, chiefly inexplicit, not possible of being aroused by other means.

Through the centuries, artists and art forms frequently have been dependent heavily upon some form of patronage for individual or functional sustenance, whether deriving from pharaohs, kings, priests and the church, the city-state, the nation-state, or individuals. Such patronage is necessary since economic successes in the marketplace cannot be, indeed should not be, unqualifiedly applied with respect to fine arts and many other cultural activities. Patronage exists in many countries today, particularly through governmental support to national theatres, orchestras, and museums.

In America, however, artists or art forms traditionally are dependent significantly upon public taste, exercised through the direct or indirect purchase of product or performance. At times taste is confused with status symbols, with the consequence that the prevailing trend of acceptance and support is indeterminate. Affluent individuals, with today's restraints upon accumulation of wealth, sometimes are less willing, or seemingly less able, to commit themselves to both pioneering and long-sustained support. Nowadays, there may be a cycle operative in which patronage once again must come from an institution or other form of social entity. Although many people advocate major governmental responsibility, many others view this course as potentially restrictive—indeed, even fatal—as inherently tending to interfere rather than to free artistic expression. American pragmatism also operates as a folkway restraint upon tax expenditures for what the mass of voters may incorrectly regard as nonessentials.

Two more recent resources for financing cultural needs are corporations and foundations. For the past half century corporations and foundations have brought about heroic advances through encouragement and support of scientific and technological research and by improved production management. Will they have the will and skill to help insure for America a brilliant, diversified future in the nonmaterial aspects of life? This is the unanswered question now being generally evaluated.

There are means, awaiting aid, which will help insure a strong cultural base to stand alongside the nation's technical and material achievements, not as an ornamental addition but as an essential part of the health and vigor of a full society. Foremost among these are support for organizations which add to the knowledge of this nation's aesthetic and historical heritage, assistance for activities of entities engaged in the performing arts, and direct support to talented individuals.

There are inherent disadvantages to most plans of direct aid to the artist. A staff of highly developed specialists necessarily would have to be acquired by any donor to select the most able or potentially talented. This is not an improper step in some situations. In other cases, this is neither feasible nor desirable. The most efficacious administrative approach for the corporate-financed foundation generally would appear to be through determination of those specialized agencies within the cultural environment which, when strengthened, might help to bring the capacities of individual artists to full bloom and thus benefit the total society. Such opportunities are comprehended in the programs, projects, and facilities of symphonic orchestras and other entities within the performing, visual, and graphic arts; by youth talent and training programs—indeed, the gamut of man's institutionalized norms for aesthetic advancement. Most hold to the view that grants to these structured approaches will insure the highest degree of development of individual artists and benefit society.

It must never be forgotten that there is a danger of neglecting talented persons at the critical phases of their development, with resultant deficiencies in our national talent and leadership and diminution of our wanted mobility and freedom of opportunity. Undue support of the social mechanisms in the cultural field, at the cost of little or no direct support, in any quarter, for gifted persons, must be avoided. But, as to both, the central strategy is *sustained* foundation and other philanthropic interest, not in-and-out, one-shot aid.

Whatever the preferred ultimate social wisdom involved, because corporations and corporate foundations generally have chosen not to provide aid directly to individuals, they have a particular responsibility to select the most promising types of operating organizations and most viable grant-in-aid methods. The growing involvement of today's population with all forms of art and music must be recognized as a major social fact, as must the roles of art and music in developing a more satisfying society. Just as the major corporate foundations already have prudently recognized responsibility in the field of education through large-scale unrestricted grants, so are many corporate foundations now preparing to expand participation in cultural areas. As this trend matures, more and more corporation executives and corporate—foundation trustees will find it necessary to appraise their forward support policies in cultural fields.

Such is prelude to cultural needs. Where are we headed? America's forward quest is at least dual: an individual search for beauty and integrity, and an individual search for safety and worthiness in daily life. The dominant cultural mores delineate the allowable scope of action. Help in finding the answers to perplexing social problems, and assistance in avoiding possible community-by-community national cultural shabbiness, offer major opportunities for enlightened action by private sectors. Some share of this large-scale task (as management executives and trustees individually determine in the light of particular conditions facing them) ought to be assumed by corporations and by corporate foundations. The economic wants and needs for three-fourths of labor force now employed by enterprise are interrelated with cultural wants and needs. These same scores of millions, culturally satisfied or dissatisfied as to the patterns of their inner growth, constitute the majority at the voting booth—out of which ultimately applied social policy decisions arise, including the freedom or limitation of freedom of enterprise to risk and to manage.

As public sectors either attempt to assume ever larger community responsibility for health, welfare, education, and science, the cultural area remains the single major, community-related and community-oriented one invitingly open for private-sector leadership and initiation of needed action. Identification of corporations and corporate foundations with the cultural objectives of the great majority of the American people would appear to be a fertile field for responsible, hopefully wise, intervention. The now planned, soon to be activated, Council of Business and the Arts, along with the many other new organizational instruments recently created in hundreds of communities portend a new day for sensible desirable support of the arts. This fruition will be a great social gain.

And beyond this the powerful concluding observation of Richard Eells in *The Corporation and the Arts* is a sobering warning and a hopeful portent of what can be.

> The Space Age lends new meaning for life in humanistic as well as scientific terms. If we can ever learn to live together without mutual extermination, mankind could be on the threshold of a far more amply dimensioned Good Life than had ever been imagined in the century of the dismal science. Then, economics could not have been more remote from art. But today, arts, science, humanistics, and business are sitting around the same table—and they are actually enjoying the experience.
> When all is said and done perhaps the most important function of art is its revolutionary function, its capabilities of helping us to overcome absurd limitations of mind which, for centuries, have prevented mankind from facing his own problems squarely so that solutions can be found. Perhaps the artist can help us to discard the blinders, to see realities where words, logic, and science have failed in getting at the kernel.[2]

---

[1] Richard Eells, *The Corporation and the Arts* (New York: Macmillan, 1967).

[2] *Ibid.*, p. 292.

The Bell Telephone Hour:

Who Needs It?

Tim H. Henney

The label on my remarks this afternoon is "The Bell Telephone Hour: Who Needs It?" I gave Bob Choate that title because, as one who has earned his keep since early college days in the writing and editing arena, I dig punchy headlines. The danger in such titles is that most television viewers if asked, "Who needs the Telephone Hour?" will quickly tell you. They'll say no one does.

In the booklet, "The Arts and the Poor," by Judith Murphy and Ronald Gross, which was sent to Symposium participants, there is a chapter called "The Unfinished Experiment." It is about television and education. The Telephone Hour is, like ETV and ITV, an "unfinished experiment." And most people are not anxious to embrace an experiment until it justifies itself and becomes no longer experimental. Rare is the fellow, for instance, who will invest his savings in a bold, new business venture. Much rarer still is the guy who gets rich because of his risk.

I feel fairly certain in assuming that a generous percentage of this audience on occasion watches the Telephone Hour. I hope as you watch the program you feel akin to that daring minority who, having invested capital in a new business enterprise, manage to come away rich. I hope that upon investing your time with the Telephone Hour, you come away feeling amply rewarded, maybe even rich, inside.

There are a lot of reasons why we continue sinking time and funds, and often frustration, into our program. At least I think there are; they're pretty intangible and thus pretty hard to pin down. We are highly enthusiastic, almost sophomoric in our spirit perhaps, about our program, even though studies and ratings show rather convincingly that the Telephone Hour experiment is likely to remain unfinished indefinitely. By unfinished I mean unjustifiable—at least by present popular standards. Let me illustrate. Here are some quotes from a recent analysis by a national organization:

"While the Bell Telephone Hour performs relatively well against the professional managerial group, its major strength appears to be in the category of unemployed and/or retired."

"Although the show has strength in upper income areas, it is not necessarily strong in peak income groups."

"We assume that AT&T is using the Bell Telephone Hour to appeal to and reach the opinion leader, which in most instances would be men. The audience of the show is skewed fairly heavily toward women."

"The exceedingly low rating levels produced by the Bell Telephone Hour will convert to a small number of people or households."

The study also said: "Those people who are watching the show really like it. The point to watch out for, however, is that some bias might arise when describing a cultural show as a favorite."

In other words, one never knows when one of those friendly interviewers might spill the beans to the neighbors about what was really being watched next door. Or, worse, he might slip the information to the prep school or college where one is determined to get one's kids enrolled. Under such uncertainties one sometimes opts for Tanglewood or the Cleveland Symphony over the dirt track drag races—just to be safe.

This same analysis went on to recommend and document with impressive figures that the Telephone Hour could reach twice as many influentials, opinion leaders, precedent setters, power elite, or whatever you prefer to call yourselves in government, education, business, and other sectors of society, by backing professional football or the movies. And we believe it.

So, in pure economic terms, the show is no champion. But, then, we've known that for ages. What, then, is the incentive? Where, if not among the grass roots of the populace, lies our bunch of carrots? Unlike ETV and ITV, *our* experiment can't even claim a growing clientele. Our audience stays about the same: small. We are not at all like virtually every candidate for the presidency of the U.S.A.—we detect no spontaneous mass draft movement from sea to shining sea which tells us, after consulting our corporate conscience, that the show must run because "The People" insist.

Some people insist, but not "The People".

A tiny part of our rationale is, I suppose, that the Bell Telephone System has been linked with television's high watermarks from the outset. We did not sponsor the first network television series. Another company did, in 1946. But AT&T backed the second such series, the following year. It was called *The Story of Seven Hilltops*, and it was about the historic topography between Boston and New York.

Our principal contributions to television, of course, have been not in programs but in the facilities that make programs possible: in coaxial cable, and microwave, and Telstar, and things of that nature. Forty years ago, for example, some Bell Laboratories engineers made possible and participated in the first public city-to-city TV transmission. Two years later a similar group at the Labs demonstrated the first successful color television. That was in 1929.

More significant than AT&T's venerable association with television innovation and technical progress, though, is the company's tradition of sponsoring good music. The Bell System's experience in network radio broadcasting began in 1940 when the first weekly Telephone Hour was produced over NBC live from Carnegie Hall. AT&T sponsored the program on radio for eighteen years before transferring to television. On radio, the Telephone Hour reached about 2-1/2 million homes during its peak period. On television, we reach about 4 million homes—better than radio at its best, but a pittance compared with, say, the Smothers Brothers.

The Telephone Hour is the oldest continuous nighttime network program, having marked its 1,000th show in February of

1964. Yet, longevity and warm feelings for what's past are not the central reasons why a communications company, with greater assets and more shareholders than any other enterprise in the world, continues to sponsor a quality music program which is clearly the world's leading Nielsen index flop.

There are better reasons for our belief in the Bell Telephone Hour. In a second pamphlet I received from your program director, one titled "Performing Arts—Who Pays the Piper," the statement is made that "economically, the arts are at bay in a technological society." This implies, or indicates perhaps, that our society cannot have both its technological guns and its cultural butter at once.

AT&T trusts that this needn't be the case. As one of the most thoroughly technological of all businesses, we put considerable energy, expense, and hope into the Telephone Hour on the premise that the arts must and will keep pace. What value or joy will society hold if we permit it to become so lopsided in favor of efficiency that we eliminate such pleasant social ingredients as people, and the performing arts?

Most of you, I realize, are not employees of giant corporations. But if you were (or if you've read your "Organization Man" and "Executive Suite" novels) you know that in big companies we always set objectives and commit them to paper, then measure our performance against these papers. Here, in one compound sentence, is the official purpose of the new Telephone Hour: *To present distinguished individual special programs related to music, which will involve the viewer in a participative way, with the primary aim of getting critical acclaim and comment for cultural effort and contribution—within which framework audience and entertainment qualities are secondary.*

With that goal in view, we are about ready to begin a second year of "involving the viewer in a participative way." Our new season, once launched, will feature such diverse programs as: *A Profile of Duke Ellington; Zubin Mehta and the Los Angeles Symphony; The Bach Choir of Bethlehem, Pennsylvania; The Aldeburgh Festival; George Plimpton Leading the New York Philharmonic; A Profile of Edward Villella; Sounds and Sights of Chicago; Portrait of Yehudi Menuhin;* and a show called *Jazz—the Intimate Art.*

Most of these, as with Telephone Hour programs already presented, will be made available to schools, clubs, and other groups as 16mm color films for nontheatrical use. The way to borrow them, as I suppose most of you know, is to write the telephone company business office. (You could call if you prefer, but I don't want to be accused of using this Symposium as a sales meeting.)

In closing, let me quote from the best rationale I've heard for our continuing sponsorship of the Telephone Hour. Some of you may have heard this already, if you were in the audience in Los Angeles recently when Walter Straley of AT&T received the Gold Baton Award from the American Symphony League. What Mr. Straley told that distinguished membership seems appropriate here this afternoon.

"Now and then a corporation should divert itself from waving its banners for the attention of great masses of people, and wave one fine banner simply because it deserves waving. It may be that not having an immediately practical reason for the Telephone Hour is very good business indeed. If this be frivolous, I say the corporation should not only permit an occasional frivolity, it ought to seek such out. To speak on commercial television, for you who speak in the language of the gods, is not impertinent to the purpose of the telephone women nor to the men who lay telephone cables and climb poles. By parading the excellence of your musicianship we reinforce our own efforts to excel, and even if we understand but dimly our full intent, and see no immediate profit at all, we know this much: the corporation must never remove itself from beauty, nor even adventure, and sententious as this may sound, our Telephone Hour provides us with a little of both. So the program you honor may not make us much money, but occasionally it produces a reason for corporate pride. And that's the most precious ingredient in corporate life."

So who needs the Bell Telephone Hour? Well, for one thing, *we* do. For another, I assume *you* do. And then there is the balance of our seven million viewers who aren't in this room. I guess *they* need it. As for the other 193 million Americans who don't watch the Telephone Hour—well, I suspect they need it too, but just don't know it.

And we are magnanimous about those things. Our attitude at AT&T is that *Bonanza*, after all, can't be *all* bad.

The United States Government, Education, and Music

Harold Arberg

Our concern this afternoon is very simply the role of government in all levels of education. I will speak primarily from the federal government level. It seems to me at this stage in the development of our society that we can use this paraphrase: "That government governs best which governs appropriately." What is appropriate for government at all levels to do in regard to the strengthening of education in the large-framework and, within that, what is appropriate for music in education? I suggest that there are three basic roles.

First, government has to serve and can best serve as a catalyst for action to help bring people together—as an encourager if you will, as a supplier of impetus and feasibility, what is possible, what can we do that we have not done previously, and how can government facilitate this. I am delighted that this meeting is being sponsored entirely by the private sector, by the MENC, the Theodore Presser Foundation, the Berkshire Music Center, and the School of Fine and Applied Arts, Boston University. This is precisely the kind of meeting which I think will serve as a remarkable catalyst. Obviously, what will transpire depends on all of us.

The second basic role: I think that government can give visibility and organization to a program of support and education. I mean by this the various agencies of government—the U.S. Office of Education in my case, and many other types of government organization.

The third role is that government can afford necessary support. Money is one form, but there are many other kinds of support—staff, personnel, and organization. For convenience, let's call it "money." I think that the cooperative relationship in this financial angle has been mentioned. It was very visibly shown in yesterday's *New York Times*. Trans World Airlines announced a grant of $150,000 to supplement a grant of $100,000 by our State Department to help support the tour of the New York Philharmonic to Europe and Israel in 1968. The proportion here is a fair arrangement; about half of the $500,000 estimated cost will come, optimistically, from the box office; TWA's share ($150,000) and the State Department's share ($100,000) will not cling to those proportions, but the government is the junior partner and does not own the controlling interest. This is fine with me. Now you know something of my bias.

What about the role of government in supporting the arts and education? First, I think the federal share should be and certainly is a relatively small one. If you know what the total expenditure of government is, national expenditure on education by the federal government is a minute portion. Dr. Turner told us this morning that he had helped to compile the figures of total foundation grants to arts and humanities during the past year; and that amount is a very small one: considerably under five percent.

Second, all are engaged in the current battle for equal rights for the arts. Equal rights for whom and for what? These include the natural sciences, the social sciences, and the humanities. The tone of this battle was established very well when Professor Northrop completed his summary by saying the scientific and aesthetic realms are not mutually exclusive but much more than compatible; they are totally integrated utlimately. To extend this concept: not only do the arts and sciences reinforce themselves, the arts — painting, theatre, drama, music — reinforce themselves. This has not been as widely recognized as it should be. I think we ought to be very much concerned with what Johnny and Jane are getting in dance education or in theatre education. If music has been waiting in the wings, so to speak, dance and theatre education have certainly been outside the stage door. I think this should be a matter of real concern to us.

Third, how does the federal government achieve these lofty goals that we are talking about: serving as a catalyst, giving visibility to the arts, and providing funds? What is the mechanism involved? To use the Ciceronian prerogative here, I'm going to pass over many other departments of government. It would be presumptuous of me to try and represent them. I have mentioned the State Department, which has a major stake in this area. Many people overlook the Department of Defense, which since its inception has not only sponsored the military band program but has supported an expanding program in the arts. Many people in our profession received very valuable experience during their military careers. The whole Defense Department is a major contributor and supporter of music, and indeed other arts.

Let me talk briefly about the U.S. Office of Education. In the past five years, the budget has gone from less than one billion dollars a year to above four billion dollars a year. When you think of growth and development, while it is a small share of the total educational effort, it has been a gigantic step forward in terms of federal commitment to education. You know what the vehicles are: the Elementary and Secondary Education Act, the Higher Education Act, and others. There is an arts and humanities program within the USOE which is an educational counterpart, if you will, to the National Endowments on the Arts and Humanities, which were created in the National Foundation Act. Two members here today representing music, Warner Lawson and Herman Kenin, are members of the National Council on the Arts, the advisory body to the Endowment. We work closely with that agency and plan to continue to do so, so there is a liaison.

We are obviously concerned with money for education. How do we get it and how do we use it? The money appropriated by the Congress for the Arts Endowment is to support the arts and nothing else. How this is divided among music, theatre, dance, and drama is a problem for the Council and for the Endowment. (On the other hand, the appropriations for education may have broad categories of funds to aid; for example, the disadvantaged and handicapped children.) There is no specific amount earmarked for music, or theatre, or dance. This is a problem. Again, the battle for equal rights for the arts has to be fought at all levels. It is fought within the Office of Education. It is fought at the state level, and as you well know at your own levels. I think it should be this way, and I hope it never changes. I would hate to have Congress say, "We will have this much money for music," because all the other arts would have every right to be lined up for their share of the money. I do not think it will happen.

The Office has several bureaus: the Bureau of Research, and the operating bureaus—elementary and secondary, higher education, adult, and vocational. A new bureau of education for the handicapped has been organized. All these have a potential for support of music and the other arts, but they do not have a specified amount of money to support these.

If I could cite a principal theme in terms of our organization and operation now, it would be "regionalization." It is a strengthening, a stiffening of the potential of the regions of our country to solve their own educational problems. This is what is taking place through a variety of means, and some of them you are well aware of. Five regional laboratories have research directors assigned and have a certain allocation of funds. They can support doctoral research. Small colleges, which frequently feel that they do not get much of a play in the national scheme of things, no longer compete; they no longer need to compete on a national level. They can only compete on a regional level.

In summary, this is some of the machinery which exists at the federal level. I hope that we will say: "Long live music, long live the arts," and then return home and do something about them with enthusiasm.

The Contemporary Music Project

Norman Dello Joio

The Contemporary Music Project for Creativity in Music Education, I believe, is most pertinent to the overall theme for this Symposium. In addition, the philosophy underlying our program is intimately related to the purpose for which the Music Educators National Conference exists.

As chairman of the Policy Planning Committee for the Ford Foundation-sponsored and MENC-administered project, I am happy for this opportunity to touch briefly on some aspects of the Project, which is now in its eighth year of existence.

The germinal idea for the Project was simple: it held that the young creative forces on the musical scene should be given an opportunity to offer their proven talent to a growing generation in the high schools over the country, a generation that, on the whole, was dimly aware of what was going on around them, musically. This condition was felt to be a legitimate area for questioning; for with few exceptions our young people are introduced to a much too restricted view of what is involved in a totally musical experience.

With the ever increasing effectiveness of our composer program, it seems inevitable that the range of interest should expand. Despite its initial premise, the young composer program forced the CMP to go directly to the heart of one of the crucial questions arising for any art in a mass culture. As a result, programs evolved that concerned themselves with a level at which we train students and disseminate information to the musically inquisitive, be it at a professional level, or in a general liberal arts sense. Together with this was a concern for the prevailing standards that for too long have been set for those who chose the career of teacher.

We have come a long way from our early days and now we have initiated many pilot projects and experiments, some successful, others less so. We are at least bringing into focus some problems that need identifying. Since 1959, with the help of many educators and professionals, we have attempted to draw attention to the fact that all music, both past and present, can be utilized as a strong and binding element between educational centers and the community.

We have long felt an arbitrary line has been drawn between the professional and the educational worlds. Our present committee on planning reflects this in its membership. We number among us theorists, historians, educators, conductors, and composers. The range of their interests reflects a full spectrum in music education, from the primary grades to the graduate level. The goodwill we have established permits us to call on many practitioners over the country, people who are increasingly aware of the implications of our program. (I might say here that we in the Project are learning. As for myself, a product of a purely professional training, my commitment to this Project has given me a further ethical basis and justification for my activities as a musician.) The natural growth of the Project is also reflected in the fact that some of our former composers serve with us now. Our administrative director, Grant Beglarian, was one of our first composers in school residence, and our assistant director, John Davies, was once a host to a Ford composer when he conducted the orchestra and band at Elkhart, Indiana.

In closing, I should mention that our six Institutes for Music in Contemporary Education, which have been functioning for a year and will continue till the expiration of the Project, presently involve approximately thirty colleges and universities and their surrounding secondary and elementary schools.

Shortly, as a result of a four-day conference held at the Airlie House in Virginia, an evaluation of our Institutes' activities will be published and made available to all interested parties.

I will now turn to Mr. Lowry, Vice-President of the Ford Foundation. I would be remiss if I did not say on behalf of the Project that whatever success we may have achieved would not have been possible without his understanding and sympathy.

A Foundation and Contemporary Music

W. McNeil Lowry

The Ford Foundation program in humanities and the arts is now ten years old, which is harder for me to recognize and remember probably than for anybody else. It still seems to me like one of the youngest and most novel and most unproved and exciting programs of activities and opportunities in the United States. It started as the smallest program in the Ford Foundation. It is now the largest activity in the support of the professional aesthetic and artistic activities in the United States that the country affords.

Last week I was in Washington testifying on the new authorization for the National Foundation on the Arts and Humanities. We all hope, particularly those of us in the Ford Foundation, that the ratio between what we do and what the government does in these fields will be totally reversed (as it has been in every other single field that the Foundation is in) and that eventually the government's program will be far greater than ours.

This program in the Foundation, way back, said nothing directly about formal education. It was based on two primary goals: first, the situation of the independent artist and artistic director; that is, opportunities for the professional, considered all the way from the potentially identified professional. Second, it put its priorities on the outlets for the professional development. It stuck therefore largely within the professional groups, companies, and artists, and artistic directors in the arts, and to this date has seldom been directly concerned or administered through programs in universities or colleges.

This did not mean that the program had no educational philosophy. If anything it was bound to have aspects and influences in the realm of education. And so it did.

It is not without accident that every commission for a new musical work supported by the Ford Foundation has been selected by either the performer, directly naming the composer, or the professional company or group, which was again selecting the composer. The Commission was not selected by laymen, nor was it even selected by composers. (However, composers *were* used in the selection of young composers to go into the high schools to write directly for performance.) In other words, we put our influence in music at that point where the artist was related both to creativity and, hopefully, to the outlet for that creativity.

It is a normal assumption on the part of every single reporter or critic who writes about music and of most people who write about foundations that a foundation is interested only in something "new" and, therefore, it will give money to do a new work but won't do one thing for those people who are concerned with the classical work or the standard repertoire. On the evidence, not only in the Ford Foundation, but in other foundations, this is nonsense. We were privileged as a foundation to make the largest single action of philanthropy in the arts that was ever made when we gave the $82.5 million to the symphony orchestra. We did not tell the various orchestras to play contemporary music, though we did so encourage them. It is up to them and, of course, must be and should be up to them. The reason that a foundation is interested in something new is:

how can you be interested in the living artist without being interested in his creativity?

In the early days, we had *ad hoc* meetings without publicity where we would lock twenty or so musicians in a room with us—or theater artists, or painters, or sculptors, or whatever—and just listen to them talk without an agenda for two days. It was in one of these conferences that Norman Dello Joio threw out the idea that even the youngest composer, if he could be tested by playing his tapes and by reading his scores for his peers, who were mature composers, could write directly for performance only in perhaps a high school orchestra or choral group and that this might be an interesting experiment to try. This finally did result in the Young Composers Program. When we said Young Composers could go to a high school, we said that they could *not* teach, and this only meant "teach" in one sense. We were not oblivious to the fact that if a composer wrote for performance and went through preparation and rehearsal with young people, that he, in fact, *did* teach. This was a kind of teaching that had to do with tearing down the wall between the creator, the composer, the professional educator, and the educational institution.

For years I wondered and for years, in a sense, I lost hope about high school systems and boards of education and communities ever beginning to use the Young Composers as this kind of teacher on their own and with their own financing. One of the most significant developments in the last few years of this project has been that at last a few high school systems and boards of education are doing just that.

Although we were not concerned immediately with the educational objective, but were thinking primarily of the young artist and his professional creative development, we were nevertheless working in a milieu that was educational. And when we allowed concert artists to select composers to write a work and then arranged with an orchestra or an opera company to put on the work, we were again motivated; and ten years later, we are still motivated primarily by the interest of the professional artist and his opportunities and outlets for development. But we have begun to see the potential implications of this for education.

After these many years (which are still frontier years for the Ford Foundation in the humanities and the arts) I am basically impressed by two things, which are very serious problems for all of us concerned with these subjects. One is the heavy toll, and to some extent the deterioration, the erosion of the personal vitality of key artists and artistic directors in this country.

In the year 1957, when we went about making the first comprehensive program on a national basis in the creative and performing arts, professional artists, people in small theaters, in small music groups, in small arts schools everywhere were quite taken by the fact that somebody had come to say to them: What are you doing? What are your problems? How do you do it? What do you think is going on in this field? Where do you get your resources financially or otherwise? Even now when so much is being invested and we have arts councils and state and national government support — even a little beginning in the corporations — so much of what is done still does not go to the purpose of the individual artist, or his development, or even his training. It goes into buildings, festivals, councils of various kinds, conferences, and seminars, *ad nauseam*. It is not going to those people who by a strong, hairshirt, personal commitment are keeping the store, are keeping things together in the creative and performing arts and making outlets for young artists and developed artists to use. Even where they have had more funds, these funds have only "stretched" them. Their objectives have been enlarged and the toll on them is incessant. It is creating a great deal of neurosis and distortion.

The second great problem is the steady erosion of craft: the difficulty of holding together that discipline and the resources for it that make for constant, ceaseless involvement with doing it over and over, with high standards of craft. We may not take out of this century the craft skills in the arts that we brought into the century; and in 1900, the United States was not in any sense thought of as being in a cultural boom or renaissance.

In many cases, novelty and sensation, so-called avant-garde material, has been used as a substitute for craft. Whether it is a classical work or an avant-garde work, it still must be judged in terms of how it is done and what is the craft.

Both of these problems have great relevance to the work of the educators in music and to the Contemporary Music Project. This project is one in which success toward the stated objectives involves both the doers of the project, the hosts of the project, and the Foundation in a further responsibility, something else that can be reached for. This project started from simply having a young composer *there* to becoming more concerned with the whole curriculum: the whole experience of a young school person. We are concerned with how that whole experience relates to the creative process and to the fact that in some of these schools the composer is not dead but alive and here in one's midst.

We are not concerned with piling up scores. We are not concerned with how many works we can say these young composers have written after the end of this project. We are concerned with whether this project can be like a rock thrown in a pool, a definitely elaborating concern with music curriculum, with the preparation of music teachers, and with the whole significance of music in the life of the young person.

VII. Music of our Time

Chairman
FATHER NORMAN O'CONNOR, National Director of
Radio and Television, Paulist Fathers, New York

Speeches
The Substance of Things Hoped For
DAVID P. McALLESTER, Professor of Anthropology,
Wesleyan University

The Revolutionary Music—Jazz
STAN KENTON, Orchestra Leader, Los Angeles

Directions in Contemporary Music
GUNTHER SCHULLER, Composer; Head,
Contemporary Music Activities, Berkshire Music Center

Special Session
Pop Music Panel
Moderator: GENE BRUCK, Coordinator,
Concert and Symphonic Repertory, ASCAP
Panel: MIKE STAHL, guitarist and leader of the
Coconut Groove; and PAUL WILLIAMS, editor of the
rock magazine, *Crawdaddy!*

The Substance of Things Hoped For

David P. McAllester

Do you feel that music is slipping out of the hands of the music educator? Has the guitar become repulsive to you because it has fallen into the clutches of the unkempt to accompany sex and hallucination?

These and other musical and social trends may be a foreshadowing of profound change in the role of music educators in the society of Western European culture. What does "educate" mean? Is the educator the creator, the preserver, or even the destroyer? Is the music educator's job to preserve the great music of the past from abandonment and decay? Is it his charge to create musical taste? Is it he who will determine what future generations will consider to be good, great, or even "cool" music? Is he the one ordained to do battle with the Philistines, to destroy bad taste and fight the creeping popularity (sometimes the galloping popularity) of "inferior" music?

The music educator has come to take the role of preserver of a certain section of his music. A corollary observation is that in most of the other cultures of the world, if they are outside the influence of Western Europe, there are no music educators as such. And yet the music thrives. There is no society anywhere that functions without art, including music. The roles of preserver and also creator and destroyer in music, and many other roles as well, are performed, not by any one profession, but by everybody who has any interest in music, and according to what that interest is.

From this fact, I suggest the possibility that if we music educators feel that music is slipping out of our hands, perhaps the truth of the matter is that it was never in our hands as much as we thought in the first place. Our conception of our role in music has been much too limited. We educators have our influence, according to our particular interests and persuasions, but we are only one of many forces shaping the course of Western European music today, and some of these are far more powerful than we are.

The first is the incredibly rapid shrinking of the world, as far as man is concerned. McLuhan made the point when he said that electric communication has changed everything. We are all in instant touch with each other. Practically speaking, we now share the same nervous system. All men are indeed brothers; in fact, we are closer than that; we are Siamese twins, like it or not. How then can we go on thinking of "music" as Western European music, to the exclusion of the infinitely varied forms of musical expression in other parts of the world? The very word "music" is destined to undergo change in our vocabularies. It can no longer mean what it has to us for so long: our musical consciousness will have, inevitably, to expand to include the entire world of music. This change of view implies a tremendous opportunity for music education to expand its influence and for the musical community to enrich its content.

Another important influence is the teen-age revolution. The prime agents for the drastic cultural changes are our own children. We are confronted not with a mere lapse of sympathies between generations, so familiar in the whole history of mankind, but with a real moral, aesthetic, even physiological revolution. Its enormous power derives from the ironic fact that the young people are beginning to practice what we ourselves have been preaching. This frightens us to death. We counsel them at their mother's knee to love their neighbors, and they become draft refusers. We urge them to be creative and original, and they suddenly do so with hair styles, clothing, art, dance, and music that we cannot stand the sight or sound of. We bid them know themselves, and they launch investigations of ideas and of their own bodies that seem to us to threaten our whole way of life. The music of this revolution is particularly interesting to us, and it is of importance as we seek greater opportunities to reach our young people and influence them in what we think are the right directions.

The third influence is the revolution that is going on right now in the arts as a whole. Dance, theater, the graphic arts, literature, and music, all seem to be reflecting great changes in our society, though just what these changes are may be hard to understand. Yet is is apparent that the great majority in our culture do not like what is going on in the arts today and hope it is a temporary aberration rather than the substance of things hoped for. Most of us really do not understand what we see and hear. It seems to us to lack design, which is to say to lack *purpose*. A theater of the absurd; music by chance, out of the bowels of computers; novels about nonheroes or anti-heroes—most of us really do not know how to react to such things, and we have grave doubts about teaching them to the young. Even if we wanted to, we would not know how. Our ideas are still based on the reasonable categories of Aristotle. We expect art to have a beginning, a middle, and an end. We expect the arts to instruct man and to elevate him.

WORLD MUSIC

Parson Thwackum in *Tom Jones* defines religion as, "The Christian religion, and when I say 'the Christian religion' I mean the Protestant religion, and when I say 'the Protestant religion,' I mean the Church of England." We can no longer afford to apply such a definition to music in this day and age.

George Harrison has been studying the sitar under Ravi Shankar and performs on this instrument on the latest of the Beatles' records. Sandy Bull has issued one whole side of a record in which he takes nearly half an hour to develop Indian ideas in Indian ways with his great skill on the guitar. India has been the first of the "exotic" musics to make a real impact on the West. By real, I mean to the extent that Westerners are now not just listening with fascination, they are beginning to dedicate careers, their lives, to the performance of Indian music. Jon Higgins, a graduate student in ethnomusicology at Wesleyan, has just returned from three years in Madras, where he came to be hailed as a savior who might help counteract the influence of Western music on India. He gave performances in Indian vocal music, an extraordinarily difficult art, to audiences of thousands of Indians. Javanese and Balinese music have been a specialty of U.C.L.A. for some years. Last year I watched an impressive performance of African music and dance in Los Angeles in which there was not one native African. There is a group performing Japanese *gagaku* music at the University of Washington, and a *nagauta* group at the University of Michigan, where a Javanese *gamelan* orchestra has also recently been acquired. One of the two authorities in the United States on the Burmese harp teaches there. Besides its specialty in South Indian music, Wesleyan has a *gamelan*, and, among its other study groups, one is in the performance of the vocal styles of several of the American Indian tribes.

This broadening of interest is not confined only to the Beatles and a few colleges. Several rock and roll groups have followed the lead of the Beatles. The popular folksinging movement now includes African and Israeli songs, and there are high school youngsters learning American Indian songs and dances. These are not imitations of Indian songs on the order of the compositions of Charles Wakefield Cadman, such as are still taught in our schools. Now there are young people who can sing like Sioux or Ponca, an impressive achievement involving the use of a powerful falsetto, intricate quavers, tremolos, and other ornaments not heard in Western music. For certain genres of song, there are sophisticated drumming techniques very different from the "BOOM-boom-boom-boom" of the Hollywood Indians. A group of Puerto Rican youngsters from Brooklyn recently won an Indian singing contest over a very good group made up of actual American Indian singers.

Why go out into these exotic musics? Granted, they are difficult, exciting, challenging, but are there not quite enough of these qualities in our own music? "How often," one might ask, "is there an artist skilled and imaginative enough to turn in a really good performance of Beethoven or Charles Ives?"

I am familiar with this argument. When I first taught ethnomusicology at Wesleyan, music majors were not allowed to take my course for credit as part of a music major. Their time was fully taken up with courses on Western music. Besides, my course was "anthropology." But the argument had to collapse in the face of world events. The challenge to our insularity is too persistent to be ignored. A musical community that fails to recognize the wide world in this day of the Peace Corps and Vietnam is face to face with the spectre of its own irrelevance to what is happening in the world.

CONTEMPORARY ART MUSIC

Our dilemma here underscores the fact that, like it or not, our society has assigned to the music educator a role of built-in conservatism. Except in the sciences, where the new is unquestioningly considered to be the good, the school is generally regarded as the preserver of our great traditions of the past. This relieves the home of a tedious job and one that all too many parents are not really interested in, except ideologically. If it is too much to expect for the parents to teach the ancestral values in the home, so the reasoning goes, then we can make it compulsory in the schools. What these values are is not too clear, but at least children should have to read the things their parents had to read: *Evangeline, Paradise Lost, Ivanhoe.* And they should have to know about "great music," which is the same as "serious music." And they should be exposed to the "serious" musical instruments. Very rarely in this situation is there room for a predisposition for new ideas in music— a music that might be written for kettledrums and peapods, or some other "nonserious," whimsical combination, or even no instrument at all in the usual sense, but the squealing of electronic devices.

Perhaps this exaggerates the conservative role assigned to teachers by parents, but I think not very much. There is ambivalence in the minds of the American people about teachers of every kind, and perhaps especially about music teachers. A latent suspicion of the arts is particularly likely to break out when the ordinary American is confronted with a "bizarre" form of expression. Suspicion turns to outright hostility. The fear that the artist is putting something over on the lay public becomes a certainty. Witness the uproar so often attendant on a new wave of ideas in painting or sculpture or at a concert by Cage or Berio.

It is possible for us to meet these difficulties head on. We have a splendid beginning in the early grades, when children are sometimes lucky enough to get acquainted with rhythm and melody on all sorts of simple and unconventional instruments. They have the thrill of exploring the delights of free creativity without a long apprenticeship in technique first. I suggest that in addition to using this device as a stimulus to get children interested in "serious" music, we might also entertain the idea that someone who never does develop skills on conventional instruments could become a gifted performer on unconventional ones. It seems possible, also, that someone who never learned to read conventional music notation might nonetheless become an outstanding composer in some medium where notation has yet to be invented, or may even be impossible to invent.

We who are most concerned with music have the most urgent need to consider the ideas of even the most extreme of contemporary composers. It is essential that we challenge young people with the ideas from the forefront of our swiftly changing culture. If the ideas are new to us as well, so much the better. The excitement of making discoveries together can replace the boredom that so often follows when we rely too heavily on the warmed-over nineteeth century.

An inspiring illustration of what is being done to acquaint both students and teachers with contemporary music is the program of the National Music Council, in which young composers are placed as visiting artists in the schools. This has given young people the opportunity to see that, though composers may still have beards, they are not necessarily grey beards. They have been able to discover a new world of sound and stimulating new definitions of the word "music." An even more exciting discovery has sometimes been that they themselves can create musical effects that may never have been heard before.

I experienced this kind of excitement at first hand when John Cage was at Wesleyan for a year. The controversy he stirred up made the music department one of the "in" places at the college, and he inspired more than double the usual number of honors projects.

POPULAR MUSIC

The popular music of our own youth embodies high art and a content, both cultural and aesthetic, that must inevitably receive serious attention from the entire musical community.

I include blues, jazz, folknik music, rock and roll, and even raga rock. Collectively, this is the music of a subculture within our own tradition, and this subculture has challenged the dominant or parent culture even more imperatively than has the music of the non-European world and the music of our contemporary composers.

The muscle of the challenge, of course, is precisely its popularity. Financially, and in the size of its audience, it is the dominant music of our era. There are features of this music and its creators that are beginning to capture the attention of the musical community as a whole. For instance, it is not only patronized ("consumed") by the young, it is also increasingly produced by them. The top composers are also the top performers, as in the oral tradition, and for the first time in our cultural history, composers are the spokesmen for, and heroes of, the young. Pete Seeger, Paul McCartney, Bob Dylan, and many others are not only composers but also the leaders of a social revolution. Sometimes covertly, but usually overtly, they are the voices of the dissent of our youth. Their criticism is really not revolutionary at all, which makes it all the harder to take—it is the accusation of hypocrisy. They protest the behavior of the dominant culture for its departure from its own ideals, and they declare the allegiance of the insurgent generation to those ideals.

Those composer-performer-heroes have a tendency to be self-taught in music. If they learn their techniques from anybody, it is from each other. It is the same way with their millions of adulating followers. Note that they are not taught through our usual avenues of music education. Yet it should be a stirring thing for anyone concerned with the arts to see the social and aesthetic force of this music. It has become international in scope, and its content is now receiving serious attention from politicians, theologians, and philosophers, if not from musicologists. It is not *just* popular music, it is the music of a social and political movement, if you think of the folk songs that accompanied the civil rights campaign in which our young people, by their courage, shamed the government into enforcing ideals that have been plainly stated in our Constitution for nearly two hundred years. Or it may be the music of a social, philosophical and *anti*-political movement, if you think of the music of the hippies in their Utopian communities.

I would suggest some practical ways in which we can take advantage of this music. We should give this music a hearing. We can include it in the recognized canon of music along with our great classics *and* world music, *and* contemporary art music. This is a very telling way to show our young people that we are concerned with the things that matter to them in this world. We can include this music, along with the others, in the classroom. An analysis of rhythm, cadence, fugue, or variation, when made with music that our students instantly respond to, ensures that it is an analysis they will be interested in and will remember. We can provide bridges between popular music in the world heritage so that we may, indeed, enrich the students' aesthetic lives. By starting from a familiar and well-loved base, we can take advantage of this music to make music education an adventure full of meaning from the start.

This is a music that must be reckoned with, in the future of the musical community as a whole. This does not mean that all of us, or even very many of us, must abandon Beethoven and "turn on" with the Lovin' Spoonful or the Jefferson Airplane. But it does mean that we must give the word "music" a still further redefinition that will include such a vital force. We must inform ourselves and give this music an understanding rather than a censorious ear. Through it we may come to understand those who are our principal concern—our young people.

PERSPECTIVE ON THE FUTURE

Taking a cue from Kahn and Wiener's book *(The Year 2000)* I predict the following changes by the year 2000, or before:

1. In mass media, not only will we have a 6' by 9' color TV screen on the wall, by 2000 we will have put information retrieval to work and be able to dial an art show, the life of Napoleon, the Tokyo Philharmonic, the Sadler-Wells Ballet, a reading of T. S. Eliot or Allen Ginsberg, or any book from the world's greatest libraries magnified and in translation if necessary.

2. The nature of the audiences will be greatly changed. Solitary viewing or watching in small groups before the Great Screen will be common. Of course, the audience will number in the millions of such small groups. The big group function, what Durkheim would call the collective representation, where the group asserts its identity by an orgiastic sense of mass, will be bigger and better. Music audiences are already filling shopping center parking lots, stadiums, and whole city parks. This kind of musical be-in will expand, and Buckminster Fuller will invent new kinds of enclosures to contain them all. Our present concert halls will be obsolete, being neither small enough nor large enough, and too primitive both acoustically and in terms of human comfort.

Electronic amplification of every instrument, as well as of the orchestra as a whole, will make possible undreamed-of tone combinations and balances and totally new ideas in composition as a result. Some of the new music will be magnificent.

3. All the media will be employed in concerts. Milton Katims and Sarah Caldwell gave us a glimpse of this. The new ways of projecting film shown at Expo '67 gave us another dimension. Film, dance, and music will surely be combined to make concerts more exciting than we think we would be able to bear at the present.

4. There will be a guaranteed income in which musicians will be graded at a high level. Freed from most of the grueling necessities they face now, they will invent new kinds of live concerts. Since most of our stationary hours will be spent waiting for planes, airports will become cultural centers with round-the-clock string quartets, and anything else you'd care to imagine.

5. Education will be unrecognizable. There will be educational automats or shopping centers. Gone will be the grade school lockstep. If a child needs an intensive week on the viola or the stero-electronophone, it will upset nobody if he takes that week and does nothing else.

With videotape playback, it will be possible to learn a musical instrument the way we now instruct in language laboratories. In ten weeks we will equal four or five years of present instruction; and the Boston Symphony will give contracts to young people with the braces still on their teeth.

6. The music educator will have leisure. With his drudgery eliminated by automation, he will have ample time to deal with music, instead of trivia. He may well have a joint appointment to the school and to the municipal government. If his inclinations lie that way, he will be a key man on the arts council, with plenty of time for it. He will be expected to do much in terms of imagination and organization for the artistic life of the whole community.

Music education will, of course, be revolutionized to train such specialists.

7. Gifted musicians of all kinds will move in and out of educational activities. A rock artist of the year 2000 will have equal status to that of any other fine musician since guild barriers will have become irrelevant.

8. The music of the whole world will be available. We will have American musicians skilled in South Indian ragas or Navajo chants, as

casually as we have people in this room who can speak French. There will be various levels of competence depending on talent and interest, just as there are with the French.

Just to give you a taste of the future, and because we have not so far had a single note of music in all these sessions, I am going to end by singing an American Indian song. It is not a Navajo chant but a corn-grinding song. The men sing it in the way of encouragement while the women grind corn. They discovered the secret of leisure, by means of music, long before the year 2000.

He ne yaheya, he ne yaheya
'Awe 'icho—wowo, 'awe 'icho—wo
Hane, hane, ha ne yaheya
etc.

The Revolutionary Music--Jazz

Stan Kenton

Somehow I think a person gets more from music than he can get from any other artistic source. Constant exposure to music makes a person grow and mature. There are all kinds of music in his life; he finds that if he keeps conditioning himself or exposing himself to music, after a few years he's looking for another music. He is looking for another music because he needs music that reaches deeper and says more to him. The most "doing," creative, achieving people I know are people that expose themselves to music all the time. They get up in the morning and have the radio on before they even clean their teeth, or fix their coffee, before they get in a car and go to the office. I think we Americans are quite lucky, because we have more music thrown at us than any other people in the world.

My mother was a piano teacher. When I was about ten years old she started me on the piano. Neither of us had heard of jazz at the time. After a couple of months she gave up in disgust and said,"Forget it; it's not worth it, nagging at you. Let's try again some other time."

When I was about fourteen years old, I was down at one of the beach cities in Southern California with my family. While we were walking around the pier, the pleasure area, I heard a band, six or seven pieces, playing a music that hit me. There was so much excitement to it. I ran up to some of the people standing around and said, "What kind of music are they playing?"

And some guy said, "Kid, that's jazz music." I never had been contacted by any music like this before. I don't recall whether it was Dixieland music or what form of jazz it was, but it was live and it hit me. So I went home and I told my mother, "I have got to start studying music again, because I want to learn about jazz."

I kept looking for jazz teachers and there wasn't any such thing. Then I started looking for phonograph records. We would find somebody clear over on the other side of town who had a jazz collection, and we would make all kinds of arrangements to get over there and hear his records. We would feel very rewarded if he would let us go in and listen to records for a couple of hours; then we would ask to come back. Gradually that is the way we started working in jazz. I started meeting other young people that were interested in it, too; and from that time on, I started studying music and hanging around beer joints and places where they played jazz to learn more about it. I was still searching around for jazz. Jazz meant so much to me that I felt jazz was the "new music." As I got older, I felt that it was going to replace all music. Not only did I believe this with all my heart, I went about proving the difference between jazz music and traditional music. This went on for a number of years, this battle of trying to prove the validity of jazz and to get people interested in it.

It was only about ten years ago that I said, "What is jazz music after all?" I started trying to analyze what it had done, and I realized jazz is not the "new music" at all, but what jazz has done to all music is something that causes all music to never be the same again. Jazz has changed the rhythmic interpretation of it.

I really believe that the music that meets the needs of modern man and man in the future will not anywhere near satisfy him aesthetically unless it has the jazz ingredient. The traditional world of music is cold to modern man. There's a certain excitement, there's something that you get from jazz music that has never been known in music before.

In the 1926-27 period there were bigger bands organized, and bandleaders at that time started to write music for their bands, to write arrangements. It was quite a struggle because they didn't know what they were doing, and the musicians didn't know how to interpret the music. For the most part, the arranger and the composer would get in front of the band and sing each part over and over again until the musician would try it and the arranger would say, "That's it. Now let's try it."

And they would try it and they would have one arrangement possibly worked out, and then they would go and work on another one. All they were doing was trying to imitate the conception of the composer as he projected it to the musicians.

This went on through all the name-band period in the thirties and in the forties. I know that all of the bands—the Dorsey bands, Miller, Artie Shaw, all of the bands in this field of American music—were actually conducting their own little schools of music in their search to find an identity. They were working on new arrangements. They wanted new sounds, and that's what gave them identity.

This went on until the war, when the bands disappeared. After that those of us that are younger started going through a change ourselves. We couldn't somehow create new music unless we started deviating from what was called "American dance music." So we started taking liberties with the music. We started using tempo changes, all kinds of time signatures, and all that sort of thing. We had a dickens of a time trying to play our music. You couldn't play it in a ballroom, because you would antagonize the dancers.

In our struggle to bring about a fresh music, we started going in new directions. By 1947, people started saying, "Stan, what kind of music are you playing?" And I said, "We are playing jazz." They were stunned because, they said, "It is not like any kind of jazz I have ever heard." I told the people, "From now on, refer to the music as 'progressive jazz.'" The name stuck, and we've used it ever since. We felt by calling it "progressive jazz," it gave us liberty with our music to create something different and fresh for the audiences.

Dancing diminished.

It was around 1948 and '49 when something started happening. There emerged a thing called a stage band. We started listening to these stage bands, and in a rapid period of time, they got better and better. I remember I used to worry about "why" this stage band. They told me it was satisfy the objection to dance music in the "Baptist belt" of the South.

Gradually we started getting interested in these stage bands. There was no place for a stage band to study. I don't know what percentage of schools had competent band directors, but it was so small that it was ridiculous. About ten years ago, we started what were called the Kenton Clinics, because there was such a need to help these young musicians become oriented in how to interpret this music and what would be expected of them in the field of jazz. They have continued right to the present day.

About three years ago, I was so bothered about the direction of this music that I said, "Something must happen with it. There has to be a greater expanse of music. Music has to have better form. We have got to get away from this eight-bar introduction, sixteen bars on a bridge, and a thing, and a thing, and then a chord. This is the third or fourth generation of men that have studied formally traditional music. They want to express themselves. This is the second or third generation of jazz composers. These fellows have studied and they know what they are doing." But there wasn't any outlet for them. They could not get a performance out of a symphony orchestra, because it wasn't written that way. It needed to be interpreted by jazz musicians.

So we went about establishing the Los Angeles Neophonic Orchestra. This happened three years ago. We took the finest jazz musicians in Los Angeles, and we organized them. We did four concerts the first year. We did four the second year. The third year we ran into financial trouble, and we hope we are back doing them again this year. We are now concerned with the development of form, and all the things that the traditional world of music has been working on for a long time, but we are in the jazz form of expression.

I began to see the point of stage bands. There was a particular thing stage bands got out of music education, and the young musician must go through it if he is going to be capable of interpreting modern music. We started looking for schools that have open minds about stage bands. Not many of them give credit for stage bands, but there are some excellent college bands and high schools bands today. We might say that the stage band is possibly the grammar school, the primary grades, of new music. And Neophonic certainly is the university. Possibly there will be another direction after that.

When rock 'n' roll came on, it baffled all the modernists in the field of jazz. None of us knew exactly what had happened. We started worrying about it because the drawing power of jazz started dropping, and rock 'n' roll started gaining popularity. I think Jerry Fielding has a beautiful theory about this. He says, "You know what happened in modern jazz? All of us in modern jazz have got the jazz music honed down so sharp and it's so 'inside' and so 'hip' that it doesn't communicate with the young people. You couldn't tell them this is a sophisticated form of modern music. They just threw up their hands and went about creating their own music." And I think to this day that is the best explanation of what happened.

Today the jazz musicians are back trying to create music with substance in it, something that will communicate to the people. It is getting back to a happy sound again. It is more complicated than it was before, but I think just as jazz caused a revolution in traditional music, rock 'n' roll has caused a revolution in jazz music. I don't know how fast things are going to be happening in the future, but I think we are now sitting in a rocket and we are moving.

Directions in Contemporary Music

Gunther Schuller

I think our most serious problem in music lies in creating an audience. We have the performers, and we have some excellent talent in the composing world, despite the negative gurglings of some of our critics. The problem doesn't lie there but in the communication gap that has been created between the audience and the performer and the composer. This communication is particularly a domain where the music educator must function and can help.

We must start building his audience, not at the level where we are now concentrating our efforts, namely in higher education, but at a much earlier level. I'm delighted when people tell me that they are taking eight-year-old children and having them sing, or play, or write a serial-technique music or aleatory music; but let's face it: this is not yet a national occupation. It is an area and a discipline of which most music educators are not aware, or indeed are not capable of teaching.

We must find a way to involve young people at the earliest possible state, emotionally and intellectually. We must take music very real and vital for them, and I think the only way to do this is by telling them the truth. Now, in music "telling the truth" means differentiating between what is quality and what is not—a very sticky subject, because it remains largely a matter of opinion. Nevertheless, there are many more objective factors in music than we often like to think; and insofar as they exist, I think it is possible to give the young student an education which will continually direct him toward the one thing that really counts: quality. Only through that can you involve them emotionally and intellectually.

When I was much, much younger, I was forced to read what I thought was a terribly dry and esoteric essay by Ralph Waldo Emerson: "On Self-Reliance." I'm sure that relying entirely on my promptings or inclinations I would never have read this essay. However, it was a required thing; and I remember having, in the reading of it, what James Joyce so marvelously called an *epiphany*—a revelation. Suddenly, the essay logic of this great piece of literature penetrated my mind. I guess I wasn't older than eleven years at that time. I have drawn on that experience, not only the particular thoughts that Emerson expressed, but the revelation that something that was forced on me was a kind of discipline that I had to accept; and that became meaningful to me. This is an important point, and I relate it to music in this way.

Musicians are still considered sort of second-rate citizens in the United States—not perhaps at the bottom of the social ladder, but certainly not near the top. While things have improved marvelously and we have very active and sophisticated music centers at the universities and some of our metropolitan cities, we still have to recognize the fact that, for example, an institution like the concert band (not to mention the stage band, which is still fighting for its existence) was initiated to perform music for football games. We still have many universities, even a university like Michigan, where they do indeed play some remarkable music with this band; but their primary function is still to play at the Saturday afternoon games.

Particularly in America we tend to regard music as an activity which is fine for professionals, who want to go into music and make it their livelihood, but not for others. For example, there is not much effort made to educate musically someone who is going into the sciences.

To go back to the example of my reading Emerson, I believe if more were required both in terms of quantity and quality in music education at all levels, and particularly at the very youngest levels, we would then create the possibility, the potential for these epiphanies—revelations which would be with these young people for the rest of their lives. There are no guarantees, but I think one needs that kind of a revelation and that kind of emotional and intellectual involvement with music as a quality thing in life, a necessity of life. If you haven't had that, there's nothing to build on, only quicksand.

We have to be much more serious about this, and we have to get away from the notion that music is mere entertainment, in the casual sense of the word. Music is entertainment in the highest sense of the word. We take the sciences very seriously, and we don't look for a way out there. We don't look for a way out with mathematics or many other subjects. But in music we are always trying to make it easier and give the impression that it really isn't necessary, that you can get through life without music. Through that is developed a sort of anti-intellectual view toward music. The average person grows up with a view that good music is really a sort of emotional bath, in which you immerse yourself in concerts of nineteenth-century music; and anything that doesn't fit into that category is eliminated. I think the music educators must find ways of breaking this kind of emotional resistance.

Related to this is the problem of our mass communications media and mass education. I am terrified by the possibilities here, because having much greater potentialities, the dangers of failing are also greater. As music education develops with these new techniques, particularly those of automation, it might set its sights for an education of the masses and might, it turn, get not a mass education, but a mass pseudo-education. The danger here is that of broadening the amount of education without the related deepening of that education.

If you teach music in the depth and breadth that this art demands, you will get a hard-core nucleus of really committed people; then you can spread that horizontally through the whole culture, through the entire society. But, if you try to operate from the other vantage point, namely of getting this mass education done, whether it be by means of computers or television, you are in danger of not involving the people emotionally and intellectually.

Related to this point is the fact that music is for all people. The *Rockefeller Panel Report* states: "The panel is motivated by the conviction that the arts are not for the privileged few but for the many, that their place is not on the periphery of society but at its center."

In a democratic society this is certainly true, but there is also this danger I just mentioned. Let's face it: not everyone is equally created, and certainly in music we can't say people are equally gifted.

There has to be a hard core from which radiates quality. Then you can get to the periphery and involve them as much as that hard core of committed people will allow. One mustn't approach it from the other end and try to get everybody involved with music, because it cannot really be done. I think the whole history of the arts proves this thousands of times.

If you music educators become involved in teaching music in the depth that it requires, there may be less people, but their commitment will be real. If you do it the other way, in a more superficial way, you get more people, but the commitment isn't as deep. It is tenuous; the first commercial music that comes along will pull them away. (I must interpolate right away that I am not opposed to commercial music. I like all kinds of music from all kinds of cultures, but we must recognize them for what they are, as subcultures.)

Another danger for music educators is to try to relate music to the other arts. This is done in a variety of ways, but all of them seem to aim at not getting involved with music as a separate art. They tend to promote a general sort of liberal arts view, such as is taught at two year colleges—which results too often in what Oscar Levant so brilliantly called "a smattering of ignorance."

Related to quality in music is taste, or judgment. This is a very difficult thing to teach. I believe it can only be taught on the broadest possible knowledge of the entire subject of music. You cannot be privileged to indulge in opinion (which you then call judgment or taste) unless you have endeavored to learn as much about the music both in breadth and depth as is possible in a human lifetime.

Along with this, I think we must begin to de-emphasize something which our orchestras and our opera houses, and to some extent even our educational institutions, are overemphasizing: the "masterpiece." We all love masterpieces and we like to listen to them. On the other hand, if you look at music history in a proper perspective, you must recognize that each period yields very few masterpieces. We tend to expect a masterpiece every time we sit down to a new piece, and this is absurd. Music is constantly growing, constantly in a state of flux (as it should be), and you cannot in this experimental stage expect a masterpiece. We must get away from this masterpiece complex of thinking that everything really should please us in the way that the Schubert's *Unfinished* is able to please us. It leads to the museum approach, which is indulged in by so many of our famous performance institutions around the country.

Music is a living art; a music score doesn't even exist until it is performed. We have to feed this art by our full, devoted attention, and support it at the highest quality level.

One thing, too, that music educators can do is to promote the notion that all of the subdisciplines in music ought to cooperate more closely with each other—theory, composition, musicology, ethnomusicology, performers, and so on. We tend to have too many educational institutions. I have inherited one at the New England Conservatory, where every little subdiscipline regards its territory like a warlord did in medieval times; and there is no communication between these various disciplines.

The way we can all get together is by the emphasis of the one common denominator: the composer, the creative impulse. He is the thread that runs through all of them. Therefore, if we support the composer, insofar as he is worthy of support, we can then all coexist much more happily together.

I believe that the music educators can create the climate for healthy survival of this listening, living art.

To speak briefly about the directions in contemporary music, I think we are entering a period of synthesis, of amalgamation, and of sifting out of the many directions and conceptions and revolutionary ideas that have been suggested in this century. As you are aware, since about 1910 music has been undergoing a continuous series of radical changes. Every time we think it's going to settle down, it seems to start up again with still further expansions and extensions of previous ideas.

I may be optimistic to say that we are going into this synthesis period, but I do see many signs of this, not only among the more established composers but particularly among the younger composers. I see, for example, a synthesizing of such opposing positions as the serial technique and the aleatory approach. I think what will happen is similar to what happened between Stravinsky and Schoenberg. When I was a young composer, these two composers and all of their disciples were not on speaking terms. But, ten or fifteen years later, it all became one common language, common not just in America, but in Japan and among the Eskimos or whatever. The same thing can happen in these two directions, aleatory and serial.

There is also the whole category of electronically generated music and computer music. We now have instruments which will make this practically a household music. We are beginning to have portable electronic instruments which can be played and which can be performed on by any individual. Here at Tanglewood, in the orchestral concert in the Fromm Festival of Contemporary Music in two weeks, we are going to do a work written for an instrument called the "Syn-Ket." This is a portable synthesizer on which you can perform. Once having programed a certain amount of material into this computer-type instrument, you can perform on it by means of toggle switches and a keyboard. It gives you several thousand possibilities at any one sitting.

Now, you can imagine what marvelous things can accrue from this. Perhaps you can also visualize the dangers. We have heard of Sunday painters. We are also going to have Sunday composers. I think with horror about all the electronic effects that people have heard in movie scores (Frankenstein movies) now being done every day on Syn-Kets. And there are several other instruments of similar manufacture. Believe me, this is not so far off. Some of these only cost a thousand dollars or so, and it is as simple as buying a tape recorder.

Nevertheless, all of these things are now being thrown into a huge melting pot. Composers are saying, "Let's sift this material out, let's see what is really viable, what is going to survive; and let's work with that." And I think what will come out of this is the kind of digestive period which, for example, preceded the arrival of Mozart, who was handed a common language and common style and, being the great talent that he was, was able to fashion one masterpiece after another.

In the future we will see the art of music at two separate levels. What you will have is this very sophisticated, very complex serious music, which will baffle the majority of the audience. If the music educators do a proper job, it will at least communicate with a small minority. Then, at a totally different level you will have the other kind of musics, and there are many of them, which will operate on a functional level, much in the sense that music functions in "primitive cultures."

I had occasion to study African music very thoroughly, for

example, and I discovered that the word "art" doesn't exist in any African language, because art is not a separate thing from life. All the music that exists in African culture has something to do with some kind of function, be it a birth, a death, preparing food, or whatever. I think we are coming to this functional level in music. I shouldn't say "we are coming to it," it exists. How this will affect music education I am not yet prepared to say. I certainly tend to think that we shouldn't exclude these other musics, which will have their own proper function in society.

We have to take it at both levels, and it would be better if we did not think of them as "higher" and "lower" but simply as different and both of very great value, of necessity to the survival of our culture and our society.

Pop Music Panel

Gene Bruck, Mike Stahl, and Paul Williams

Gene Bruck: Before introducing the two panelists, I would like to say that my qualifications as moderator follow the axiom that a good moderator is a person who knows very little about the subject but has a tremendous amount of curiosity. Perhaps there is something in the so-called popular music which is complex, more lasting, and more involved in the daily patterns of both young life and life than the "popular music" before, and perhaps there is something in rock that might help us all.

Therefore, we have two young persons involved in rock here to tell us not so much what it is, but what it is for and what it is about. Let me introduce first Mike Stahl, who is a guitarist and leader of a group, The Coconut Groove, now playing at the Bonsoir in New York. He is attending Wilkes College in Pennsylvania as a political science major, and plans to be a musician, a rock 'n' roll musician. He is 21. Mike, is that old for a rock musician?

Mike Stahl: No, I don't think so.

Bruck: Paul Williams, our second panelist, is the editor of *Crawdaddy!*, a rock magazine that has existed for quite a while. Mr. Williams serves the function here not of a musician, but of critic, apostle, historian, and perhaps even creator of a new language and literary form, in relation to rock. To start off, Paul, how about some perspective of rock (and I presume it's rock and not rock 'n' roll)?

Paul Williams: Rock, pretty much now, yes.

Bruck: What happened to roll?

Williams: It dropped off for simplicity.

Bruck: To simply start off, How does rock relate to the other current popular trends, such as country and western, and folk, and blues? What is its relationship to those forms, if any?

Williams: Well, rock is by far the most popular music in this country and I think in most of the Western world right now in terms of mere numbers of people listening to it, buying records, and so on. And what has developed into what we call rock, in other words rock since the Beatles, is a very eclectic music, very consciously eclectic, very consciously reaching out for as many possible influences and new ideas rather than old rules. So you have, for example, country and western as a considerable influence; it's always been an influence on vocal styles. Country and western is one of the indigenous vocal styles in the United States, and the Beatles learn directly from people like Buddy Holly and the Everly Brothers. The Everly Brothers are almost an example of country and western singers turned into a popular rock 'n' roll group. There are groups where you can pick out various specific things. The Byrds and the Buffalo-Springfield Strings have taken a lot from country music. The Beatles, for that matter, split from country artists like Carl Perkins. The early Beatles stuff, and anytime they do a song like, "Everybody's Trying To Be My Baby," they are taking very much from what is country and western in this country.

Blues is probably the most central influence on rock 'n' roll, mainly because the blues has somehow been the central influence on all American music; in many ways it's the oldest native American music. Its influence on rock 'n' roll was clear at the beginning; rock

'n' roll was originally Negro music. The term was invented by a white disc jockey who gave it the name of rock 'n' roll. When it started catching on, white artists would record the same songs that had been a hit in the Negro market, with the same arrangements and the same vocal style. You take an Arthur Big-Boy record and then you take Elvis Presley and show him how to do everything the Big-Boy did, and then you release stuff like "All Right Mamma" or "Hound Dog," and Presley is essentially those same songs, only coming out of a white face instead of a Negro face, which was important in those days. Then, it can sell to the white market and be played on the radio and everything else.

Eventually, of course, Negro artists became important in the white market, too. Fats Domino was maybe first of all. But this Negro music wasn't at that time blues either; it was what we call rhythm 'n' blues. It was blues that took on the aspects of the city—just like the people themselves who had come North, say, up from Mississippi to Chicago. Sonny Boy Williams, in the 20's and 40's, started playing amplified harmonica, and amplified guitars began to creep in. The model for the modern rock 'n' roll band comes from the Chicago rhythm 'n' blues band which began to develop in the late 40's and early 50's. People like Muddy Waters came up from Clarksdale, Mississippi, and instead of playing solo bottleneck guitar or singing with a couple of friends, they would have an actual band system where there would be a drummer, and somebody would play the harmonica, which was usually amplified. There would be a guitar, a piano, and a singer, and you had essentially the basis of what is now considered a group—amplified music.

The reason for the amplification, as much as anything, was its equalization. On stage, a guitar and a piano are not really matched against each other very fairly. So you get into the concept of an electric guitar with changing modulation and volume, and a good deal more control over the type of sound you get.

Bruck: And folk music?

Williams: Well, when you have a group concept in playing, immediately you need more than amplified instruments. The reason for the amplification was for more versatility.

Bruck: And what about folk music, the great protest folk?

Williams: Looking back on it now, the great folk protest boom wasn't anywhere near as real as all the fuss was. In other words, the term "folk music" certainly wasn't the proper term to apply. It was a form of pop music, and because everybody called it folk music, they thought this was the beginning of something where Frank Crockett would become as popular as Elvis Presley, and everybody would start listening to the roots of America; but this never happened. Most of the folk music was just pure pop stuff. However, the folk music boom gave us the first clear example of a singer/ composer, of the people who wrote and sang their own songs, which is now very basic in modern rock 'n' roll. A real difference between rock 'n' roll today and ten years ago is that now most of the important artists are writing their own material.

Stahl: I think today rock is completely different. What is melodic and what is not melodic means a lot when you are writing a song. As part of the Coconut Groove, I know when we sit down and listen to a song, we say, "Boy, I like that sound; it hits me right in the ear." Now it agrees with Coconut Groove. The Coconut Groove likes that. So, the next time we go out, we say, "Let's see if we can write a song to capture that same song." First we try to get the music, because we like to get an infectious melody. You can listen to it once and you can remember it; the words come later. I think lyrics today are very important, much more so than they were. There used to be a very hard-rock beat that everybody would listen to; today, I think the words are much more important. The beat doesn't have to be the hard rock, but it does have to have something that will stick in your mind. It has to catch you. Trying to find a sound for a group is very difficult today. You can't be imitators. Anybody can imitate, but you have to be original to make it. No group can make it on material that another group has written, because they won't sell it to them. It's that simple. You have to have your own material.

Bruck: What about words? Do you know what rock is about? What is the relationship between words, the meaning, and the people who listen to it?

Williams: The words are a part, but not necessarily a literal part. You won't understand a rock 'n' roll sound by reading the lyrics. Actually, rock 'n' roll is moving much more toward traditional music, where it is not really valuable to take the words literally; rather you feel it on an artistic, on an aesthetic level. You don't have to hear the lyrics; I mean, there's nothing necessarily wrong if you hear the sound and can't figure out the words.

Bruck: What I'm aiming at is that we all hear about rock, that it reflects a certain way of life, adopted mainly by the young, and an attitude toward the world—a form of companionship and protest for young people. What is it about?

Williams: I'm not sure I know what you mean.

Bruck: All right, to put it another way: Aside from the fact that you like it that way, is there any other reason why your hair is long? That's part of it, I assume!

Williams: Right, right. The long hair has probably been discussed much too much already. It's a social thing and nothing more. It's a style. You dress a certain way to show people that you are a certain way. As for lyrics . . . it would take a long, long time, you know, to explain everything. On the back cover of one of the Beatles' albums the lyrics were actually printed to make it easier for people. Their song, "Fixing a Hole," purposely comes close to being nonsense, because that's part of the feeling they are trying to get out.

[Williams reads the lyrics of "Fixing a Hole."]

Bruck: It's a long way from nonsense. We've had great experience with nonsense verse, and that's hardly it.

Williams: Well, it's literal, but it's also meant to be silly in a certain sense. It's meant to give a feeling of easiness. I think you get more out of listening to the track musically without the words than just reading the words. Neither is valid alone. It's the whole thing that communicates. The Beatles throughout this whole album—*Sergeant Pepper's Lonely Hearts Club Band*—are essentially reaching out and telling the listeners, "It's ok. We understand where you are." People are getting older and things are getting more complex and they are getting involved with different scenes. People begin to feel disoriented. They may feel very good about what is going on directly, but at the same time they have great doubts and begin to think: Am I losing track of what's going on? Am I losing track of myself? And

here the Beatles are saying, "We know where you're at; it's all right; it's groovey." They are reaching to comfort, they are putting an arm around your shoulders and saying, "Don't worry about it, it's ok. It's great." And this is the whole nature of this album. It's very strange, and these lyrics would have been even more strange a couple of years ago.

Bruck: I have to break in here to ask either of you: Who listens to rock? Who takes rock seriously among the young people, and is it so far away from the older generation that they will never comprehend it? I'm trying to bring it to the point where we might find some use for it.

Stahl: I would say that the young people who grasp it the most are the ones that are really looking for something to grasp. They are alone. They need something more than they are getting, and they turn toward this rock music.

Bruck: Isn't that a typical adolescent attitude?

Stahl: Maybe so, but I think it might be more dramatic if you walked down to Greenwich Village. There are quite a few different types of adolescents in the Village, and maybe they need this type of stimuli. Maybe they are finding in this rock what they can't find in other places. Maybe it's the long hair, maybe it's a form of rebellion, maybe it's something else. Maybe they can just express themselves through rock 'n' roll.

Bruck: As listeners or performers?

Stahl: I'd say either way.

Bruck: Do you think that the number of performers will grow? After all, there isn't that much professional competence required to be a rock 'n' roll musician, or is there?

Stahl: Oh! I would say that is one of the biggest fallacies going: that rock 'n' roll musicians don't have to be good musicians. Listen to the Jefferson Airplane and listen to the Beatles. George Harrison is now a world-renowned player of the sitar. Many of the rock musicians have a lot of formal music training.

Bruck: Do you ever conceive of an institution or a curriculum for rock 'n' roll?

Stahl: Well, music is music. I think to get people interested in music, the main thing is to offer them something they like. If they like rock 'n' roll, have them study rock 'n' roll, and maybe they can go on. That's exactly what I did. I took piano when I was in the third, fourth, and fifth grades, and I practiced every day, and I couldn't stand it. I didn't want any more of it. Then in the ninth grade, all of a sudden I wanted to play the guitar; so I picked up a guitar, and I played it for five years. Nothing else. Then I was playing in bands and everything else. Now I know there is so much more to the guitar than what I can accomplish just by listening to records and playing by ear. I am now starting to take lessons and learn how to read music.

Williams: The reason people enjoy studying music, after all, is that they are interested. It communicates. You can express yourself with it. If you teach them piano by teaching "Clair de Lune," they are not going to be expressing themselves very fully. It's like playing the typewriter with no words coming out of it. The whole reason we value music is its capacity to communicate, if you are a listener, and its capacity to express, if you are a creator or a performer. So, to keep people interested, you've got to give them the reality, music as music, and allow them to really express themselves. I think the only way you can do this is to relax and find out from the kids themselves how they feel and what they would like to play. Ask them to whistle something. Find out what it is. Teach them how to play that.

Bruck: That seems to me a very germane statement. In an article in the *Saturday Evening Post* on pop music, you say very much the same: the rock is absorbing everything, but that doesn't eliminate everything else. The people who are in rock are becoming more open-minded toward what's really good, and they are getting turned on to other sorts of things like Billie Holiday, John Handy, and even early Baroque music. As a result, even modern contemporary jazz and classical composers must try to measure up.

By this, do you mean that young people no longer have to be simply idolizers of Frank Sinatra, or whatever idol who comes along, but should be interested in the rock form that is growing more and more complex? Obviously if rock has changed, in ten years it will become more complex and worthy of a professional. Do you see this as an educational system, and what can we do to measure up?

Williams: I think it's definitely educational, and what you can do depends on what you want to achieve. First of all, let me ask a question: What goals do you specifically want to achieve as music educators? I mean, is it a greater understanding of the history of music, or of the nature of music, or notes and so forth?

Bruck: I think that the ultimate goal of music education is to involve as many people as possible and to give them the opportunity to grow into any direction as either listeners or performers. I think you will agree that this is a good goal.

To move on, I would like to read an excerpt from a criticism in *Crawdaddy!* by Sandy Pearlman. I read it this morning to the group and they were quite astonished. "The Byrds, being a group, have real formal constancy. From time immemorial, they have ground their music in what are or what seems to be obviously regular rhythmic patterns. It is out of this ground that all developments and variations seem to rise, as it were, to the surface. This sound is dense, but not obviously or impressively complicated. That is, it is very coherent. It works because of its unity and not out of an accumulation of contrasting effects such as volume changes or syncopations. Here the contrasts inherent in any rhythmic pattern are not at all emphasized. The changes in the basic rhythm patterns are not necessarily gradual but rather nondramatic." This is a very complex and advanced way of describing a popular form. I've never quite read anything like it. How did it arise? What is *Crawdaddy!?*

Williams: Well, Sandy arose quite suddenly from a school called the University of New York at Stony Brook, which is very advanced and allowed him to become a rock star while he was there. After I had been publishing a rock 'n' roll magazine for a while, somebody put me in touch with him, and I discovered there are a lot of people in universities across the country who have been studying rock 'n' roll on a fairly simple level, or studying the history of it. What Sandy had actually done was to begin to formulate in his own mind, and with his friends, a critical basis for understanding what the music is and how it communicates. In doing so, he changed the nature of the magazine quite a bit. The magazine itself was started about a year and a half ago with the idea that rock 'n' roll deserved serious commentary because there are people who are interested enough to want to discuss it. As editor, it's pretty much my decision as to what I think is important to our listeners. In other words, I will eliminate one group and set up another strictly on my judgment of what's musically important. What we've done is to get into the concept, I guess, of rock music as art. One thing we have tried to do, which I think is very important, is *not* to formalize it. Sandy has taken a formalized approach, but not

the magazine itself. There's another writer who takes a different formalized approach, Richard Nautzer. He is very concerned, for example, with transitions in music. Other things we write are not as intellectual, but I consider them equally important.

Bruck: Who reads *Crawdaddy!?*

Williams: To some extent, rock 'n' roll groups, themselves. In general, I would say it has an age category of about 16 to 25, with quite a number of people older than that. I suppose that a great many people who are actually playing the music found themselves becoming very interested in it.

Bruck: If the reason why I have pursued this is because this is a literary expression rather than a musical expression, then perhaps it leads us to wonder how, as educators, we might bring back rock into the colleges. Mike, if you should come to my campus and talk to my musicians, what would you do?

Stahl: I've found so many educators that are against rock 'n' roll musicians and rock 'n' roll, just in general. They feel that it's not the thing that should be taught. It would be great if I could go to a college dean and say, "I'm a rock 'n' roll musician; I would like to learn some more about it." I would probably get thrown right out. I think it would be fabulous if people would say. "Fine, come on in; let's see what you have to offer," or "Let's see what I have to offer you."

Bruck: I think, although we have much more to say, with such short time, we will open up the floor to serious questions.

Father O'Connor: I have a tremendous sense of history today, because on my right is a childhood idol, not maybe in childhood, but in my early teens. I made a discipline of collecting the works of Stan Kenton, and what I can remember is literally hundreds of hours of musical missionary work in which I actually brought in my friends. When the new Kenton record arrived, there was a kind of a religious silence in the front room, and if there were any disturbances, I would hate these. There is no noise while Stan Kenton is going on; it is a deeply religious kind of attitude. Now, I have just recently become a fan of the music that you spoke of as complex. When the Jefferson Airplane came along, that's when I got it—I love it! But there's a concentration problem that I have because of the simplicity of the textures. Now, you've spoken of this music, both of you, as gradually becoming more complex; and yet it seems to me that what we had, let's say fifteen years ago, was much more complex. Mr. Kenton's music seemed to me (and I was a performer then and a writer) enormously complex. Everytime I heard "Laura," I heard some progression that I just couldn't figure out. This music, however, as our culture has become more complex, has seemed to become extremely simple.

Do you envision now, through study and scholarship, the National Institute of Rock 'n' Roll, or a Ph.D. in rock 'n' roll, or something like that? Do you imagine that perhaps this form will gradually evolve into the more complex forms of the earlier music we enjoyed, or do you think we will be able to keep this marvelous simplicity that sets rock 'n' roll apart from the greatest jazz of the past?

Williams: I think that, while musically most rock 'n' roll is not as complex, there is as much complexity in it, if you mean by complexity that the implications are on a great many levels at once and you continue to go back and get new implications and new discoveries in the music because rock 'n' roll has become the beauty of finally having an art form that is also of pop music. At least something about pop music is that it takes on a social complexity as well as a musical complexity. There are implications in a rock 'n' roll song which can be close to infinite, and which can be really beautiful and can operate on a social level. I'll give you an example of what I am talking about: "Respect" by Aretha Franklin. It is a very well done piece. Basically this material has been done a number of times before; it's a very good arrangement. Aretha Franklin has been recorded as she should be: as a gospel singer singing hard rhythm and blues for a white and Negro audience. The backup is perfect. Atlantic has the best Negro musicians working for their label and the best producer in that field. It's still the traditional pattern—the horn break in the middle of the song, a basic drum pattern, and so forth; however, the song can be considered almost historical in its value of the nature of words as an examination of the English language today.

The whole nature of the song, if you take it and study it, is the taking of a word, "respect," and the reduction of it to, first, specific metaphorical meanings, and then all meanings, and then no meaning. By the end of the record, when she spells out the word r.e.s.p.e.c.t., it has been used to the extent that it can have any meaning you want it to. Because of all this, the implications in rock can be very complex and very deep, and very beautiful; and this is what is being achieved with the song, "Respect."

Bruck: We've come a long way from Irving Berlin, I must say.

Joan Gaines: Assuming that the moment might come when it is decided to bring rock into the classroom: With the very serious attention that has been paid to the new album, *Sergeant Pepper's Lonely Hearts Club Band,* do you feel that the music teacher is equipped to teach the Beatles' music?

Williams: I think, as with everything else, you've got to do your summer reading. By all means, subscribe to my magazine! Try to get certain, specific records and listen to the radio, even if most of it is not very good. Get the feeling of what top-40 radio is, having it going as people do in their cars while driving around during the summer. Notice the way the top 20 hits work in and out from one week to the next. Every week there are a few changes; five changes one week, five the next.

To understand the nature of rock 'n' roll, you've got to get used to hearing it. Naturally, any kind of music doesn't sound like anything the first time you hear it. For example, to appreciate *Sergeant Pepper's* you can listen to it carefully, on one level. However, to really be able to reach it, I think it would help to listen to earlier Beatles music, also to listen to the Rolling Stones. It's important right now to listen to the Beach Boys, who are certainly one of the most creative rock 'n' roll groups in records. The Beach Boys have synthesized a number of different things in the record, "Good Vibrations," and the same sort of synthesis is used in the composition of post-Baroque works. You could work from the Beach Boys back to Bach in explaining to a student how music is composed. I'm sure there is a lot of listening to be done.

Bruck: We have time for another question.

Max Kaplan: I have two questions: One is aesthetic, and the other is sociological. Would you not run a risk by having your new tradition incorporated in the academic framework, since the very nature of your work seems to be rapid and spontaneous? Secondly, sociologically, what do you think is the relationship of your movement, if that's what you call it, to the hippies?

Williams: The first question is very easy. It's simply a matter of self-confidence on our part. You definitely run a risk, but I think that getting the academic into rock 'n' roll would speed up the academic,

which I think is necessary.

Bruck: I think Mike wants to talk about hippies.

Stahl: If it wasn't hippies, I think rock would be connected with something else. Maybe people consider hippies have long hair, and rock 'n' roll musicians have long hair, so that's the connection.

O'Connor: The strange variations in audiences with regard to white rock and Negro rock in which you don't find them crossing the boundaries, so to speak, so often on the Beatles I would call conventions, and the audience is dominantly, almost exclusively white as the case offers. I was wondering if this has significance or misinterpretation. Also, I would like to see you express to this audience something of what you feel are the energies which could be of value to them in terms of their classroom techniques in teaching and particularly in regards to modern contemporary music of the classic composers, the jazz composers, and all this sort of thing.

Williams: Well, the first question is quite interesting. Negro music is just as popular among whites as Negroes.

Stahl: I would say even more so.

Williams: But it doesn't work the other way. It's beginning to. "Grooving" by the Young Rascals, "A Whiter Shade of Pale" by Procol Harum, are making it to the top of the rhythm 'n' blues charts. It's taken a long time. This is merely for social reasons. To a certain extent, of course, people who've been listening to the Negro stations aren't ready for *Sergeant Pepper's,* because they haven't heard the other Beatles records. They have specifically become accustomed to one kind of music. But it's mostly social. There's a pride which operates, which means that you listen to the radio station that represents your community. This is really not a musical problem.

Stahl: I think white audiences like to hear Negro music from a white band even though a Negro band could play it much better. This again is a social problem, but you find it so apparent that many white rock 'n' roll bands today are incorporating so much more, they call it Negro soul music, within themselves, because they find that it appeals more to white audiences. And these white audiences would rather hear the Negro music from a white band.

O'Connor: Do you think rock 'n' roll will influence other musics, other contemporary composers? How do you see yourself developing? Do you see a Gershwin rhapsody or a Mike Stahl rhapsody in rhythm 'n' blues?

Stahl: I don't know. I'll have to wait and see how things develop. You can't just say: When Beethoven was writing the *First,* could he see the *Ninth?* I can't jump ahead that far.

Williams: It's very difficult because rock 'n' roll is an eclectic music and some of the forms that rock 'n' roll is taken from are not eclectic; so for that reason, I don't want to talk about Baroque music. I'd just make a fool out of myself. Indian music and Eastern music are making a strong impact on the Beatles and certain other modern rock 'n' roll groups. Rock 'n' roll is not making much musical impact on Eastern music for the simple reason that Eastern music is very traditional, not eclectic at all. It's very beautiful music and based on a great history and certain techniques which must be followed. Therefore, rock 'n' roll is very unlikely, at least for a long period of time, to affect that music or affect in any way the music that Ravi Shankar plays. Rock 'n' roll has given him many more listeners, and a more attentive audience. It's affected his career, but it hasn't affected his music because his music is not eclectic and it can't absorb rock.

Bruck: I suppose it isn't the responsibility of the rock musician to impinge his music on anyone else.

O'Connor: Well, I think that one of the problems we face in terms of evaluating is to define the substance of rock.

Williams: Just because of its eclecticism, it does not have substance; it's rather a style. If you pull the style out, then you would actually be creating rock. Igor Stravinsky was creating rock when he wrote "L' Histoire du Soldat" because this style is a rock style. Rock may actually become synonymous with music, not because all music will be like this but rather because it's a growing thing which is going the other way. It's a style of approach to music in which the basic thing is the ability to take from all music and present it in a way that can relate to all people.

Bruck: That's a very fundamental objective of all music, to find a style that will amalgamate and be popular.

Williams: I think it's working toward a universal music, which does not mean the elimination of any music, by any means.

David McAllester: Two observations: One is that Ravi Shankar is influenced by Western music in his musical style. More traditional classical musicians in India criticize him. He's a great writer of film music in India, which is popular classic music, and the old style classical musicians are very much distressed by it and consider it degraded. The other observation was to come back to the matter of complexity. I thought your responses were important, because in a group like this we have a very narrow, traditional definition of what is musical complexity. You illustrated with the analysis of text an area that we have hardly discussed in music, and there are other areas, I think, in rock 'n' roll and in other musics of the world where things like vocal texture are so complex that we hardly know how to discuss it. I think rock 'n' roll is an area where this is true, too. Vocal and instrumental texture, and the use of electronics in rock 'n' roll music permit an instrumental sound texture that has enormous sophistication, and we don't even have the vocabulary to discuss it except perhaps in your magazine.

Bruck: Well, Milton Babbitt can probably discuss it quite well. I think we have time for one more question.

Donald Shetler: Young men like you are younger versions of what we once were; and in our youth, those of us who were jazz musicians, and who played Stan's charts, and who worked the road, always contemplated the possibility of having a crack at the music educators. Well, now's your chance, Paul and Mike. If you had a message to give us, what would it be, outside of tuning up and winding up, and playing something for us and maybe trying to reach us that way? What would you have to say for us?

Stahl: I expressed it before, but the point is I hope you have a more open mind. I know specifically in my college, Wilkes College in Wilkes-Barre, Pennsylvania, rock 'n' roll music is taboo. We just don't mention it here; and if I could walk into the music department and say, "I'd like to learn how to read music, or to learn some kind of voice control to help me sing rock," the dean would throw me right out on my ear.

Question: How do you define true white and black rock?

Williams: Well, I think we try not to use definitions in general.

Question: But they are different.

Williams: Yes, historically. Rhythm 'n' blues is the euphemistic term in the trade for Negro pop music; it is played on stations with Negro disc jockeys with a predominantly Negro audience. In the 30's the term was race music, and the records were only produced to be sold in the South. Today there are records made only for the rhythm 'n' blues stations; but these records also sell largely to the white market. Probably one-third or maybe forty percent of rock 'n' roll that the white market buys is actually Negro music that is also successful in the Negro market; the only difference is in the traditions. In other words, rock 'n' roll includes a number of things other than the specific traditions such as rhythm 'n' blues. There's Motown, there's the Memphis sound.

Barry Gordy, who is a Negro and the owner of Motown records in Detroit, is now putting on all his albums "Climb Every Mountain" and as much Broadway stuff as he can. That's totally irrelevant. The Four Tops, the Temptations, Smokey Robinson, and the Miracles are among the most brilliant artists we have, and they are being destroyed because Barry Gordy somehow believes that these people belong at the Copa Cabana, and he doesn't even realize that the people at the Copa Cabana would rather hear the Supremes sing "You Keep Me Hanging On" than "The Girl from Ipanema." Now Gordy, the man most important in Negro music, is being produced by Atlantic records, particularly by Stacks and Bolt, which is staffed by Negroes, but the people in charge, those who see that it all goes right, are mostly white. Right at the moment it looks as though it may be necessary for whites to preserve Negro music.

VIII. Basic Issues

During the first week of the Symposium, all participants were requested to meet with one of five Subject Area groups, which considered particular issues or areas of critical concern to the profession. On the following pages are the reports of these five committees.

Committee Reports

A Philosophy of the Arts for an Emerging Society

Music of Our Time

Impact and Potentials of Technology

Economic and Community Support for the Arts

The Nature and Nurture of Creativity

Subject Area I

A Philosophy of the Arts for an Emerging Society

Members of the committee on A Philosophy of the Arts for An Emerging Age: Max Kaplan, Chairman, Page Bailey, William H. Cornog, Alvin C. Eurich, Freda Goldman, William C. Hartshorn, Warner Lawson, Father Norman O'Connor, and Ralph W. Tyler.

The general charge put to this committee was titled "Values: Music as Means and Ends," and "Music in the Emerging Society."

The working paper that constitutes a prologue to the Symposium notes that the term *values* has enlivened and plagued philosophical discussions for many generations. The writers note also that in community or educational circles, and whenever there is competition for time, budgets or governmental assistance, the general feeling of warmth for the arts as valuable must somehow be translated into terms that can be grasped.

The committee came to the Symposium with no illusions that it could, in a limited time, grapple seriously with either the broad issues of values, or a translation of its deliberations into clearly understandable terms for purposes of strategy. It hoped neither to enliven nor plague, but to bring to the Symposium a degree of focus upon highly important issues.

The general positions on major issues. The following propositions or positions set the general terms and issues for the committee. They emerge from the experience we brought to the conference; they were sharpened during the many addresses by Symposium speakers at plenary sessions; they permeated, in part, our committee discussions; and with the sequence or even a direct consequence of the report, these position statements point toward the material that follows:

1. We look upon a vast body of social change, as do many in other disciplines, and see enormous upheavals in every phase of life. These changes occur in objective aspects, such as greater abundance in goods, faster travel, quicker communications, more services, decaying cities, civil strife, large-scale cybernated economic production, growing government, and continual international tensions.

2. Perhaps more than in some other fields, leaders in education and in the arts see in these changes the even more disturbing impact on personal and social values, described in such terms as anomie, rootlessness, "killing time," waist-high culture, "alienation, anonymity, and a whole range of emotional illnesses. Many observers are more deeply concerned with the strengthening of human dignity, love, and self-realization than with the mere accumulation of goods, speed of travel, or television sets. They are especially concerned with the strengthening of family ties and the quality of living that would characterize them.

3. In addition to these positive *concerns,* there are elements in the current order of change that can be used to utilize change in support of constructive *values.*

4. Among those means that provide transition to new human conditions are the arts, which reflect positive values, for they are deeply rooted in human needs, in man's nature, in all of his history, and even in his new, post-industrial technology. For example, access has been provided to a broad range of recorded music for almost everyone. Quantitative evidence abounds everywhere of concerts in halls, schools, clubs, parks, and community centers. Quantitative criteria are more subjective and, therefore, the quality of much that is presented may be debatable.

5. It is incumbent upon music educators to bring higher quality into new and familiar contents of quantity, by developing audiences as well as performers — audiences that extend far beyond the school, that touch all age groups and all segments of the community.

6. This enlarged commitment of music education comes at a period in American life when there is an increased need to prepare us for more leisure time. There is a clear need for education, at all levels, to approach music as one major prototype value for leisure alternatives.

7. Thus the statement of "values" that becomes a foundation for articulating and implementing musical experience in the school is increasingly germane and significant for *all* ages, and most especially in an era of revolutionary change. These values, spelled out early in the report, must be grounded on what Northrop calls the "immediately apprehended" as well as the objective or "inferred" meanings. As this eminent philosopher calls for a synthesis between these on the broadest panorama of world cultures in his *Meeting of East and West,* so this duality is dynamic for purposes in music education, and calls equally for a new, conscious synthesis.

8. The emerging world of new social tools, institutions and sources of power is paralleled in emerging musical forms; and indeed, some of the "new music" is as much a manifestation of intergenerational breakdown of communications as it is of radical sounds *per se.* Thus, there is need for a new aesthetics, or at least a reappraisal of familiar aesthetics, to confront and understand music that now emanates from new technology; there is also need for a close inquiry into the place of musical styles and fads in the value systems of young people. Altogether, music educators must take clear positions about temporary music, characterized by this double-headed fact of life among youth.

9. The reconstruction of schools at all levels is a movement that relates directly from new technology, urban growth, and other external societal changes; but also, from better understanding of young people, theories of learning, methods of teacher preparation, rapport of philosophy and of social sciences with education. It is

now incumbent on music education to examine in depth how its characteristic purposes and its inherent nature as an art can best contribute to new educational directions. On the other hand, music and the arts are not only uniquely *creative,* and thus grounded in constant self-change and creative exploration; they are also *preservative* and are, symbolically, direct links with the past. Change may have value for the sake of change, but primarily in a situation of boredom or satiety. Tradition also has value in itself, but primarily in a situation of complacency. What is needed are new formulations or pragmatic directions that recognize continuities and ongoing human and social needs, as well as new, even disturbing tendencies that are irrevocable, provocative, and hopefully significant.

10. The reconstruction of the larger society parallels in many ways the changes close to the teacher and the student. We take the position that the school, and music education, must become more sensitive to social processes and take a more vigorous part in directing social change or in contributing to a recognition of its potentials for good.

11. Finally, we wish to assert a belief that in periods of transition, a national professional organization must itself face a re-examination of its roles, its strengths, and its potential relationships to all of the issues of the report.

Committee procedures. The model for the committee, in its total of fifteen hours, was the string quartet. Such a model provided a degree of freedom for each participant within the larger unity. We first discussed the general issues as stated in the working papers. These were then reduced to major clusters of issues, and taken over by various members of the group in terms of respective expertness. Committee time was then allocated for individual writing, followed by group reaction, and again by individual activity.

Dr. Tyler assumed major responsibility for the opening discussion on values; Professor Bailey, on the "new aesthetics"; Dr. Cornog and Mrs. Goldman, respectively, on education in general and education for adults; Dr. Kaplan, on social change; Dr. Lawson on special problems of music education in the city; Father O'Connor, on attitudes toward change; and Dr. Hartshorn, on the applications of Northrop and Broudy for music education.

I. SOME CONSIDERATIONS TOWARD A PHILOSOPHY OF ART IN AN EMERGING SOCIETY

The increasing rapidity of change in modern industrial society has many implications for education in the arts but several seem of major importance. Greater productivity is increasing the incomes of the majority of American families with corresponding increase in their aspirations, not only for material goods, but also for the intangible "goods" that have heretofore been largely reserved for the most affluent. We may expect most American families to aspire to participate in the arts and to expect their children to include the arts in their education. In this sense, music education must include all or nearly all children.

New attitudes favoring research, innovation and change, combined with expanding worldwide communication, provide a climate favoring new music: new forms, new sounds (Eastern as well as Western), new musical instruments and techniques, and new contexts in which music will be performed. Music education in the future will be able to draw upon these new developments.

The range of technologies and technological devices available

to schools and colleges, and a new interest in research and development of educational procedures, devices, and programs will furnish music educators with a wider range of means for carrying on education in music.

Increased hours of non-work time, coupled with the lengthening of human life and the higher level of education of adults, will provide a background for continuing education in the arts. The hope that schooling serve only as a beginning for a lifelong education can become more nearly a reality. Music education can be conceived as a long-term process with the period in school representing the development of interests, initial understanding, and basic skills requisite to carrying on more or less independent learning in the future.

Increasing specialization in occupations and the relative anonymity of modern life afford greater opportunities for the arts to serve in helping the individual find meaning in human life and to share with others by participating in the arts. The realization of such possibilities depends upon relevant selections of musical experiences and musical content, for they will need to lend themselves to these purposes.

The preceding comments are suggested as a general background against which more specific ideas and proposals can be considered. Another general perspective is needed relating to human values, since the arts themselves are valued by many if not most Americans, and they also serve to represent and to enhance other values.

Some types of values. From the standpoint of the individual, a value may be defined as something he cherishes and seeks. The importance of values lies in the fact that much of human behavior is directed by the concepts one has about what he cherishes, that is, by what he "values." Anything can be valued by someone; thus, a specific list of human values would be limitless. Even a listing of main categories of values that serve to activate Americans today is likely to be incomplete. Nevertheless, the following list of kinds of values may serve to illustrate their variety:

1. To belong to a "society" in contrast to being alone or an outcast.
2. To "get ahead," to gain status and respect from those whose judgments count.
3. To possess or to use material things.
4. To help other people, or to see other people happier. (altruism)
5. To perceive and enjoy aesthetic qualities in an object or an experience.
6. To live in accordance with one's sense of what is right. (moral values)
7. To satisfy curiosity, to understand things. (intellectual values)
8. To use one's abilities effectively, that is, to be active, and to be skilled. (craftsmanship)

This list is obviously incomplete, but it suggests the possibilities that young people may recognize and the choices they make as they grow up in building their own hierarchy of values. These choices are often unconscious unless instruction is planned to help young people to identify and to evaluate their values. Fortunately, most of the types of values listed above are cherished by many young people, although their relative importance to the individual differs markedly.

Values as means and ends. In addition to the values themselves, human beings direct their behavior in various ways to attain values that are cherished. Thus, to some persons, the way to gain respect and status is to be a patron of the arts. Their actions in supporting and attending musical performances reflect this view of art as an instrument of status. This fact has relevance in music education, both to indicate objectives and to suggest some additional ways by which students may be initially involved in musical experiences. It is possible for students who enroll in music courses to be motivated initially be values other than those appropriate to music, but it is also possible to plan educational experiences in such a way that some of these students develop genuine interest in music and cherish musical values. Thus, it is important to isolate those values that derive psychologically from the experience of hearing or creating music from those values that relate musical experience sociologically to external or dependent values. Further, each of these types of values have their own criteria and distinctive implications for the teaching of music and for its place in school and society — both of which have always been dynamic factors of music.

As it will be noted in Section V of the report, both dimensions of values are related to trends in the emerging American and world society. It is not the fact that the psychological approach is related to music as an end — music in its "independent" functions — and that the sociological approach leads only to consider music in its dependent, secondary, or referential functions. Both branches of the social sources deal with this duality, for just as individual and social values are functions of each other, ends and means in music blend in the actual experience.

There is, however, a current trend (and, in this committee's judgment, a sound development) to restore some balance in the *validation* of music as an integral body of experience in the school by re-emphasizing the inherent, or aesthetic, values as an educational end.

Developing behavior that is supportive of values. In opening up the consideration of values in relation to music education, it should be clear that teaching values is not necessarily *indoctrinating* or forcing new values on students. But because the meaning of "teaching values" is often unclear, it is less ambiguous to talk about the "learning side"; that is, to consider what students can do that will help them in developing more significant values and in gaining more enjoyment from them. The following partial list will serve to illustrate what students can do in their learning that may be important in the field of values:

1. Participate in activities that *explore* values new to the student.

2. Try to *discover* things in these experiences that are interesting and meaningful.

3. Reflect upon past experiences to *compare, contrast.* Evaluate the things in them that are satisfying, meaningful, or disappointing.

4. *Practice* abilities and skills useful in gaining values. (For music, there are likely to be skills involved in identifying aesthetic elements, in gaining understanding of the work, or increasing sensitive apprehension of features in the work.)

5. Listen, respond, recall other similar or related experiences so as to *enhance* both the meaningfulness of the musical experience and the emotional responses made to it.

6. Relate the emotional response being made to several kinds of meaning found in the musical experience so as to *discipline* the emotional responses in relation to their meaning and their consequences.

These comments are intended to suggest the relation of values developed by individuals to the dominant values of a society, a culture, or a subculture within that society. From the point of view of educators, their efforts are to assist the individual in developing values that are uniquely his while at the same time they are helpful in enabling him to participate constructively in the common life of the society. *The emphasis should be to help the individual to be able to explore, identify, and develop new values throughout life — ones that help him to be more fully human.*

From this general discussion of individual and social values that are supported by music, we turn to the object itself, to music, from the view of its aesthetics. On the one hand, there is a venerable literature on aesthetics as a branch of an enormous literature in philosophy. Committee deliberation, whether by inherent wisdom or in the interests of time (itself an American "value"), cannot with impunity ignore this tradition. Yet on the other hand, music itself has changed in basic sounds and internal organization; hence, we consider the need for an aesthetics that seeks to build upon its heritage so that it may deal with the new music. It is not a question as to whether music education should be concerned with an aesthetic system, for every classroom in which music is heard or explained is a communication that is grounded, knowingly or not, in aesthetic premises. It is well to sensitize the teacher of music, if not the listener, to his assumptions as an interpreter.

II. A NEW AESTHETIC FOR MUSIC

Aesthetic theory has, in the past fifteen years, been profoundly attacked by advances in technology, cultural anthropology, and communications. Modern technology has made it possible to produce electronic instruments such as the Moog, Buchla, Syn-Ket, and Trautonium. These are capable of ranges and varieties of sound never before thought possible. Gunther Schuller remarked recently that electronic instruments such as the Syn-Ket may soon be available at prices that will bring them within the range of many American families.

Cultural anthropology has made the music of exotic cultures available to us all. Ethnomusicologist David McAllester, of Wesleyan University, has said that: "The music educator of the future will not only teach the music of exotic cultures, but will be proficient in the performance of the music of the culture he deals with."

Today the phrase "instant communication" has taken on new meaning. Not only are we instantly in touch with events around the world via communication satellites, but we have before us the project now being carried on by the American Telephone and Telegraph Company which, if successfully completed, would make available to educators intradisciplinary information from computer storage centers via special telephone lines capable of both voice and picture transmission. The prospect of instant access to music from numerous cultures, never before considered in the educational system of Western Europe, places the music educator in the center of yet another manifestation of learning in this postindustrial era.

Toward a new conception of the aesthetic. It is hardly surprising that such an age prompts us to the consideration of a new aesthetic theory which is: a) sufficiently general to account for aesthetic experience rooted in electronic music and in the music of exotic cultures, and b) sufficiently exacting to meet the epistemological standards that the scientifically-trained young person has come to expect from that which is presented to him under the general rubric of "knowledge."

Aesthetic theory before 1950 was very much under the influence of the work of Plato, Aristotle, and Immanuel Kant. For purposes of this discussion we will speak of this line of thought as the "old aesthetic" as distinguished from one possible aesthetic which, for purposes of convenience, we will now refer to as the "new aesthetic." No pretense is made that all forms of the new aesthetic follow the description given here.

The old aesthetic (and one does not need to be reminded that such a phrase commits the sin of oversimplification) carried on discussion of works of art in terms of four interests which were thought to correspond with four elements which are, supposedly, to be found in all works of art: 1) form, 2) matter, 3) purpose, and 4) the relations that exist between the first three. The *tools* for the discussion were the tools of common language, although in the case of Kant the common language was enriched considerably for the treatment of aesthetic judgment. The *method* by which discussion was carried on was what might be thought of as a pyramid technique; one of the four traditional interests was made fundamental to all the others and the philosophy consisted of an explanation of just how the one element selected is, in fact, fundamental to all the others.

The weakness of such a procedure is twofold: a) words from common language are multidimensional entities and are, by nature, history, and actual use, incapable of referring to singular entities; and b) the choice of one of the four elements supposedly existing in all works of art is an arbitrary one for which no justification is ultimately possible.

The new aesthetic. The new aesthetic can be understood by looking directly at a) its "interests," b) its method, c) its materials, and d) its purpose.

The old aesthetic concerned itself with *four questions,* each requiring description in terms of either the species of work being discussed or a particular work: What is form in this genus or work? What is the purpose of this genus or work? and What is the relation that holds all of these together? The interests of the new aesthetic is singular and can be expressed in the question: Is the object under consideration to be admitted to the genus for which membership has been suggested? In music this question then takes the following form: Is the work X a musical work?

The *method* of the new aesthetic is descriptive, but it is well to observe that it is not without normative content. Words from common language are replaced by symbols which have a positive mode of reference, that is, a clearly defined range of reference. If the work X involves sound, is a candidate for admission to the genus of objects called "musical," and can be described by a formal language (symbolic language), then the work X is said to be a "musical work." This criterion which refers us to the possibility of description in a formal language is known as "the criterion of expressability."

The *materials* of the new aesthetic are the formal languages (symbolic languages) which are suggested to test the describability (expressability) of the musical work.

There are five *purposes* toward which the new aesthetic is directed:

1. It directs the attention of the student to the factual, or public, character of the object before him.

2. It directs the attention of the student and the teacher to the development of the capacity to hear detail in a "musical" work, and to express this detail accurately and in a symbolic language that is consistent and creative. The student might be encouraged to develop the symbolic language himself; the language will become richer as the student hears more details in the musical work and seeks to describe them.

3. It places the work of the general music student (the development of descriptive-evaluative skills) on the same level as the skills of the performing musician.

4. With the development of descriptive-evaluative skills by the general or special music student, a knowledgeable audience may be more assured for the future of music. The objection is sometimes raised that although such a system might, in fact, guarantee a knowledgeable audience for music, it would not guarantee that the audience would "appreciate" music. Here the proponents of the new aesthetic reply that "appreciation" is not teachable, and that concern with such an indefinite attitude is not the proper interest of the music educator. The music educator is to deal with the factual, public, measurable content of musical works. Such appreciation as the individual student is capable of will come about through the choices and responses that are the proper object of his experience and are not public. The job of the music educator is to put the student in contact with the objects, the skills, and the capacity for response that might be called appreciation but, when real understanding is present, ought to be more accurately described as *wonder* and *love*.

5. The shift from interest in the appreciation of a work to the knowing of a work is designed to place music again in that role in the academic program of a liberal education, which it has not occupied since the Middle Ages. To say, "I appreciate the musical object X" is to say nothing that has any public meaning. To say "I know the musical object X" is to say, " I can describe, with a unique description (applicable to one and only one object) the musical object X."

The teaching of the new aesthetic. The new aesthetic is pointed toward the development of skills available to the general music student who does not read music or play an instrument. This student must be given an extensive set of particular exercises which teach him: a) to make particular public judgments which uniquely describe the musical phenomena before him, and b) to express these judgments in a formal (symbolic) language.

The development of descriptive skills (particular public judgment and the expression of these judgments in a formal language), and the application of these skills to the vast sea of possible musical objects available for discussion, are both exciting and creative. William Cornog suggests below that music educators are, even now, being asked to "dance a new tune." We suggest that the new aesthetic will be most useful in keeping music education in step with that tune, whether it be from the culture of the American Indians, South Sea Islanders, or from the Moog, Buchla, Syn-Ket, or Trautonium.

The values for which music is taught, and the aesthetic approach to its teaching are primarily functions of the school. Music in this country has been increasingly sanctioned by public educational policy since the Boston breakthrough in 1838. It would be unrealistic to suppose that the large proportion of American children are exposed to music on any regularized basis. The facts show quite the contrary. Yet, with changes in the home, and with a more comprehensive curriculum in the past 130 years, the school has clearly emerged as the major institution in which large numbers of children obtain some exposure to the arts and music.

Various speakers of the Symposium, particularly Samuel Gould, drew in some detail the projections of the schools of tomorrow as they will be affected by technology. The present curriculum, addressed to classes, will become radically flexible; computerization will serve individual needs; bodies of knowledge (as now in engineering) will be outdated within a decade.

In the paper that follows, a straightforward statement sets forth the case for music that is pertinent in any school, anytime, with any degree of "formlessness," any size, or any budget.

III. MUSIC IN THE SCHOOL

"She Walks in Beauty." If a justification must be constructed for music either as a performing art or an aesthetic experience in the curriculum of American education, it can be done on the basis of postulates regarding the nature of a school, the nature of man, and the relation of music to both.

1. Schools exist to pass on the cultural heritage of their society. Music is a part of that heritage. Music belongs in the curriculum.

2. The nature of man demands certain cultural and aesthetic outlets and some means of creative and re-creative expression. Music from earliest history, and apparently in all times and places, has been a major means of experiencing both sensuous-emotional and intellectual-aesthetic feelings and a means of expressing "thoughts that lie too deep for words."

3. The nature of music is infinite variety and adaptability — qualities assured by the almost limitless scope of sounds audible, malleable, or recognizable, by man.

Thus, if one asks why music should, nay *must*, be part of formal education, if we accept the postulates, then one says that as a subject of study or inquiry: 1) music belongs with the social and cultural heritage, 2) music is profoundly related to the nature and the man, 3) music is in itself, by its nature and by reason of its extraordinary fluidity and plasticity, one of the great challenges to the mind and spirit. Like the arts generally, its province is as wide as the world of man and as deep as the heart of man.

Since a school curriculum, however specifically child-centered or community-centered, must forever be *man-centered,* music is amply justified as a part of it.

So far as a school has problems of educational presentations, music teaching must be organized, though music has always taught itself more and often better than it has been taught.

The principles of organizing music teaching are not unlike those applicable to other subject teaching. The differences arise from the specific skills and innate gifts that characterize mastery of a performing or a fine art, as distinguished from other disciplines. It is, of course, the business of music educators to find out how music may be taught and to do it.

How much music should be taught and to whom are questions that we think have no valid generalized answers. However, much personal prejudice presses us to say, "as much as possible to everybody." How much, to whom, at what point in the school's program depend largely on 1) the community, 2) the energy, forcefulness, and competency of the music teachers, and 3) the presence or absence of administrative and other reactors or obstacles.

The basic question for the future of music in America is how well prepared the music teacher will be, and how well supported by inner and external strengths. Will tomorrow's music teacher be prepared — that is, not merely *trained* but emotionally and intellectually ready to meet challenges such as:

1. A radically changed society, both in physical terms and in its value system.

2. A radically free state of the art of music.

3. A radically different kind of teaching and performing equipment, including the lavish gifts of technology and sophistication.

4. Students with more musical sophistication as in every other way, by reason of the electronic revolution and the impact of mass media.

A final question for the music educator in an emerging society is: When that society emerges and says, Shall we dance?, **who leads?** At that moment of truth, which is not far off if it is not already upon us, music educators as a profession had better know the new steps and tune in on the new beat. They can only do this for themselves. But we know that if they don't, not all their scholarship, nor status, nor expertise, nor pride, nor wit will save them from wallflowerdom and that old rockin' chair.

The lady music is of much ritual adoration. She often slips past the virgins who *guard* her *shrine* and goes dancing in the street.

The reticence, the humility, the defensiveness of some music teachers resemble the fearing and behavior of faceless acolytes or pallbearers.

If music is to have a rebirth, or is to be born in America, it is the music educators who should first raise the cry, "She lives!"

To do that they must let themselves see her radiant face. This will take courage and faith, and a good deal of spiritual and intellectual stamina. But more and more teachers now have seen the lady and report that she indeed walks in beauty like the night, /Of cloudless climes and starry skies."

The lady who "dances in the streets" reminds us that her home is everywhere. Music is one of those experiences that can become an easy carry-over into the home and beyond. The relationship of home and school has long been an issue in music education. It always will be. But a new, related problem now emerges: the role of the music educator in reaching out to the adult directly. The basis for such a concern is our next topic.

IV: THE LARGER SCHOOL: EDUCATION OF THE PUBLIC

Underlying premises on which we talk and argue need to be stated explicitly. Thus, several assumptions were noted in the preceding section:

1. Education has always been the means of passing on skills of survival from one generation to the next.

2. In more complex societies, we pass on not only skills but values, that is, the culture we wish to preserve.

3. Music is part of a culture, serving both utilitarian and spiritual needs. Larger underlying assumptions about our American culture as a whole also need to be recognized, such as:

    a. The democratic tradition that we accept at the theoretic level has implications for the pretraining level in education.

    b. Thus, we believe in equality of opportunity for all, and have come to reduce this to a concept of serving all the children.

    c. The schools are a means to "success," serving as elevators to status and happiness.

The emerging society and purpose in lifelong education. As an educator approaches the task of setting policy for his area of education, he accepts a certain view of the contemporary culture and points his subject area to it. This is particularly so when considering the adult, for he is deep in the affairs of the world. Thus, in deciding what part music should play in education, we begin with one or all of the following characterizations of the contemporary (and emerging) culture, indicating in broad outlines the new demands on education the characterization reveals. One may characterize the contemporary society in a number of ways. Three characterizations seem fruitful and valid:

1) This is an age of science and technology. While the development of science promises a vast number of additional improvements in the life of man, it has challenged man's inner image of himself. Viewed scientifically (mechanistically), man seems in his own eyes a dull creature, surrounded by and limited by machines that diminish his sense of personal worth.

The imperative for music education, as inferred from the above characterization (much oversimplified though it is), is that music along with other arts and humanities, should be explored by educators as a possible countervailing force to the prevalent emphasis on things and abstractions, restoring a sense of subjective individuality.

2) Modern American society has also been characterized as the "affluent" society, and therefore as the leisure age, or the age being sought, and a philosophy of leisure is likely to develop.

The imperatives flowing from this characterization of our society are that we need to bring music (and art) into the lives of people so that we help them change the style of life itself. In the affluent society, people need to find in the cultivation of music an occupation that can provide, in part or in the whole, the values now derived from work: identity, commitment, a central pole for one's life.

3) Still another way in which the modern age is characterized is as the "age of anxiety." Man is unsure of his ground; he has given up the traditional safeguards against fear and loneliness (religion, rationalism, and so forth), and he has only a vague suspicion of what can comfort him. In the face of an illiberal, even anti-liberal spirit, he seeks in aesthetic experience not only pleasure but also a new understanding of himself and his spiritual place in the universe.

Implications. Dealing in broad generalities and attempting no one-to-one relationship between date and implication, one may arrive at a number of inferences for content, audience, and form of music and arts education from the analysis above.

With respect to content, we might say that we must prominently include the contemporary in the curriculum. In selection of educational experiences, we ought to adopt a "now" attitude, not only preparation for the next step but with satisfaction now. But along with this "be" experience, there is need for continuity in learning what must today characterize all education, that is, aiming to go beyond formal schooling.

With respect to audience, the conclusion from the analysis of the modern world given here is that all men (young and old, bright and dull) must have access to music education. But this does not mean that all need the same opportunities, nor want the same things. A comprehensive design is needed that covers all needs, but a flexible approach that makes it possible to fit different kinds of experiences to different needs. Examples of audience groups are: teachers of music; producers and performers; listeners and "friends" of music bodies; amateur performers, and young amateur composers, retired businessmen, and disadvantaged youngsters.

A note on adult and community education. All that has been written above also applies to adult education; but a special note is necessary. First, a special premise has to be accepted: The music educator's philosophy should encompass a responsibility to the adult community in relation to two kinds of educational needs. *Remedial* education is the traditional form of adult education — the school attempts to provide an opportunity for people to "catch up." The aim is to remedy the effects of deprivation, to offer chances that were available to others in an earlier time in life. Students here include new arrivals, second-chance seekers. Education, for them, provides a place to acquire basic skills and information. Another form of education that fits under this heading is the upgrading education, catching up, keeping-up — all "further" education; (for example, professional education for teachers or producers of music).

Already observable and implied in most analyses of the future, is the decline of the form of education that provides remedies in favor of a form we may call *continuing* education — education that provides uninterruptedly throughout life. This kind of education is mainly informal in nature. What was needed and available only to a governing aristocracy in the past is now accessible to wider sections of the population. For the present population, this education must be structured and offered formally through schools and other educational institutions.

The program desired, however, should be flexible, offering the already "educated" man a chance to continue his preparation for a more thorough experience of living. It should call on resources of music institutions as well as of the school. As an example of music education programs for adults, Milton Katims told the Tanglewood Symposium of the seminars that the Seattle Symphony has offered during the season's annual performances.

What should be the direction of a program of continuing education in music?

To persons of all ages, it should offer an opportunity to move as far in depth or in breadth as each man can, through a comprehensive program of music that will equip him to live in the modern world.

Music should be offered to adults both for instrumental purposes, to satisfy psychological, religious, and vocational needs, and for expressive purposes, to help each individual find means for self realization, either as creator or as participant audience.

We should have as a possibility in the educational program for those who want it, developing a "leisure occupation" in the music sphere. This means developing the role of audience member (for the nonmusician) by being not only a listener but also a tastemaker, by not only enjoying but also sharing in determining the destiny of music.

All we do should be part of an organic whole, with a beginning and a future direction implied. Continuity in educational purpose is a keynote of an appropriate response to present day objectives.

While agendas for such ends cannot be laid out in advance, a variety of activities that are often unorganized in this kind of program may be anticipated:

Learning to listen
Learning to perform, read, and write music
Getting the opportunity of going to concerts
Learning to analyze and discriminate
Learning to judge and define taste
Enlarging the extent of commitment
Learning to integrate music into life

V. MUSIC IN THE SOCIETY: SOCIAL FORCES IN MUSIC

Approaches to social change. The underlying theme of the Symposium has been social change and its implications for music and music education. Implicit in the analysis of this theme is the corollary assumption that music and the arts are integral elements of the "culture," as this term is used technically in the sociological-anthropological sense. From these major assertions flow several important positions that are implied, but need to be made explicit:

1. "Social change" refers to the entire range of institutions, ideologies, traditions, and patterns of behavior: economic, political recreational, religious, familial, scientific, and technological. One of the responsibilities of any profession is to develop an ongoing procedure for viewing these changes for relevance to its own purposes; another is to determine philosophies, policies, and implementations by which a) relevant changes are brought to bear on the profession, b) the profession seeks to bring its own philosophy and functions to bear upon the society.

2. Although observations about the elements of society and its processes of change are made by all of us, a major characteristic of the twentieth century is the presence of sources and disciplines devoted to such special analysis. The Symposium has therefore called upon experts from several fields with primary functions outside of the arts (labor, business, church, mass media, and the like) and specialists (in sociology, psychology, philosophy, and anthropology) who study the relationships of interests, values, and institutions. An apparent recommendation, implied in the Sym-

posium formulation itself, is that this dialogue with other interests and social sciences should continue in other meetings, conferences and publications.

3. Every session of the Symposium that dealt with social trends made apparent that the revolutionary character of social trends, such as in technologies and education, may reach into every aspect of music as a dynamic force and as a vital facet of the society. Thus, any profession must be prepared to re-examine its most cherished beliefs and revise its most encrusted practices. This attitude is peculiarly pertinent to behavior of music due to: a) its product, music itself, which can be viewed as a body of elements (forms, style, colors, genres) that can be analyzed independently of social factors; b) the fear by some that the attempt to view the arts amidst other human interests will inject spurious judgments into aesthetic areas.

It is possible to take any segment of change, and move from it to music as an aesthetic and social process. Thus, areas for study might be internationalism, urbanization, communications, and transportations, leisure, mass culture, mass education, expanding government, cybernetics, and similar areas mentioned by speakers of the Symposium. Each of these contains major implications for music.

An alternative approach is to move from categories of music as an institutional phenomenon outward toward the elements of social change; this gives us at once a relationship of music education to the factors of *creators, distributors,* and *consumers,* and also a more specific way of extracting pertinent elements from the enormous range of "social" changes.

Relationships of music education to music as social process. An important change of the past few decades is that elements of the musical community that were often isolated from each other are drawing together: practicing musicians and musicologists; professional orchestras and educational forces; labor unions and the direct preparation of string players; libraries and performers. These tendencies toward cooperation are in themselves partly a result of social factors that come from the "outside," such as the changing character of the school, or the larger responsibilities of government. We turn to each element noted above, creator, distributor, consumer, and educator, to characterize very briefly: a) some "social" aspects of each role, b) some relationships of each role to social change, and c) some general conclusions on relationships of *change to music education roles.*

Creators

Familiar questions cluster around the determination and the destiny of the creator: What are his roles in the total aesthetic process? How does he compose or perform, and how do these roles interact? How does he conform or deviate from traditions of his art? Where and how is he best prepared? Can the actual realization of a work of art be described and generalized into a science or lore about creativity? What are his materials, restraints, and types of commitments in various kinds of societies — primitive or sophisticated, urban or rural, democratic or autocratic? Who are his publics, his critics, his economic patrons, his social and aesthetic colleagues?

Few if any of these questions can be answered in a social vacuum. Composer and performer are related to higher economic affluence. Federal predications (prepared for the outdoor recreation resources review commission) are that average family incomes will go to over $14,000 annually by the year 2000, based on present purchasing power. The industrialization that underlies our present affluence and productive capacity has also contributed, and will contribute to higher literacy. Max Lerner projected for the Symposium a college-graduate segment of 85 percent of the population at the end of this century. Can we, then, continue to think of "mass culture" when, within recent months, the 20th Century Fund study by Baumol and Bowen finds a high correlation between high income, college education, and concert attendance?

A further set of projections asserts that the rising productivity and personal comfort has been achieved, in part, through technologies that are simultaneously reducing work hours. The 72-hour week familiar to American life (mostly rural) a century ago has given way to the long weekends, the long vacation, and the 40-hour week. Hardly a session of the Symposium passed without some reference to this matter of leisure, one that was most appropriately symbolized by the aristocratic, old-fashioned, rural setting in which the meetings were held.

There is a continual concern as to the "quality" of taste that the present and the future "masses" will display amongst the increasing array of private, commercial, and publicly-sponsored alternatives. Again, many speakers turned to the training of new and large audiences in the light of more affluence, time, literacy, and (hopefully) a more natural aspiration or expectation for the arts. The emphasis on music-making in the American high school is being questioned in some circles as the new interest emerges for audiences of discernment.

Not unrelated to the creator and performer, who by economic or other criteria is called professional, is the growing place of the amateur. Whether in the musical content of home, recreation center, retirement village, concert stage, or church, the body of capable and committed amateurs continues to grow. As a recent issue of *Arts and Society* (University of Wisconsin, Extension Division) made clear, there is need for studies of new relationships that have developed between amateur and professional, as in many community orchestras. Given the increase in non-work time, their interdependence may become of increasing interest to music educators in respect to their own goals and involvement in serving community needs.

Economic issues affecting the composer and performer are of such central importance that a separate Symposium group confronted this issue. Federal legislation in recent sessions has contributed slightly to the professional segments of music and enormously to its educational segments. These funds, together with foundation grants, arts councils, and other emerging artistic agencies, will have numerous indirect effects far beyond direct economic or education goals. One impact may be on the destiny of poor children, a subject to be discussed below. To the degree that the poor, and especially the Negro poor, are motivated toward the arts by ongoing or special efforts, this minority will find greater access to the values outlined earlier — values at the core of musical experience.

Distributors

Links between creators and the public in music, are found in such roles as that of impresario, patron, club program chairman, publisher, librarian, the entire mass media industry, the church, the AF of M, the community center, and the recreation system.

Major issues may be drawn, such as the power that is exerted over creators. Motivations can be examined. The schools, especially the universities, have in many cases become major middlemen, providing audiences as well as performers and composers.

We may expect some drastic changes in methods of distributing music, changes resulting in large part from new technologies. However, aside from techniques, social values may be directly affected, as lower-economic groups begin to approach the fine arts as natural to anyone, rather than as the special possession of the upper classes. Music, from this view, is an important social power, albeit in symbolic form. Like many churches, many music education programs do not touch the lives of community segments that might be reached. In this regard, the Symposium profited from the recital of the United Auto Workers plans for leisure-time programs. One development that is fairly safe to project is the growing concern of labor unions in the use of time by its membership, thus moving them closer toward the tradition of European unions.

Consumers (publics)

Sufficient reference has already been made to vital issues here, such as mass media, increasing time and affluence. The committee on technology will undoubtedly report on projected electronic devices that will contribute to more individual desires in provisions for music. All elements of musical life have an interest in such possibilities, but perhaps the "programing" of such cybernetic devices and preparation for intelligent uses of previously unknown magical resources will draw music educators closer to the scientific disciplines.

The essence of such prospects has bearing on attitudes toward music, and perhaps on the psychological and social values that may arise from such significant changes. The music educator cannot be a Luddite, for it is a strategic position now to prepare for 1) the technological revolutions, and 2) the psychosocial impact of such rapid changes.

Even the commercial mass media industry, with its vast research apparatus, has told us little about the qualitative impact of its programs upon children. As educational television expands, perhaps in line with recent Ford and Carnegie Foundation proposals, an enormous potential for music education will suddenly develop. *It is highly important that the profession look forward to this prospect with utmost care.*

About the year 1972 will see a generation of parents grow to the age of 26, old enough to have been themselves raised by television. This will give rise, for the first time in history, to a parent-child relationship that is totally immersed in values related to television. Yet it is apparent that even then the mass media in the home will hardly have passed its infancy. For the central fact of present television is that the viewer is completely dependent on the machine (and its sending station), subject to a time schedule of images outside of his control. The time will come when the *viewer* will be the scheduler, fitting any program to his whims, just as he does so now with his use of phonograph records. He will, perhaps with a "subscription" per month or year to the telephone company, bring to his large wall-screen any film, dramatic or musical performance that is stored in some file. Thus, the quality of the family's taste in the arts and music will be complemented by equipment and by electronic repertoire far beyond those possessed by most schools today.

Discussions about the public cannot remain only on the level of new electronics. Well over two-thirds of the American population today are on a poverty level of existence. Even if this group owns radios and TV sets, and many do, studies by Oscar Lewis and others have called attention to a "culture of poverty." Various subcultures, whether in terms of age, race, or poverty, approach music and its instruction from a background that is often different from that of the W. A. S. P. child. Although this issue is considered shortly in this report, it serves to remind us that the familiar phrase "music for every child" arose from a political, democratic ethos of a former era. Do we mean by the phrase cello lessons for the child whose family can hardly afford inside running water, much less an expensive instrument? The real significance of Title I of the Elementary and Secondary School Act is that we are closing the gap between aspirations and possibilities. This Act alone has put into the hands of music educators a democratic tool of the highest import. It has enabled a beginning from which the public to a serious art can be developed from all classes and economic segments of America.

Educators

Educators are the fourth element in this classification of the process of music. Its many relationships to the social fabric of American life permeate every phase of the Symposium.

We turn directly to two phases of the music program related to the general observations above. The first deals with music as a social value for the whole society and the general obliviousness of colleges in providing a sanction for this value by the very nature of admission policies. The second deals in more detail with the culturally disadvantaged child.

The widest social base for music. In spite of expanded and greatly increased interest and activity in the arts, music and the arts are not yet generally accepted as necessary components of our everyday life. The federal government has offered a new dignity to the artist through its unprecedented action in establishing the National Council on the Arts and the Humanities. It has given approval and significant support to the purposes of art and the needs of the artist through the two great education bills of 1965. But so long as music remains on the periphery of our lives as a frill and as an extracurricular activity, it will continue as a peripheral subject in the curricula of our high schools, colleges, and universities.

Requirements for entrance to our colleges and universities almost entirely ignore credits in music and the arts as proper admission units. In the fight to meet ever toughening standards of admission, college-bound students have no time or interest for other than those subjects enjoying the category of major necessity. This fact not only has robbed high school classes, bands and orchestras in many, many instances of participation by our best students, but admittedly, content and presentation methods of our courses in general music, literature and even theory are hardly worthy of unit credit with other major disciplines such as English, physical sciences, and the social sciences.

Thus, music and the arts remain on the periphery of the high school curriculum, relegated to the status of minor areas and unacceptable to the college. It would seem, therefore, that if we are to achieve major subject status for music in the secondary curriculum, we must use the weight of Music Educators National Conference, the National Association of Schools of Music, and the National Council on the Arts in achieving this goal by directly influencing the College Entrance Board to regularly include questions on music and the arts appropriate to the student of talent as well as to the general education student. Such a step might give assurance to the public that music and the arts are indeed valid in terms of the kinds of knowledge a young student should possess upon entrance to college; such a requirement might then give us the means by which such courses as mentioned could be strengthened and made worthy of credit. It would give us the means by which we could force secondary schools to re-evaluate and tighten course content and revise outworn methods of presentation.

As an equally important step, we must also turn our attention to psychological teaching with a view toward developing tests that will give opportunity to evaluate the potentials of the talented student. At the present, all such tests are geared exclusively toward the academically-oriented student, without regard for those whose creative and re-creative potentials can not now be measured as a valid basis for consideration on the college level.

The culturally disadvantaged child. Such programs as Upward Bound and Head Start have demonstrated the tremendous potentials in the disadvantaged and poverty stricken child. We have also found that the middle class Negro teacher can no more cope with the disadvantaged child than can the middle class white teacher without specialized training and appropriate conditioning. There is no way for either group to bring the understanding, empathy, and patience (as the psychological tools) necessary to overcome the terrible scars caused by poverty, illiteracy, and listlessness on the part of parents, insufficient food and inadequate housing, and replace these with hope, belief, pride and confidence. We cannot continue with isolated, crash, gimmick programs. We recommend that sound solutions to this problem, which threatens the very survival of our nation and our culture, can only be gained by our intensive study involving the best brains in the country in a re-assessment program in teacher preparation.

Attitudes toward social change. It is a familiar dictum that social change is often resisted, misinterpreted, feared. The pace of change was illustrated by several speakers of the Symposium, as in Samuel Gould's report that all chemistry books written before 1958 are useless, or that the engineer's education is completely obsolete in ten years, or in Thomas Malone's statement that knowledge had doubled from Christ's time to 1750, and then doubled by 1900, by 1950, and again by 1960.

One member of the committee, reflecting on the speed of social change, prepared a set of general observations that are as relevant to music educators as to other fields. His wisdom, we felt, should be shared with the music profession.

If one participates in change or renewal in its planning, in the possible choices that make it occur, then there is little fear, or hesitation or irritability on the part of members in a society.

Each proposed decision must be as rationally based as

possible. This does not necessarily mean a delineation of the logical consistency of the decision. This means that the desired decision be aired in all its details and all its literature.

The leaders must have a sense of the historical significance of what they are about. Good leadership is constantly putting its hands into the future; it is constantly assuming new roles and new trusts; the dynamic of a vital society demands that this take place. Renewal cannot happen unless leadership makes contact with tomorrow; no matter what tomorrow may bring, then an attempt has been made to prepare for it. The leaders then speak in tones that convey the seriousness of the task, the tensions of the task, but also the great odds that favor the accomplishment of the task.

The word "change," or "renewal," is a rallying word only when it has been placed in a setting of reason and sensible expectation.

No matter how well prepared for, change will bring a certain friction. Some members will not accept it. They don't withdraw; they remain quiet. Change also releases energies for dreams. Expectations become greater than reality can ever contain. Once the future starts to become the present, and the dreams appear unfulfilled, then bitterness sets in. A current example is in the present Negro plight. A certain amount of this frustration is inevitable. Leadership must be prepared to accept this; direct contact with it will quiet the flames usually.

Renewal (or change) also causes splintering and separation. Energy is so aroused that some members take off, they become the nucleus of splinter groups, but they are small in the big picture, and they are annoying in present society because the communication systems provide quick, available platforms.

Renewal (or change) must be forthright, honest, and related to practical goals, done in full public light; there can never be any sign of behind-scenes maneuvering. This will occur inevitably and when it does, morale falls and hostility rises. Membership accepts decisions, knows they must be made, but they are to be made publicly, for the benefit of the society, and personal gain on the part of individual leaders must not, can never be, a priority.

The platform of change or renewal must be thoroughly understood by the leadership, otherwise individual commitment will falter. Just as the individual moves through to a full individual actualization of self by a lifelong decision of excellence that never wavers, so too do societies achieve excellence by a decision of commitment to excellence. That commitment is made by leadership, personified by leadership.

Particularly in respect to relations of music education to the complexities of social change in American life, we think back to our caveat in the early pages of the report; indeed, we do well to ask the right questions.

It is on two dimensions of analysis that these changes take root: on the *meanings* of music to our lives, and on the *introduction* of music to young lives, so that more sensitive meanings may be nurtured. Our subject, after all, is music. And like the sonata that still sounds right when the movement returns to the core of its theme, the report returns, finally, to music. As the Symposium itself began with the philosophers Northrop and Broudy, and the philosophy of art as value, the relevancy of these systems of thought is now explored for purposes of music education.

VI. FINAL LESSONS FROM NORTHROP AND BROUDY

In *The Meeting of East and West,* F. S. C. Northrop states that man has an inherent need for aesthetic experience, as deep-seated and as urgent as his need for food. He points out the value of aesthetic response to natural beauty: streams, lakes, sunsets; and he places great importance upon art and music as stimulators of exceptionally rich aesthetic response.

Northrop cites two types of aesthetic components. The first is identified as a radical, empirical component which is immediately apprehended and can be directly inspected. It consists of the materials used by painters, musicians, and poets, such as colors, sounds, flavors, and sensed spatial and temporal reactions. Under certain conditions these immediately-experienced items are conveyed as they are, purely; thus, we have purely abstract art and music. This is what Northrop calls "the aesthetic" in the nature of things. Responses to this aesthetic component are comparatively intuitive and at the level of feeling.

Northrop's second component is designated as theoretical. It conveys inferred meanings, analogies, and symbolisms together with theoretical elements in the aesthetic "object" or work of art perceived. Involvement in this component is primarily intellectual.

The two components must be considered together, for there is an essential interaction between them, so that both components are necessary to a complete aesthetic experience. In like manner, responses to aesthetic experiences are more complete when they involve both feeling and intellect.

The basic human need for aesthetic experience requires the provision of such experiences in the curriculum of public education. In like manner, the duality of aesthetic components and of human response has direct implication for the content of a program of aesthetic education, and the content are activities that should characterize it.

In addition to Northrop's statement, Harry S. Broudy, an educational philosopher, suggests that if aesthetic education is to be for all young people, it must be varied to meet the widely divergent societal, cultural, and intellectual backgrounds of children and young people. Broudy, too, has recognized the importance of both the perceptual experience and the response to it at the level of feeling on the one hand, and the theoretical, analytical, intellectual response on the other.

Broudy's position on behalf of more and better aesthetic education for all children and youth refers to two of the questions raised in the "Introduction to Issues" prior to the Symposium.

Is it possible to maintain qualities of artistic excellence in a program of education which, by mandate, must be for all children? Or, as so many critics insist, is a "mass culture" of necessity of low calibre, if not utterly impossible?

The answer to the second question is negative and the response to the first question is affirmative provided that:

The integrity of music as an art is maintained.

The music selected for study conforms to a generally accepted standard of artistic quality appropriate to the age group involved.

Performance of the music — a simple, short song in the primary grades or a more advanced composition to be sung or played in later periods of instruction — is appropriately expressive in quality of tone and interpretation (including phrasing, tempo, and dynamics) and is also accurate in such matters as rhythm and intonation.

Recorded music to be heard possesses artistic worth of an order recognized by the connoisseur, and related information is authentic.

The nature of pupils' responses to the music is consistent with the nature and structure of the music.

Prerequisite to the achievement of the foregoing conditions are the depth, breadth, and quality of the teacher's education, including musical skills, knowledges, concepts, and attitudes, as well as the development of specialized abilities in helping students who do not possess skills in musical performance to understand the nature and structure of music. Artistic excellence can be maintained in a program of music education for all children if the institutions responsible for teacher education, recognizing the value of this goal, insist upon adequate preparation in this area before issuing the teacher credential. School districts also have an obligation, in this connection, to provide in-service education focused upon the unique needs of students whose backgrounds and musical abilities are atypical. Barring physical handicaps, they can achieve a degree of artistic excellence.

Returning to Northrop's concept of the dual components that exist in the nature of the aesthetic experience, it is useful for music educators to recognize the necessity for instruction which will evoke responses both intuitive and intellectual.

This points a questioning finger toward another issue raised prior to the Symposium: What is meant by the phrase, music is an academic discipline?

In what ways is music a discipline? We all recognize and respect the discipline required for musical performance of a high quality, a self-discipline no less rigorous than for many other fields. The first method of inquiry will be by the aural perception of the music. This will be reinforced by the visual perception of musical notation. Analysis, reading, discussion, and aural evaluation will be additional processes of investigation, during which the music will be heard repeatedly. These activities and others of a similar type relate to the second of Northrop's components in aesthetic experience, namely the analytical, theoretical, and intellectual aspects of aesthetic learning as well as their inferred meanings. Note, however, the activities of the the second component are constantly reinforced by repeated sensory control with the first component in Northrop's theory, namely the *sound of music,* purely and empirically.[1] This is of utmost importance, for music is the thing to which the concept refers, and there must be repeated aural perception of the referent (music) if the musical concept is to be clear in the mind of the learner. Additional compositions, illustrative of the original concept, will also be heard and analyzed to reinforce and clarify the learner's concept of this segment of the discipline.

It is of paramount importance to note that this approach to the study of music must be based upon and grow out of a genuine

experience with the sound of music. The ultimate source of musical knowledge is in music itself. The literature of music, as heard through live or recorded performances, validates what is read about it and what is learned of its theory.

A sensible program of music education must recognize the practical nature of its academic aspects and the disciplinary nature of its musical aspects. So-called "practical" musicians may, according to their musical and educational insights, suggest that the academic is unmusical, but academic learning can serve highly useful purposes. This paper takes the position that the theoretical is essential to the practical, and that intellectual understandings of music are indispensable to the musician whose performance is to be coherent, even to himself. In reacting to this paragraph, Ole Sand recently wrote, "Theory without practice is empty; practice without theory is blind. Theory and practice illuminate one another."

Every aspect of the program of music education should preserve and strengthen this duality. A program that stresses either at the expense of the other is not only out of balance, but it is seriously shortchanging its pupils. Although we are often able to reach the hearts of young people through music, we too often neglect, or underestimate, their minds.

Let no music educator complain because the best students are concentrating upon a program of rigorous academic studies at the expense of participation in musical activities. The best minds want to be challenged, and they will go where they can find that challenge. We must have a program that will stimulate them.

RECOMMENDATIONS

1. We recommend that there be established machinery within the music education profession by means of which an ongoing communication is established with all other relevant disciplines and interests. Further, we recommend that such discussions should be built into the agenda of professional meetings, and increasingly, in *Journal* articles.

2. We recommend that the MENC encourage and guide schools to bring into their teacher training the fruits of research in philosophy and the social sciences. A staff member of MENC should be assigned to this responsibility.

3. We recommend that special attention be paid by the music educators profession to the theme of leisure that ran through many sessions of the Tanglewood Symposium. It is essential that music education turn seriously to this development to make available to the public the fruits of its research for the formulation of a public and private philosophy for the significant use of time free from work.

4. We recommend that as one result of the regional meetings, the Symposium, the state and national meetings, MENC adopt or develop a set of official positions as a basis for communication, for decision making in policies, and for guidance of all elements involved with music. Such declarations will be valuable for self-understanding, and will immeasurably strengthen the image of MENC, measure of its influence, and the establishment of confidence in the direction it is taking.

5. We recommend that the music education profession

---

[1] The remainder of this section, somewhat edited, is quoted from *The Study of Music as an Academic Discipline,* by William C. Hartshorn, MENC, 1963.

reopen official and informal relationships with the Adult Education Association of the United States of America, so that cooperative activity and understanding may result. This might take the form of special sessions on adult activity in music meetings and of music sessions in adult education conferences so that researches and demonstrations might result.

6. We recommend that MENC and its related agencies initiate or cooperate in large scale studies of audiences. Evidence indicates the importance of this issue in view of social changes noted in the body of this report. Such studies, valid in their own right, need always to be related to school education and to trends of increasing educational interrelations between school and community.

7. We recommend that there be established a national commission on music education comparable to commissions in other fields; its purpose would be to confront all of the issues treated in this Symposium, but in the detail that these issues deserve, and with the full-time staff that such inquiry necessitates.

Subject Area II

Music of Our Time

Members of the committee on Music of Our Time: Wiley L. Housewright, Chairman, Grant Beglarian, Gene Bruck, Wilson Coker, Rose Marie Grentzer, Wayne S. Hertz, Milton Katims, Stan Kenton, Harry Lantz, John T. Roberts, and Edwin E. Stein.

The principal tasks of Group II were to identify, describe, and examine the crosscurrents of music in American life, to identify the segments of the population which support them, and to estimate the strength of their impact.

Broudy has said that music does for people just about what they want it to do for them. The American people want it to do a great deal. Those who believe with Northrop that a cultivated taste is better than a raw one prefer art music, the great music of the past, established masterpieces, or standard repertory. But there is revolution today in all the arts, and one of the most violent is in art music: the avant garde using traditional materials experimentally, aleatory music, nonhuman electronic music, music concrete, and serialization.

The taste of another segment of our population is mainly for some type of jazz: ragtime, dixieland, big band swing, bop, the combos and their improvisation, funky jazz, third-stream, hard rock, and soul rock. Jazz began as a simple type of music but now has mutations so numerous that its composers and performers have reached out into foreign cultures for new instruments and new scales to accommodate changes in styles.

Between these two musics is environmental music (commonly called wallpaper music) intended to enhance factory production, encourage buying, or aid digestion, while at the same time begging to be ignored. While "functional music" may succeed in its pernicious design, it breeds inattentiveness and boredom in the listener.

Affected both by tradition and the groundswell of experiment are the musics of the church, musical theatre, films, and television, and the folk song of social protest.

Our insatiable appetite is no longer satisfied with the parochial music that surrounds us — the immediately available. Americans young and old are studying, singing, and playing the musics of ethnic and national groups halfway around the world. Instant communication and rapid travel have opened a rich new ethos of endless variety.

The vast amount of music today suggests that Americans have a great hunger for music. The plurality of musics suggests the presence of a plurality of tastes. The quantity and variety of musics required to fill our needs are staggering. In Stan Kenton's words, "People are absorbing music as they absorb air." There is a music for the young, one for the rich, one for the housewife (if she is at home), one for the dropout, and one for the professional man. And most music is consumed ritually, no matter whether with costumes, beads, feathers, and flowers, or with bath, deodorant, and tux or tails.

The directions our musics are taking have been indicated. But the years ahead will bring music not yet imagined. The survival rate of music is a commentary on its popularity, its craftsmanship, or its promotion. The mortality rate of much popular music may be attributed to its lack of essential substance, to a change in fads, or again to the promotion factor. The presence of diverse music in a society satisfies the variety of tastes and various levels of emotional and intellectual maturity. All music is germane to the mainstream of American life and should be written, studied and performed in our schools and in private teaching studios.

The mob-scene music festival, *Messiah* performances, or peace jubilee-type sing alongs appear to be diminishing in favor of soloistic music performed either as a solo or in small ensembles. The trend is observable in popular as well as art music. An implication for educational goals is clearly for greater performance expertise.

Man reaches for one music, then another, then another throughout life. But youth will say, "The music today is completely different." And so will music be, as long as people are different, and as long as there is another day. And no man will write nor teach the music which has total mass appeal. The music of today and tomorrow will be for a special group or for an individual taste. If we respect the human being or the human element in music, we will respect man's right to his own taste and his equal right and privilege to change it.

The human element is being challenged in an age dominated by technological change, but music, more than any other art, has become ubiquitous through that change. What is the content of the technology, the nature of the change?

In terms of machines and tools, music moves from the commonplace of radio, recordings, phonographs, tapes, and television to the electronic synthesizer and computer. So vast is the array of machines that the musician, educator, layman, and student may, indeed, find that the medium "massages" him at every waking and sleeping moment. But it may be that the medium is *not* the message. And the new technology of creating music is the main part of the medium.

Until recently most of the innovation in music by our artists was too tough to take, too much to assimilate, too hard to appreciate, happening too fast to grasp. The mainstream of change is associated with the "emancipation of the dissonance," as Schoenberg put it and, as Gunther Schuller suggests, the freedom of the creator to fashion his work with completely new techniques. The salient technologies of the composer *now* are the serialization of any or all facets of music by set theory, the aleatoric lining out of music, and the electronic-computer synthesis of a work.

With completely serialized music the techniques tend to lead to the elimination of the performer as a creative interpreter, or, in electronic music, to the eradication of the performer. With chance music, the techniques lean toward minimizing the control over actual sounds by the composer, or the near elimination of the composer's duties in improvisatory music.

The technology of music looming large now is the electronic synthesis and presentation of music. Direct communication from composer to listener may overtake us before we educators even can explain how electronic music is made, let alone understood, appreciated, or taught. Serial, aleatoric, improvisatory, and electronic techniques command the conscientious educator's attention. Their nature must be grasped and presented to students of all levels: elementary, secondary, or collegiate. The computer and synthesizer, which we know are here to stay, cannot be ignored forever, although some music educators may retire before new electronics threatens many musicians with obsolescence.

Today, with computer and synthesizer hooked up, a composer can create and program a work of extreme complexity in a reasonably small amount of time. And, at the click of a switch, his work is synthesized on tape and played back, virtually instantaneously. Who will sell lessons on the cornet when the band is comprised of transistors and tapes, programed by IBM, led by Ampex, and played on a Clipshorn or Electro-Voice? To the educator, the computer and synthesizer will soon demand curricular attention.

Not only will the new electronic music require attention in our schools, the electronic music will need full explanation in higher education. Teachers, not just composers, must be given a fair chance to learn how to make the music, to program the computer, to operate the electronic console. As one took brass methods before, computer and synthesizer methods and techniques are next to be required for credential certification.

In vocal music, the traditional base for early phases of music education, new directions are especially apparent. The new image of vocal music is the conception of the choral ensemble as a soloistic chamber music group (with a separate part for each singer). Moreover, increasingly modern vocal music departs from its former dependence on setting the ideas and mood of a text. The textual verbal message either becomes minimal or irrelevant, feeling alone seems to be expressed, to the extent it is involved. Nonsense, or merely phonetic and other oral sounds, largely suffice for their timbral and articulative force alone.

The new musical technology encompasses the new music recognized. We "rock" with lead, harmony, and bass guitars and electric piano. We "groove" with the sitar, nose flute, and temple gongs.

The new dimensions in musics of our time demand new dimensions in value judgments. Music is cutting across musical form, styles, texture, timbre, dynamics, and traditional functions. The expressive elements of the musics are unique and revolutionary. The electro-acoustical discoveries have tumbled the old foundations and laid grounds for new ones. Value judgments may be delayed because today's avant-garde do not write for the lay listener. They write for composers. For the most part, their works are difficult to perform, which limits the number of performances; and performances are necessary in order to arrive at competent musical judgments.

But the avant-garde music is only a small segment of all the musics which surround us. There are different kinds of musics existing side by side with relative degrees of aesthetic values. Separate musics have separate functions; and the functions are multiplying. There are happenings all around us, on the street corners, in churches, events both political and social. They pose the problem of value judgments, not only of the quality of the music, but quality within the function of the musics. Can we and should we assign a hierarchy to various music?

We are reminded that time available to us as teachers is geometrically diminishing compared to the geometrically increasing amount of new music and techniques. Time for reflection, decision, and action is critically short; we are forced to formulate value judgments and make decisions now. We have a strong obligation to know and communicate newly emergent facts. Our obligation to raise new issues and study new problems is no less urgent.

Subject Area III

Impact and Potentials of Technology

Members of the committee on The Impact and Potentials of Technology: Allen P. Britton, Chairman; Edward A. Bowles, Arnold Broido, Curtis W. Davis, Tim H. Henney, Warner Imig, Ole Sand, Donald J. Shetler, and Maurice C. Whitney.

The committee on The Impact and Potentials of Technology might well have been titled "The Committee on Revolution." The word revolution, which appeared in most of the addresses, either boldly stated or defined by Max Lerner as "a highly accelerated pace of change" may properly be used to describe our current situation. Never before have the forces of change spun with such speed. The explosion of knowledge, which applies much more to the exact sciences than to the social sciences and humanities, may account in part for our comparative lack of involvement in the swiftly moving tides of technological change and development.

Music educators are not alone in this situation. The techniques and devices which will be used to individualize and improve music teaching will also be used to alter the educational strategies of the entire school curriculum, change the training and retraining of teachers, and redesign the structures and organization of the school itself.

Time is the most urgent factor as the gap widens between the availability of knowledge and the ability of the school, our ability, to cope with it.

At the start, our committee was faced with the problem of whether to concentrate on the hardware, or on the implications of this hardware for society — a problem which plagued the meetings held on this subject at the six divisional conferences as well, meetings whose reports proved a useful parallel to our own work. It was decided that we must see them in a complete relationship, consider both man and machine.

A paragraph from the introduction to the book *Automation, Education, and Human Values,* by William Brickman and Stanley Lehrer, may be useful to set the stage:

> So it is with our attempts to convey the wizardry, the radically progressive magnitude, novelty, and pervasiveness of the technological changes with which we deal. Nothing less than the lexicon of superlatives and absolutes will do; and, as the term *wizardry* itself suggests, nothing less will do than a vocabulary borrowed from the never-never land of high romance. *Radical, revolutionary, unprecedented, sweeping, mushrooming, explosive, catastrophic, titanic, gigantic, astronomic, meteoric, cosmic, phenomenal, breathtaking, astounding, astonishing, fascinating, wonderful, marvelous, magical, miraculous, fabulous, incredible, fantastic, limitless, boundless, infinite,* these are some of the highest-powered and most gorgeously colored terms that are used, soberly, to suggest, modestly, the present preludial accomplishments and the predicted or guaranteed infinite potentialities of the phenomena with which [we are] concerned.[1]

The list of media and materials considered by the committee in a greater or lesser depth is extensive. We shall touch on them all with comments and explanations where we explored in depth.

Music educators should be aware of the many books and studies available on the current state of educational technology.

We will deal with two kinds of materials: those that are currently available and in use, which makes up the greatest part of the list, and those which are still in developmental stages. There is a direct sequence of development from each area to the next.

1. DUPLICATION
   Printing, all varieties
   Spirit duplicators
   Ditto machines
   Electrostatic copiers
   Thermal copiers
   Photographic processes
   LDX — Long Distance Xerography (This is the technique of using existing phone lines to transmit images. The American Telephone and Telegraph Company is presently considering a process which uses phone lines in a business-run variant of ERIC, for the transmission of educational information and research.)

2. AUDIO RECORDING AND TRANSMISSION
   Electronic amplification
   Disc recording
   Tape recording
   Cartridge recording
   Optical sound (on film)
   Tone generation machines
   Tone analysis machines
   Acoustics — architectural
   Acoustics — artificial (audiophonics)
   Tone synthesizers — such as the Moog, Buchla, Syn-Ket, and Trautonium

(These tone synthesizers point the way toward school and home instruments, which could popularize the idea of electronic composition.)

3. RADIO
   AM
   FM and FM stereo
   Miniaturized — solid state, printed circuitry

4. VISUAL OR VIDEO (Still and motion projectors)
   Opaque projector
   Overhead projector
   8 mm, 16 mm film projector
   8 mm (format M, or Super 8) Single Concept film
   35 mm Filmstrip projector
   35 mm 2" x 2" Film-slide projector
   Tachistoscope (controlled pace) projectors
   Microfilm and Microfiche and the newest developments: 70 mm format and Tape-stripped film

5. CLASSROOM TEACHING AIDS
    Metronomes (as the Bilotti Multi-beat)
    Tuners (and micro-tuners)
    Stroboscopic and oscillographic devices
    Audio-video tape analysis (of performance)
    Electronic pianos and organs
    Electronic music boards
    Intonation trainers

6. TELEVISION
    Black-and-white and color transmission
    Closed circuit
    Educational TV (ETV) — National Educational Television (NET) non-commercial open circuit
    Instructional TV (ITV) classroom, closed circuit or open. NCSCT — the National Center for School and College Television
    Functional TV. The video component of Information Storage and Retrieval systems
    VHF — UHF and 25 MHZ transmission
    The immediate future holds out:
       Pictures up to 6′ by 9′ on a wall screen
       Hi-Fi multi-channel sound
       Many additional channels in use
       Satellite transmission. One 24-channel satellite in fixed orbit could blanket the entire U.S. Three or four would blanket the world.
       Videotape recording using quad or helical scan for home use.

E. B. White, the author, in a recent letter to the Carnegie Commission on Educational Television said:

> I think television should be the visual counterpart of the literary essay, should arouse our dreams, satisfy our hunger for beauty, take us on journeys, enable us to participate in events, present great drama and music, explore the sea and the sky and the woods and the hills. It should be our Lyceum, our Chautauqua, our Minsky's and our Camelot. It should restate and clarify the social dilemma and the political pickle. Once in a while it does, and you get a quick glimpse of its potential.

While the technology of television is perfectly adequate for ETV or ITV, recent assessments in the music education field find that current programs are not of high quality to do the teaching job. There are not a sufficient number of trained personnel for the development of proper programing. Directors, producers, and all the other jobs are not being filled by people equal to the task. Money and direction are needed to set up training programs in both current and developing techniques.

There is a slightly brighter horizon in arts programing on both NET and commercial channels. The *Bell Telephone Hour,* as we have heard, continues to produce exciting musical shows, despite ratings which would usually be considered dismal. NET promises a continuing series of musical shows at the level of the *Golden Ring.* TV abroad, especially England, Germany, and Japan has moved far ahead in the field of music programing; and the trend toward compatible tape playback equipment should make it possible for us to judge for ourselves soon. The new techniques, huge screen, and first-rate multi-track sound, should enable television to assume its obvious and necessary place in the

educational scheme; but only if the problems of personnel and content are solved. The National Center for School and College Television (NCSCT) is interested in everything happening here and abroad. It is looking for the best material available, and is also concerned with finding or developing evaluation techniques.

The impact of the new Corporation for Public Television is still two or three years away, but it *may* provide a source of support for all kinds of programing, as well as funds for training personnel.

7. INDIVIDUALIZED INSTRUCTION
    (usually called P. I., or programed instruction)
    Linear: Skinnerian — traditional
    Branching: Crowderian — scrambled
    Computer Assisted Instruction (CAI)
    Individual carrels: wet (electronic) or dry
    Multi-sense or multi-media programs with immediate student-teacher effect measurement.

But of all the tools and all the technologies, it is the computer that calls forth the adjectives of our opening quotation.

8. COMPUTER
    Storage and retrieval machine.

It is a completely reliable, continuously available memory bank for any material programed into it; and it is available to store everything. The contents of all our libraries, all our collections of music, will eventually be programed into computers to be available whenever and however needed, all at an incredible speed. It may accomplish in a short time what formerly might have taken years or decades of research if, indeed, it were possible at all!

ERIC, the Educational Research Information Center, is one example of this kind of use. A monthly catalog of resumes of all reports and projects filed with ERIC is available from the U. S. Office of Education and copies of the reports stored in ERIC's computer memory banks may be had either in hard copy (the printed version) or on microfiche, which is a 4″ x 6″ film card containing up to 60 pages of text and requiring a special "reader" for use.

Professor Barry S. Brook of Queens College has produced computer indexed abstracts of all the important current musical journals of the world.

Professor Harry Lincoln of SUNY has prepared indices of various musical repertoires for purposes of identifying anonymous works, finding duplications and borrowings.

Professor Alan Forte of M. I. T. has done an analysis, by computer, of structural characteristics in order to produce an adequate analytical description of the atonal, pre-12 tone works of Schoenberg, Webern, and Berg.

These examples give a small indication of the kinds of operations possible using the storage and retrieval aspects. Imagine when libraries at any great distance may be tapped from one's own terminal, the material searched at incredible speed and, if desired, hard copies of needed information produced via LDX. The scholar is unlocked, and a high school student may do as an exercise what would now be a major piece of scholarly research. Graduate students in music education at the Eastman School now take a course in Fortran programing as part of their graduate research.

It is possible to create sounds with the computer. By means of a digital, analog computer and auxiliary equipment, electric pulses are created which will play back through a loudspeaker. David Cohen of University of Alabama, Max Mathews of Bell Laboratories, and others have worked in this field producing the techniques and programs necessary.

Sound synthesizer. It is also possible now for a student to write or even compose music directly on the cathode ray face of the terminal of an I. B. M. 2250 using a light pen. The tube has the ability to display information stored on a disc and the notes drawn on the face may be transferred to the disc and both instant sound output and hard copy output are available.

Computer assisted instruction (CAI). The huge information processing capacity of computers allows them to adapt mechanical teaching routines to the needs and past performances of the individual student, who may study, learn and progress at his own rate of speed. It is especially valuable for handling routine tasks and facts, with all the information on the student's learning history as a guide to the machine. The interface of the student and machine makes for a high rate of student interaction with the material. Other electronic and audiovisual aids, such as the cathode ray tube and light pen for display of charts, microfilm, pages, and so on; earphones for audio, and the typewriter keyboard terminal which allows direct question and answer access to specially programed material, combine with student interaction to provide for almost any situation.

Industry applications. The computer promises to solve bottlenecks in the preparation of copy for printing, work which has always been done by time-consuming hand processes. Stefan Bauer-Mengelberg is now translating music into machine-readable form which is printed out on a special Foton printer adapted from type to music faces. His technique promises to extract parts from a score, or reverse the process and create a score from the parts. Others, too, are working on this and a commercial venture in New York is promising to produce 150 completed music plates a day, ready for the camera, before the year is over.

That the computer is *not* a "thinking machine" needs to be stressed. It can only do what it is told to do and the word "GIGO" coined by the computer people points up the necessity of storing the proper material in the proper way. GIGO stands for "garbage in, garbage out!"

Using a computer requires clear, lucid thinking and a disciplined approach to the learning process. It requires a new vocabulary. "Hardware" for the machine and "software" for the material are obvious; but would you guess that "wetware" stood for the human brain that produced the software?

Computers pose many problems in use. One is causing concern to the entire publishing industry and to the legislators who are working on copyright revision. Somehow, the authors and composers must be compensated for the use of their creations and no one has as yet solved the riddle of "how."

It is obvious that books could be written (and have been) on the relation of computers to education, but this look at a few uses should give us some sense of urgency, of getting on with the business of relating our field to the new technologies. We have to come to terms with them, we have to become knowledgeable about them and acquire proficiencies in their use. With this in mind the committee makes the following urgent recommendations:

RECOMMENDATIONS

1. Activate a major committee within MENC on Advanced Educational Technologies. It would be the duty of this committee, as it is with the parallel committees already established in most disciplines, to keep the entire membership informed on developments and how they are or might be applied to music education. The pages of *Music Educators Journal,* the *Journal of Research in Music Education,* special brochures and whatever else is necessary should be made available to this committee for the dissemination and coordination of information.

This committee should be responsible for a continuing dialogue with (for example) IBM and the other major manufacturers, to bring our needs to their attention. It is axiomatic that industry will not move on the development of hardware or programs until it is convinced of a true need. The committee would relate to and cooperate with the Division of Educational Technology of NEA.

2. The key people in MENC (probably the directors and officers), should be provided with a one-time, 3-day exposure to computer concepts as have the leaders in other disciplines. In this way they will be able to evaluate projects and provide needed leadership. A training program for music educators in this field should be devised and disseminated by all practicable means: college courses, workshops, clinics, and the like. Programing, computer techniques, non-numerical computer languages suited to music uses such as PL/I or Snowball would serve as the content of such programs.

3. The ERIC clearinghouse proposals should be put into operation as quickly as possible to provide computerized indices (such as KWIC) of all materials in music education and related fields. This will help provide an interface between music schools and the music researchers.

4. Preparation of new teachers, and in-service experiences for working teachers in these technologies should be a major concern of MENC. Specific courses and programs should be planned to bring this information with force and urgency to the general membership. The short-range objectives might be accomplished by the development of short-term summer workshops and institutes. However, the long range objectives can only begin to be dealt with in a revision of our teacher training curriculum to provide experiences with the whole range of concepts and processes of education in the 1970's, instead of doing quite well what was widely acceptable 40 years ago.

---

[1]William Brickman and Stanley Lehrer, *Automation, Education, and Human Values* (New York: School and Society Books, 1966) p. 14.

Statement:

The Impact of Technology

Edmund A. Bowles

Within the past dozen years or so, the computer has made itself felt in every aspect of our society. Indeed, Issac Auerbach has characterized the invention of the computer as being comparable to that of the steam engine in its effects upon mankind. He predicted that the computer will have a far greater constructive impact on mankind during the remainder of the twentieth century than any other technological development of the past two decades.

In the field of scholarship and education there is hardly an area that is not now using data processing techniques. In music, the computer is being used as a tool in indexing and thematic retrieval, musical and harmonic analysis, music theory, and composition. Present trends suggest that the computer will come to play an important role in programed teaching as well.

In order that this opportunity be fully exploited, the music faculty must be able to use computers in teaching in all academic levels. The student, in turn, must be given the opportunity to apply the techniques of data processing in his own course work. In order to achieve these stated aims, it is recommended that: 1) various training programs be established in computer concepts or programing for deans of music schools, music supervisors, and music teachers; 2) a committee on computer technology or computer applications be set up within the framework of MENC; 3) a task force of music educators develop a set of guidelines for computer-assisted instruction in music; and 4) the MENC establish a continuing working relationship with the computer industry in order to take advantage of this new tool.

Subject Area IV

Economic and Community Support for the Arts

Members of the committee on Economic and Community Support: David P. McAllester, Chairman, Harold Arberg, Herman D. Kenin, Olga Madar, Gene Morlan, Emmett Sarig, Everett L. Timm, W. Homer Turner, and A. Verne Wilson.

I. THE SEARCH FOR A WIDER AUDIENCE

The performing arts in general do not earn their way with sales and admissions. Even a popular idiom, such as jazz, rarely commands enough of a paying clientele to make this important art form an adequate mode of earning a livelihood. Except in the case of a few of the most popular forms of the performing arts, only a small proportion of our population (estimates range from five percent to as little as three percent) is interested enough to attend performances.

For financial reasons, but also because of the value of the arts to the life of any society, we recommend that the musical community seek every means to reach the mass of our population with the widest possible spectrum of musical experiences.

A Cooperative Campaign of Selling. The growth of arts councils, arts leagues, and similar organizations seems to promise a wide spectrum of cooperation. We recommend that these planning and organizing institutions broaden their representation to include every appropriate segment of the community. They might well include representatives from the school boards, local labor (perhaps through their departments of recreation), local chapters of the National Federation of Music Clubs, the mass media, the music industry, the municipal government (especially its recreation department), local business organizations and churches. Cooperation with arts programs in colleges and universities has already taken place and will increase as these institutions extend their commitment to the performing arts.

An illustration of an unexpected ally in supporting the arts is the proposed construction of an arts center by the Garden State Parkway Authority in New Jersey.

II. CHANGING THE ATTITUDES OF THE GENERAL PUBLIC

The basic work of the cooperating agencies mentioned above is to change attitudes —— to create a vital interest in the place of indifference. Two areas of attack are through established educational channels and through public programs of such high interest that they themselves will capture the imagination and change attitudes.

Education. Education in the arts, and education in music in particular, can be made increasingly persuasive and attractive. We recommend that the boundaries of music education be enlarged to include a greatly increased recognition and use of many styles of music, including popular music, world music, and contemporary music. Such breadth of musical fare may be especially appropriate in the Inner City, where ethnic enclaves are likely to be found. A model for the use of musics from many traditions may be found in Honolulu, where both schools and recreation programs in the parks teach young people to appreciate and to perform songs and dances from the varied cultures that make up the community.

Not only greater breadth but also greater depth will do much to stimulate and maintain interest. We noted, for instance, the drop-off in interest in band and other kinds of music in the later years of high school and transition to college. One reason may be the limited repertory of many performing groups which soon ceases to challenge the most promising players.

We recommend a continued improvement in the use of teaching aids of high quality and a drastic change in the scheduling of the music teacher's time. Since the long-term purpose of the music educator is to help create an informed and interested music community, we urge that his work program be restructured to include a major role in consultation and leadership in the musical life of his municipality.

The musical education of adults has an important bearing on the search for a wider audience. Many mature people fail to cultivate their interest in music, sometimes even after considerable musical activity in school, for lack of opportunity. Still another population for whom music can be extremely important are people of retirement age. The concern of labor unions for retired workers, as well as for younger people with leisure due to shortened working hours, should be matched by an equal concern on the part of music educators. We recommend that continuing education have a prominent place in the search for a wider music audience.

Public programs. Untried and imaginative ways of stimulating interest in music will help to achieve a wider audience. We recommend a search for new ideas in combinations of the arts, and appeals, with high quality material, to popular taste to attract audiences to music — not because it is good for them but because it speaks to them irresistibly.

Ways might be explored of making musical performances more available in mobile form close to where people live. A jazz-mobile, piano-mobile, dance-mobile, and a chamber-music-mobile are examples. Group involvement is a way to make the musical experience take on deep meaning. A simple device quite often used in an open-air evening concert, is to ask everyone in the audience to light a match. Music in which the audience can participate is a means of engagement.

The rural sector should not be forgotten in the search for a wider audience. Traditionally isolated from the cultural advantages of population centers (and therefore often relying on their own somewhat different cultural advantages), country people can be brought into the larger audience, not only through television and other mass media, but also in personal contact with the arts by means of mobile shows, or by centers which, like regional schools, can serve large areas of sparsely settled country, now that transportation is swift and easy nearly everywhere.

III. THE FUNDING OF THE ARTS

1) **Local, State and Federal Government Support.** The mayor of a western city, when approached, was reluctant to agree to municipal support for a series of band concerts because of his conviction that such concerts "had gone out with button shoes." The local musicians union, however, took the financial risk of an initial series of concerts, giving them wide publicity. From the resulting audiences, numbering in the thousands, enough petitions were collected to persuade the mayor. Municipal support was added to union funds and the program has maintained its popularity for fifteen years. A gratifying further indication of public acceptance came when county funds were also added to the support of this program about four years ago.

Municipal or state support can sometimes be achieved by matching grants or challenging grants. This principle, used frequently by foundations, will help insure broad community participation and support. Our committee discussed the question of what happens when an expensive program gets started and the supporting grant expires. This could, of course, result in the collapse of a program. One safeguard is to make the community share equal to estimated continuing costs. Thus the community will have demonstrated its ability to carry this load. Or the money raised may be sufficient for initiating expenses and also for an endowment that will contribute towards the subsequent costs.

The increase in federal appropriations for the arts was taken as a hopeful portent for the future, especially since it implies public recognition of the importance of the arts in our society. Our committee agreed, however, that the federal government should be a junior partner, the principal support coming from state and local government and, of course, as many other local sources as possible.

2) **Support from Corporations and from Corporate Foundations.** There are more than 1500 large corporations, and the extent of their expenditures in various causes, outside of their business interests, is impressive. They exceed the philanthropies, enormous as they are, of the Big Five private foundations, and even those of such giant federal foundations as the National Institutes of Health or the National Science Foundation.

Much of this money is spent by the corporation itself for purposes that relate rather closely to their commercial interests. At the most, it is good for business, like a covered bridge donated by a lumber company which also sells the recipient the lumber. Or it may be a somewhat less direct gain due to improved public relations after some conspicuous public contribution.

The corporate foundations, on the other hand, are legally independent of the corporations and are under no formal obligation to think of corporation interests. In a long-term but basic sense, the ultimate influence on corporate foundation appropriations is the aspirations of their own labor force. These employees, who constitute three-quarters of the working population of the U. S. A., can influence the fate of the country by their overwhelming voting power. Free enterprise as our way of life will continue only as long as this population is convinced that it should. Whenever this labor force considers it desirable that corporations support music, a very impressive response can be predicted.

Five hundred corporate foundations have been united for some twenty years in the National Council of Foundations which constitutes a forum for their common interests. It behooves the musical community to find the way to a broader support than it has yet received from this source.

We recommend that the MENC add to its staff a full-time specialist to coordinate information on all possible avenues to the funding of music. In the regional reports, an urgent need was expressed for the widest distribution of information about financial support available for research, training, and performance. We urge that the MENC funding specialist be given the resources to see that this information goes directly to the appropriate regional and local offices and the general membership.

Subject Area V

The Nature and Nurture of Creativity

Members of the committee on The Nature and Nurture of Creativity: Karl D. Ernst, Chairman.; Frank Churchley, John Davies, Ernestine Ferrell, Charles B. Fowler, E. Thayer Gaston, O. M. Hartsell, Gerard L. Knieter, and Dorothy Maynor.

In its most fundamental sense, "to live" means that life is continually creating and re-creating itself. A hypothetical status quo world would be static and dead, a negation of creativity. "To be alive" means that man continually reconstitutes his environment into new and more satisfactory formulations. To place value on creativity is to embrace change as an inevitable and ubiquitous fact of twentieth-century American civilization.

Certain other social dimensions of life in the United States also point to a need for the development of each citizen's creative potential. The automation and over-organization of life, and the stifling and inhibiting socialization process tend to robotize and dehumanize man. In a democracy, strength lies in diversification.

Each citizen must be provided the opportunity to develop his individuality, to discover his humanness, and to achieve self-confidence in his special role.

The United States is a mobile, but not completely integrated society. Acceptance of differences and respect for the dignity of others are traits related to creative behavior. Flexibility and adaptability, openness to new ideas, and freedom of artistic expression, are necessary national characteristics that, at least in part, assure that democracy will not only survive, but flourish.

Man largely makes his civilization. He creates himself. Quality in life requires imagination. Traditional forms of life demand periodic refertilization; existing institutions require constant rejuvenation, and new social problems call for continual invention of appropriate social agencies. Creative thinking is needed in every area of American life, from the making of new laws to the tasteful decoration of the home. Man's full use of his creative potential will inject vitality and meaning into every facet of American society, bringing a degree of cultural richness never before achieved. An education in music that emphasizes creative development will make a major contribution to the realization of these potentials in American society.

NATURE OF CREATIVITY

The culture of man begins when he is born. Most of his growing years are spent learning the ways and skills of his culture. He must attain a sufficient amount of conformity in order not to come into conflict with his fellow man. But, his culture in no way excludes individual creativity. Creativity is a valued ingredient of life, particularly in this present age. Hence, we will do all we can to promote the development of every child's creative activities. Creativity leads to peak experiences which highlight life. For these reasons the school and community will provide an environment which induces creative behavior.

Of all life on this earth man is the only creative animal, and superbly so. It is this creative ability that has enabled him to survive and to come to his present state and it is this creativity also that makes possible the democratic process. Because of the necessity of creativity to man's life, we will do all that is possible to encourage its expression in the home and in the school. Therefore, it is appropriate for teachers to identify and to stimulate creative musical behavior.

Creativity comes into existence in many different ways. It is a human characteristic existing in all, but varying only in degree. It may result from a unique way of looking at a problem — musical or otherwise. It may be simple or it may be complex. The same creative behavior may be observed in children as well as in composers. The difference is in degree of complexity.

The creative student is one who, at times, may not conform. It is this lack of conformity which so often distresses the teacher. The teacher has to decide whether the nonconforming student is one seeking to express himself creatively, or one who is acting out grievances. Certain personality traits of the creative student may not endear him to his peer group or his teacher. The creative child who is quite flexible in some areas may be rigid in others.

He is ordinarily not the most intelligent child in the class. Studies have shown that 70 percent of our most creative children would be excluded if they were evaluated solely on the basis of IQ tests. The creative child is divergent rather than convergent in his thinking. Such a student is independent and seeks his own style.

What should be understood is that although the individual requires a structure in which to grow, this structure must be sufficiently flexible so that it does not inhibit creative development. Since children and teachers are unique, each situation requires individual interpretation. In critical situations — where there is doubt — thorough consideration should be given to the behavior to determine its nature.

PROVIDING AN ENVIRONMENT FOR CREATIVE EXPRESSION IN MUSIC

Living life to the fullest suggests providing an environment for acquiring the skills needed for creative living. Whether or not parents realize it, they play a significant role in establishing in the home not only an environment for creative development, but equally important, an attitude of interest in and a tolerance for creative expression. Much can be accomplished by the parents prior to the time the child enters nursery school or kindergarten. For example, parents and children can be drawn together through singing, listening, or moving to music.

The point of view that children are born with the capacity for creative response and that such response can be elicited emphasizes anew the responsibility of the school in establishing a classroom environment and planning instructional experiences which are consecutive, continuous and conducive to the many facets of creative expression. In the years ahead, as patterns of school organization become more flexible and place increasing emphasis on individualizing the instruction, music can be the subject area which adds dimension, variety and satisfaction to creative expression. The teacher holds a strategic place in this creative development.

At any level of school organization, the creative teacher possesses many desirable characteristics, some of which are:

A respect for children as individuals

The ability to relate to or establish rapport with children

A flexibility in adapting to the needs of children at all times

An enthusiasm for learning and living, which is reflected in the response of children

The acumen to lead children to experience the wonder of music through personal discovery

An interest in helping children discover the social relevance of music

The ability to recognize some of the earmarks of creativity in children

The capacity to arouse a curiosity about music that won't let go until it is satisfied

A confidence and security resulting from adequate preparation and experience

The knowledge to plan wisely for each stage of a child's creative development

A capability for making the study of music exciting and meaningful

An awareness of the importance of using community resources

The insight to appraise children's work objectively and to provide encouragement for additional experiences

A knowledge of materials and instructional procedures and the ability to use both for maximum results

An awareness of the importance of being attractive in both personality and dress

Music is taught and experienced in a variety of physical settings. The spatial, acoustical, and locational requirements of the classroom must be in keeping with the type of instruction being provided. The area used for instruction in music must be functional in design, attractive in appearance, and meet the specific needs for creative musical expression. Just as science cannot be taught without appropriate equipment, likewise, music cannot be taught effectively without necessary equipment. Creative teaching demands sufficient instructional materials and library resource materials for reference and research. The possibilities of using new and different technology in teaching music creativity are limited ONLY by the teacher's imagination and willingness to keep up to date.

PRE-SERVICE AND IN-SERVICE PREPARATION FOR CREATIVE TEACHING

Creative teaching in the elementary and secondary schools will not be realized to any great degree until it is experienced more frequently at the tertiary level. Teachers usually teach as they have been taught. College and university teaching often ignores the research which is beginning to make many elementary classrooms both exciting and dynamic. Some of the same techniques utilized successfully there will gradually be implemented in the college classroom, too many of which are still dominated by the lecture. Ole Sand, in *Schools for the Seventies,* said that education must move "from memory, to inquiry; and from spiritless climate, to zest for learning." The future will witness greater use being made of the rich resources outside the classroom. As Maslow so aptly stated: "The classroom atmosphere must be changed to include more time for talking about what students do outside the classroom."

The college music teacher is immersed so completely in his subject field that he has not taken time to consider more creative ways of bringing to the experience of his students that which has so deeply engrossed him. College and university faculties of the future will find ways of sharing, not only their intellectual and aesthetic ideas, but they will also communicate with one another their methods for motivating learning and for evaluating the results.

In developing the college music curriculum it is expected that, as prophesied by Symposium speakers, more of what is now taught during the first year of college will be moved into the high school. This will include music fundamentals, sightsinging, ear training, music literature, survey, and beginning class piano. When this is accomplished, it will be possible for music majors to be educated as broadly in the sciences and humanities as those who major in most other subjects. Present music curricula are notoriously anemic in those general studies which are needed to enable the music teacher to relate his subject to history, literature, anthropology, sociology, and the related arts. Interdepartmental courses, based around the humanities, which will become a more important factor in the secondary school, require not only a superbly trained musician, but one who is also a generally well informed person. Even the conductor of performing groups will be expected to have the ability to include academic and intellectual content in the rehearsal.

In the total music program there will be a trend toward greater synthesis of courses. Music performance, both individual and group, will become the laboratory; and its relation to theory and literature will be similar to that of the science laboratory to the lecture hall. Ensembles will plan performances which will illustrate what is studied in theory and literature. Teachers of theory and literature will cooperate with applied teachers in selecting suitable works for this purpose. All teachers will be involved in some way with performance, which is the essence of music.

Contemporary music will receive increasing attention as we move into the last third of the twentieth century. All art is a reflection of the times which produced it. Contemporary music, in all its variety, is the music of our time and will be considered within the common musical heritage. The music teacher's own musicality will emanate from a broad, comprehensive base of musical knowledge and skills so that he will have a full understanding of music of all periods and styles. All musicianship studies will relate contemporary thought and practice with those of former times. Contemporary music will be taught as a part of the same continuum that has produced all other music. The teacher has a responsibility to his students to provide a comprehensive sampling of this total musical heritage. Theory classes will no longer limit themselves exclusively to the study of harmonic practices which have their origins in the music of the eighteenth and nineteenth centuries. The changing musical concepts of the twentieth century will be given the attention which they deserve. Analytic study and performance of representative contemporary literature will be an integral part of all musicianship training. Conducting experiences which involve the metrical and notational problems of this new music will be provided.

Theory and literature will be taught more as one subject, and in a laboratory setting. Students will perform, write, analyze, and discuss music at the same time as they develop a historical perspective. Music history will become a live and vital part of the education of the music teacher. The studio and practice room will be more than a place to develop technical skills. It will become an exciting kind of laboratory.

There will be opportunities to explore the music of other cultures, and to gain some skill in hearing and playing instruments of those cultures. There will also be provision for contact with the more simple instruments of our Western culture, which are important as recreational instruments in providing creative outlets for the greatly increased leisure time. Fretted instruments, recorders, and other instruments which were common in the period before performance was a profession will be taught.

Student teaching will bring the apprentice teacher into direct contact with young children as early as the freshman or sophomore year. Such early contacts are important and they will be more than detached observation. They will be more like the kind of clinical supervision which is a part of medical education. Early teaching efforts will utilize tape recordings and other new technological means which might make it possible for the young teacher not only to hear, but to see his strengths and weaknesses. Ways will be discovered for him to have a laboratory teaching assignment which will make possible some kind of innovative teaching without the discouraging and pessimistic attitude of a tired master teacher.

The rapid changes that are affecting our schools and society make it evident that teachers educated ten to fifteen years ago are already in need of updating their education. Those now being prepared as teachers will even more rapidly find themselves unable to meet the new challenges, which we cannot now anticipate. Schools and colleges will work together to provide creative ways for a continuous program of in-service growth. Teachers in elementary and secondary schools will be given leaves of absence at frequent intervals and be expected to obtain the added training which is necessary in order to meet the changes in the explosive years ahead. Those who teach at the tertiary level will be expected to have sufficient direct contact with both elementary and secondary schools to insure that their objectives and techniques in methods and procedures classes are fresh and timely. The constantly changing society will necessitate new approaches each year, with new and innovative materials.

IX. Problems and Responsibilities

The music educators and consultants remained to appraise the summaries and conclusions of the Tanglewood Symposium. Included in this section are their formulated implications and possible directions for music education in the United States.

Committee Reports

Critical Issues

Implications for Music in Higher Education and the Community

Implications for the Music Curriculum

Implications for the Educational Process and for Evaluation

General Recommendations

The Tanglewood Declaration

Critical Issues

Members of the committee on Critical Issues: Max Kaplan, Chairman; Page Bailey, William C. Hartshorn, Warner Lawson, John T. Roberts, and Louis G. Wersen.

MUSIC AND THE INNER CITY

The complex problems of the inner city and the civil rights movement raise grave and compelling issues for the totality of education. Music educators are not properly prepared to cope with the severe problems created by poor housing, unemployment, poverty, and other intolerable conditions that exist in cities throughout the United States.

We recommend that teacher-education programs in music be modified or expanded to include the skills and attitudes needed for the specialized tasks required in the inner city. These tasks call for (a) a person whose solid musical background is equal to that expected of all music teachers in the schools; (b) a person with positive attitudes toward himself, toward children, and toward society, with a commitment to his task and with a sense of responsibility toward music as well as an empathy for the social needs and conditions for other people; (c) a person who possesses the initiative and imagination to relate the school and his skills to the unique needs and resources of the families and traditions of the neighborhood he serves; and (d) a person who is informed about conditions and trends in the community, including those of minority groups, and who has the skills to apply his insights in a flexible way to the societal problems he faces.

We recommend the formulation of a new curriculum for teacher-training institutions that will attract such persons and educate them in actual community situations during the pre-service period. This curriculum might include (a) courses from the social sciences that are most relevant to community structure and change, group relations, and family life; (b) direct experience in the application of music to the community during the training period, and especially in the student-teaching period; and (c) continuing experiences by teachers in the field along these directions to meet problems of conflict and change in the community that will continue and perhaps become more pressing in the years ahead.

We recommend the convening of a national conference on the problem "Music and Critical Issues of the Urban Community." Among others to be designated in planning sessions, this conference would be attended by (a) successful school and community leaders of music and music education in such areas as Watts and Harlem; (b) government officials of such programs and agencies as Head Start, the Office of Economic Opportunity, the Office of Urban Affairs and the Office of Education; (c) national leaders of minority groups and community welfare, recreational, church, labor, and business organizations; (d) administrators of teacher education programs, counselling and teacher-placement services, and supervisors; and (e) social scientists or scholars from other disciplines who can make significant contributions to the conference. Although obtaining funds and planning the conference will require time, we urge that plans be initiated quickly so that the conference can be held in the winter or spring of 1967-1968.

We recommend that a special workshop on this problem be held during the summer of 1968. This workshop would use as its theme, "Internship-Workshop on Critical Community Issues for Music Education," and would be composed of a limited number of music teachers, administrators, and other educators from cities throughout the nation who presently confront or who wish to become involved with the problems of the inner city. It would meet for a sufficient but relatively brief period in an appropriate setting to consider the issues of and techniques for relating music to the community. The members might then disperse in sub-groups to various communities of the country where they could observe and participate in actual community situations. They would then reconvene to exchange experiences, initiate action to meet evident problems, and plan for future workshops, or other forms of internship and training. We would hope that teachers who come to this workshop will receive full expenses, and, whenever feasible, credit and ongoing salary from their respective school systems.

We believe that music educators must address themselves immediately and boldly to this problem on national, state, and local levels by establishing a clearer understanding of the facts, trends, prior experiences, and researches throughout the country, and knowledge available from other agencies and professions.

MUSIC STUDY FOR ALL STUDENTS IN THE SENIOR HIGH SCHOOLS

Because of existing academic pressures, college entrance requirements, and rigid scheduling, less than twenty percent of high school students in the United States are engaged in the systematic study of music as an art. The need for aesthetic experience is a basic characteristic of human life that education at every level is obliged to meet.

We recommend that MENC, using its publication *Music in General Education* as a base, (a) utilize such existing media of communication as the *Music Educators Journal* and its national, divisional, and state meetings to promote a greater recognition of music education's importance for the "non-performing" student and to further an understanding of appropriate materials and strategies of instruction by music educators at the senior high school levels; (b) establish a commission to develop a content of instruction and processes of teaching that will in fact, make the study of music in the secondary school comparable in quality to that of other subjects; (c) develop a dialogue with personnel at the university level to promote a reform in teacher-education curriculum that will adequately prepare students to teach music as a part of general education; (d) initiate conferences with appropriate representatives of the American Association of School Administrators, the National Association of Secondary School Principals, and public school curriculum authorities in order to promote programs of instruction that will bring the values of education in music to vastly greater numbers of young people; and (e) gather and disseminate data regarding successful plans for flexible scheduling that may be useful in providing additional time in the school day for the study of music.

MUSIC FOR THE CHILD
WHO IS THREE TO EIGHT YEARS OF AGE

Music has played a less significant role that it should in the lives of children, aged three through eight.

We recommend that MENC, recognizing the unrealized potentials of education in general and particularly of music in the lives of children from the ages of three to eight, (a) establish a commission that would cooperate with recognized leaders in the field of early childhood education and of Head Start and of other programs to develop a systematic plan of action and content for the effective use of music; (b) apprise college and university music departments of the necessity to work closely with experts in early childhood education to prepare music education students to teach music to three-to-eight year old children from all economic, social, and cultural backgrounds; and (c) charge its Music Education Research Council with the responsibility of defining areas of research related to the use of music for this age group.

MUSIC FOR TEEN-AGERS

Required music classes in secondary schools seldom challenge the boundless energy, emotional resourcefulness, curiosity, idealism, and creative ability of teen-agers.

We recommend that a commission within MENC be established to deal directly with this age group, to evaluate successful experiences in music and in other disciplines, to develop conference sessions on this topic, to originate research studies or pilot projects, and to disseminate its findings to the entire profession. This problem is crucial for all economic and ethnic groups in schools throughout the United States. Action must be initiated immediately.

Implications for Music in Higher Education and the Community

Members of the committee on Implications for Music in Higher Education and the Community: Wiley L. Housewright, Chairman; Wilson Coker, Rose Marie Grentzer, Wayne Hertz, Warner Imig, and Emmett Sarig.

COLLEGE ADMISSION, TESTING, AND THE MUSICALLY TALENTED

Rigid college and university admission policies sometimes deny talented and capable high school music students the privilege of advanced study.

We recommend that the music education profession promote the recognition of pre-college music study by college and university admission boards. It is essential that MENC and other professional agencies communicate directly with education testing services for the specific purpose of accomplishing a better balance between the quantitative disciplines and the humanistic and creative disciplines that are to be examined. MENC is urged to cooperate with the Association for Higher Education in its project to effect better articulation between high school and college study of the arts. We further recommend that admission to college music study be based on flexible standards that recognize and honor creative efforts — not merely the ability to reproduce cold-storage knowledge on call.

RELATIONSHIPS WITH OTHER DISCIPLINES—INTER- AND INTRA-MUSICAL

Compartmentalization and lack of communication between various segments of the music field preclude intra-disciplinary stimulation and professional unity.

We recommend that MENC establish continuing liaison committees with composition, musicology, and performance disciplines to encourage the free exchange of ideas that may be mutually beneficial. We further recommend that sub-committees be designated by the MENC Research Council to serve the same function for extramusic disciplines, and that they report periodically on the information that is relevant to the music teaching profession.

MUSIC IN THE GENERAL EDUCATION OF THE COLLEGE STUDENT

College students often fail to relate to the musical heritage of American culture.

We recommend the inclusion of music in the general education requirements of every college and university student in the United States. Basic in formal education is the study of or inquiry into the social and cultural heritage of the past and the present as it profoundly relates to the nature and needs of man. As secondary school music offerings improve, such requirements would be reexamined periodically to insure that collegiate music study is sufficiently challenging.

GOALS OF AESTHETIC EDUCATION

College courses in the arts are seldom accepted as an integral part of a liberal education.

We recommend that MENC maintain a standing committee on music and aesthetic education in order to keep abreast of research in the field and to disseminate information to the profession. We further recommend that the study of music aesthetics and philosophy be added to the customary studies in psychology and human growth and development in the education of music teachers. It is imperative that the necessity for developing citizens who have discrimination and taste be recognized.

CREATIVE TEACHING OF MUSIC

Current practice does not include sufficient procedures for helping music educators to become creative teachers and to accept the challenges of new technologies and new social, educational, and musical trends.

We recommend that professional meetings of music educators more fully utilize creative scholars from other fields. Interaction with composers, master performers and master teachers is essential. Research on creativity in other fields can be studied and related to music. We urgently request that music educators open themselves to change, prizing it not for its own sake but for the new knowledge of music and education it brings.

THE NEED FOR HIGHLY TRAINED SPECIALISTS IN MUSIC

Many music teachers find their skill and knowledge inadequate to meet the current demands of the music education profession.

We recommend that educating and reeducating for specialized functions be initiated at all meetings of MENC and at college and university summer sessions. We further recommend that long-term goals be met by new undergraduate and graduate curricula in all specialized areas that demand more than basic professional competency.

Teachers must be trained and retrained to understand the specifics of a multiplicity of musics: avant-garde, art music, various mutations of jazz, and ethnic musics. The findings of recent research in musicology and theory must be communicated to them without delay. The speculations of philosophy, the theories of sociology, and the experiments of psychology — especially those relating to the teaching-learning process — must be taught when they are cogent.

High levels of achievement and precise critical standards must be expected of everyone who enters music as a profession. A great nucleus of experts must be trained who can lead the profession in every area of responsibility, especially those requiring the greatest originality, invention, and imagination. Our passion for democracy is not inimical to a corresponding passion for excellence. Music must be on the cutting edge of knowledge. The university must be a forerunner in experiment and research.

MUSIC AND LIBRARIES

The music holdings of public school and college libraries are generally not adequate for the broad type of music education that is currently advocated.

We recommend that teacher education programs make students more aware of their responsibility to insure that schools serve all students and faculty, from the passive listener to the most advanced performer.

We recommend that music teachers concern themselves with all types of music materials and their availability to students. They cannot limit their interest to music for performing groups but must assist the school librarians in building up collections of books about music, recordings, scores, and pictures. Adequate facilities for listening to music and doing research in music are the joint responsibility of the music educator and librarians.

CONTINUING EDUCATION IN MUSIC

Communication between the school music program, the family, the community, and society in general is inadequate.

To reinforce the place of music in continuing education, we recommend that (a) chamber music and small ensembles be stressed at all levels; (b) school music performing groups be used to enhance the music education of those who do not perform; (c) emphasis be placed on music's role in the development of the whole man; (d) humanities courses in secondary schools be encouraged, and colleges urged to make the satisfactory completion of such courses an essential part of their entrance requirements; (e) colleges be urged to offer more courses in music for all students; (f) schools provide more musical performance opportunities for the student who does not aim for a music career; (g) music educators assume leadership in developing continuing music opportunities for their communites; (h) music educators prepare leaders for community music activities; (i) these educators strive for better communication with parents concerning the true objectives of the music program; (j) the scope and perspective of youth concerts be broadened to include participation of children, parents, and other community members; (k) mass media be used more extensively to enhance communication between the school music program and the community; (l) teacher education programs be developed in the area of adult and continuing music education; (m) music educators seek active roles in Arts Councils, Arts Leagues, or any other organizations concerned with the promotion of the arts. MENC should encourage this participation at local, state, and national levels. Other agencies with which cooperation may not only be appreciated but even urgent are churches, Upward Bound programs, leisure committees of labor unions, and mass media.

Implications for the Music Curriculum

Members of the committee on Implications for the Music Curriculum: Karl D. Ernst, Chairman; Ernestine Ferrell, O. M. Hartsell, Harry Lantz, and A. Verne Wilson.

THE MUSIC CURRICULUM FOR CHILDREN

Elementary music instruction has often been splintered into separate activities that are unsystematic and lack cohesiveness.

The committee recommends that a new music curriculum at the elementary level place a major emphasis on the study of music in four broad areas of music experience: (a) understanding many types of music through guided listening or performance; (b) studying music through singing, playing instruments, moving to music, or a combination of these; (c) arranging and composing music for instruments and voices; and (d) understanding and using music notation. The optimum ages for developing musical interests, skills, and attitudes of young children are now viewed as being three through eleven. This recommendation is based on the assumption that experimental programs will be developed, and appropriate publications will be designed and prepared for the music education profession. These publications might be developed cooperatively with such organizations as the Association for Supervision and Curriculum Development, and Association of Childhood Education International, or the Department of Health, Education and Welfare. The study of music for children aged three to eleven must be reorganized to reflect recent innovations, appropriate technology, and trends in the school curriculum.

We further recommend that MENC, through appropriate committees at the national level, plan to make an appraisal and an evaluation of present emphases in elementary music education and to develop curricular guidelines for the new music. In turn, these guidelines would be implemented through divisional and state meetings and through state departments of education, and disseminated through the official publications of MENC.

THE NEED FOR UPGRADING THE QUALITY OF MUSIC TEACHING FOR CHILDREN

Qualitative musical experience for children in the elementary schools can seldom be provided by a generalist. Teachers cannot teach what they do not know, or that which lies outside their major interest or conviction.

We recommend that MENC officially take the position that a teacher with strong music preparation is needed for each school dealing with children of ages three through eleven. The music education profession should be moving away from the concept of the self-contained classroom to the idea of the self-contained school, and from the teacher as a general practitioner to the teacher as a clinical specialist. It is urgent that MENC, through publications and conference planning, assume a more active role in giving direction and support to maximizing quality education in music during the children's formative years in school. Continued

neutrality on such critical issues can only be interpreted by the education profession at large as a lack of interest and concern on the part of MENC in helping to eliminate the deplorable musical-opportunity lottery, in which each year a child must chance whether or not he will have a worthwhile experience with music in his self-contained classroom.

THE MUSIC CURRICULUM FOR ADOLESCENTS

A general music course is often required in many junior high schools, but it is too frequently poor in quality, boring, immaterial, and irrelevant to the art of music. At the senior high school level, opportunities for music study are often inadequate.

We recommend that all junior high school students be required to study a general music course that constantly illuminates that nature of music as an art, involves participation and performance, and teaches skills, understandings, and attitudes.

High schools should include at least one arts course as a part of graduation requirements. Such a course would be taken even by those who participate in performance groups.

We also recommend that colleges and universities prepare a third type of music teacher: one who will be, foremost, a superb and sensitive musician and one who will have concentrated intensely on music history and literature, music analysis, cultural anthropology, ethnomusicology, and aesthetics.

State and sub-state music associations in cooperation with state departments of education and colleges and universities are obliged to engage in upgrading the entire field of general music, understanding of music, and related arts courses. This will require a massive effort to reeducate teachers who are currently in service.

More studies can be made in the areas of humanities and related arts at the high school level to ascertain whether they are more effective than separate arts courses in developing aesthetic attitudes and judgments.

THE OTHER MUSICS — THEIR SELECTION AND USE

Traditional music literature dominates and overbalances the present music education repertoire.

We recommend that teachers be encouraged to experiment with and utilize many types of music in their instructional activities. In-service education programs instituted on a regional basis, could equip teachers with the materials and techniques necessary to present a wider variety of music to children. The fulcrum of the repertoire should be shifted to include more of the many varieties of contemporary popular and serious music as well as music of other cultures.

Historically, the instrumental program has developed entirely around the standard orchestral instruments. It is incumbent upon music educators to reevaluate this position and to consider the validity of adding other instruments, particularly those social instruments having a considerable effect upon American culture.

Implications for the Educational Process

and for Evaluation

Members of the committee on Implications for the Educational Process and for Evaluation: Donald J. Shetler, Chairman; John Davies, E. Thayer Gaston, Everett L. Timm, and Maurice C. Whitney.

IDENTIFICATION AND PREPARATION
OF THE PROFESSIONAL MUSIC EDUCATOR

The recognition of prospective music educators often occurs too late to prepare them for the expanded content of programs in teacher education.

We recommend that music educators immediately open avenues of communication with guidance personnel in order to develop effective means of early identification and guidance for all prospective music educators. High school guidance and music departments can efficiently screen students who are considering careers in music education. Colleges, also, must overcome their reluctance to drop students who do not show an aptitude for music teaching.

We recommend that MENC develop materials that will assist high school counselors in identifying potential music teachers and in helping these students to understand the advantage of an early commitment. Early in the college curriculum students should be oriented to the opportunities in music education and be provided with opportunities to observe superior music educators at work.

An immediate and continuing reevaluation of teacher education programs is imperative. Some of the traditional patterns in this area require reexamination. Experimental approaches need to be encouraged, and the results widely disseminated.

EFFECTIVE UTILIZATION OF NEW TECHNOLOGIES
AND APPROACHES IN THE EDUCATIVE PROCESS

Music educators have not effectively applied new technological developments to their discipline.

We recommend the implementation of the recommendations of the Tanglewood discussion group on "The Impact and Potentials of Technology." This report could profitably be consulted for further examples of utilization. With this in mind the committee makes the following urgent recommendations: (a) A major MENC committee on Advanced Educational Technologies should be activated. The duty of this committee, as it is with the parallel committees already established in most disciplines, would be to inform the entire membership of developments and how they are

or might be applied to music education. The pages of the *Music Educators Journal*, the *Journal of Research in Music Education*, special brochures, and any other medium that is necessary should be made available to this committee for the dissemination and coordination of information. A continuing dialogue with major manufacturers would be initiated in order to bring the needs of music educators to their attention. Axiomatically, industry will not develop hardware or programs until it is convinced of a true need. The committee would relate to and cooperate with the division of Educational Technology of NEA. (b) As have the leaders in other disciplines, the key personnel of MENC should be provided with a one-time, three-day exposure to computer concepts. Knowledge of these concepts will permit them to evaluate projects and to provide the necessary professional leadership. A training program in this field for all music educators should be devised and disseminated by every practicable means: college courses, workshops, clinics, and the like. (c) The ERIC clearing house proposals should be put into operation as quickly as possible to furnish computerized indices of all materials in music education and related fields. This system can provide an interface between the music schools and the music researchers. (d) Preparation of new teachers and inservice experiences for working teachers in these technologies should become a major concern of MENC. Specific courses and programs can be planned to bring this information to the attention of the general membership with force and a sense of urgency. The short-range objectives might be accomplished by the development of short-term summer workshops and institutes. However, the long-range objectives can only begin to be dealt with in a revision of teacher-training curricula that will include experiences with the whole range of concepts and processes of education in the 1970s, instead of doing quite well what was widely acceptable forty years ago. (e) Research into the most effective structure and content of individualized instruction should be carried out cooperatively by qualified music educators and specialists in programed instruction.

IMPROVEMENT OF THE TEACHING PROCESS
IN GROUP INSTRUCTION

Many group-teaching methods are not in keeping with current trends to humanize instruction. Opportunities for learning by individual inquiry are often minimal in large groups.

We recommend that teachers in every area of music instruction seek effective resources and inaugurate techniques that will render large group instruction, including the rehearsal, more relevant and valuable. The widely deplored lack of carry-over into adult music-making points up the need for a reevaluation of present practices. Demonstrations and pilot projects can be developed and tested to explore innovative approaches to group instruction.

MEASUREMENT OF MUSICAL BEHAVIORS

Measurable areas of musical achievement at elementary and secondary school levels have not been determined, nor have criteria for assessment been developed.

We recommend that evaluative devices for the measurement of musical behaviors be developed at every level: elementary, secondary, higher education, and adult. This suggests the establishment of a committee of experts, adequate funding, and multi-disciplinary resources.

ACCOMMODATING INDIVIDUAL DIFFERENCES IN LEARNING

Creativity and individuality in students are frustrated and stifled by existent rigid instruction.

We recommend that pre-service and in-service teachers adopt flexible approaches that will accommodate individual learning differences in students. The creative learner thrives best under the imaginative, resourceful teacher. Every culture demands certain conformity but at the same time rewards individual creativity. An urgent need exists for disciplined research that will develop criteria for the identification of creative behavior in both the teacher and the student.

Curriculum Must Assume a Place

at the Center of Music

A Minority Report by David McAllester

The MENC has become increasingly aware that the entire Music Establishment is the perpetrator as well as the victim of a hoax. Ralph Ellison has identified it best in *The Invisible Man*, where he points out that the controlling middle class in the United States does not *see* the lower classes and the poor among them. Such euphemisms as "the inner city" (slums), "the disadvantaged" (the poor), "institute for living" (lunatic asylum) are linguistic evidence that the middle class is profoundly unwilling to face the invisible culture.

Most of the Establishment is unaware, or unwilling to admit, that the invisible culture has a rugged vitality of its own. When social workers and crime commissions consider the invisible culture at all, they mistake invisibility (their own inability to see) for emptiness.

In a democracy, class barriers are uncomfortable. The Establishment, seeing that its entertainments, customs, and values are not shared by everybody, makes a limited effort through the schools to impart the love of Shakespeare, T. S. Eliot, and Schubert to the poor. This endeavor is a failure because these great expressions of the cultural heritage of the Establishment have little to do with the cultural heritage of the poor. This endeavor is a hoax because in the name of communication and the elimination of class barriers we insist that only one cultural language be spoken

and that the natives on the other side of the barrier do not, in fact, really have a language at all.

We of the Music Establishment believe that there must be real communication, especially in the arts, between all sectors of a democratic society, if it is to remain healthy. The evidence of a crisis in the health of our society is clear enough. In Dorothy Maynor's words: "It would be tragic indeed if, while we are striving to weave a cloak of democracy for Vietnam and the rest of the world, the fabric of Democracy were torn beyond repair right here within our own borders."

In view of these matters, we affirm that is is our duty to seek true musical communication with the great masses of our population. While we continue to develop and make available, to all who are interested, the great musics of the middle class and aristocracy, we must also learn the language of the great musical arts which we have labeled "base" because they are popular.

When we have learned that any musical expression is "music," we hope to be able to reduce the class barriers in our schools and our concert halls. The resulting enrichment of our music will, we hope, give it a new vitality at all levels, and provide a united voice that can speak, without sham, of our democratic ideals.

The Tanglewood Declaration

The intensive evaluation of the role of music in American society and education provided by the Tanglewood Symposium of philosophers, educators, scientists, labor leaders, philanthropists, social scientists, theologians, industrialists, representatives of government and foundations, music educators and other musicians led to this declaration:

We believe that education must have as major goals the art of living, the building of personal identity, and nurturing creativity. Since the study of music can contribute much to these ends, *we now call for music to be placed in the core of the school curriculum.*

The arts afford a continuity with the aesthetic tradition in man's history. Music and other fine arts, largely nonverbal in nature, reach close to the social, psychological, and physiological roots of man in his search for identity and self-realization.

Educators must accept the responsibility for developing opportunities which meet man's individual needs and the needs of a society plagued by the consequences of changing values, alienation, hostility between generations, racial and international tensions, and the challenges of a new leisure.

Music educators at Tanglewood agreed that:

(1) Music serves best when its integrity as an art is maintained.

(2) Music of all periods, styles, forms, and cultures belongs in the curriculum. The musical repertory should be expanded to involve music of our time in its rich variety, including currently popular teenage music and avant-garde music, American folk music, and the music of other cultures.

(3) Schools and colleges should provide adequate time for music in programs ranging from preschool through adult or continuing education.

(4) Instruction in the arts should be a general and important part of education in the senior high school.

(5) Developments in educational technology, educational televison, programed instruction, and computer-assisted instruction should be applied to music study and research.

(6) Greater emphasis should be placed on helping the individual student to fulfill his needs, goals, and potentials.

(7) The music education profession must contribute its skills, proficiencies, and insights toward assisting in the solution of urgent social problems as in the "inner city" or other areas with culturally deprived individuals.

(8) Programs of teacher education must be expanded and improved to provide music teachers who are specially equipped to teach high school courses in the history and literature of music, courses in the humanities and related arts, as well as teachers equipped to work with the very young, with adults, with the disadvantaged, and with the emotionally disturbed.

Members of the Committee: Allen Britton, Arnold Broido, and Charles Gary.

General Recommendations

Members of the committee: David McAllester, Chairman; Robert A. Choate, Vanett Lawler, and Louis G. Wersen.

1. The Role of the Music Educator in His Community

A constant theme of the Tanglewood Symposium was the central role that the music educator should assume in the musical life of his community. Both in and out of the schools, he must show the imagination as well as the technical knowledge to promote interest and enthusiasm for music.

We recommend that music educators continue to seek cooperation with a wide variety of local organizations with musical interests. The rapid increase of local Arts Councils suggests one of the many promising avenues for such cooperation.

2. Corporate and Government Foundation Support

Out of the Tanglewood Symposium came a new awareness of the number of large corporations and corporate foundations that are actively engaged in the major support of programs designed to serve the public welfare.

We recommend that MENC establish a commission made up of leading thinkers in music, both professional and non-professional, to explore with corporate and government foundations the role of music in the enrichment of our national life.

X. Participants

Olga Madar, Executive Board Member, Director of Recreation and Leisure Time Activities, United Auto Workers, Detroit

Abraham H. Maslow, Professor of Psychology, Brandeis University, Waltham, Massachusetts

Dorothy Maynor, Founder and Executive Director, Harlem School of the Arts, Inc., New York

David P. McAllester, Professor of Anthropology, Wesleyan University, Middletown, Connecticut

F.S.C. Northrop, Sterling Professor of Law and Philosophy, Emeritus, Yale University, New Haven, Connecticut

Ole Sand, Director, Center for the Study of Instruction, National Education Association, Washington, D.C.

Gunther Schuller, Head, Contemporary Music Activities, Berkshire Music Center; President-elect, New England Conservatory, Boston

W. Homer Turner, Vice-President, U.S. Steel Foundation, Inc., New York

Ralph W. Tyler, Chairman, National Assessment Program, Chicago

CONSULTANTS

Max Kaplan, Chairman, Subject Area I: "A Philosophy of the Arts for an Emerging Society"; Professor of Sociology, University of South Florida

Wiley L. Housewright, Chairman, Subject Area II: "Music of Our Time"; Dean, School of Music, Florida State University

Allen P. Britton, Chairman, Subject Area III: "The Impact and Potentials of Technology"; Associate Dean, School of Music, University of Michigan

David P. McAllester, Chairman, Subject Area IV: "Economic and Community Support for the Arts"; Professor of Anthropology, Wesleyan University

Karl D. Ernst, Chairman, Subject Area V: "The Nature and Nurture of Creativity"; Chairman, Division of Creative Arts, California State College at Hayward

SYMPOSIUM MEMBERS

Harold Arberg, see Speakers

Page Bailey, Professor of Philosophy, Eastern Baptist College, St. Davids, Pennsylvania

Arnold Broido, Director of Publications and Sales, Frank Music Corporation, New York; President, Music Industry Council, MENC

Wilson Coker, Composer, Associate Professor of Music, San Jose State College, San Jose, California

William H. Cornog, see Speakers

Curtis W. Davis, see Speakers

Ernestine Ferrell, State Supervisor of Music, Department of Education, Jackson, Mississippi

E. Thayer Gaston, see Speakers

Rose Marie Grentzer, Professor of Music, University of Maryland, College Park

O.M. Hartsell, Professor of Music, University of Arizona, Tucson

William C. Hartshorn, see Speakers

Tim H. Henney, see Speakers

Wayne Hertz, Chairman, Department of Music, Central Washington State College, Ellensburg

Warner Imig, Dean, College of Music, University of Colorado, Boulder

George M. Irwin, see Speakers

Milton Katims, see Speakers

Herman D. Kenin, see Speakers

Stan Kenton, see Speakers

Gerard L. Knieter, Professor of Music Education, College of Music, Temple University, Philadelphia

Harry Lantz, Supervisor of Orchestras, Houston Independent School District, Houston, Texas

Warner Lawson, Dean, College of Fine Arts, Howard University, Washington, D.C.

Olga Madar, see Speakers

Dorothy Maynor, see Speakers

Father Norman O'Connor, National Director for Radio and Television, Paulist Fathers, New York

John T. Roberts, Director of Music Education, Denver Public Schools, Colorado

Ole Sand, see Speakers

Emmett Sarig, Director, Extension Music Department, The University of Wisconsin, Madison

Donald J. Shetler, Professor of Music Education and Coordinator for Research and Development, Eastman School of Music, University of Rochester, New York

Edwin E. Stein, Dean, School of Fine and Applied Arts, Boston University, Boston, Massachusetts

Everett L. Timm, Dean, School of Music, Louisiana State University, Baton Rouge

W. Homer Turner, see Speakers

Ralph W. Tyler, see Speakers

Maurice C. Whitney, Coordinator of Music, Glens Falls City School District, Glens Falls, New York

A. Verne Wilson, Supervisor of Music Education, Portland Public Schools, Portland, Oregon

RESOURCE PARTICIPANTS

Edward A. Bowles, Manager, Professional Activities Department, Department of University Relations, International Business Machines Corporation, Armonk, New York

Gene Bruck, Coordinator, Concert and Symphonic Repertory, American Society for Composers, Authors and Publishers, New York

Oliver Daniel, Assistant Vice-President, Concert Music Administration, Broadcast Music, Inc., New York

Freda Goldman, Center for the Study of Liberal Education for Adults, Brookline, Massachusetts

Mike Stahl, guitarist and leader of "The Coconut Groove," featured at the Bon Soir, New York

Paul Williams, Editor, *Crawdaddy!* Magazine of Rock, New York

OBSERVERS

Frank Churchley, President, Canadian Music Educators Association, University of Saskatchewan, Regina Campus, Regina, Saskatchewan, Canada

Leonard Feist, Executive Secretary, National Music Publishers Association, New York

Wilbur D. Fullbright, Chairman, Division of Music, School of Fine and Applied Arts, Boston University, Boston, Massachusetts

Craig McHenry, Dean, School of Music, Ithaca College, Ithaca, New York; Second Vice-President, Eastern Division, MENC

John R. Ott, President, Theodore Presser Foundation, Philadelphia, Pennsylvania

Abraham A. Schwadron, Chairman, Department of Music, Rhode Island College, Providence

MENC STAFF

Vanett Lawler, Executive Secretary

Charles L. Gary, Associate Executive Secretary

Gene Morlan, Associate Executive Secretary

Charles B. Fowler, Editor, *Music Educators Journal*

Joan Gaines, Director of Public Relations

Grant Beglarian, Project Director, MENC Contemporary Music Project for Creativity in Music Education

John Davies, Assistant Director, MENC Contemporary Music Project for Creativity in Music Education

Dorothy Regardie, Administrative Assistant

Rose Glanz, Secretary

SYMPOSIUM STAFF

Cara Mandeville, Secretary to the Director, Tanglewood Symposium Project

Edward J. Drew, Assistant; School of Fine and Applied Arts, Boston University

Joaquim Manuel, Assistant; School of Fine and Applied Arts, Boston University

XI. Appendix

Music in American Society: Introduction to Issues
(Reprinted from the Music Educators Journal, April 1967.)
ROBERT A. CHOATE, Professor of Music,
School of Fine and Applied Arts, Boston University
MAX KAPLAN, Professor of Sociology,
University of South Florida

Tanglewood Symposium Program

The Music Educators National Conference is of sufficient age—three-score years—to have developed respectable traditions, history, perhaps even ritual. Its size, now well over the 50,000 mark in membership, is not only significant in quantity, but its quality lies in the capable leadership of its members who are hopefully independent as well as respectful of traditions. Here arises a major internal tension within the dynamics of the music education profession. How can it carry on a success from past assumptions concerning objectives in music education in a way that is flexible enough to meet new and unforeseen conditions? Can the generations within MENC carry on a meaningful dialogue? Can sensitivity to new conditions of American and international life be made into an explicit cardinal virtue of a large professional group, or does the large group necessarily give in to bureaucracy that finds both stability and defense in familiar patterns?

These issues arise from the strength of the public school movement—a success due to such factors as capabilities of teachers, administrative and community support, cooperative efforts, urbanization and suburbanization of our populations, and to aspirations for the children of new middle class families. Urgent problems and challenges are now facing the entire profession however, which arise from social, economic, and cultural developments of the last decades. Our strengths will serve us well, but re-assessment and appraisal of our programs and positions are indicated. As a professional organization we have fulfilled the traditional functions of any professional association: a machinery for communications among all members; a structure for creating effective regional, state, and local groups; representations from the large association to other professions; conferences and clinics; publications of researches and general materials; participation among international bodies; consultation with governmental bodies in the passage of legislation; productive relationships with publishing and manufacturing industries.

It can be asserted, with the *prima facie* evidence of its own achievements, that the MENC has been in line with an emerging ideology and maturity of the nation as a whole. The ideology was in good part responsible in the first instance for bringing music into the public school: the democratic right that every child has to be exposed, under qualified leadership, to the accumulation of man's aesthetic heritage. The maturity is evidenced in a sharper insistence on the essence of quality alongside democratic exposure.

I

Now, larger issues have emerged more clearly for the nation as a whole: *First,* what is the desirable ideology for a post-industrial society; to what extent is it a continuity of or a break from familiar sets of goals and values that went with a work-oriented economy based on scarcity, or a local-oriented family life that went with pre-television and pre-computerized communications and processes? *Second,* what are the desirable directions for a maturity that seems increasingly concerned with the arts as one form of personal and group awareness in a departure from a highly activist, materialistic, or pragmatic society? *Third,* what should be the *ends* or purposes of education in such a society? What are the *means* for attaining these? *Fourth,* what are the values, the functions, and roles of music and other arts in such a society? In education? What contributions are they making or can they make to the needs of people and to the totality of our American society?

These larger issues of ideology and maturity hardly need documentation. They are being discussed in all intellectual circles and within many professions. Perhaps education more than other fields has become intensely aware of its stake in the conceptualization of issues and in its internal response. For education is at the center of a whole stream of conditions, from population explosions to cultural explosions, from the invention of technologies to their application in the lecture hall, from the centrality of mass education to equalitarian styles of consumption. All levels of education from the primary grades to doctoral seminars are concerned with the capacity of their students to ask new questions, to prepare themselves for a generalist type of mind that is adaptable to rapid obsolescence of knowledge, and to consider the nature of "creativity" —a term that seems central to autonomy for the individual as opposed to passivity, alienation, or emptiness. Thus, educators in the arts, who were until recently often interlopers and part-time colleagues of traditional educators, have become—or have the potential for becoming—major contributors to the "cultural condition" of a society in its search for ideology, maturity, and attainment of its potentials.

II

The real meaning of all this for music education is that our major concerns for techniques and implementations, although of continuing concern, are rapidly becoming secondary to a greater cognizance and perhaps reformulation of (1) our basic goals and objectives, (2) communication with others, and (3) a common search for a more vital contribution to the developing society. National and regional conferences are based primarily on performances and broader musical opportunities for students through concerts and upon mutual self-help sessions of "how-to-do-it." These activities are important and typical of most professional meetings. We have been concerned with "what" we should teach, and "how" we can teach more effectively; the "why" and "how effective we have been" have received less attention. We have reached a crucial time for re-examination of the most basic assumptions of everything music education stands for, and *may want to stand for in the decades ahead.* Considered in the light of identifiable issues, this appraisal becomes a categorical imperative.

Fundamentally, then, these are the purposes of the entire Tanglewood Symposium Project: to re-appraise and evaluate our basic assumptions and beliefs about music education; to become more concerned about music activities in our entire culture; and to explore possible ways and means by which we may be more effective, seek new dimensions for our profession. Every music teacher should become involved as deeply as possible in such an appraisal. This is his professional commitment. The MENC, his professional organization, merely serves as a catalyst, a central focal point for such a process.

III

It is possible, but highly improbable, that the MENC might emerge from the totality of the self-appraisal more secure than ever in its present course. It is possible, but highly improbable, that the MENC's basic premises will be shown as unrealistic or outdated. It is possible, and entirely probable, that from the experience will come a reformulation of the place of music education in respect to projections into the future.

It is the nature of social change that should dominate every phase of the planned program; and a major implementation that could be easily envisioned—if less easily implemented—is an ongoing, built-in system of exchanges with other disciplines and fields of interest. It may also be predicted that a major issue which will arise, in sharper focus than it has already, is the degree of leadership that music educators want to take, or can take, vis-à-vis (1) the educational program within the school, (2) inter-disciplinary relationships in higher education, (3) the musical life in its totality, (4) community and national life—including the family and neighborhood, (5) such special segments of the population as the retired and aged, the "culturally disadvantaged," or those unemployed through increasing forces of technology and automation.

From the entire discussion there might also emerge a bold but flexible "model" or Utopian view of what music educators would like to see in the U. S. by 2,000 A.D.; such a model is presently missing, but could encompass all assumptions of purposes in a dramatic way.

Most profitable, as an end result, might be a general structure of thought that could become a framework around which MENC and the profession might focus more pointedly its body of activity. The rapid growth of MENC, as in its proliferation of publications, may have an inherent tendency to move with dash and confidence in a multitude of directions. On the other hand, a somewhat rigid structure of regional conferences can easily result when much of the planning comes from a national organization. Thus, rigidity and proliferation can be healthy, each in its way, but only if the central trunk is recognized so that the limbs and the leaves have a point of reference. The "central trunk" is now in a forest where other trees co-exist— the tree of the sciences, of urban forces, of movements for civil rights, trees that look across the sea at other cultures. The young person in school, and then as an adult, walks between all of these trees, some providing more shade and protection than others from the harsh daylight of images and conflicts. The problem now for the tree of music, and its undergrowths and roots of music education, is to draw upon the nurturing waters and minerals that are feeding the other trees and to recognize the paths that can lead one easily

and creatively from one part of the forest to another, indeed, ultimately to see the whole forest as more than any group of trees.

IV

The following six large areas were selected by the planning committee to give focus to both our "inward" and "outward" reaches—that is, to crystallize directions for examining music and music education in their relation to general trends in American life.

A short *introduction* to each topic states the issue in general terms. A larger discussion of each at this point would be presumptuous; each is of immense importance and complexity.

Some *questions* are formulated to initiate discussion of the area from our experience as music educators. These questions are tentative. You may have more pertinent ones. Members should feel free to treat the issue according to their interests and understanding.

A brief *bibliography* related to issues is suggested. These sources may serve to extend ideas or information about the subject.

No discussion group should feel unsuccessful if it comes to no consensus. Indeed, many more questions may arise than those given. Your comments, when put alongside more than forty reports from the six regional meetings, will help establish a broad picture of where the music education profession stands at present, its clear points of concern as well as consensus, its internal differences, the desirability of communication with other fields, and its possible contributions to the directions of American social and cultural change.

I. Music in the Emerging American Society

The panel is motivated by the conviction that the arts are not for a privileged few but for the many, that their place is not on the periphery of society but at its center, that they are not just a form of recreation but are of central importance to our well-being and happiness . . .—Rockefeller Panel Report, The Performing Arts, *p. 11.*

Introduction

■ Music and other arts have been expressions of men in all societies, used for many purposes, considered "peripheral" or "ornamental" by many and an essential esthetic component of the "good life" by others. Although negative attitudes exist in this country toward the arts, many believe we are on the threshold of a cultural renaissance. Post-World War life in our country has been marked not only by rising affluence but also by a more positive control over our social destinies; the programs of the Great Society have reached deeply into the fibre of American political, social, and educational life, whatever our personal convictions about its motivations and effectiveness. What should be the *quality* of life in a democracy? The famous *Triple Revolution Report* speaks of the revolutions in cybernetics, human relations, and weaponry that have transformed our concepts of social change; they have reshaped the power structures among nations of the world; with industrialization as the fundamental underlying change in the lives of a growing portion of mankind in both East and West, the Toynbees, Sorokins, Mullers, and Mumfords have helped us all raise basic questions of human directions. Without question, music and the arts are affected by these momentous changes.

Questions

• How do music and the other arts affect the "condition of man?"

• What, if any, are the interrelations between the ideals of a democratic society, the arts, and mass education?

• To what degree do the "power structures" (decision-makers in national, state, and local governments, those in education, and other community organizations) affect developments in the arts? In what manner? What should be our relations with such "structures?"

• To what degree should the federal government become involved in support of music in the country? Should subsidies for artists, composers, opera companies, and musical organizations be granted?

• How do concepts of the functions and roles of music in this country compare to those of Eastern cultures?

• What are the most serious obstacles to the development of a wide musically literate public in America?

• Is it possible to maintain qualities of artistic excellence in a program of education which by mandate must be for all children? Or, as so many critics insist, is a "mass culture" of necessity of low calibre—if not utterly impossible?

Bibliography

Arts Councils of America. *The Arts: A Central Element of a Good Society.* New York: Associated Councils of the Arts, 1564 Broadway.

Arts in Society. Issued by: Extension Division, University of Wisconsin. See especially: Vol. 2, No. 4, "Government in Art"; Vol. 2, No. 3, "University and Creative Arts"; Vol. 3, No. 3, "Institutions of Art."

Broudy, Harry S. "Aesthetic Education in a Technological Society: The Other Excuses for Art." *Journal of Aesthetic Education,* Vol. I, Champaign, Ill.: 118 Fine Arts Building, University of Ill. 1966.

Dorian, Frederick. *Commitment to Culture.* Pittsburgh: University of Pittsburgh Press, 1964.

Edman, Irwin. *Arts and the Man.* New York: Mentor Books, 1950.

Fuller, Buckminster. "The Music of the New Life." *Music Educators Journal,* April-May 1966 and June-July 1966.

Gores, Harold B. "The Schools of Tomorrow: Ten Trends," *The Instrumentalist,* Vol. 20, No. 4, November 1965.

Jacobs, Norman. *Culture for the Millions.* Boston: Beacon Press, 1964.

Johnson, Lyndon B. "Art Belongs to the People," *Music Journal,* Vol. 24, No. 3, March, 1966.

Kaplan, Max. *Foundations and Frontiers of Music Education.* New York: Holt, Rinehart, and Winston, 1966.

Langer, Suzanne K. "The Cultural Importance of the Arts," *Journal of Aesthetic Education,* Vol. I, No. 1. Champaign: University of Ill., 1966.

Mumford, Lewis. *The Condition of Man.* New York: Harcourt, Brace and Co., 1944. (See introduction.)

Northrop, F. S. C. *The Meeting of East and West.* New York: The Macmillan Co., 1946.

Read, Herbert. *The Redemption of the Robot.* New York: Trident Press, 1966.

Rockefeller Panel Report. *The Performing Arts: Problems and Prospects.* New York: McGraw-Hill Book Co., 1965.

Rosenberg, B. and D. M. White (eds.). *Mass Culture.* Glencoe: Free Press, 1957.

Source Book III. *Perspectives in Music Education.* Washington: Music Educators National Conference, 1966. Various articles.

Toffler, Alvin. *The Culture Consumers.* New York: St. Martin's Press, 1964.

The Triple Revolution, prepared by an *Ad Hoc* Committee and submitted to Pres. L. B. Johnson, March 22, 1964. In *Socialist Humanism,* editor, Erich Fromm. New York: Anchor Books, 1966, pp. 441-461.

Villemain, Francis T. "Democracy, Education, and Art." *Journal of Aesthetic Education,* Vol. I, No. 1. Champaign: University of Ill., 1966. Also in E. W. Eisner and D. W. Ecker. *Readings in Art Education.* Waltham, Mass.: Blaisdell Publishing Co., 1966.

II. Values: Music as Means and Ends

To the frequent charge that the humanities are impractical and that they must give way to narrow concern with those studies which seem more immediately connected to economic opportunity for the individual or to survival in a world whose instruments of power are based on the specific applications of science, we would assert that the humanities play a uniquely effective role in determining a man's behavior and values. Included in the humanities are those studies that help man find a purpose, that endow him with the ability to criticize intelligently and therefore to improve his own society, and that establish for the individual his sense of identity with other men both in his own country and in the world at large. . . . Those who understand the humanities also lead more rewarding lives both within their own hearts and minds and in their relations with their neighbors and associates, their communities and their countries. . . Whenever a student leaves school, it is important to him and to society that he be allowed to receive, as fully as his potential permits, the heritage which is his in the humanities. While the school is not the only agency to accomplish this task, there is no other in America today that bears so heavy a responsibility for it.—Report of the Commission on the Humanities, pp. 19, 20.

Introduction

■ The term "values" has enlivened and plagued philosophical discussions for many generations. No society can look at itself without asking, on levels of group or of individual life, about its purposes, its meanings. *Abundance—for what?* asks David Riesman; Victor Frankel speaks of *Man's Search for Meaning;* and currently, especially since the wars of this century, philosophers in every part of the world address themselves more directly to every man and every nation. Participants in the arts are assured and feel secure in the knowledge that they represent some of man's highest aspirations and accomplishments; yet, as economic creatures in the marketplace they are sensitive to their lower level in the hierarchy of workers. Further, in community or educational circles and whenever there is competition for time, budgets or governmental assistance, the general feeling of warmth for the arts as valuable must somehow be translated into terms that can be grasped. The musical world, dedicated to a nonverbal form of expression, faces the difficult task of articulating its reasons for being or defining its unique functions.

Questions

- What are valid, *unique* values of music for the individual?

- Is it important for the individual to distinguish between "play" activity, relaxation, and "appreciation" of music? Should music be "escape from reality?" Is there conflict between artistic standards and recreational activity?

- What are the meanings and implications of the increasingly greater concern for "aesthetic education" in schools and colleges?

- How may understandings of philosophy and aesthetics afford direction for formulation of objectives in educational, church, or community groups? How might such understandings affect music utilized and processes of teaching?

- Given increased leisure time, what functions can music fulfill for the individual? Amusement arts fulfill a socially useful function of relaxation, but this is quite the opposite of "bracing" or re-enforcing or enriching one to meet times of stress or tension when inner resources are needed. Could the study of music as "humane art" with greater understandings of intellectual and emotional imports of finer music better serve the individual? In other words, in what ways may music be considered one of the humanities?

- What is meant by "music is a discipline?" By the phrase, "Music is an academic discipline?"

- In an era when the development of "human relations" and understandings of all peoples are paramount, what do you discern the roles of music might be?

- In varying ways, music is being used in programs for the aging, in adult and continuing education, as therapy in many types of institutions, included in urban development plans, receiving greater emphases in programs for retarded children, in industry, and virtually omnipresent in stores, elevators, etc. What criteria might be determined for the validity of these uses of music? What concerns might be expressed?

- What are the historical roots of negative attitudes concerning the validity of music performance in schools and colleges? Are such attitudes defensible in our present society? What are *means* and *ends* in music for developing musical understandings?

Bibliography

Bloom, Benjamin S. (ed.). *Taxonomy of Educational Objectives: Handbook I: Cognitive Domain.* New York: David McKay Co., 1966.

Boenheim, Curt. "Music and Group Psychotherapy," *Journal of Music Therapy,* Vol. III, No. 2, June 1966. Lawrence, Kansas: The Allen Press, pp. 49-52.

Dejager, H. "Musical Socialization and the Schools," *Music Educators Journal,* February 1967.

Engleman, Finis. "The Arts and American Education," *Music Educators Journal,* February-March 1964.

Ernst, Karl and Charles Gary. *Music In General Education.* Washington: Music Educators National Conference, 1965.

Frondizi, Risieri. *What Is Value?* LaSalle, Ill.: Open Court Press, 1963.

Henry, Nelson B. *Basic Concepts in Music Education.* Chicago: University of Chicago Press, 1958.

Jones, Howard Mumford. *One Great Society.* New York: Harcourt, Brace and Co., 1959. Humane Learning in the United States.

Krathwohl, David R., B. S. Bloom, and B. B. Masia (eds.). *Taxonomy of Educational Objectives: Handbook II: Affective Domain.* New York: David McKay Co., 1965.

Langer, Suzanne. *Philosophy in a New Key.* Cambridge: Harvard Univ. Press, 1942.

Leonhard, Charles. "Philosophy of Music Education," *Music Educators Journal,* September-October 1965.

Margolis, Joseph. *Philosophy Looks at the Arts.* New York: Charles Scribner's Sons, 1962.

Meyer, Leonard B. *Emotion and Meaning in Music.* Chicago: University of Chicago Press, 1961.

Mueller, John. *The American Symphony Orchestra: A Social History of Musical Taste.* Bloomington: University of Indiana Press, 1951. See: Chapter 7, "Musical Taste and How it is Formed."

Museum of Modern Art. *Art, Art, Art, Art, Art.* New York: Doubleday and Co., 1964. Three important essays: "Art as the Measure of Man" by George D. Stoddard; "Art as Education" by Irwin Edman; "Art as a Personal Vision" by Bruno Bettelheim.

National Association of Secondary School Principals. *Arts in the Comprehensive Secondary School.* Washington: NASSP, 1962.

Read, Herbert. *Education Through Art.* New York: Pantheon Books, 1958.

Report of the Commission on the Humanities. New York: American Council of Learned Societies, 345 East 46th Street. (no charge)

Revelli, William D. "Goals for the Future—Music Performance," *The Instrumentalist,* Vol. 21, No. 1, August 1966.

Sand, Ole. "Schools for the Seventies," *Music Educators Journal,* June-July 1966.

Schwadron, Abraham. *Aesthetics: Dimensions for Music Education.* Washington: Music Educators National Conference, 1967.

Source Book III. *Perspectives in Music Education.* Washington: Music Educators National Conference, 1966. Many valuable references related to this subject.

Taylor, Harold. "Music as a Source of Knowledge," *Music Educators Journal,* September-October 1964.

III. Music of Our Time

The modern and the old have always been.—Ferruccio Busoni

Introduction

■ The music(s) of the twentieth century present a wide and bewildering array of developments. Perspectives become difficult to gain or maintain if sound judgments are to be made. Horizons of sound have opened with breathtaking rapidity; changes which would have been spread over generations in past years are telescoped into a single lifetime. Since the closing years of the 19th century, assaults have been made on our traditional concepts of all elements of music, and the roster of important composers who have developed distinctive styles and techniques, more or less independent of major trends, is impressive. Exploration of tonal, harmonic, melodic, rhythmic, and structural possibilities; new mixtures of sound; and developments of new types of sound generation have expanded aural comprehension and created music vastly different from the "masterpieces" of earlier years. Our sense of what "music" can be is altered and extended. Our technology affords new musical outlets and resources for experimentation.

American jazz has influenced serious music, not only in this country but also abroad; operetta, musical comedy, comic and folk opera, ballet music, the meteoric rise of interest in folk music, church music, music for films, and many shapes and forms of "popular" music, and music of other countries converge into a maelstrom of musical interests which are prevalent in our society.

Questions

• What are the responsibilities of the contemporary composer to society? Of society to the composer?

• Are there imperatives for the use of more contemporary music in schools and colleges? Students have been found responsive to the sounds and forms of this music of our time. What factors hinder its uses in schools? What implications are there for education and re-education of teachers—in theory, history, performance, and composition?

• What responsibility does music education have for the development of musical taste and judgment?

• Should education in music consist largely of the "great masterworks" or should a greater pluralism of tastes be recognized and furthered?

• Is there a "high" function of "popular" art which gives the same degree of emotional satisfaction and perhaps the same kind of intellectual stimulation as "classical" art? If so, are the "popular" forms then the province of education?

• In half a century, American jazz has undergone numerous transformations and ranks with sports and philately as the realm of the self-made expert; it appeals to certain sophisticated tastes and fulfills certain demands of a new industrial urban culture. Is it more symptom and pastime rather than "unperishable utterance?" What are the obligations, if any, of the educator?

• If the functions of music interests of teen-agers are primarily "social," or afford opportunities for identification with performers as "personalities," or help him to conform to his "peer culture," to what degree should the music teacher further such interests?

• In what ways do music industries affect development of musical life in the country? What is their balance between commercial and artistic commitments? Who determines?

• Polycultural curriculums are developing rapidly. Should music of other cultures be included? For what purposes? Few centers exist in this country for such studies. What are the implications?

• What functions should the music critic perform in the community?

• Insularity, rigid departmentalization, and adherence to tradition characterize many music schools. Would music and society be better served by a greater mutuality of concern and interests of theorists, composers, musicologists, educators, ethnomusicologists, and performers?

Bibliography

Austin, William W. *Music in the 20th Century*. New York: W. W. Norton, 1966.

Babbitt, Milton. "An Introduction to the R.C.A. Synthesizer." *Journal of Music Theory* (Winter, 1964).

Benson, Warren. *A Creative Approach to Developing Musicianship*. Washington: Music Educators National Conference, 1967. A report of pilot projects sponsored by the Contemporary Music Project at Ithaca College and the Interlochen Arts Academy.

Cage, John *Silence*. Middletown, Conn.: Wesleyan University Press, 1961.

Chase, Gilbert. *America's Music*. Revised second edition. New York: McGraw-Hill Book Co., 1966.

Contemporary Music Project. *Report of the Seminar on Comprehensive Musicianship*. Washington: Music Educators National Conference, 1965.

Contemporary Music Project. *Experiments in Musical Creativity*. Washington: Music Educators National Conference, 1965.

Copland, Aaron. *Music and Imagination*. Cambridge: Harvard University Press, 1952.

Dallin, Leon. *Techniques of 20th Century Composition*. Dubuque: William C. Brown, 1964.

Hiller, Lejaren A. and L. M. Isaacson. *Experimental Music: Composition with an Electric Computer*. New York: McGraw-Hill Book Co., 1959.

Hood, Mantle. "Music the Unknown," in *Musicology* by Frank Harrison, Claude Palisca, and Mantle Hood. Englewood Cliffs: Prentice-Hall, Inc., 1965.

Judd, F. C. *Electronic Music and Musique Concrete*. London: Neville Spearman, 1961.

Kostelanetz, Richard. "Milton Babbitt and John Cage are the Two Extremes of Avant-Garde Music." *New York Times Magazine*, January 15, 1967.

Lang, Paul Henry (ed.). *Problems of Modern Music*. Princeton Seminar in Advanced Musical Studies. New York: W. W. Norton, 1962.

Machlis, Joseph. *An Introduction to Contemporary Music*. New York: W. W. Norton, 1961.

Marquis, G. Welton, *Twentieth Century Music Idioms*. Englewood Cliffs: Prentice-Hall, Inc., 1964.

Meyers, Robert G. "Technical Basis of Electronic Music." *Journal of Music Theory*. Spring 1964, 2-53. New Haven: Yale School of Music.

Nettl, Bruno. *Theory and Method in Ethnomusicology*. Glencoe: Free Press, 1964.

Palisca, Claude V. (ed.). *Music In Our Schools: A Search for Improvement*. Washington: U. S. Government Printing Office, 1964. Superintendent of Documents Catalog No. FS 5.233:33033.

Schwadron, Abraham. *Aesthetics: Dimensions for Music Education*. Washington: Music Educators National Conference, 1967.

Seeger, Charles. "Nationalism, Traditionalism, and the American Composer." In *Report of the Second Inter-American Conference on Ethnomusicology*. Bloomington: Indiana University Press, 1966.

Sessions, Roger. *The Musical Experience of Composer, Performer, Listener*. New York: Atenaeum Press, 1962.

Ulrich, Homer and Paul A. Pisk. *A History of Music and Musical Style*.

Vega, Aurelio de la. "Electronic Music: Tool of Creativity." *Music Journal* (Sept., Oct., and Nov., 1965).

Wen-Chung, Wen. "Varese: A Sketch of the Man and His Music." *The Musical Quarterly*. Vol. LII, No. 2, April 1966, pp. 151-170. New York: G. Schirmer, Inc.

Wiora, Walter. *The Four Ages of Music*. New York: W. W. Norton, 1965.

IV. *The Impact of Technology*

We have entered a new era of evolutionary history, one in which rapid change is a dominant consequence. Our only hope is to understand the forces at work and to take advantage of the knowledge we find to guide the evolutionary process.—Jerome Wiesner, Massachusetts Institute of Technology

Introduction

■ Cybernetics, computerization, electronics, automation—these are new terms; the technology they represent has the potential of altering our economy, our educational system, our capacity to handle information, communications, science, government, and our personal and social life. Eric Fromm and Lewis Mumford hold that the machine has not been controlled adequately by man and that the values of technology have produced man's alienation and destroyed his relationships to nature and to other men. Such values have further dramatized the impersonality of work, and are reordering the economic and social structure and creating leisure to a degree hitherto unknown.

Music and the other arts can hardly escape the implications of technology in such matters as the growth of governmental functions, the rising affluence, proliferation and potentials of communications and mass media, the use of electronics, and greatly expanded distribution of art works. Computer-based teaching systems, learning machines, television systems, and numerous ingenious automated devices now allow unprecedented breakthroughs in group as well as individualized instruction.

Questions
• What are some prospects for further technologies in the teaching process? What aspects of the learning process, or of teacher-student relationships may be most affected?
• What are some implications of electronics, as a creative element in music, for our concepts of developing taste, discrimination, sensitivity to sounds and structures?
• Considering a virtually unlimited potential of television (commercial, educational, instructional), what steps might be taken to realize the potential for music?
• What seem to be some portents of the "new leisure" for a wider use of the arts and music?
• How may music industries be affected by developing technologies?
• What are research potentials in music and music education utilizing advancements in technology?
• What place should electronic or computer music have in education?
• How can technology be utilized to bring music to a wider audience?

Bibliography
Buckingham, Walter. *Automation: Its Impact on Society*. New York: American Library, 1961.
Carlsen, James. "Programed Learning in Melodic Dictation," *Journal of Research in Music Education*, Vol. 12, No. 2, Summer 1964.
de Grazia, Sebastian. *On Time, Work, and Leisure*. New York: The Twentieth Century Fund, 1962.
Goldiamond, Israel and Stanley Pliskoff. "Music Education and the Rationale Underlying Programed Instruction," *Music Educators Journal*, February-March 1965.
Holland, James G. and B. F. Skinner. *The Analysis of Behavior*. New York: McGraw-Hill Co., 1961.
Kaplan, Max. *Leisure in America: A Social Inquiry*. New York: John Wiley and Sons, 1960.
Lumsdaine, A. A. and Robert Glaser. *Teaching Machines and Programed Learning*. Washington: National Education Association, 1965.
Mager, Robert F. *Preparing Instructional Objectives*. Palo Alto: Fearon Publishers, 1962.
McBride, Wilma (ed.). *Inquiry: Implications for Televised Instruction*. Washington: National Education Association, 1966. Contains articles by Joseph J. Schwab, Richard Suchman, Jerome Bruner, and others.
Moles, Abraham. *Information Theory and Esthetic Perception*. Urbana: University of Illinois Press, 1966.
Roucek, Joseph S. (ed.). *Programed Teaching: A Symposium on Automation in Teaching*. New York: Philosophical Library, 1965.
Schultz, Morton J. *The Teacher and Overhead Projector*. Englewood Cliffs: Prentice-Hall, Inc., 1965.
Spohn, Charles L. "New Media for Improved Music Education," *The Instrumentalist*, Vol. 19, No. 5, December 1964.
Wyman, Raymond. "Audio Media in Music Education," *Music Educators Journal*, February-March 1966.

V. Economic Support

The performing arts in the United States are not and cannot become self-supporting, and recognition of this fact is essential if Americans are to develop a vibrant cultural life. The basic difficulties arise not from such traditionally identified sources as inflation, union demands, or mismanagement, but rather from the nature of the economic structure of live theater, opera, music, and dance in a technological age.—Performing Arts—The Economic Dilemma, William J. Baumol and William G. Bowen.

Introduction

■ The Twentieth Century Fund study of the economic "dilemma" of the performing arts confirms in great detail what the music world knows from the American Symphony Orchestra League bulletins, the reports of the American Federation of Musicians, various Senate hearings, from every local campaign for the local symphony, or from the musician's own experience. Yet new sources of support and sympathetic concern are recently familiar—from foundations, state and local arts councils, and the Federal government. Colleges and universities during the past two decades have taken major steps in affording leadership in arts by establishing schools of fine arts and, in many instances, arts centers which serve wide areas. University campuses have become economic bases for many artists and musicians. Public schools for many years have served as subsidizers of artists and musicians as well as educators of audiences. Although music is not the poorest of the arts, it faces serious economic issues in the emerging America.

Questions
• What are some of the implications of Titles I and III for music education a decade from now? For the professional music field?
• Should the Federal government become more involved in support of musicians, orchestras, and opera companies, as in many European countries?
• How effective have foundations been in promoting, supporting, and encouraging activities in music?
• Does the precarious economic future for the professional musician hold any implications for the college music department?
• Is one approach to the economic problem that of developing wider, informed audiences through programs of general education in music in our public schools and colleges? How can this best be done?
• Is there adequate support for programs in music in public schools of our country? Is a part of the difficulty a lack of adequately prepared music teachers?
• Why do not large corporations and businesses support music and other arts more generously?

Bibliography

Arberg, Harold. "Music and the New Federal Legislation—Challenge and Opportunity," *Music Educators Journal,* June-July 1966.

Associated Councils of the Arts. Publications and Documents. 1564 Broadway, New York, New York.

Baumol, William J. and William G. Bowen. *Performing Arts—The Economic Dilemma.* New York: Twentieth Century Fund, 1966.

Brademas, John. "Government, the Arts, and the Public Happiness," *Music Educators Journal,* April-May 1966.

Lang, Paul (ed.). *One Hundred Years of Music in America.* New York: Grosset and Dunlap, 1961. See Chapters, "Government and the Arts" and "The Dilemma of the Music Publishing Industry."

Rockefeller, David. "Corporate Interest in the Arts," *Music Journal,* January 1966.

Rockefeller Panel Report. *The Performing Arts: Problems and Prospects.* New York: McGraw-Hill, 1956.

Stevens, Roger L. "National Council on the Arts Defined," *Music Journal,* March 1966.

VI. Creativity:
Its Nature and Nurture

The nation that neglects creative thought will assuredly have its nose ground into the dust of tomorrow.—Fred Hoyle, British scientist.

Creativity is in each one of us. That is to say, creativity was in each one of us as a small child. In children creativity is a universal. Among adults it is almost non-existent. The great question is: What has happened to this enormous and universal human resource? This is the question of the age. . .—Harold H. Anderson.

Introduction

◼ In all times and societies there has been recognition of the specially gifted and endowed, whether these become known in their culture as the "shaman," the "genius," or the "artist." Folklore, poetry, philosophy, anthropology, sociology, psychology, psychiatry, and even economics have taken a hand in seeking to describe and understand the creative set and person. Science more recently has sought to hurry our understanding, so that we might more efficiently uncover potential creators in the schools and turn their training toward mastering such skills as mathematics, physics, and chemistry. Yet there persists, in both lore and experiments, a considerable opinion that the arts, as major prototypes of creativity, hold clues that may be valuable for all types of manifestations.

Although creativity is usually defined in terms of either a process or a product, more broadly considered, it may also be defined in terms of a personality or an environmental condition. As research continues, concerning the nature, measurement, and development of creativity, it is time that those in music join forces with other disciplines in common exploration. In a period when "mass culture," "conformity," and "alienation" are familiar terms and diagnoses, the quality of our society is enhanced not only by identification of the specially gifted but also by re-structuring our teaching processes and re-ordering the environment of our classrooms and schools.

Questions
• What are some generalizations that have emerged from the behavioral sciences about the highly creative person or the art of creativity?

• What are the meeting points of the arts and of science on issues affecting creativity?

• How is creativity manifested at different educational levels? What pattern of development do the creative abilities follow?

• What is meant by creative ways of learning? How can music teachers provide opportunities for development of more flexible, imaginative, and productive learnings in music? Should we be more concerned with formulation of skills and strategies of inquiry, discovery, and problem-solving in music teaching? Might these apply at all levels of education?

• What are the most common blocks to creative development?

• What should be the goals in guiding creativity? How influential are the attitudes and preparation of the teacher?

• How can imaginative approaches be utilized to teach students fundamental *musical* understandings and knowledges of music?

Bibliography

Anderson, Harold H. (ed.) *Creativity and Its Cultivation.* New York: Harper and Bros., 1959.

Andrews, Michael F. *Creativity and Psychological Health.* Syracuse: Syracue University Press, 1961.

Benson, Warren. *A Creative Approach to Developing Musicianship.* Washington: Music Educators National Conference, 1967. A report of pilot projects sponsored by the Contemporary Music Project at Ithaca College and the Interlochen Arts Academy.

Berdyaev, Nicolas. *The Meaning of the Creative Act.* New York: Crowell, Collier, and Macmillan, 1962.

Bruner, Jerome. *The Process of Education.* Cambridge: Harvard University Press, 1960.

Contemporary Music Project. *Experiments in Musical Creativity.* Washington: Music Educators National Conference, 1966.

Contemporary Music Project. *Report of the Seminar on Comprehensive Musicianship.* Washington: Music Educators National Conference, 1966.

Daedalus. "Creativity and Learning," Summer 1965. American Academy of Arts and Sciences, 7 Linden Street, Harvard University, Cambridge, Massachusetts.

Fowler, Charles B. "Discovery Method: Its Relevance for Music Education," *Journal of Research in Music Education,* Vol. XIV, Number 2, Summer 1966, p. 126.

The Creative Arts in American Education. Includes two lectures: "The Interrelation of the Arts in Secondary Education" by Thomas Munro and "Third Realm of Education" by Herbert Read. Cambridge: Harvard University Press, 1960.

Lowenfeld, Viktor. *Creative and Mental Growth.* Third edition. New York: The Macmillan Co., 1957.

McBride, Wilma (ed.). *Inquiry: Implications for Televised Instruction.* Washington: National Education Association, 1966. Includes articles by Joseph J. Schwab, Richard Suchman, Jerome Bruner, and others.

Miel, Alice. (ed.). *Creativity in Teaching: Invitations and Instances.*

Neilson, James. "Educational Creativity and Title III," *Music Journal,* April 1966.

Parnes, Sidney J. and Harold F. Harding (eds.). *Source Book for Creative Thinking.* New York: Charles Scribner's Sons, 1962.

Read, Herbert. *Education Through Art.* New York: Pantheon Books, 1958.

Read, Herbert. *The Form of Things Unknown: Essays Toward An Aesthetic Philosophy.* New York: Meridian Books, 1963.

Schwadron, Abraham. *Aesthetics: Dimensions for Music Education.* Washington: Music Educators National Conference, 1967.

Zirbes, Laura. *Spurs to Creative Teaching.* New York: G. P. Putnam's & Sons, 1959.

Tanglewood Symposium Program

July 23 to August 2, 1967

SUNDAY, July 23

All day	**Registration.** Heaton Hall.
10:00 a.m.	Berkshire Music Center Chamber Music. Tanglewood Theatre.
2:30 p.m.	Concert, Boston Symphony Orchestra. ERICH LEINSDORF, Conductor.
5:30 p.m.	**Opening Session.** Chamber Music Hall. *Chairman:* HARRY J. KRAUT *Introduction of the Speaker:* LOUIS G. WERSEN *Address:* "Music in a Changing World," ERICH LEINSDORF
6:30 p.m.	Reception for members of the Tanglewood Symposium and faculty of the Berkshire Music Center. Chamber Music Hall.

MONDAY, July 24

9:00 a.m.   **Plenary Session I—"The Role of the Arts in a Changing Society"**

Chairman: LOUIS G. WERSEN
Introductions by ROBERT A. CHOATE, Director of the Tanglewood Symposium, of the sponsors of the project.

Address: "The Theoretic and Aesthetic Components in Western Civilization," F. S. C. NORTHROP

Address: "The Case for Aesthetic Education," HARRY S. BROUDY

1:30 p.m.   **Plenary Session I (continued)**

Chairman: MAX KAPLAN

Responses: OLE SAND, WILLIAM C. HARTSHORN, and RALPH W. TYLER.

Discussion: Symposium participants

3:30 p.m.   **Organization: Symposium Subject Areas**

Subject Area I: "A Philosophy of the Arts for an Emerging Society," Chairman: MAX KAPLAN, Recorder: WILLIAM C. HARTSHORN

Subject Area II: "Music of Our Time," Chairman: WILEY L. HOUSEWRIGHT, Recorder: ROSE MARIE GRENTZER

Subject Area III: "The Impact and Potentials of Technology," Chairman: ALLEN P. BRITTON, Recorder: ARNOLD BROIDO

Subject Area IV: "Economic and Community Support for the Arts," Chairman: DAVID P. McALLESTER, Recorder: EVERETT L. TIMM

Subject Area V: "The Nature and Nurture of Creativity," Chairman: KARL D. ERNST, Recorder: GERARD L. KNIETER

8:00 p.m.   **Dimensions I—"Potentials for the Arts in the Community"**

Moderator: ALVIN C. EURICH

Panel: DOROTHY MAYNOR, "The St. James Program"
WILLIAM H. CORNOG, "These Essences"
OLGA MADAR, "A Program for Leisure and Recreation"
GEORGE M. IRWIN, "Arts Councils and the Expanding Arts Scene"

Inquiry: Symposium participants

TUESDAY, July 25

9:00 a.m.   **Plenary Session II – "Toward the Year 2000"**

Chairman: WILEY L. HOUSEWRIGHT

Address: "The Emerging American Society," MAX LERNER

Discussion: Symposium participants

Address: "Reflections on the Impact of Science on Cultural Interactions Among Nations," THOMAS F. MALONE

Address: "The Quest for Quality," ALVIN C. EURICH

2:00 p.m.   **Plenary Session II (continued)**

Chairman: ALLEN P. BRITTON

Address: "The Arts in Higher Education: Valid or Valueless?"—SAMUEL B. GOULD

3:15 p.m.   **Dimensions II—"A Foundation and Contemporary Music"**

"The Contemporary Music Project," NORMAN DELLO JOIO

"A Foundation and Contemporary Music," W. McNEIL LOWRY

8:00 p.m.   **Dimensions III—"Prospects for the Future: Television-Symphony-Opera"**

Moderator: LOUIS G. WERSEN

Panel: CURTIS W. DAVIS, "National Educational Television: Fulfilling the Artistic Potential"

MILTON KATIMS, "The Problems, Concerns, and Projections for the Symphony Orchestra in the United States"

SARAH CALDWELL, "The Future of Opera in the United States"

Inquiry: Symposium participants

WEDNESDAY, July 26

9:00–12:00   **Symposium Subject Areas I-V**

1:30 p.m.   **Plenary Session III–"Perspectives on Music and the Individual"**

Chairman: KARL D. ERNST

Address: "Music, Education, and Peak Experiences, ABRAHAM H. MASLOW

Discussion: Symposium participants

3:00 p.m.   *Address:* "Expanding Dimensions in Music Education," E. THAYER GASTON

Discussion: Symposium participants

8:00 p.m.   Concert, Berkshire Music Center Orchestra, Tanglewood Conducting Fellows.

THURSDAY, July 27

9:30–12:00   **Symposium Subject Areas I-V**

1:00 p.m.   **Special Session–POP MUSIC PANEL**

Moderator: GENE BRUCK

Panel: MIKE STAHL and PAUL WILLIAMS

1:30 p.m.   **Dimensions IV–"Economic and Community Support: Perspectives"**

Moderator: OLIVER DANIEL

Panel: HERMAN D. KENIN, "The AFL-CIO and the Arts"

W. HOMER TURNER, "The U.S. Steel Corporation and Music"

TIM H. HENNEY, "The Bell Telephone Hour: Who Needs It?"

HAROLD ARBERG, "The United States Government, Education, and Music"

3:15 p.m.   **Special Session.** "The Rationale for Nationwide Assessment of Music Instruction," RALPH W. TYLER

8:00 p.m.   **Dimensions V–"Music of Our Time"**

Moderator: FATHER NORMAN O'CONNOR

Panel: DAVID P. McALLESTER, "Music of World Cultures"

STAN KENTON, "The Revolutionary Music–Jazz"

GUNTHER SCHULLER, "Directions in Contemporary Music"

Inquiry: Symposium participants

FRIDAY, July 28

All day   **Symposium Subject Areas: I-V**

7:00 p.m.   Weekend Prelude. Music Shed, Tanglewood. Concert by CLAUDE FRANK, LILIAN KALLIR, with singers.

9:00 p.m.   Concert. Boston Symphony Orchestra, RAFAEL KUBELIK conducting.

SATURDAY, July 29

9:00–12:00   **Plenary Session IV–"The Tanglewood Symposium: Summary and Recommendations"**

Chairman: ROBERT A. CHOATE

A report of principal concepts, issues, and Symposium and group deliberations with recommendations will be given by designated reporters. Symposium members will appraise and approve the proposed recommendations. Minority reports will be accepted. "Evaluation of the Tanglewood Symposium," ALVIN C. EURICH. Closing statements by LOUIS G. WERSEN.

POST-SESSION–APPRAISAL. Saturday, July 29 through Wednesday noon, August 2

(The fifteen music educators and consultants will remain until Wednesday noon to appraise the summaries and conclusions of the Tanglewood Symposium.)

MONDAY, July 31

9:00 a.m.   **General Session**

Chairmen: LOUIS G. WERSEN and ROBERT A. CHOATE

"The Report and Recommendations of the Tanglewood Symposium"

10:30–4:00   **Study Groups**

TUESDAY, August 1 — Study Groups

WEDNESDAY, August 2

9:00–12:00   **Final General Session.** *Chairman:* ROBERT A. CHOATE

Reports and Recommendations of Study Groups: "Implications of the Tanglewood Symposium for Music in Schools, Colleges, and Communities."

Discussion and Acceptance of the Report

Closing statements: LOUIS G. WERSEN